SPORT PSYCHOLOGY ESSENTIALS

Dave Collins, PhD
Andrew Cruickshank, PhD

Editors

HUMAN KINETICS

Library of Congress Cataloging-in-Publication Data

Names: Collins, Dave (Sports psychologist) editor. | Cruickshank, Andrew
 (Sports psychologist) editor.
Title: Sport psychology essentials / Dave Collins, Andrew Cruickshank,
 editors.
Description: First. | Champaign, IL : Human Kinetics, Inc., 2023. |
 Includes bibliographical references and index.
Identifiers: LCCN 2021050992 (print) | LCCN 2021050993 (ebook) | ISBN
 9781492599432 (paperback) | ISBN 9781492599449 (epub) | ISBN
 9781492599463 (pdf)
Subjects: LCSH: Sports--Psychological aspects. | Athletes--Psychology.
Classification: LCC GV706.4 .S81855 2023 (print) | LCC GV706.4 (ebook) |
 DDC 796.01/9--dc23/eng/20211020
LC record available at https://lccn.loc.gov/2021050992
LC ebook record available at https://lccn.loc.gov/2021050993

ISBN: 978-1-4925-9943-2 (print)

Copyright © 2023 by David Collins and Andrew Cruickshank

Human Kinetics supports copyright. Copyright fuels scientific and artistic endeavor, encourages authors to create new works, and promotes free speech. Thank you for buying an authorized edition of this work and for complying with copyright laws by not reproducing, scanning, or distributing any part of it in any form without written permission from the publisher. You are supporting authors and allowing Human Kinetics to continue to publish works that increase the knowledge, enhance the performance, and improve the lives of people all over the world.

To report suspected copyright infringement of content published by Human Kinetics, contact us at **permissions@hkusa.com**. To request permission to legally reuse content published by Human Kinetics, please refer to the information at **https://US.HumanKinetics.com/pages/permissions-information**.

The web addresses cited in this text were current as of October 2021, unless otherwise noted.

Acquisitions Editor: Diana Vincer; **Senior Developmental Editor:** Cynthia McEntire; **Managing Editor:** Shawn Donnelly; **Copyeditor:** Joanna Hatzopoulos Portman; **Indexer:** Ferreira Indexing; **Permissions Manager:** Dalene Reeder; **Graphic Designer:** Dawn Sills; **Cover Designer:** Keri Evans; **Cover Design Specialist:** Susan Rothermel Allen; **Photograph (cover):** Emilee Chinn / Getty Images; **Photographs (interior):** © Human Kinetics, unless otherwise noted; **Photo Asset Manager:** Laura Fitch; **Photo Production Specialist:** Amy M. Rose; **Photo Production Manager:** Jason Allen, **Senior Art Manager:** Kelly Hendren; **Illustrations:** © Human Kinetics, unless otherwise noted; **Printer:** Versa Press

Human Kinetics books are available at special discounts for bulk purchase. Special editions or book excerpts can also be created to specification. For details, contact the Special Sales Manager at Human Kinetics.

Printed in the United States of America   10   9   8   7   6   5   4   3   2   1

The paper in this book is certified under a sustainable forestry program.

Human Kinetics
1607 N. Market Street
Champaign, IL 61820
USA

United States and International
Website: **US.HumanKinetics.com**
Email: info@hkusa.com
Phone: 1-800-747-4457

Canada
Website: **Canada.HumanKinetics.com**
Email: info@hkcanada.com

E8125

Tell us what you think!
Human Kinetics would love to hear what we can do to improve the customer experience. Use this QR code to take our brief survey.

To my own Famous Five: Lily, Ruby, Rosie, Judy, and Joe. Plus Hels Bels.

Dave Collins

To all of our contributors, and to all at Human Kinetics and at home who supported us. We got there!

Andrew Cruickshank

CONTENTS

PART III ENHANCING TEAM PERFORMANCE POTENTIAL

PART IV   PREPARING INDIVIDUALS AND TEAMS FOR OPTIMAL PERFORMANCE

PREFACE

Sport Psychology Essentials is for anyone who is considering incorporating psychology into their work as a coach or athlete. Of course, involving a psychological perspective in training is also important for a parent or other primary supporter of an athlete. This input ensures that young athletes are not only more likely to progress effectively and achieve more in their sport but also more likely to develop skills and attitudes that will benefit other aspects of their lives (e.g., school, or their dual or postsport career). In short, incorporating sport psychology in an athletic program results in development *through* sport as well as development *of* and *for* sport.

Regardless of your starting position, as a reader of this book you probably already recognize the importance of psychological training in promoting development and performance. However, you may be concerned about the amount of extra work it takes to implement all—or even an effective subset of—the ideas offered in this book. Intentionally incorporating a mental side to training athletes is actually not as time consuming as you might think. In fact, the more deliberate and intentional you are in incorporating sound mental principles, the more effective your training becomes. As editors of this book who are also sport psychology consultants, we are confident that the benefits will far outweigh the costs of your time and effort.

Whether you are picking up this book as a relative novice, occasional dabbler, or full-fledged follower of sport psychology, we hope you enjoy the investment of reading this book. Most importantly, we hope you enjoy plenty of returns from integrating the contributors' ideas and advice into your training and performance.

PART I | MAKING SPORT PSYCHOLOGY WORK

1 | Blending Mental Training Into a Performance Program

Dave Collins

Grey Matters UK and University of Edinburgh

Andrew Cruickshank

Grey Matters UK

You can improve the mental aspects of your sport in two broad ways. First is the isolated way, whereby you target and train specific psychological factors, such as motivation, concentration, or imagery skills, in a particularly direct manner (e.g., through specific sessions with a sport psychology consultant or training sessions that are focused on specific psychological factors). Second is the integrated way, whereby you still target and train specific psychological factors, but you do so more in tandem with your physical, technical, and tactical activities. Which way is better? The answer is that it depends.

Generally, both the isolated and integrated approaches are necessary for optimal progression and performance. Although neither requires a sport psychology consultant (discussed in the epilogue), a good one can often help. In this respect, the chapters in parts II and III of this book are dedicated to more isolated mental factors from individual and team perspectives; they offer ways to improve or refine your current approaches. Although mentions of integrated work also exist in those chapters, the concept of integration becomes more prominent in part IV, in which contributors discuss the preparation of individuals and teams for optimal performance. As such, the purpose of this opening chapter is to provide some early framing on how the factors in parts II and III, which can be targeted in isolation, can also be integrated with work on your physical, technical, and tactical goals.

Relevance

How you blend mental training into your wider training and performance program affects its usefulness within the program. For example, finding ways to combine all of your activities can deliver at least a double dose of positive effects. In simple terms, psychological principles can not only be incorporated into your usual work (or, in many cases, incorporated more systematically) to improve in those specific principles but also make other relevant elements (e.g., physical, technical, tactical) more effective as well. Learning to set more effective goals can lead to an increase in your overall motivation, but it will likely also lead to better focus during your technical sessions because you're clear about what you're trying to achieve. Similarly, developing leaders across a team can have positive effects on the way that a group interacts on competition day, but it also influences the grasping of tactical information in the training sessions leading up to that day (e.g., by leaders directing teammates to the most salient cues in different game situations). Therefore, designing, developing, and using what the sport psychology literature describes as a psychologically informed environment (PIE) can make an overall contribution to everything that you do physically, technically, and tactically. Consequently, part IV returns to the theme of integration and discusses how psychological principles can be blended, rather than siloed, within wider processes.

Whereas Boris Blumenstein and Iris Orbach cover the teaching, development, and incorporation of psychological skills over different phases of time in chapter 18, this first chapter examines how all the different elements of training and preparation optimally fit together. Chapter 18 shares ways to develop and prepare specifically psychological skills (to primarily achieve the best *psychological* outcomes), and this chapter looks at ways in which using psychology can help develop and prepare your other core performance skills (to primarily achieve the best *physical, technical,* and *tactical* outcomes). In chapter 15, Tom Willmott shows you how a mental health program is integrated as a total package. The present chapter focuses on the psychological factor of how the elements can be planned and presented so that athletes fully buy into and commit to the program.

This chapter underscores the importance of integrating any work with a psychologist into all the other things that the organization (coach, athlete, or entire team) is involved in. Research in this field has shown that psychological input is most useful when it is channeled through the coach. In addition, securing understanding and buy-in from all participants is essential. This old joke exemplifies the concept: *How many psychologists does it take to change a light bulb? Only one, but the light bulb must really want to change*. Whether you are a performer, caregiver, coach, or sport psychology consultant, ensuring that your psychological work is well integrated into the overall training and performance package is both sensible and essential if you want to optimize the return on your investment. As you digest the content in this chapter, look for ways in which you can practically and effectively integrate the various elements of training and performance. To pursue this worthy goal, first consider some of the literature that can underpin your approach.

What We Know

This chapter stresses the importance for everyone concerned to gain a common understanding of the goals and development methods within a performance program. As the famous baseball coach and catcher Yogi Berra said, "If you don't [all] know where you're going, you'll [all] end up someplace else." In other words, progress usually requires a target outcome. Our addition of *all* in brackets is a reminder that it is a team effort; a well-integrated program will ensure a common understanding, or shared mental model (SMM), for all concerned (Collins & Collins, 2010). Indeed, without that common understanding, it is very likely that either (1) everyone involved will end up in different places or (2) frustration and miscommunication will lead them all to give up on the journey well before the end.

Therefore, when integrating various elements into a coherent program, a key factor is that everyone involved understands and, ideally, buys into the plan. As you consider and apply the ideas in this chapter, remember that communication is key.

Combining Elements: Nested Planning

In the nested planning approach pictured in figure 1.1, you build on Yogi Berra's quote and work backward; in other words, you begin with the final outcome of integrating the various training elements into an overall plan.

In nested planning, different agendas are attended to simultaneously, and they are nested (smaller versions fit into larger ones). The idea started with work done in performance psychology (e.g., Martindale & Collins, 2005, 2012) that offered a means for practice to focus on immediate goals; decisions were made to facilitate achieving them. Additionally, however, week-to-week tasks (called the micro level) are fit into a block of weeks or months with medium-level targets (meso level). In turn, these intentions fit into a longer-term (annual or even quadrennial) plan of overarching goals (macro level).

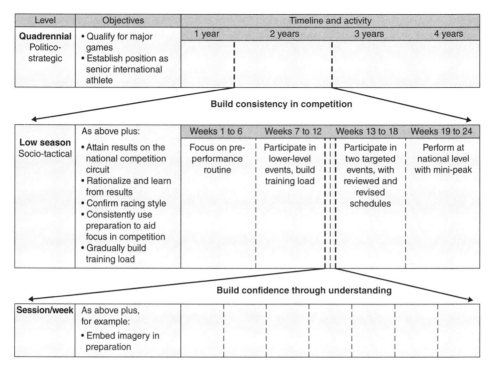

FIGURE 1.1   Example of nested planning.

Since its inception in performance psychology, nested planning has become a common feature of work in coaching (Abraham & Collins, 2011), leadership (Collins & Cruickshank, 2015), and other support disciplines including strength and conditioning (Collins, Downes, & Moody, 2021). In all cases, the principles are the same; they are a hierarchical assembly of goals with activities designed to achieve them, nested together to provide a carefully planned and coherent experience for the eventual target, individual athlete, squad, or team. You might consider the further use of this tool as an integration of the various support processes as described in chapter 15.

The logic of nested planning is sound. Any single training session is challenging for the athlete, coach, parent or caregiver, and sport psychology consultant, and it is necessary for maintaining motivation and perceived progress. However, each session is part of something bigger than one occurrence. For example, as shown in figure 1.1, the athlete is also always working toward longer-term targets, both developmentally and as outcomes themselves. Accordingly, whoever is planning and directing the sessions needs to allow an encapsulation of short-, medium-, and long-term targets to influence their decision making, even minute to minute. This attention helps to ensure that the long-term targets are catered to and kept in focus. It also prevents short-term challenges from dominating the process. If you don't view goals from a nesting perspective, you can allow immediate needs to overshadow longer-term targets. In short, you can overlook the big picture and, in turn, lose the potential scale of return from your efforts to improve physically, technically, and tactically.

The athlete in figure 1.1 has some macro-level targets across the four-year period, which is a common plan in Olympic and Paralympic sports. During year 2 of the quadrennial, the meso-level target is to build consistency in competition. Therefore, the athlete is focusing on a micro-level target this week—enhancement of imagery processes. This target is nested in the goal of building consistency; in turn, consistency is nested in the higher-level quadrennial performance goals.

Now, think of those plans from the perspective of the coach: As a coach, your sessions this week include a lot of emphasis on the use of imagery, so you build imagery into the athlete's training routines. You keep in mind the meso targets, ensuring that you relate the imagery embedded in the practice approach toward an effective and consistent preperformance preparation. The goal of consistency is implicit in what you do. At the same time, your coaching style ensures that you also stay focused on where you are going with this plan—the macro goal of achieving a qualification standard and selection to a place at the target major championships.

As a coach, you are careful not to make the athlete feel too busy by mentioning all these goals at once. The macro goal is probably something you discussed in the planning process (see chapters 10, 15, and 18), during which the athlete and coach sit down to set some targets for the year within the career focus. The meso target of consistency is another feature that would have been fixed away from the pitch, track, or pool, and it doesn't need to be consistently emphasized. Indeed, the meso goal should be referenced just enough to keep the athlete knowing why they are doing what they are doing and promote application of the weekly focus into a greater whole. In terms of bang for your buck, also note that the athlete's psychology work is therefore both acute (e.g., building imagery into their routines) and chronic (e.g., optimizing focus and deliberate practice through their continued awareness of the big picture).

Generally, the evidence that applying nested planning principles helps to provide the athlete with a more coherent and ultimately effective training program is increasing. Therefore, the next issue to consider is how different elements of the program may be combined to achieve this nested hierarchy within optimal time frames.

Physical Periodization

An old and well-established approach to the planning and execution of physical training, this version of periodization is based on the ideas of Selye and his impactful work on stress and how the body responds to it (Selye, 1956). The simple idea is that under any type of pressure (such as physical training that challenges an athlete's capacity), the body's systems are supressed but then bounce back to counter the challenge; this process is called supercompensation. If another stressor is applied at the right time, the process results in more supercompensation, leading the athlete to become stronger or fitter. Timing is crucial in this process. Apply the second stimulus too early, and the system gets run down; apply it too late, and the system has already returned to its previous level, so no training benefit occurs.

This idea has existed for decades. Indeed, work in the 1950s and 1960s, based largely in Eastern Bloc countries, drove the approach significantly. These developments related mostly to the timing and phasing of the loading—in short (micro), medium (meso), and longer (macro) terms. Texts and applications from this time to more recently—including the work of Counsilman (1968), Verkhoshansky & Siff (2003), and Bompa (e.g., Bompa & Haff, 2009)—saw the ideas become well established in sport training. Some of the ideas are sound and even have face validity. One such idea is that work phases should build from the general to the specific, with loads initially high in volume then lowering in parallel to increases in intensity and leading to a peak at the time of the event. Even more basic and sound is the idea that training loads need to vary across micro-, meso-, and macrocycles. Without variation, which Bompa saw as worthy of special attention, training benefits will be suboptimal or even non-existent.

In recent years, these classic ideas have faced criticism. In an erudite and detailed review, Kiely (2018) criticized what he described as the over-simplistic if–then perspective offered by classic periodization theory; in particular, the linearity of the process (e.g., "Do *this*, and you will get *that* from every athlete in every context") can be problematic. The paper is open

With an individualized approach, coaches track each athlete to evaluate the exact effect of training and rest on an athlete's progress.

access (free to download) and is well worth a read. Kiely, among others in the field, sees the process as requiring individualization—carefully tracking each athlete to evaluate the exact effect of the balance of training and rest on their progress, making consequent adjustments to optimize the adaptation process. Interest has increased in the monitoring of training readiness, a preventive approach to overtraining and, in general, a much more nuanced perspective, albeit many of the same principles of variation and progression toward peaking still apply. These ideas are addressed later (see the section titled Optimization). For now, the key message is that general principles of physical periodization will be optimally effective for individuals only if they are applied in an individualized way.

Physical Training Content

Although an apparently simpler construct, deciding on the content of the physical training program is as important as the finer design detail inherent in its periodization. Following the principle of specificity, the aim is to ensure that the athlete is physically training the components or fitness that they will need to perform optimally at their chosen sport. At first glance, this idea might look simple; after all, runners run and swimmers swim. However, once you add in the increasing emphasis on other elements, things become more complex and even a little bit more confusing. For example, both track athletics and swimming now recognize the importance of including other elements, most notably strength work, in the overall package (e.g., Karp, 2010). When you get into team sports, this mix can become even more complicated. For example, consider the ratio of aerobic to anaerobic or sprint work that a soccer player should pursue. It will inevitably vary across position, team playing style, and age.

   Although this book is not a strength and conditioning text, it is worth emphasizing that the physical conditioning side of athlete development and preparation carries its own complexities, which must be accounted for simultaneously with other elements, necessitating a nested approach to planning. These complexities are also crucial to appreciate if your *explicit* psychology work (as per the ideas presented throughout the rest of this book) is to be integrated in the best way at the best time for the best purpose and if your *implicit* psychology work (e.g., to establish a PIE) is to have an optimal effect (see Optimization, later in this chapter). The following section considers the need to also blend your explicit and implicit psychology work with your technical or tactical work.

Technical or Tactical Periodization

Originally developed by Vítor Frade at the University of Porto, tactical periodization is a methodology that links training evolution to specific phases of the target activity, most typically a team game. The approach has become popular; soccer coaches such as José Mourinho and Andre Villas Boas have famously used and promoted it, and it has been detailed in several texts on rugby (e.g., Tee et al., 2018). Reading a book that explains the subject (e.g., Tamarit, 2015) is recommended.

Tactical periodization employs the same general-to-specific progression identified earlier. Generally, the target sport is split into a model of several phases, each of which is then trained through an increasingly specific progression of training exercises and drills. As emphasized earlier, these considerations must be incorporated with the psychological work.

Other Ideas

In addition to the broad physical, technical, and tactical aspects described so far, a number of other factors affect the athlete's development to enable optimal progression and performance. Looking at the targets presented in figure 1.1, you can see the full biopsychosocial range of factors that must be considered. As a consequence, probably several different types of periodization are occurring within the development journey. For example, chapter 15 presents emotional periodization as a necessity to vary the intensity of challenge that athletes experience in high-risk adventure sports (Collins et al., 2018). Across all levels of involvement—and certainly for grassroots participants—psychosocial aspects of training will also need to be considered both explicitly and implicitly as well as chronically and acutely.

Regardless of the aspects involved, the main factor to consider is how to incorporate mental training with these other elements. Indeed, psychology as a discipline does and can make a significant contribution to them all. Aspects of motivation, anxiety management, and simply the reassurance gained when a performer knows why they are doing all the things they are doing—in that order—are important concerns. In sum, putting more thought (or different thought) into the psychological aspects of your training can benefit psychological outcomes and, when done well, physical, technical, and tactical outcomes too. The following section focuses on a couple of linked and particularly key ideas from which this integration should start, namely, how athletes view themselves and the ultimate outcomes they are trying to achieve.

Assessment

Assessment functions to help you check the mental models used by all concerned—whether athlete, coach, support staff, parent or caregiver, or manager—at the start of the planning and periodization process and then throughout the consequent action phase. If all parties involved don't see eye to eye on the best balance of training from the beginning, even the best integrated program in the world will misfire. Simply put, people need to agree with and buy into even the best ideas. As such, developing a successful and optimal integration depends on good communication and alignment between athletes and those who set the structure to which they aspire. Therefore, any method that provides a basis for conversation on the balance of training is worthwhile in progressing toward the SMMs that underpin well-designed and well-integrated programs.

Encouraging Common Understanding

Linked to this concept and from a leadership (e.g., coach or manager) perspective, the point of the second half of this chapter is to help you design, sell, and operate the best program. The middle word—*sell*—is crucial. Many coaches, managers, and even sport psychology consultants do a good job at design and operation. Unfortunately, however, far fewer do the comprehensive sales job that helps to ensure the fullest buy-in from all concerned. They may have limited interpersonal skills (e.g., to sufficiently understand how the athlete will receive the ideas); they may have beliefs about what the relationship between the athlete and the coach, manager, or sport psychology consultant should be (e.g., "I design, you follow"); or they may be following certain social norms (e.g., they don't want to appear as a salesperson). For clarity, *selling* refers to the ability to effectively explain why the program is relevant, robust, and rewarding for the athlete or team for which it was designed, not for the designer. Indeed, as covered in chapter 14, developing and providing an integrated program on this basis is an important consideration for anyone. The horizontal integration described in chapter 14 helps to get everyone involved at that particular stage onto the same page with a clear rationale. Once achieved, this coherence supports motivation and directs focus. However, if it is neglected, athletes will miss out on the multiplicative benefits that a well-integrated program brings (cf. Simonton, 2001). Furthermore, and especially against the increasingly diverse messaging provided through social media, athletes, parents or caregivers, and other stakeholders will be susceptible to distractions that inevitably affect progress.

Evaluating Common Understanding

Reflecting on these ideas and others throughout this book (e.g., points made by Artur Poczwardowski in chapter 4), the best line of assessment is to check for a common understanding between all concerned on what they are doing and why. Levels of agreement can be shown in three ways—what scientists call a triangulation. If all three methods provide the same or similar answers, the gold standard has been achieved. If one measure stands out as different from the others, it is still valuable information that can inform on that particular issue. Some important principles for assessing the mental models of those involved in blending psychological training with physical, technical, and tactical training follow. First, consider the common-sense tool of simply talking.

Effective conversations are a great tool for evaluating the commonality of ideas, yet they are often underplayed and sometimes even avoided. Indeed, coaches who share and promote their philosophy with their athletes are often viewed as more effective and have greater influence. This important factor is discussed in chapter 11. Even if you subscribe to the all-too-common application of great person theory (cf. Fliegel, 2015), you should note that this tool won't work unless the athletes and other stakeholders buy into the idea. The effective coach is usually a good salesperson; they sell what is best for the buyer and the buyer's (or *our*) goals.

Selling can be direct through verbal persuasion, or it can be indirect. A good example of indirect selling is through the reputational capital of the coach (cf. Collins et al., 2012). Charismatic coaches are often successful, especially once they have a few medal-winning athlete performances under their belts.

Nevertheless, the best sale can be accomplished through two-way conversation, a factor that lends support to work on coach–athlete relationships. Openness and communication are often the best ways to enhance both this profile and the positive relationships that enable it (see the work of Sophia Jowett and colleagues, such as Jowett et al., 2012, and chapter 14). Often, however, talking may not be enough. Clearly, athletes—or coaches, managers, or other leaders—might not tell the truth. More likely, their understanding of certain constructs or factors may not match other people's. This idea of shared mental models (SMMs) is a consistent and important feature

FRANCK FIFE/AFP via Getty Images

Conversations between coach and player can be a great tool for evaluating the commonality of ideas.

throughout many chapters in this book, so promoting SMMs is an important step. Recognize that understanding is a powerful tool, especially when it underpins agreement. What tools can you use to check for and promote it?

Tool 1: Performance Profiling

When it comes to evaluating what might need to be integrated into a training program, performance profiling offers an established tool for athletes and their support staff alike. Performance profiling became fashionable as a tool in the late 1980s and early 1990s and was grounded in Kelly's personal construct theory (Butler & Hardy, 1992). It is important for our purposes because personal constructs are the structures an individual uses to conceptualize an area of their experience or beliefs; in short, they contribute to why people think what they think. Consequently, performance profiling offers a tool to evaluate the constructs that each person thinks are relevant to achieving their goals, then to compare and contrast among individuals to see how well their ideas agree.

Table 1.1 shows one variation of this very common sport psychology tool (cf. Jones, 1992), presenting data for an imaginary single-seat motorsport driver.

This example depicts the constructs that this hypothetical motorsport athlete thinks are important for driving at the Formula 3 level. First, the athlete is asked to propose characteristics or constructs that would be important for performance in their chosen domain; they are listed in the left-hand column. Next, the athlete rates their perceived ability with that factor, with 10 being high; this number is entered in the *Current rating* column. Next, they are asked to rate the importance of that factor (once again, 10 is high), and this number is entered in the *Importance rating* column. The next entry calculates the discrepancy between the perfect 10 and the athlete's personal rating. Finally, discrepancy (*D*) and importance (*I*) are multiplied. This final product provides a priority rating, showing where the athlete and coach should place each factor in their planning. Larger numbers are deserving of more attention, at least according to the athlete's personal rating. It is probably

TABLE 1.1 Discrepancy Approach to Performance Profiling

Factor	Current rating	Importance rating (*I*)	Discrepancy (*D*)	*D* × *I*
Aerobic fitness	6	9	4	36
Neck strength	8	6	2	12
Nice hair	3	1	7	7
Reactions	4	7	6	42
Track knowledge	3	8	7	56
Braking	7	7	3	21
Commitment	8	8	2	16

no surprise to learn that reactions and track knowledge should be receiving more attention than nice hair.

For a young emerging driver, this breakdown might be useful. It is also informative for the athlete's coach. For example, how do the athlete's own ratings match up with that of the coach? Or the importance allocated to each factor? Or even what factors the athlete chooses (nice hair notwithstanding)? If coach and athlete have different perceptions of what is important, they will rarely agree on the design of the training program. Indeed, even if the coach pulls rank and dictates the content, the athlete's heart may well not be in it. Consequently, it will limit the program's effect. The same concerns exist if athletes, coaches, and managers or administrators have different perceptions. Once again, the horizontal coherence essential for effective progression will just not exist.

Of course, differences in score may come from differences in perception. They might also indicate differences in understanding or a lack of SMMs. As such, it is always important for all concerned to have a debriefing to explore reasons why a particular difference exists and even to check the reasons why a certain similar score or factor has been chosen. In short, they need to evaluate the structures that are being used; in psychology, these structures are called schemata.

Tool 2: Performance Reviews

This method for checking and building understanding can be used once the SMM is established through performance profiling or even as an approach to establishing levels of SMMs in itself. Once again, regular use of these approaches will facilitate communication. An example is shown in figure 1.2, an annual review sheet developed for use in a variety of sports. Originally designed for individual sports, it is easily tweaked for use in team invasion games. For the purposes of this chapter, the figure uses a profile for a fictional Formula 1 driver and coach.

The categories in this template are completely open for your development. The main consideration is that rankings on important categories are established and shared, leading to an in-depth conversation.

You can develop and use this approach at any level and with almost all age groups. Given that its main aim is communication, you might want to add in exemplary athletes for each category. Individuals known to the athletes completing the profile (better to use athletes from a couple of years ahead rather than world-class performers) can be briefly described, thereby further clarifying the meaning of each construct.

Although you can use forms such as the two examples described earlier, it doesn't need to be a paper and pencil exercise. For some, this will be useful; for others, using the templates to inform a conversation from the beginning (or a warm-up conversation with someone else) might be best. Either way, the aim is to initiate conversations about what each person's constructs are and why the differences or similarities have occurred. Once these constructs become common, you can have a series of positive conversations about the

Athlete Performance/Potential Template (APPT)

Athlete: Lewis Schumacher

Event: Motorsport—Formula 1

Coach: Stirling Fangio

	Factor	Rationale	Score
OUTCOME	**Consistency** High scores reflect consistent performances at, or close to, personal best. Score is based on 4 best performances that season.	Excellent consistency as shown by frequent P1 placings in practice and qualifying.	Score 1 to 10 **Actual score: 10**
	Progression Provides a point score, based on lap times compared to the top three drivers in his formula.	This driver has arrived! Importantly, however, he continues to look for the next edge.	Score 1 to 10 **Actual score: 9**
	Technical/tactical ability Related to technical models developed by team engineer and/or independent evaluation by motorsport authority.	Strengths: Exceptional focus in races; strong cornering and pace. Areas for development: Sometimes aggression can take over in situations where he feels disrespected.	Score 1 to 10 **Actual score: 8**
	Competition placing Based on place in the major competition that year as agreed with the PM, first place scores 16, second 15, and so on.	Can't get higher!!	Score 1 to 16 as a reverse item **Actual score: 16**
PROCESS	**Professional attitude** The driver's manner, especially in interaction with support professionals and fellow competitors in training and events.	Completely focused on motorsport.	Score 1 to 10 **Actual score: 8**
	Program commitment Rate the driver's willingness and commitment to involvement in relevant programs, including testing, squads, etc.	Excellent attitude toward team; largely adheres to managerial instruction.	Score 1 to 10 **Actual score: 8**
	Training commitment Rate the driver's work ethic in training. Score should be substantiated by exemplars and third-party evidence.	Strong work ethic; can occasionally overcommit to program based on natural enthusiasm for the sport. Adheres 100% to training or rehabilitation when it is required.	Score 1 to 10 **Actual score: 8**
	Sport commitment Rate the driver's commitment to progress in chosen sport, as opposed to other areas of endeavor, including academics and other sports/activities.	Full-time driver with little competing life apparent; it might be an issue in future years.	Score 1 to 10 **Actual score: 9**

> continued

FIGURE 1.2   Athlete performance/potential template (APPT).

— > *continued* —

	Factor	Rationale	Score
PROCESS	**Physical resilience** Reflects the fragility or injury proneness of the driver. Remember that past weaknesses may explain lack of progress rather than predict it.	Strong physical presence, which has been his strongest and weakest asset so far.	Score 1 to 20 **Actual score: 13**
	Mental toughness Reflects the driver's ability to produce the goods in major championships and other pressure situations. Use data and exemplars to justify score.	Has shown excellent competitive edge in key crunch races. Good mental strength in dealing with injury focus of past few years.	Score 1 to 10 **Actual score: 7**
	Lifestyle Reflects the driver's commitment to, and execution of, an appropriate lifestyle (an important but hard-to-define construct). Justifications for ratings need to be particularly clear here.	Nightclub attendance and tabloid revelations reported in the past; now seems completely committed.	Score 1 to 10 **Actual score: 7**
	Environment Closely linked to lifestyle; relates to the level of support enjoyed by the driver across various areas such as finance, emotional support, facilities, etc.	Home life increasing in stability. Financially very comfortable. Seems committed to team but seems to need frequent contract clarification.	Score −5 to +5 **Actual score: +1**
	Coaching quality Based on observation, quality of coach's planning/peaking and technical input, and commitment to this driver.	Unsure about sources of coaching, but performance seems to suggest effective input.	Score 1 to 20 **Actual score: 16**
	Coaching development Reflects the coach's willingness and commitment to personal development, especially as pertaining to increasing their capacity to improve this driver.	Unable to evaluate; needs closer communication with driver.	Score 1 to 10 **Actual score: 4**
ATHLETE CHARACTERISTICS	**Physical suitability** Reflects the driver's suitability for the ultimately targeted competition, based on an estimation of their fully mature body shape and size.	Generally excellent leg, core, and neck strength, plus cardiovascular fitness, relative to progression markers.	Score 1 to 10 **Actual score: 9**
	Feeder championship potential Based on Final placing in team, scoring table, and number of starts	Potential to score if involved; may not commit.	Score 1 to 20 **Actual score: 10**
	Major championship potential Top formulas...open wheel, saloon car, etc.	If injury-free; has possibility of a world-level performance.	Score 1 to 20 **Actual score: 16**

FIGURE 1.2 *(continued)* Athlete performance/potential template (APPT).

balance of training (as detailed in the first part of the chapter), which can be tweaked to best effect.

Tool 3: Projection

Conversations on performance constructs (schemata) can be driven by almost any measure. The methods already described use subjective ratings between athletes, between athletes and a coach, or, in the second case, between coach or manager and athlete. Other options include use of performance analysis data; performers talk through strengths and weaknesses and the coach listens to the constructs they use. Indeed, some academies get young players to cut their own tapes of good and poor plays and share during a debriefing with coaches and peers, which is a fantastic way to build understanding over time. For younger athletes, coaches and caregivers can use a projection technique. Rather than ask the young performer to rate their performance, subtle inquiries can request their opinions about another player they are watching. The idea is that the young performer will use their own thoughts as the basis for their interpretation, projecting their thoughts. For example, consider a coach and athlete observing an excellent performance by a competitor, from which the coach picks up most on the preparation routine and core technical skills of the competitor, whereas the athlete picks up most on the competitor's physical stature and the support being provided to them by teammates and family members in the stands. Once again, you are getting an insight into the constructs they (and you) think are important—a balance you can use to check understanding and tweak as needed.

Optimization

So far, this chapter has made clear the benefits of integrating psychological training into your physical, technical, and tactical training, ideally in an individually periodized manner. It is important for this work to be grounded in the personal and shared mental models of all involved. Assuming you have both of these important elements sorted, how will things look in an effectively integrated program? The first characteristic will be that all the constructs identified by and agreed with the athletes will be featured in the program.

Second, the balance of these elements is likely to vary according to the phases of the season. However, that variation over time, plus the weighting of the different elements within a particular microcycle, will also fit with the structures and principles that the athletes have agreed to.

Third, whatever the particular balance at any particular time, a few other principles should apply. You may have heard of the idea of representative design. Originally developed as a way of designing experiments to make them more representative of real life (cf. Brunswik, 1955), the idea received a broad coverage and developed into an excellent principle for experimentation (e.g., Dhami et al., 2004). Since then, however, the idea has been somewhat misappropriated by some popular authors to suggest that unless a training medium is closely aligned with the real-life task, it lacks worth. This idea is somewhat oversimplified. What *is* true—and it offers the third principle for your checklist—is that efforts must be overt to largely relate training mediums to the target skill. For instance, strength and conditioning uses a feature called combination training; in this case the exercise will be immediately followed by another, which promotes the transfer of the training benefits to the skill. Judo athletes use a pulling exercise (e.g., bench pulls) followed by fast action pulls on a judogi (judo jacket) as the first part of a throw. Javelin throwers will combine bent arm pullovers with standing throws whilst sprinters will complete power cleans followed by sprint starts. From a psychological perspective, these combinations will encourage or even require athletes to employ a similar mental state for training to what they would use for competitive execution. In short, it is a focused and aggressive execution that matches training to the competitive demands of that particular sport. In summary, effective training will *mostly* match the training stimuli to the target activity.

Fourth, keep in mind that representative design is a sound principle, and it should certainly be a feature of a well-integrated and planned program—but not entirely. There will always be content that exists for other reasons, contributory but not necessarily falling into the representative design principle. On the strength side, there may be exercises to build joint integrity, especially at the early stages and through growth spurts. As another alternative, fatiguing exercises may be used in combination with technical practice, either real or in imagery—a different sort of combination training. Or there may be sessions as described in the assessment section, conducted with the specific aim of increasing understanding and buy-in from athletes. This principle is simply related to the *why* question. For every element, in whatever form, combination, or balance, always ask what it is designed to do and whether it can be tweaked to fulfill that aim more effectively. Don't just look at behavior; always consider it in combination with the rationale and intent presented. Recent work has started to view this idea as the RIB principle (see chapter 14).

The fifth concept relates to variation and enjoyment, both of which are as experienced by each athlete. The importance of variation—avoiding too much routine in the training regimen—is already clear. It is also important to include activities that the athlete enjoys. Otherwise, motivation is likely to erode (see chapters 5 and 8). This idea fits in with the previous one: Some elements might be included largely (or even sometimes entirely, at least for a while) because the athlete enjoys them. For example, the authors work with several athletes across individual sports who have built indoor climbing into their program. Even though transfer (through representative design) is not clear nor equivalence complete, there are lots of benefits (both psychological and physiological), which, together with the athlete's satisfaction, make it a positive inclusion.

Success Story: Catering to the Mental Side in an Olympic Sport's National Squad

This book offers case studies to illustrate successful real-world applications of the theories discussed. Because confidentiality is a major concern, these studies do not identify the participants or teams involved unless they have given their express permission. The following success story is a montage of examples drawn from different real-life cases. As you read it, be reassured that every element has worked in high-performance settings.

This case study describes a small national squad from an Olympic sport with a focus on the processes by which a shared understanding was built to support an effective focus and blend of training.

Consisting of 15 athletes, three coaches, a physical therapist, a strength and conditioning specialist, and a psychologist, the team had all moved to a new national center. This process involved most moving to accommodations in the new area. As one of the first actions in the new center, the head coach met with each athlete individually, talking them through the nested program that had been developed. Then, the athletes formed a small steering group made up of four elected seniors who acted as a feedback mechanism to the coaches.

Early on, the steering group raised the issue of the level of training severity. The athletes were training two or three times a day, with physical training, technical and tactical work, and practice and simulations combined into a challenging program. Practices were run by different coaches or the strength and conditioning staff, and the athletes were finding all sessions taxing; in fact, several athletes showed signs of overtraining. Two solutions were designed and implemented. First, the coaches committed to color coding sessions to facilitate communication and expectations across the team. Green sessions were designated as technical, with target heart rates set low. Amber sessions were a mix of tasks focused on aerobic intervals of work. Red sessions, limited in number, were full-out hard work. These categories were explicitly stated on the monthly program, and they varied week by week.

Second, training readiness measures were introduced. Completed first thing every day, this evaluation included questions about sleep quality and muscle soreness, a simple reaction-time task, and a power test (a standing jump for height). Large decreases in these measures resulted in an adjustment to the planned program.

Monthly tests were also included, offering athletes an opportunity to gauge their progress. These were followed by one-to-one debriefing sessions with plans adjusted collaboratively. Performance profiles were further completed every three months, and more formal reviews followed. Goals were set based on the stage of the season but also against each athlete's progress toward achieving their goals for the forthcoming Olympics.

Finally, and as a key proactive element, the physical therapist directed the separate preventive exercise program for each athlete, communicating regularly with other staff to ensure a well-understood mental model of practice.

As a result of these integrated tweaks, athletes, coaches, and support staff expressed their satisfaction with the improved processes. Indeed, all concerned felt that they were closer as a team. Outcomes were also positive at the European, World, and Olympic levels.

Conclusion

This chapter has stressed the value of intentionally and systematically including a mental side to your performance program. Indeed, as well as delivering specific psychological benefits, building in more (or better) mental work can also have a significant effect on your physical, technical, and tactical development and performance. The chapter also highlighted the foundational role of clearly identified and then openly discussed personal constructs. Indeed, few key pillars exist to any effective training environment, and communication based on these constructs is one that you should prioritize highly and monitor carefully. These messages and suggested tools offer ideas for you to try in your own situation as well as a lens through which to view the chapters that follow.

2 Case Conceptualization: Strategies for Assessing and Conceiving

Amanda Martindale

University of Edinburgh

Sport psychology consultants commonly use needs analysis, issue conceptualization, and case formulation to determine the key areas of development for individual athletes and how best to devise an effective plan of action. Athletes and coaches can also use one or all of these tools and strategies, albeit with a slightly different emphasis, to guide their practice. This chapter explores the relevance, knowledge base, assessment, and optimization of these key strategies for assessing and conceiving, thereby providing evidence-based guidelines to assist you with case conceptualization and applied practice.

Relevance

At all levels of sport, sport psychology consultants, athletes, and coaches assess the athlete's developmental needs, consider their issues, and formulate plans to aid this development. Of course, the extent to which people use these strategies, how formally or informally they may be applied, and how effectively they are used will vary greatly. Consequently, the aim of this chapter is to show you how to optimally use each of these case conceptualization strategies in your own pursuit of performance enhancement.

The importance of these strategies should not be underestimated; choosing the proper strategy has a significant effect on the success of the interventions designed and subsequently applied to the identified issues. For example, incorrectly identifying (or failing to identify) an underperforming gymnast's area of need, insufficiently building a picture of the main issues affecting a deselected rugby player, or formulating an ineffective plan for a judo player returning from injury can easily lead you down the wrong path or, even worse, to a dead end. In such cases, the needs and concerns can become (and may remain) persistent if not suitably addressed. Athletes, coaches, and sport psychology consultants also may experience damage to their relationships from following the wrong paths to dead ends. Effective use of needs analysis, issue conceptualization, and case formulation strategies are key skills highly prized by athletes, coaches, and support practitioners who seek to reach peak performance and identify possible further gains, however marginal.

The following sections outline a number of relevant principles to consider when using these strategies most effectively.

Validity of Data

Because it is a fundamental aspect of effective performance enhancement, the data used to identify needs must be logically and factually sound. To effectively ensure validity of data, you have to perform a comprehensive analysis of need and consider various sources of data. For example, a field athlete's perception that poor performance is down to poor technique would logically require triangulation with other sources of evidence (e.g., video footage, coach observation) to corroborate the theory. *Triangulation* means to include at least three sources of data. It allows for an internal consistency check to make sure the same area of need is apparent from each data source. In turn, it allows for more certainty that the need identified is indeed factually correct and not loosely based on a single observation.

In some cases, different answers may emerge from different sources. This observation is still relevant because it can lead to further questioning and consideration of how the identified factors may be interacting; for example, is another overarching factor—which is the root cause— showing itself through the two (or even more) factors being observed? The point is that in any situation, triangulation is useful even when the first picture is frustratingly complicated.

Applicability of Data

A sound appreciation of the athlete's needs (e.g., likely contributors to performance) and the specific task demands (e.g., physical, technical, tactical, and psychological) is required in order to ascertain which aspects of their performance are most likely to be applicable or attributable to the outcome. For example, focusing only on the physical and technical aspects of a cyclist's injury recovery, but not paying due consideration to psychological aspects such as fear of reinjury, may delay the reestablishment of the athlete, because data regarding their mental approaches to recovery are also relevant. Alternatively, for a diver who is struggling to learn a new technique, focusing on the development of psychological skills (e.g., positive self-talk such as *I can do it*) may not be as advantageous as an analysis of exactly where the skill breakdown is occurring (e.g., perhaps the coaching methods are failing to generate sufficient understanding of the new skill) and why (e.g., perhaps the core strength required is lacking). Your ability to discern the most applicable data is underpinned by declarative knowledge; in simple terms, the *why* and *why not* support the knowledge of what might relate to the performance challenge. This conceptual (descriptive) knowledge allows the athlete or coach to describe why a particular factor is important to develop and how it relates to the overall performance. Thus, in order to determine the athlete's needs and concerns most effectively, a sound understanding and appreciation of the performance task demands (and, therefore, the likely applicability of the data to be gathered and used) is required.

Rigorously Measuring Significance of Data

Related to gauging the applicability of data is the requirement for measuring the significance of the data (the extent to which it is important or worthy of attention) in a thorough and careful way. The question is whether the data is relevant or worthy of attention for this particular performer. For example, the use of match analysis statistics that show a particular soccer player lost or gave the ball away on a high percentage of occasions may indicate fatigue or lack of recovery rather than insufficient skill level or lack of motivation. Alternatively, it might be a feature of the player's high-risk style, especially if this trait is why the player was selected. Thus, data should be interpreted with caution and careful consideration so as not to draw incorrect conclusions regarding areas of need. Such misinterpretation could instigate a chain of intervention that is less likely to be effective or useful to the athlete (e.g., additional ball possession practice rather than additional recovery or conditioning). The use of triangulation helps in this situation also; performance can be monitored over time (e.g., a number of matches), and it can take into account other sources of data, such as performer views and physical therapy or strength and conditioning reports.

Operationalizing Efforts in the Right Direction

The importance of assessment and conceptualization strategies is best demonstrated through the importance of operationalizing efforts and resources in the right way or toward the right aspects of performance. A sound needs analysis, thorough conceptualization of the issues, and careful case formulation are more likely to accurately determine the most effective course of action and conversely prevent unnecessary time, efforts, and resources directed toward less fruitful areas. For example, a plateau in a target shooter's performance development may not occur because of insufficient psychological skills but rather because of insufficient flexibility in the deployment of those skills. In this case, continued efforts and resources to increase skill level may be futile and potentially wasted without due consideration of the development of the essential concomitant psychological flexibility and adaptability. On a larger scale, determining the needs of a team or squad of players will lead to operationalizing considerable efforts and resources; as such, the importance of using them in the right direction and for the right purposes escalates considerably.

Using a Design Aid for Planning

Within high-level sport, operationalizing efforts and resources occur in discrete time phases (e.g., weeks, series, seasons, years, cycles) that vary from sport to sport. Regardless of the particular time phases involved, undoubtedly the requirement exists for short-, medium-, and long-term planning. Strategies for assessment and conceptualization for working with athletes can inform this planning process and offer a design aid for planning. For example, a number of phases are likely to be involved in a judo player's return from injury (e.g., grief and coping, rehabilitation, return, and reestablishment; see Success Story 1: An Elite Judoka's Return From Injury). This nested planning approach is described in chapter 1 and shown in other contexts in other chapters (e.g., chapters 14 and 15). Conceptualizing these phases at an intervention level can assist with a nested planning approach to ensure that individual sessions are aligned to the relevant phase and that the injury recovery intervention is conducted in a manner that is conducive to the overall program of support (e.g., to foster independence and empowerment in the athlete). The use of professional judgment and decision making (PJDM) is key; it ensures that a coherent plan for change can be implemented alongside the nested planning for discrete phases. How the athlete or coach frames the injury recovery period (e.g., as an opportunity to upskill or develop uninjured areas) will aid the planning process depending on what best fits the unique context.

Success Story 1:
An Elite Judoka's Return From Injury

This case study is an example of needs analysis, issue conceptualization, and case formulation as applied to an elite judo player recovering from injury. Corrin (a pseudonym) sustained a ruptured anterior cruciate ligament (ACL) in her knee just before a major international competition that would have represented the pinnacle of her judo career to date.

The *needs analysis* in this case study used triangulation with a range of tools, including a diary and thought log, regular semistructured interviews, informal interviews with social support, regular consultations with the physical therapist, and observations of physical demeanor and body language. It was immediately apparent that support would shift from predominantly focusing on performance to assisting with recovery from serious injury and all the personal, social, and practical consequences of it.

In this example, *issue conceptualization* was aided by the practitioner's awareness of Corrin's personality and lines of reinforcement; understanding of her life situation and social support systems; use of mainstream psychology, sport psychology, and sport science knowledge bases; and empathy for the needs of rehabilitation and performance environments. Given that rehabilitation from injury typically follows a series of phases, psychological support to Corrin was considered more likely to be effective if it matched (and evolved) with these phases:

Supporting an athlete recovering from injury involves multiple processes, including needs analysis and issue conceptualization.

> *continued*

> *continued*

1. *Grief and coping*: upset and loss, acceptance of injury, adjustment
2. *Rehabilitation*: overeagerness, frustration and dejection, sense of time dragging, loss of judo
3. *Return*: timing of return, decay of or interference with technique, fear of reinjury, preference for safer techniques
4. *Reestablishment*: technique adaptation, loss of confidence, scrutiny regarding recovery

This process of issue conceptualization led to the formation of intentions for impact and therefore directly influenced subsequent implementation.

In terms of *case formulation*, planning took place to ensure that support of the athlete remained cohesive throughout intervention and individual sessions. This emphasis on planning and the gradual layering of support enabled the intervention to stay on track and meet the needs of the athlete during all phases of recovery. In this case, the implementation of support was designed to address the main issues in each phase, progressing in sequence and flowing logically from phase to phase as follows:

1. *Grief and coping*: provision of comfort and support, use of counseling, use of motivational videos
2. *Rehabilitation*: reinforcement of the physical therapist's messages, goal setting, personal development, performance simulation
3. *Return*: realistic perspective, performance simulation, positive imagery
4. *Reestablishment*: use of technical coaches and videos, systematic desensitization, attribution restructuring

It is important to establish the scientific rationale as part of issue conceptualization before proceeding with an intervention to ensure that this action is well informed. For more detail on this case study, see Martindale & Collins (2012).

What We Know

The key strategies for assessing and conceiving are needs analysis, issue conceptualization, and case formulation. As mentioned in the introduction, these tools and strategies are commonly used in sport psychology (e.g., Martindale & Collins, 2012), are increasingly used in coaching (e.g., Abraham & Collins, 2011), and are growing in other sport sciences such as strength and conditioning (e.g., Downes & Collins, 2021).

Needs Analysis

The needs analysis typically involves an initially broad assessment of the performer, the task, and the environment, and it becomes more specific as it progresses (see Applicability of Data). Preliminary assessment objectives include gaining awareness of any presenting (obvious) issues, strengths, areas for development, and any contextual or situational demands. The aim is to establish the psychological skills required to perform the task and to identify any skills that may require development or improvement. For example, if a hockey player experiencing a performance slump falls into a negative mindset, it is worth exploring what particular aspects are involved (e.g., negative self-talk, negative imagery, or poor relations with teammates). Adopting a scientist-practitioner standpoint to determine the areas to investigate will facilitate a test-and-adjust approach to uncovering the areas of greatest need. In short, the coach or athlete adopts an investigative approach, trying out possible solutions to see which one offers the best fit to the data (Schön, 1991). Later in the process, this same approach requires the coach to experiment, trying out solutions and checking to see which ones generate the best outcomes.

Issue Conceptualization

This important, though often neglected, mediating phase comes after the needs analysis is complete and before any intervention begins (Poczwardowski et al., 1998). Basically, during this phase you pause and think about the data to make sure you are reading it correctly. Issue conceptualization provides the essential bridge in evidence-based practice and effectively represents the scientific rationale for any proposed intervention; in other words, it's about *why* you are doing what you are doing. Of course, it is important to establish this rationale before proceeding with an intervention to ensure that this action is well informed. This stage can also usefully include why you are choosing *not* to do what you are not doing. Continuing the scientist-practitioner approach, you might also try out your reasoning with another person who can check your arithmetic.

In addition to the needs analysis and assessment data, the use of a range of knowledge bases is important. Psychological, scientific, personal, and situational knowledge are relevant. You may need to consult relevant literature and research about the identified areas of need or reach out to specialists in each area of interest. This approach builds on the idea that more heads are better than one. It is analogous to a builder who studies building regulations, seeks advice from other builders who have done similar jobs, or consults a specialist such as a structural engineer. A sport-related example involves a long-distance swimmer whose attention is wandering during performance; in this case, it would be worth exploring contemporary literature on what tools or techniques can be most effective for attentional control in endurance events. This scientific knowledge base combines with a personal knowledge base from past experience and your skilled intuition. As Kreber (2002) suggested, knowledge base alone does not determine expertise; rather, the ability to utilize that knowledge in practice in the most effective manner does. Therefore, issue conceptualization provides the opportunity to consider why any proposed action is likely to have a positive, performance-enhancing effect. This declarative knowledge—being able to describe *why* a particular factor is important and *how* it relates to overall performance—will be embedded in how the performer's issues have been conceptualized.

Case Formulation

Case formulation is generating a set of hypotheses about the causes and maintaining influences of a performer's psychological, interpersonal, and behavioral issues (Eells, 2002). In other words, it represents your proposed explanation of what may be going on for a particular performer based on the data or evidence you have gathered. Case formulation skills include obtaining relevant data (see Validity of Data, Applicability of Data, and Rigorously Measuring Significance of Data) and integrating that information into a conceptualization of the athlete's main issue(s) (see Issue Conceptualization). Further case formulation skills include the extent to which a coherent plan for change follows logically from the conceptualization, and the extent to which interventions are in sequence or context as specified by theory. In short, does everything seem to flow logically and follow from stage to stage? For example, in the case of the injured judo player (see Success Story 1: An Elite Judoka's Return From Injury), an understanding of the main issues (adjustment, loss, interference with technique, and fear of reinjury) enabled the development of a phased approach to intervention (grief and coping, rehabilitation, return and reestablishment) and the evolution of skill development throughout (use of imagery for performance simulation).

In pursuit of accurately identifying areas of need or concern, a comprehensive approach to assessment and measurement is required. Unidimensional approaches such as performance profiling (Butler & Hardy, 1992) can be a good place to start, particularly to gauge the athlete's perspective of what is important and what they think they need. The use of a multimodal approach known by the acronym BASIC I.D. is particularly helpful for a broader assessment (Lazarus, 1997, 2003). It involves the following seven interactive modalities: behavior, affect, sensation, imagery, cognitions, interpersonal functioning, and drugs and biological functioning. The following section considers what questions (adapted from Lazarus, 2004) are relevant to explore, and what tools and techniques can be used to assess or measure each of these seven modalities.

Behavior

What is the athlete doing that is getting in the way of their performance or fulfilling their potential (e.g., self-defeating actions, unhelpful behaviors)? What does the athlete need to stop or start doing (increase or decrease)? A range of tools, including self-reports, observation, video analysis, and pre-competition checklists, can gauge behavior.

Affect

What emotions (affective reactions) does the athlete experience? To what extent? What seems to generate any negative affects experienced (e.g., cognitions, images, interpersonal conflict)? How does affect interact with the other modalities (e.g., how does the athlete respond or behave)? Affect can be assessed through self-reports, observation, and psychometric scales (e.g., anxiety scales).

Sensation

What positive (e.g., visual, auditory, tactile) or negative (e.g., tension, pain, tightness) sensations and sensory experiences does the athlete report? Sensation can provide an indication of the athlete's attentional focus. Techniques to measure sensation include self-reports, self-monitoring, and psychophysiological assessment (e.g., electrodermal activity).

Imagery

What spontaneous images does the athlete report? Do they have specific images of success or failure? Do they have negative images? How are these images connected to the other modalities? What is the athlete's self-image? Imagery can be measured using self-reports, guided imagery, self-monitoring, and psychophysiological assessment (e.g., electroencephalography [EEG]).

Cognitions

What are the athlete's main values, attitudes, and beliefs? Does the athlete display functional (helpful) or dysfunctional (unhelpful) beliefs? To what extent are these beliefs flexible or adaptable? Is self-talk generally positive or negative? Does the athlete have any automatic thoughts that potentially undermine performance? Cognitions can be accessed and assessed through self-reports, self-monitoring (e.g., audio or thought logs), and simulated recall (e.g., using video footage).

Interpersonal Functioning

Who are the significant others in the athlete's life? What is expected in each of these interpersonal relationships? Which relationships are rewarding for the athlete, and which ones cause tension or distress? Interpersonal functioning can be gauged through self-reports, interviews with significant others (with consent), and observation.

Tim Clayton/Corbis via Getty Images

While sharing many similarities, all athletes have unique characteristics and needs that should be considered in the case formulation process.

Drugs and Biological Functioning

Is the athlete functioning well biologically and physiologically? Do they have any medical issues or injuries? What details are relevant regarding diet (nutrition, hydration), weight, sleep, prescribed medication, and alcohol or other drug use? This modality can be measured using self-reports, medical evaluations, and physical therapy evaluations.

To operationalize the BASIC I.D. approach, consider the example of a tennis player who overtly displays aggressive behavior (e.g., slamming a racket) when losing a point. The athlete self-reports a high degree of anger and frustration, affects and emotions that contribute to the behavior. Sensations when losing a point are mainly those of tension and tightness connected to feelings of rage. Losing a point can lead to images of failure and contribute to the athlete's negative self-image. Cognitions are highly self-critical; they contain thoughts such as *must*, *ought to*, and *should have*—beliefs that are rigid, unrealistic, and extreme. Self-talk is negative and unhelpful. Interpersonal relationships are tense with support staff, parents, and life partners, who are dismayed at the player's regular outbursts and obvious discontentment. The athlete is carrying a few minor injuries and is unable to train to the maximum, which fuels further self-criticism.

As this example demonstrates, the use of the BASIC I.D. approach allows for a thorough assessment of the areas of need and concern (e.g., aggressive outbursts, feelings of anger and rage, negative self-image, and irrational beliefs) and contributes to the identification of the likely issues (e.g., maladaptive perfectionism, low self-esteem, and low frustration tolerance). In simple terms, it offers a checklist to make sure that you consider everything that is relevant rather than rush to address a single (if obvious) element of the overall problem. A multimodal approach using BASIC I.D. and related techniques can inform the issue conceptualization and case formulation processes that follow; therefore it has significant implications on the subsequent planning of support.

Assessment

The previous section introduced the multimodal BASIC I.D. approach and identified tools and techniques for measuring each modality. This section summarizes the most common assessment techniques. It is crucial that you follow principles of good practice regarding assessment (e.g., use of valid and reliable measures, triangulation), so assessment guidelines are offered too. Finally, this section provides some suggestions for assessing your issue conceptualization and case formulation.

Techniques for Assessment

The scope of potential assessment techniques is vast, and it can be difficult to navigate selection of the most appropriate tools. This section outlines the main categories of assessment techniques, namely interviews, surveys, questionnaires, observation, and techniques to access cognition. This section also provides a rationale for each technique and some pointers for what to look out for in implementing them.

Interviews

Semistructured interviews with athletes are instrumental in the assessment toolkit. In fact, you can use this form of self-report for any or all of the BASIC I.D. modalities. You can use questions that are formal, informal, direct, or indirect in order to uncover relevant information about each modality. Using a semistructured approach allows you to have a set of predetermined questions while also having room for flexibility depending on the athlete's response and where the conversation ultimately goes. You can also informally interview significant others (e.g., parents, peers, teammates, physical therapists) with the athlete's permission. Sample questions for athletes include asking how things are going in training, during events, with peers and teammates; asking about any specific challenges or concerns; and asking about current goals or targets for performance.

Surveys

Using surveys provides valuable data. Surveys are key to understanding peak behaviors (e.g., through a comparison of best and worst performances) and critical issues or moments in task performance. The use of surveys offers an internal consistency check with which to triangulate behavior, interviews, and the perspectives of others. For example, the use of a preperformance survey (e.g., asking whether the performer has a clear preevent strategy in the buildup to performance) offers valuable information about the athlete's awareness of their preperformance preparation and whether this awareness is consistent with the observed preperformance behavior. You can also use surveys as the basis for projective questioning to uncover certain behaviors (e.g., *Why would that happen? Can you tell me a bit more about that?*).

Questionnaires

You can use a vast range of questionnaires or psychometric tools as part of an assessment or needs analysis. The skill is to select which ones are likely to offer a valuable insight or additional source of data on a particular issue rather than to subject the athlete to paperwork overload. Some athletes are happy to sit and complete a questionnaire or scale; others are skeptical or cynical about their worth. Indeed, athletes who are savvy and those who are anxious may even try to guess what is being measured and fake good on the results. In such cases, using valid and reliable measures and making sure athletes are informed about the benefits and limitations of each tool are invaluable. Questionnaires that gauge psychological characteristics (e.g., Psychological Characteristics of Developing Excellence Questionnaire [PCDEQ]; MacNamara & Collins, 2011) are a great starting point. From there, tools that are more specific can be selected as appropriate. For example, if anxiety or confidence are concerns, you can use the Cognitive and Somatic Anxiety Inventory 2 (CSAI-2; Martens et al., 1990) to investigate further. Also, consider questionnaire tools that can offer an insight to wider team and coaching processes, such as the Talent Development Environment Questionnaire (TDEQ; Martindale et al., 2010). As with any measure, triangulation is a key step. Although a questionnaire may offer some clear and objective data, you still need multiple perspectives to keep it in check.

Observation

Observation, especially over time, offers a key window to athlete responses in the performance environment. You can observe the athlete in a range of settings, such as in training; before, during, and after performance (in real time or through video footage); and in a range of scenarios (e.g., winning, losing, best possible circumstances, and suboptimal circumstances). Observation offers an invaluable source of information and data to consider, particularly for gauging behavior, affect, and interpersonal functioning. For example, how is behavior affected when conditions are not ideal? What emotions are experienced, and to what extent? How does interpersonal functioning differ under conditions of high or low stress?

Techniques to Access Cognition

Sport psychology consultants are especially interested in the athlete's thought processes (cognitions); however, the intangible and private nature of cognitions makes them difficult to observe or evaluate. Fortunately, you can use a range of techniques to make an athlete's thinking visible as part of your needs analysis. These techniques include informal self-reports (e.g., the athlete discloses what was going through their mind before, during, and after performance) and the use of diaries or thought logs, in which the athlete records their thoughts and cognitions in a more structured fashion to allow for later reflection with a coach or teammate. Video footage can also be used for the purposes of stimulated recall (e.g., video is paused and the athlete is asked to recall what was going through their mind at any given time during the performance). In certain contexts, think-aloud protocols may be relevant or appropriate; for example, they have been used in training for endurance events. Sometimes you may be interested in accessing the athlete's macrocognition—higher-order functions and processes such as planning, sensemaking, decision making, and coordinating. In these cases, cognitive task analysis (CTA) techniques can be helpful. CTA techniques involve analyzing the cognitive task (e.g., the demands involved in decision making) rather than performing a cognitive analysis of the task, which is a common misperception. These techniques can shed light on how athletes assess situations and also what cues and strategies they use to guide their actions.

Guidelines for Assessment

The following assessment guidelines (adapted from Heil & Henschen, 1996) are helpful to consider as part of this process. First, you should share your views on the role of assessment in order to explain its limitations, allay any fears the athletes may have (e.g., about how the data will be used), and confirm arrangements for confidentiality and access to the data (tell them who will see it and for what purposes). Athletes might have some preconceptions about testing and the influence of any assessment undertaken (e.g., on selection), so take the time to explain it clearly.

Use only assessments you consider essential to the process. Try to use assessments that are applicable to the focus (see Applicability of Data). Ensure that you use valid, reliable, and specific instruments (see Validity of Data). Explain the results of any assessments in a simple, clear, and concise way, and use examples when interpreting the results. Allow ample opportunity for follow-up questions and discussion. Finally, whenever possible, use triangulation as part of your assessment process (see Rigorously Measuring Significance of Data).

Assessing Issue Conceptualization and Case Formulation

You can use the BASIC I.D. approach to perform a comprehensive needs analysis, adhering to the principles of good practice and the recommended assessment guidelines. However, how can you accurately assess issue conceptualization and case formulation? Assessment can come from oneself (e.g., critical reflection), peers (e.g., peer support and mentoring), and others (e.g., support staff).

In terms of critical reflection, carefully consider the justification or rationale for the issues taking precedence and for the plan or intervention that you are devising. The central questions are related to the logic and flow of the issues and proposed actions (e.g., are they embedded with knowledge and theory as well as a practical understanding of the task?). Checking your issue conceptualization and case formulation with a respected and trusted peer can be a valuable source of support or mentoring and is a common part of a community of practice (CoP) approach. Finally, it is also important to test these ideas with the athletes (if a coach) or with support staff (if an athlete) to gauge accuracy, receive feedback, and secure buy-in for the change to follow.

Optimization

This chapter has highlighted many of the strategies for optimizing needs analysis and issue conceptualization. For needs analysis, it is important to consider the relevant principles (validity of data, applicability of data, measuring significance of data in a rigorous way, operationalizing efforts in the right direction, and using a design aid for planning). It is also important for the needs analysis to be comprehensive and multimodal (BASIC I.D.). Finally, it is crucial to follow principles of good practice with regard to assessment (e.g., use of valid and reliable measures, use of triangulation) and to follow assessment guidelines (e.g., regarding awareness of limitations and clarifying confidentiality).

For issue conceptualization, give due consideration to this aspect of the process before proceeding with an intervention to ensure that the action is well informed. This pause to reflect on your thinking makes a difference on the eventual outcome. Consulting with relevant literature and with peers or mentors can help to ensure that this phase has been covered appropriately. Your own knowledge base (in relation to the performer, the task, and the environment) and your declarative knowledge about why any proposed action is likely to have a positive or performance-enhancing effect are both vital components. During this critical time, check your own chain of decision making—the rationale for your proposed action, the intention for impact, and the behavior required to make this change. The remainder of this section focuses on case formulation and how this strategy can be measured and optimized in performance.

Measuring Quality of Case Formulation

You can measure the quality of case formulation using these eight criteria: comprehensiveness, formulation elaboration, precision of language and terminology, complexity, coherence, intervention plan elaboration, goodness of fit (of the formulation to the intervention plan), and systematic process (Eells et al., 2005). These criteria offer a useful reflective tool for measuring the quality of case formulation. They also provide a useful set of prompts for consideration during the development of case formulation. As with the development of any skill, the more they are used and practiced, the more automatic and consistent their use becomes.

Comprehensiveness

Comprehensiveness is the range of information categories discussed in the formulation regardless of the extent to which the ideas were elaborated. The range of categories includes *insufficient information*, *very little comprehensiveness*, *little comprehensiveness*, *moderately comprehensive*, and *highly comprehensive*.

Formulation Elaboration

Formulation elaboration describes the extent to which the athlete's issues were articulated and developed. The range of categories includes *not present*, *present but not elaborated*, *present and slightly elaborated*, *present and moderately elaborated*, and *present and highly elaborated*.

Precision of Language and Terminology

This term refers to the extent to which language was used to describe an individual athlete (formulation tailored to the individual athlete). It refers to the degree of articulation and specificity in the use of language and terminology but not to the quality or amount of information covered. The range of categories includes *insufficient information*, *very little precision*, *little precision*, *moderate precision*, and *high precision*.

Complexity

Complexity describes the extent to which several facets of the athlete's issues were integrated into a meaningful presentation. Highly complex formulations either integrate several aspects of the athlete's issues and functioning or develop one or two themes extensively. The range of categories includes *insufficient information*, *very little complexity*, *little complexity*, *moderate complexity*, and *high complexity*.

Coherence

Coherence describes the extent to which the formulation provided an internally consistent account of the athlete's issues. It is the extent to which the formulation could be summarized in a short, meaningful sentence. The range of categories includes *insufficient information*, *very little coherence*, *little coherence*, *moderate coherence*, and *high coherence*.

Intervention Plan Elaboration

Intervention plan elaboration describes how well the intervention plan was explained or developed. The range of categories includes *insufficient information*, *very little elaboration*, *little elaboration*, *moderate elaboration*, and *high elaboration*.

Goodness of Fit

Goodness of fit is the extent to which the intervention plan was consistent with the formulation. It describes the extent to which the intervention plan addressed the issues raised in the formulation. The range of categories includes *insufficient information*, *very little consistency*, *little consistency*, *moderate consistency*, and *high consistency*.

Systematic Process

The systematic process reveals the degree of evidence that a predetermined, structured approach was used to organize the athlete's information into a formulation. The range of categories includes *no evidence or nearly no evidence*, *little evidence*, *moderate degree of evidence*, *clear and convincing evidence*, and *evidence beyond a reasonable doubt*.

Optimizing Case Formulation

Research in cognitive science has shown that experts process information differently than novices. For example, experts have superior pattern recognition skills, they use problem-solving strategies that emphasize comprehension, and they represent problems in more meaningful conceptual ways than novices (Glaser and Chi, 1988). Therefore, you can expect the quality of case formulation skills of expert coaches to be superior to that of novice or inexperienced coaches. This evidence forms part of the rationale for accessing a mentor or peer who may be more experienced with case formulation as part of the quality checking process.

In considering the question of what cognitive processes enable the expert to produce better formulations, Eells et al. (2005) offered the following explanations that can be contextualized to a sport performance setting: Expert coaches perceive meaningful patterns in their analysis, probably due to the organization of their knowledge base. Expert coaches can see and represent issues in their sport or discipline at a deeper level than novices who are more likely to represent an issue by its surface features. Expert coaches have strong self-monitoring skills, so they are more aware of when they make errors and when they need to recheck their solutions.

Success Story 2: A Junior Judoka's Quest for Performance Enhancement

This case study provides an example of needs analysis, issue conceptualization, and case formulation as applied to an elite junior judo player. He was a member of the national development squad and actively sought sport psychology consultation for performance enhancement following variable results in competitions.

The *needs analysis* in this case study used triangulation of a range of tools including interviews, training observations, competition observation, and performance profiling. The BASIC I.D. framework was used to develop a detailed picture of the athlete's presenting issues in training and competition. In this case, psychometric assessment (questionnaires) was not used with more ecologically valid assessment techniques preferred. In this example, the client was unsure about where he specifically wanted to improve, but he identified confidence, dedication, and professionalism as areas where gains could be made.

In terms of *issue conceptualization*, the primary issue identified by the consultant was a significant lack of self-belief. It was particularly the case for throwing techniques (nagewaza) as opposed to ground techniques (newaza), and it was evident in his negative thoughts and beliefs and avoidant behavior. A pervasive lack of self-esteem was also identified as an issue following the needs analysis phase. Intentions for impact were formed at this broad program level to optimize self-efficacy, facilitate self-acceptance, and facilitate autonomy and self-regulation in training and competition.

Following a break in the consultation process to allow the performer to reevaluate his goals and intentions, complete an outstanding academic course, and move to a location nearer to the coach and training facility, further specific intentions for impact were formed to optimize physical development, perceptions of control, and process-focused perceptions. Importantly, each of these intervention-level intentions were consistent with the broad program-level intentions to optimize self-efficacy and self-regulation.

As part of *case formulation*, a nine-week intervention package was developed as a coherent plan for change that followed logically from the case conceptualization. The plan included work on fitness and power to optimize physical development, a number of strategies to optimize perceptions of control (e.g., self-talk, formulation of fight plans, use of performance simulation, and prefight preparation), and optimizing preevent confidence through refinement and reinforcement techniques. The intervention package was sequenced in three blocks, and it was underpinned by supporting literature, theory, and research. For more detail on this case study, see Cruickshank (2013).

Conclusion

When addressing an athlete's issue, it can be very tempting to jump to conclusions and get started on sorting the obvious problem. This approach is understandable, especially when the sport psychology consultant or the coach is keen to make a difference for the performer. However, reflecting carefully and allowing sufficient time to formulate a proper plan of action will reap better results than a hasty reaction will, even if a quick reaction is initially welcomed as evidence of your dynamism and concern for your athletes. In fact, as you practice the case conceptualization process, your results will become quicker, more accurate, and more effective.

3 | Integrating Athlete- and Performance- Centered Approaches

Andreas Küttel

University of Southern Denmark

When people think about elite athletes, they typically imagine someone young and fit who is at the pinnacle of their sport career, achieving great results, and celebrating victories. They might also imagine someone overwhelmed by emotion after a defeat or a disappointing performance. Elite sport is about winning, but success is never guaranteed. Furthermore, athletes are more than machines that produce results. The typical elite sport narrative, *The only way to athletic success is through a single-minded dedication to sport* (Carless & Douglas, 2013), is promoted by many stakeholders, which generates an expectation for athletes to focus and commit 100 percent of themselves to sport in order to be successful. Using this perspective, commitments in other life domains (e.g., education, work, relationships, hobbies) are seen as distractions from what is important (athletic success and results) that consequently should be reduced to a minimum. Kidman (2005) describes such an approach as coaches controlling athletes' behavior not only through training and competition but also beyond the sport setting, hence disempowering the athletes. Kidman further highlights that many coaches applying this approach believe *they*—the coaches—are expected to win and that successful coaches should be hard-nosed and discipline oriented. Coaches are not the only ones who promote this approach. In biographies, articles, and through social media, retired elite athletes have stressed that this sole focus was central to their success (e.g., Kobe Bryant and the Mamba Mentality; Harrison et al., 2016).

In contrast, the athlete- or person-centered approach is consistent with social constructivist theories of learning in which coaches and athletes are both centrally involved in the learning process. Athlete-centered coaching aims to empower athletes to become self-aware and independent, and responsible for their development and decision making within and outside the domain of sport. A fundamental belief of this holistic perspective is that each person is a compilation of multiple selves. Athletes have their own roles, responsibilities, needs, wants, and stressors, and they all interact and affect each other.

This chapter emphasizes the importance of supporting athletes holistically from a whole person perspective, thereby making them more resourceful in sport and life. The reasoning is grounded in the author's experience as a former elite athlete, research stemming from studies about athletes' (dual) careers as well as mental health, and applied experience as a sport psychology practitioner and career advisor in high-performance sport. This chapter discusses relevance of athlete-centered approaches and what we know about them. Next, it presents various tools for assessment. Finally, it offers recommendations for optimization for athletes, coaches, and environments.

Relevance

This chapter is relevant for athletes, coaches, and sport psychology consultants. Athletes can find inspiration to create an optimal balance between sport performance and other life domains, which can lead to career excellence in sport and life beyond it. Furthermore, athletes can realize that ongoing preparation for a second career while competing is doable and meaningful. Coaches can further develop their coaching skills by integrating a caring approach (Dohsten et al., 2020) and use their influential role to support athletes aiming for career excellence. Sport psychology consultants can expand their toolbox beyond the principles of psychological skills training related to performance enhancement and use a holistic-ecological approach when working with clients or organizations.

Since early 2020, the COVID-19 pandemic brought unexpected challenges to athletes and other stakeholders in sport. Closed facilities, canceled competitions, and limited group sizes for training brought uncertainty to all involved. Clearly, not only were athletes' sport schedules, sport goals, and motivation affected, but the pandemic also had a considerable effect on their psychosocial development (isolation, relationships, living situation), financial situation (reduced income from sponsors, no prize money), and psychological level (reduced well-being, challenged athletic identity). In general, crisis situations disturb the equilibrium of the status quo but may also provide an opportunity for change and development. Resourceful athletes who are able to apply relevant coping strategies and have high adaptability and life skills have better chances of emerging stronger out of poor situations when those situations return to their previous conditions.

What We Know

The following sections provide an overview of the whole-career and whole-person perspective, challenges in sport and other life domains as opportunities to enhance life skills and personal characteristics, the roles of coaches and the coach–athlete relationship, and athlete- and performance-related issues at the Olympics.

A Whole-Career and Whole-Person Perspective With a Dual-Career Focus

Contemporary views on athletes' careers embrace the notion of athletes as whole persons (persons who engage in sport and other life matters such as studies, work, family); athletes' development as holistic (athletic development complemented by other layers that influence each other in multiple ways); career transitions as crucial turning phases in career development (coping with transition demands leading to more successful or less successful outcomes); and athletic career as part of life career. The concept of athlete career excellence, defined as the ability to sustain a healthy, successful, and long-lasting career in sport and life, was introduced to complement the established concepts of performance and personal excellence (Stambulova et al., 2020).

The holistic athletic career (HAC) model (Wylleman et al., 2011) is a framework that provides an overview of the development stages and normative transitions athletes go through on their sport pathway through interrelated layers (i.e., athletic, psychological, psychosocial, academic-vocational, financial, and legal). While early phases in the sport career are characterized by playful activities and sampling of different sports, specialization and increasing training load with a focus on results and winning are typical for later stages. Career transition frameworks (e.g., Schlossberg, 1981; Stambulova, 2003) can help to explain how various factors (e.g., demands, resources, barriers, situation, support, coping strategies) interact to create different transitional outcomes. Career assistance covers various intervention types provided by sport psychology consultants or career assistance programs (for an overview in 19 countries, see Stambulova & Ryba, 2013).

Globally, many elite and semi-elite athletes are engaged in a dual career (DC); in other words, they have two major foci—one on sport and the other on studies or work (Stambulova & Wylleman, 2019). While the U.S. collegiate system has been the predominant pathway for U.S. athletes toward elite or professional sports (90% of the 2012 U.S. Olympic team members were student-athletes), DC pathways in other countries are more diverse and depend heavily on local sport systems and DC possibilities (Küttel et al., 2020). A variety of benefits are associated with a DC, such as developing a multidimensional identity and a sense of well-being (Brewer & Petitpas, 2017; Pink et al., 2015). Findings from a recent review suggest that student-athletes develop academic identities, albeit these identities are likely to be less important to their definition of self when compared with their athletic identities, particularly in earlier university years (Steele et al., 2020). Successful athletic retirement (Küttel et al., 2017) and increased life satisfaction after sport (Lavallee & Robinson, 2007) are further potential benefits. Indeed,

UpperCut Images/Getty Images

Many elite athletes are engaged in a dual career: sport and studies.

focusing on an alternative career has also been described as a relief from the pressures of sport and provides a broader perspective (Aquilina, 2013; Pink et al., 2015). DC athletes have mentioned higher levels of motivation to maintain endeavors in both sport and education to obtain these benefits (Aquilina, 2013; Cosh & Tully, 2014).

In terms of athletic performance, student-athletes seem to have better medal prospects than those who have not attended university. For example, in London 2012, 40 percent of the Australian team were student-athletes, and they won 63 percent of the medals. Similarly, the 30 percent of the French team who were student-athletes won 56 percent of their team's medals (Knapp, 2012), and 80 percent of the Danish medals in Rio 2016 came from the 36 percent of the team who were student-athletes (Bundgaard, 2016). These numbers indicate that engaging in an alternative career does not harm performance at major sport events.

Clearly, the demands DC athletes meet are many, and they require time and effort. DC athletes have to prioritize (e.g., school during the exam period or sport when approaching competitions) and make shifts depending on life situations to find an optimal DC balance (Stambulova et al., 2015). Conscious shifting of domain-specific identities across time may also be an important strategy in reducing role conflict, supporting well-being, and achieving goals in both sport and academic domains. For instance, during athletic competition, the athletic identity is likely to be dominant in the individual's sense of self, whereas during university exams, academic identity is likely to be more central. Student-athletes who can rapidly shift the salience of their academic and athletic identities as they complete different types of tasks are better at achieving this DC balance (Yopyk & Prentice, 2005). However, athletes' ability to manage a DC is described as heavily dependent on support from significant others (Knight et al., 2018), a well-functioning DC environment (Henriksen, Storm, et al., 2020), and the possession of DC competencies (De Brandt et al., 2017).

Some negative aspects of pursuing two career goals simultaneously have also been reported. DC pursuits can be very challenging because of the great time effort (80+ hours per week) and the intense pressures on physical and mental energy (Sorkkila et al., 2017). Thus, DC athletes have reported feeling compelled to compromise one of their pursuits (Cartigny et al., 2021) and find it difficult to maintain a DC balance. Role conflict may also occur when the demands of one role interfere with meeting the demands of another (van Rens et al., 2018). In addition, DC athletes generally feel underequipped. For example, in a quantitative study of 107 Flemish elite student-athletes, DC athletes rated their DC competencies as lower than the level they perceived as needed to deal with the various demands on them (De Brandt et al., 2017).

Success Story:
Sport and Life Through a Dual Career

This case study is autobiographical; it comes from the author's own experience. My career as a member of the Swiss national ski jumping team (which won the World Championship title in 2009) lasted for 15 years. Following a DC pathway, which luckily my coaches supported, I received a master's degree in sports sciences in 2006. Combining my ski jumping career (150 travel days per year) with the study schedule was an intense challenge. It demanded high flexibility of my learning style, agreements with coaches to accommodate my training plans, and constant negotiations with tutors concerning assignments. Adapting to this DC lifestyle took time. It required that I improve my planning and prioritizing competencies and gain higher awareness of my different roles as student or athlete. While training camp days are packed and study time is limited, competition days follow another rhythm; generally, they allow for more spare time. Instead of worrying (or trying not to think) about the upcoming competition the whole day, I used this time as an opportunity to dive into my textbooks, focusing me on a different challenging task. Switching back to the athlete mindset when preparing for the competition, I felt recharged and ready, knowing that on that day I had developed as a person no matter how the competition would end.

My transition out of sport in 2011 was a turbulent phase in which I had to deal with changes on different levels (e.g., social, vocational, financial) along with adapting to the challenges of moving to another country with my family. During my first year living in Denmark, learning the local language and taking care of our child were my primary tasks. Looking for a new challenge, I reached out to the local university, proposing my research idea. After funding was in place, I started a PhD in 2013. My thesis focused on athletic retirement from a cultural perspective. Many of the competencies gathered in and through my DC (e.g., perseverance, seeking help, planning and organizing, and balancing intense intellectual efforts with daily regeneration and a healthy and active lifestyle) were essential to successfully completing my doctorate degree.

Challenges as Opportunities to Enhance Life Skills and Personal Characteristics

For elite athletes involved in chronic high-pressure and goal-oriented environments, the ability to manage reactions to all types of stressors can have major effects on performance and well-being (Bryan et al., 2019; Küttel & Larsen, 2019). When developing resilience-associated resources (e.g., support, self-efficacy, optimism, coping skills, motivation, perspective) in both sport and work, you need to consider what effect it will have both on the long-term development and upcoming adverse circumstances. How competencies and skills learned in the sports domain can be used in nonsport settings and vice versa is another relevant consideration (Lebrun et al., 2018). Life skills can be behavioral, cognitive, interpersonal, or intrapersonal. They are defined as "internal personal assets, characteristics and skills such as goal setting, emotional control, self-esteem, and hard work ethic that can be facilitated or developed in sport and are transferred for use in non-sport settings" (Gould & Carson, 2008, p. 60). A prevailing myth held among many coaches and parents is that sport participation automatically teaches athletes life skills. However, these skills must be intentionally taught and fostered throughout the sport experience with coach characteristics, teaching strategies, and athletes' assets mediating this process (Turnnidge & Côté, 2016).

Contrary to the linear development of athletes' careers described in the HAC model, empirical research on athletes' careers has shown that development is not linear; it is characterized by performance slumps and nonlinear progression. Considerable research highlights the importance of psychological characteristics and competencies as central to the development process for athletes on their rocky road to the top (Collins et al., 2015). *Psychological characteristics of developing excellence* (*PCDEs*) refers to a skill set that can both facilitate the process and optimize the outcome of the talent pathway (MacNamara, 2011). PCDEs describe skills and characteristics that enable young athletes to cope with the many ups and downs of development and transitions, maximize growth opportunities, and learn from setbacks in both sport and life (Collins et al., 2016).

In a retrospective study comparing *super champions* (winning several medals at international events) with *almosts* (players who had achieved well at youth level but then reached much lower levels as their highest senior achievement), Collins et al. (2015) found that super champions were characterized by a strong positive reaction to challenge, both proactively and in response to injuries or sport-related setbacks. They also had higher levels of self-reflection that supported their development. The authors concluded that the super champs' experience of facilitative (rather than directive) styles of parenting and coaching contributed to their proactive approach toward challenges.

Role of Coaches and the Coach–Athlete Relationship

Coaches play a central role in how athletes experience sport. They are like architects of sport environments, carrying a responsibility to design and nurture athletes' learning and development (Rynne et al., 2017). However, athletes have reported coaches' behaviors as sometimes unhelpful for their athletic and personal development or mental health (Küttel & Larsen, 2019). Effective coaches integrate professional, interpersonal, and intrapersonal coaching knowledge, and they foster athlete development in terms of competence, confidence, connection, character, and caring. Depending on the development stage, coaches serve different roles and functions in athlete development. While coaches working with emerging athletes have a significant role in offering care and support, demonstrating excellent people skills, and helping athletes develop PCDEs (Collins et al., 2016), they also have a large influence over the most common factors related to athletic dropout (e.g., too much emphasis on winning, showing favoritism, lack of fun). High-performance coaches play a key role in supporting athletes to navigate the many tensions and challenges characteristic of elite sport. However, because financial support for elite athletes and coaches is primarily based on results, coaches in high-performance sport often experience dilemmas concerning the crucial balance between the athletes' focus on the pressure to perform with health and well-being issues, as well as the DC pressures alluded to earlier (Dohsten et al., 2020).

However on all athletic levels, the coach–athlete relationship is at the heart of coaching; coaches and athletes are inseparable entities, whether in participation or performance (Jowett, 2017). Jowett and Poczwardowski (2007) proposed a conceptual model to understand the quality of the coach–athlete relationship; it involved *closeness* (mutual respect, trust, appreciation), *commitment* (maintaining a close relationship over time despite ups and downs), *complementarity* (athletes' and coaches' corresponding behavior of affiliation), and *co-orientation* (degree of empathic understanding and the established common ground in their relationship), known as the *4 Cs*. It

Plumb Images/Leicester City FC via Getty Images

A coach's conversations with athletes—both on and off the field of play—increase the quality of relationships.

clearly takes time to foster these 4 Cs and to build up a close coach–athlete relationship. Additionally, group size and type of sport are important parameters to consider (Lorimer & Jowett, 2013).

Different aspects of coaching climate (task/ego-involvement, autonomy-supportive, and controlling) can affect athletes' development and motivation. For example, a Finnish study among 414 DC athletes used latent profile analysis to group participants based on measures of coaching climate and symptoms of burnout. DC athletes whose coaches emphasized that everyone has an important role on the team, valued each athlete as a person, and listened to athletes' thoughts and feelings, experienced lower symptoms of burnout in both sport and school (Into et al., 2020). In contrast, controlling coaching and punishing athletes for making mistakes were associated with higher levels of burnout. Learning conditions and motivational processes have been examined among Norwegian elite performers (Haraldsen et al., 2020). A performance-oriented climate and a controlling coaching style unfolded as a two-sided result: They could provide a boost of competence development and a strong, nurturing source of motivation for ambitious performers underpinned by high demands, hard work, and professionalization. However, when facing failure and adversity, these performance-oriented practices and culture revealed a downside. Stagnation and failure were challenges that put the performers' quality of motivation to the test.

Athlete- and Performance-Centered Issues Concerning the Olympic Games

The Olympic Games are usually the culmination of an athlete's career. They can provide an opportunity to justify years of hard work for this moment of glory in the international spotlight. However, while much is at stake, being your best at the Games is no easy task. The four-year cycle offers few opportunities to gain experience and acclimatize to the unique mental challenges of the Olympic environment (e.g., distractions in the Olympic village, feeling of living in a bubble, security procedures, and constant media attention). Some sport psychologists argue that "at the Olympics, everything is a performance issue" (McCann, 2008, p. 267). However, the range of issues that potentially arise at the Games often lay outside the sport domain and concern interpersonal conflicts (with coaches, agents, spouses, or teammates), crisis management in the personal domain (e.g., death of a family member, marriage crisis, uncertain future after the Games), and clinical issues (e.g., obsessive-compulsive thoughts and behaviors, eating disorders, depression). Supporting athletes in such critical situations (a crisis at the Games cannot be put off until later) demands that sport psychology consultants and coaching staff have skills for dealing with the immediate problem together with an understanding of the athlete's overall situation and underlying cause(s).

The post-Games phase is also challenging regardless of an athlete's level of success at the event. Athletes must decide whether to continue for another quadrennial or retire from elite sport, prioritize work or study, or perhaps start or expand a family. While some athletes will receive increased attention and the opportunity to capitalize on their results, others will have to deal with intense emotions and mood fluctuations resulting from underperforming. Each post-Games phase is different depending on the career stage and the results and expectations of the past events. For instance, take this example from the author's experience on Switzerland's ski jumping team:

In Salt Lake City in 2002, one of my teammates unexpectedly won two gold medals, and I finished with a satisfying sixth place. When the team arrived home, the sudden public interest and hype around the sport was overwhelming for us. Four years later at the Torino 2006 Games, I had become a medal favorite. However, finishing fifth and sixth this time was a huge disappointment. It took more than six months to appreciate this performance and to find the motivation to set new career goals. When I returned from the Vancouver 2010 Games, I had to accept my mediocre results knowing that they had been my last Olympics. My thoughts were circling around the *what's next?* questions concerning my sport career as well as my life and work career. Additionally, I had to deal with the challenges and expectations of being a young father who had been away from home too much during the Games and preparation phase.

With the multiplicity of issues and high vulnerability of athletes who experience the so-called post-Olympic blues, this phase must be targeted as a unique and crucial time for mental health support (Henriksen, Schinke, et al., 2020). However, support for athletes after the Games is typically reduced while coaches and sports officials also experience their own post-Olympic blues; they, too, need time off after the intense Games phase. Hence, the post-Games phase should be considered as the final (and equally important) part of the Olympic cycle. During this phase, athletes should be monitored in terms of mental health challenges and changes. Dedicated support experts should assist both athletes and coaches (whose contracts might be terminated) in dealing with specific issues. In addition, they should provide opportunities for continued light training and team gatherings to maintain some familiarity with existing daily sport processes.

Assessment

Validated scales used with easily obtained questionnaires or online tools can support working with an athlete-centered approach. For example, athletes' identity can be assessed by the Academic and Athletic Identity Scale (AAIS) (Yukhymenko-Lescroart, 2014). Even though it is more challenging to assist athletes with strong athletic identities on nonsport commitments, it might not be the case if athletes are constantly preparing and taking their time to plan their next careers (Harrison et al., 2016). A valuable tool to encourage reflection about prioritization of different life domains in the present and near future is the five-step career planning strategy (Stambulova, 2010); it builds on the HAC model and sociocultural learning theory. Using this instrument can help athletes and coaches in career planning and goal setting, preparing for a career transition, and improving social support systems.

Athletes on their way to becoming elite can optimally benefit from developmental challenges by assessing characteristics associated with effective development. The Psychological Characteristics of Developing Excellence Questionnaire, version 2, (PCDEQ2) (Hill et al., 2019) is a psychometric tool that measures these seven factors: adverse response to failure, imagery and active preparation, self-directed control and management, perfectionistic tendencies, seeking and using social support, active coping, and clinical indicators. These factors can help to identify areas that require support for individual athletes or monitor intervention impact and effectiveness. Most sports require athletes to have social skills in order to compete successfully, and adolescent athletes and coaches have described communication skills as the most important transferable skills (Jones & Lavallee, 2009). However, athletes may not be aware of the skills they have developed, so they may not transfer across life domains. Tacit knowledge of skills developed through sport such as verbal communication, relationships, team commitment, responsibility, and nonverbal communication can then be made accessible through guided self-reflection and structured feedback (verbal and written) from both peers and coaches.

Another interesting tool to self-assess competencies related to managing DC challenges (De Brandt et al., 2017) can be found at www.dualcareer-tools.com. On this website, student-athletes, DC support providers, and athletes planning their transition from elite sport to the job market can get an evaluation and a personalized feedback report. Environments that aim to facilitate athletes' holistic development can make use of the DC development environment (DCDE) model (Henriksen, Storm, et al., 2020) as a lens to become more aware of how different key stakeholders from sport, study, and the private domain interact and communicate around the athletes. Using these models in workshops with coaches, teachers, parents, and athletes can spur discussion about relationships, responsibilities, and communication pathways.

Acknowledging that the coach–athlete relationship is a dynamic process that can fluctuate over time (Jowett, 2003; Sandström et al., 2016), coaches need to find the right balance between being friendly and demanding (being able to impose, direct, and persuade). The quality and satisfaction of the coach–athlete dyad can be assessed by the 11-item Coach–Athlete Relationship Questionnaire (CART-Q) (Jowett and Ntoumanis, 2004), available in a coach and athlete version. Coaching climate can be measured with the Empowering and Disempowering Motivational Climate Questionnaire

(EDMCQ-C) (Appleton et al., 2016). This questionnaire concerns what the coach does and says and how the coach structures the environment in training and competitions. Regarding athletes' mental health, the IOC mental health working group has developed a sport-specific screening tool (Gouttebarge et al., 2020). Together with observations by coaches and sport psychology consultants, such instruments can help to detect changes in athletes' mental health so that tailor-made interventions can be started in good time if needed.

Optimization

Different areas of optimization can be outlined to enhance the athlete- and person-centered approach for athletes, coaches, and club and team environments. However, keep in mind that the efforts should be supported by an appropriate organizational culture that facilitates the interventions on all levels and supports the interplay between the various actors (Maitland et al., 2015).

For Athletes

Athletes should constantly engage in self-reflections (see chapter 10) in terms of athletic goals, life in general (*What is meaningful?*), and concerning their roles and identity (*Who am I? How do I want to be?*). Value-driven approaches can help to answer such questions (Küttel, 2020). To find the right DC balance, different DC competencies are essential. In addition, working with one's weaknesses in terms of both interpersonal and intrapersonal skills is required. Social support networks in and outside the sport domain are essential, but because athletes often travel and have busy schedules, these contacts need to be carefully and actively maintained. Focusing on the here and now and determinedly striving for success are important qualities of successful athletes. These qualities need not be in opposition to proactive career planning, which has the potential to enhance athletic performance (Lavallee, 2019) and can facilitate overcoming transitional barriers in any career stage. Bearing in mind that life after a career in sport can be as demanding as the career within it, it is recommended that athletes embrace a whole-career and lifelong learning perspective in which they can use the life skills gathered in and through their engagement in sport.

For Coaches and Practitioners

This chapter has highlighted the benefits of athlete-centered coaching and creating a climate in which athletes can contribute to mutual learning. By being authentic, the holistic and person-centered coach demonstrates humility that can act as a catalyst for establishing and maintaining a well-functioning coach–athlete relationship. Showing interest and understanding what is going on in other spheres of an athlete's life while constantly working on the elements of closeness, complementary commitment, and co-orientation are key elements for a sustainable collaboration.

Coaches should not be afraid to gather ongoing feedback from their athletes and peer coaches about how they communicate, what climate and culture they foster, and how their behavior affects team members. Coaches can further provide opportunities for athletes to promote their life skills (e.g., expertise from their studies) by leading workshops, involve them in creating team visions, and involve them in planning related to training and competition. Pushing athletes to their limits while simultaneously caring about them as persons often generates dilemmas. Coaches are advised to build their practice on a solid philosophy (see chapter 4) and discuss such dilemmas with others whom they trust. Besides enhancing athletes' performance mindset (described in chapters 5-10), assisting them in building resources to cope with transitional demands, and helping them to navigate between different life domains, sport psychology consultants have an important role in supporting coaches to apply an athlete-centered approach by challenging their practice and basic assumptions.

For Club and Team Environments

Clubs can foster a hypermasculine culture (e.g., ignoring injury, denying vulnerability, sacrificing individuality), which has to be met to gain acceptance and approval from the club's player and coaching hierarchy (Coulter et al., 2016). On the other hand, research in successful talent development environments has shown that proximate role models, inclusion, knowledge sharing, and focus on long-term development increase the chance to develop elite athletes while fostering their mental health (Henriksen et al., 2010; Ivarsson et al., 2015). Creating an athlete-centered club culture demands that the espoused values and the artifacts expressed by the organization are built on basic assumptions of athlete career excellence described earlier. Effective DC environments are characterized by a dedicated DC support team that focuses on individualized solutions, applies an empowerment approach, and has a deeply rooted and shared philosophy (Henriksen, Storm, et al., 2020). Outcomes of a DC should therefore not only be measured by athletic success, study completion, or drop-out rates but also by athletes' DC satisfaction and their mental well-being. Furthermore, organizations and clubs aiming to apply an athlete-centered approach should be cognizant of the periodic nature of the sport and academic calendars, where athletes need different kinds of support (related to their performance, their mental well-being, and their development in nonsport domains). To reach this overarching goal, it is helpful to provide staff with expertise and possibilities for ongoing education on how to optimally support athletes depending on their career stage and their unique profile.

Conclusion

This chapter has stressed the need to perceive and treat athletes as whole persons and support their development in sport and other spheres of life. The road to the top in elite sport is full of obstacles and challenges that provide athletes with opportunities to enhance their life skills and competencies. Coaches play a key role in providing a motivational climate that supports athletes' lifelong learning. Quantitative and qualitative assessment tools described in this chapter include career planning, DC skills development, and the coach–athlete relationship. When supporting athletes to sustain a healthy, successful, and long-lasting career in sport and life, coaches and sport psychology consultants need to integrate both athlete- and performance-centered approaches and also incorporate athletes' environment (family, clubs, schools) in a coordinated manner.

4 | Putting Into Practice Sound Philosophical Approaches to Sport Psychology

Artur Poczwardowski
University of Denver

Delineating one's professional philosophy has become an important tool in the hands of reflective practitioners in both sport and performance psychology consulting (e.g., Poczwardowski, 2019; Poczwardowski et al., 2004) and high-level coaching (e.g., Collins & Collins, 2016; Webb et al., 2016). In particular, the alignment of a coach's philosophy with their day-to-day activities has been proposed as a way to enhance the coach's expertise and effectiveness. Such alignment can be viewed as coherent coaching (Webb et al., 2016). Deeper self-examination (asking not only *what* and *how* but also *why* you do what you do) and context-focused judgment and decision making (the answer is *it depends*) also position coaches to better prepare for the complexities of their work through moving from competence to expertise (Collins et al., 2015). From an athlete perspective, features of the performance environment (including social media) also encourage these groups to consider the question *Why do I do what I do?* In short, increasing evidence shows that the success of *what* an athlete or coach does (including psychological practices or mental work) depends on *why* they are doing it. In this respect, the biggest returns usually arrive when the philosophy behind a person, principle, or tool engaged with for psychological purposes (e.g., to feel more confident) is directly matched to the beliefs, goals, and needs of the coach or athlete.

Increases in the application of sport psychology principles to sport training, as well as more common hiring of providers of sport psychology services in elite sports, call for athletes' and coaches' reflections on the utility of this trend in their own work. Of particular importance is establishing their ever-evolving philosophy–action alignment with regard to the role and applications of sport psychology into their daily operations. This need is accented further in high-performing systems that aim to operate and thrive in the very demanding context of elite sport.

Based on these needs, the content of this chapter focuses on putting a sound philosophy of sport psycholo*gy* into practice by high-level coaches and athletes. The emphasis on psycholo*gy* (rather than psycholo*gist*) is intentional and important. More specifically, this chapter is relevant for those who use the services of a sport psychology consultant because it clearly relates to work that they do with their clients. However, in all cases (including when a sport psychology consultant is not used), high-level athletes and coaches apply principles of sport psychology for their development and performance. Many of these principles are presented in other chapters (e.g., goal setting to direct motivation in chapter 5 and performance optimization to mentally peak on competition day in chapter 16). As such, this chapter explains how examining the philosophy behind these principles can help athletes and coaches to examine *why* the principles might work for them or *how* they need to be tailored to work for them.

Ronald Cortes/Getty Images

For coaches and sport psychology consultants, delineating one's professional philosophy has become an important tool.

Relevance

Another of this chapter's underlying assumptions about high-level coaches and elite athletes is that they do not bluntly hire a sport psychology consultant with no involvement in the process. Instead, they are adequately engaged in shaping the hiring process as well as monitoring and adjusting the sport psychology service delivery practices to maximize the output of their numerous investments (primarily time, money, and increased expectations for athletic success).

In elite sports in particular, the culture of high-level performance and the culture of mental training need to be coherent; otherwise, the investments of time and money will not produce desired results (e.g., performance enhancement, personal growth). Consequently, a culture change to better match these philosophies might be required (Cruickshank et al., 2015; Eubank et al., 2014). On the other hand, congruence between individual philosophies and the larger culture (team, club) can contribute to increased motivation in athletes to acquire, practice, apply, and perform

- mental skills (e.g., positive self-talk; concentration on relevant aspects of the task at hand),
- team skills (e.g., effective communication, appropriately distributed leadership), and
- life skills (personal excellence).

The latter set of skills are accomplished in a counseling setting where the aim is to support the athlete in pursuing performance and personal goals. This broader approach is even more relevant for adult athletes in elite sport contexts (see chapter 3). All in all, when the philosophy behind psychological practices or mental work is clear, the chances of progress are elevated. Indeed, it is much easier to commit to *what* you're doing—and do it well—when you know *why* you're doing it.

In this respect, sport psychology literature has widely discussed the need for coaches and athletes to have positive attitudes or a certain type of buy-in toward sport psychology services if these services are to have positive and lasting effects (e.g., Ravizza, 1988; Poczwardowski et al., 2020). Similarly, support from the high-level club (team) management is vital in allocating various resources for sport psychology. When a sport psychology consultant arrives, the head coach or manager can choose how to respond: Leave the room without participating; say something dismissive such as "The shrink is here"; sit passively in the room when the consultant is working; or actively engage with the material. These choices indicate levels of philosophical alignment and ultimately the systemic nature of whether sport psychology will make a positive difference on coaching and athletic performance. Once again, aligning philosophy is important because it means that everyone can be clear about *why* they are doing what they are doing.

If coaching philosophy builds on the assumption that athletic performance benefits from whole-person development, sport psychology consultants who stimulate athletes to expand nonsport identities and activities will be in alignment with the coach's convictions, adding to coherence in coaching. Additionally, coaches (especially those who know their athletes and team well) can be strategic in addressing the needs of their athletes as people. For example, they might offer hobby sharing summits or family barbecue events. The former scenario, in which a coach's assumptions and sport psychology consultant's actions are compatible, expresses an external alignment (you and your system together with the consultant); the latter scenario, in which a coach invites families' or significant others' attendance to a team barbecue, expresses an internal alignment (you as a coach think and act congruently; see figure 4.1).

Similarly, athletes also need to expand their awareness and understanding of the application of psychological principles into optimal functioning in sport (practice, competition) and in life. As noted earlier, this well-grounded understanding is critical in discerning sound principles and tools from the overabundance of noise on what enhances mental performance. This understanding is needed regardless of collaboration with a sport psychology consultant; the latter option is more likely to offer solid scientific foundations. In line with the previous example, an athlete who volunteers their time to an organization of their choice (e.g., a charity that helps the elderly) will derive a sense of accomplishment from these community-focused activities. This sense of achieving something valuable rests on both the external alignment (coach's practices) and internal alignment (athlete living according to their values). This lack of conflict can be contrasted with thinking that through volunteering, they would waste time in the overall pursuit of their athletic goals. As a result of this holistic view of themselves, athletes can freely engage in nonathletic pursuits (but without undermining their goals as an athlete).

	Internal alignment	External alignment
Coach	Your practices as a coach are aligned with your philosophy.	You as a coach and your system are aligned with sport psychology consultant/ sport psychology principles.
Athlete	Your training and competing practices as an athlete are aligned with your philosophy.	You as an athlete and your training and competing philosophy are aligned with sport psychology consultant/ sport psychology principles.

FIGURE 4.1 Alignment (compatibility) and misalignment (incompatibility) quadrants relating to the philosophy behind psychology services and psychological principles.

Furthermore, because they face no internal conflict, their self-esteem grows and becomes a psychological resource in their overall resilience, which in turn supports their athletic pursuits.

On the other hand, misalignment in all four quadrants (i.e., athlete-internal, athlete-external; coach-internal, coach-external) contributes to either limited or no impact of psychological processes and mechanisms underpinning individual and team performance. For example, given tough circumstances (e.g., a losing streak), coaches and athletes might have trouble putting a great deal of value in focusing on the process of preparation and performance; instead, they become preoccupied with the outcomes (lack of winning). Conversely, most (if not all) sport psychology consultants operate with the fundamental commitment to process (while pursuing the outcomes/wins). Clearly, if this misalignment is not recognized and worked through, issues from the gap between the sport psychology principles and the team's reality will be present both internally and externally. This lack of added value to overall and sport-specific functioning often results in underperformance, and it may contribute to unproductive conflicts. Clearly, a cost–benefit ratio in applying sport psychology principles (or using a sport psychology consultant's services) is unfavorable in this situation. Notably, a productive clash of sport versus psychology worldviews could occur, and the athletes, coaches, and organizations can choose to learn from it. For example, in 2020, individual and systemic adjustments related to the COVID-19 pandemic resulted in athlete mental health moving to the forefront of sport psychology service delivery, and performance shifted somewhat to the back. This shift was in part because of publicly and widely available advice from sport and performance psychology organizations (e.g., United States Olympic and Paralympic Committee [USOPC], Association for Applied Sport Psychology [AASP], International Society of Sport Psychology [ISSP]).

This first section provided reasons to understand the importance for both athletes and coaches to understand the benefits of alignment between their own philosophy of sport training, competing, and long-term development and the philosophy that underpins any sport psychology principles or services in their environment. As the notion of *what* the coach or athlete does depends on *why* they are doing it becomes clearer, the next section explores how to identify the philosophies that are currently at play in the sport environment.

What We Know

Various philosophical positions can underpin sport psychology services or sport psychology principles. The ones covered in this chapter are more mainstream; thus, the likelihood is high that you have encountered (or will encounter) one of them in your environment. Table 4.1 includes essential descriptors of three typical philosophical positions. A *holistic* (person-centered or humanistic) approach attends to all aspects of the athlete, those directly related to fulfilling the role of an athlete and delivering high-level athletic performance, and aspects of life that are not directly related to sport (e.g., interpersonal relationships, hobbies and interests, other activities) (Hill, 2001; Orlick, 1989; Prochaska & Norcross, 2013; see also chapter 3). Thus, growth, long-term development, and a great deal of autonomy are other characteristics of this person-centered philosophy. These features can be evident in the work of a specific sport psychology consultant or in the application of sport psychology principles in general (e.g., individual athlete

TABLE 4.1 Three Philosophical Positions in Approaching Behavior Change

PROFESSIONAL PHILOSOPHY ELEMENT	PHILOSOPHICAL POSITION		
Theoretical paradigm	**Holistic**	**Solution focused**	**System**
Beliefs and values	Every person is unique; personal responsibility for behavior change; autonomy; long-term growth and self-actualization	Solution to a problem behavior can be replicated from exceptions to the problem; efficiency; focus on what works; both athlete and coach are experts	Collaboration of all stakeholders is required; the whole is greater than the sum of the parts; interconnectedness of all parts (roles, values); multiplicity of solutions to a particular problem
Primary models of practice	Counseling; individual sessions; nondirective (following the client's lead)	Psychological skills training (PST); directive and instructional	Organizational/systems approach; immersion; prolonged engagement
Intervention goals	Whole person is addressed with goals expanding athletic performance pursuits to mental health and post-career goals; performance enhancement and personal growth	Productive behaviors isolated as solutions to the presented problem; decreasing or eliminating problem behavior and increasing productive behavior	Involvement of all levels of the team and organizations in deciding about and implementing organizational change; emphasis on improving processes (leadership, communication, etc.); collective empowerment and effectiveness
Intervention techniques and methods	Establishing a working alliance as the platform for making change; support and positive regard; conversing and dialoguing; highly individualized goals and objectives	Shifting from problem-talk to solution-talk; looking for and exploring exceptions; developing clearly formulated behavioral goals (as solutions); setting up a concrete evaluation plan; short-term interventions	Culture change; clarification of the organizational vision and mission; aligning values and norms; role and goal clarification

plans that identify goals for performance and also goals for broader life). An exclusive focus on producing fast (but unstable) behavioral changes, glorifying winning, and centralizing athletic identity at the cost of other roles and pursuits would be an undesirable contrast to the more widely embraced (and practiced) holistic approach.

In contrast, a *solution-focused* approach typically isolates a given problem that requires fixing and seeks solutions in the athlete behavior (Hoigaard and Johansen, 2004). The proposed solutions are built on exceptions (when the problem is not there or borrows behavior patterns from before the problem started). This approach can be apparent in the actions of a sport psychology consultant and also in the application of sport psychology when no sport psychology consultant exists. For example, in an environment where mental training is typically driven by the problems experienced in the last competition, coaches and athletes look for situations when a certain problem did not exist in order to explore exceptions (e.g., keeping 100% commitment to come back offensively after losing a point) to isolate what worked, translate it into a clear behavioral plan for the next game, and put in place both preparation goals and execution reminders for game day.

Often, a sport psychology consultant can work with the entire system (athletes, coaches, staff across the whole organization) (Henriksen et al., 2011). This *system* approach is especially valuable in high-level performance settings. A collaborative style, immersion (the sport psychology consultant being part of the interdisciplinary support staff), and prolonged engagement are other features of this philosophy. Similarly, sport psychology can also be applied in a systemic way when no sport psychology consultant is involved. For example, leaders may consider principles of motivation on an organizational level, such as how to recognize and reward desired behaviors in middle management (Cruickshank et al., 2015).

To be able to compare and contrast how these or other approaches fit (or not) into your own philosophy of training and performance (i.e., *why* you train and perform the way you do), it is worth knowing what these philosophies reflect and what they comprise. One approach is to consider how professional philosophy is defined in the practice of sport psychology consultants. Indeed, this approach can help you to think about the philosophy of any sport psychology consultant that you work with and also the philosophy behind the psychology principles applied by others in your environment.

More specifically, the sport psychology consultant's philosophy, as conveyed in figure 4.2, consists of the following elements (Poczwardowski et al., 2004):

- Personal core beliefs and values
- Theoretical paradigm concerning behavior change
- Models of practice and the consultant's role
- Intervention goals
- Intervention techniques and methods

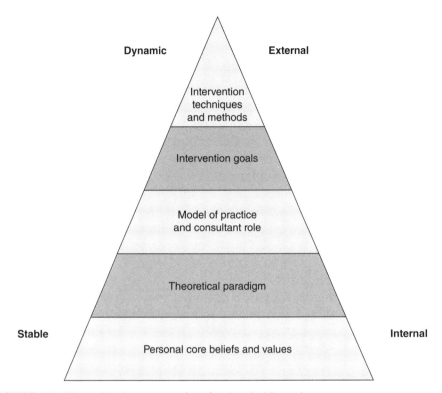

FIGURE 4.2 Hierarchical structure of professional philosophy.

Reprinted by permission from A. Poczwardowski, C. Sherman, and K. Ravizza, "Professional Philosophy in the Sport Psychology Service Delivery: Building on Theory and Practice," *The Sport Psychologist* 18 (2014): 415-429.

The first and most stable element of professional philosophy is personal core beliefs and values. From the perspective of working with the athlete, the consultant can view many of these beliefs and values as the athlete's fundamental rights; they include freedom, autonomy, dignity, equality, privacy, and safety (physical, emotional, cultural). Other values shaping sport psychology consultants' work can be growth, connection, honesty, respect, diversity, integrity, excellence, and balance from short- and long-term perspectives. From a performance standpoint, a predominant belief among sport psychology consultants is that task-relevant practices and processes powerfully contribute to athletic success. Focusing on the present when executing a skill rather than thinking about a desired (or undesired) outcome of it is a fundamental currency of performance (Haberl, 2012). In short, the philosophy behind the psychological principles in the environment—whether they are applied by a sport psychology consultant or someone else—reflect the fundamental beliefs and values of those who deliver them.

The second element of professional philosophy is the theoretical paradigm of behavior change—how individuals believe that behaviors can be modified to optimally pursue their goals, such as higher levels of performance.

An example of a theoretical paradigm concerning behavior change is a cognitive behavioral approach, which is known in the field of psychology as cognitive behavior therapy (CBT) (Prochaska & Norcross, 2013). Within this widely used framework, a sport psychology consultant engages the client in examining and changing their beliefs (about succeeding, losing, coming back from an injury, playing on a team, etc.) so that the client can manage their thinking. Managing thoughts leads to ability to manage emotional reactions. The aim is for these modified thoughts and emotions to be task relevant and to facilitate performance. Another approach gaining in popularity is the mindfulness-acceptance-commitment (MAC) approach (Gardner & Moore, 2007), which originated from acceptance and commitment therapy (ACT) (Hayes et al., 1999). The psychological principles of the MAC approach, available from various sources (e.g., smartphone apps) or from a sport psychology consultant, propose that the athlete can focus on the task at hand (e.g., penalty kick in soccer) regardless of the rising thoughts and emotions in any given moment (e.g., *last chance to win the match*).

The middle element in the hierarchy of professional philosophy involves sport psychology consultants operating based on a certain model of practice or their own combination of models (Aoyagi & Poczwardowski, 2011). For example, a psychological skills training (PST) model primarily focuses on mental (psychological) skills as relevant for quality practice and successful performance during competition. A counseling model would also include nonathletic pursuits and overall growth and well-being, which is similar to the person-focused (holistic) paradigm described earlier in the chapter. In the interdisciplinary sport science model, sport psychology consultants collaborate closely with other sport science and medical staff to integrate their sport psychology services with other sport preparation specialties, such as strength and conditioning, recovery and sleep, nutrition, biomechanics, and injury prevention or rehabilitation. Resulting from this collaboration, some coaches and service providers (e.g., nutritionists) are willing to apply selected elements of the sport psychology consultant's knowledge to their own practice (e.g., promoting autonomy in sticking to a new nutrition program). In this so-called train the trainer model, a sport psychology consultant may, for example, empower a coach to use communication strategies that facilitate athlete commitment and motivation to some challenging aspect of their training (e.g., additional cardiovascular training for winter sports during the summer). Finally, depending on the situation regarding problematic issues in athlete mental health, a sport psychology consultant (with appropriate credentials) operating from a medical model will be needed to address identified psychological problems (e.g., depression, disordered eating, substance use). Overall, expert sport psychology consultants can adjust their theoretical approaches to look for the best fit with an athlete, coaching style, and organizational culture and to deepen their focus on what is of the highest importance.

Moving from more abstract to more specific elements of professional philosophy in sport psychology, the intervention goals are as much a reflection of the consultant's philosophy as they are a function of what the coach or athlete most needs. These goals, which are not mutually exclusive, are as follows:

- Athletic performance enhancement (e.g., through teaching stress management skills, assisting the athlete to direct their focus to the task at hand based on their committed action plans in relation to their core values as individuals and athletes)
- Health and healthy lifestyle (e.g., changes in diet, rehabilitation after injury)
- Personal growth and development (e.g., self-exploration for asset searching and identifying areas for personal fulfillment)
- Daily living (e.g., anger management, reducing time spent on browsing through social media)
- Team effectiveness (e.g., team cohesion, team communication)
- Organizational service (e.g., applying a sport psychology perspective to administrative decisions and policy making)

Similarly, expert sport psychology consultants select intervention techniques depending on athlete and contextual features; for example, to facilitate concentration, they might use a performance resonance model (Newburg et al., 2002) so that the athlete can actively connect with their dream feeling versus addressing a gap between value and action (Haberl, 2012). Similarly, they have a choice of methods, and they can vary the frequency of group versus individual sessions to further individualize their approach.

The main idea of this chapter is that coaches and athletes benefit from putting a sound philosophy of sport psychology into practice—one that works for the individual. The individual knows *why* they are using certain sport psychology principles and tools over others. The structure described could be one among many starting points for moving in the direction of expanding self-knowledge and self-awareness. Once accomplished, the individual athlete can move toward aligning internally with (seeking coherence in) coaching and performing philosophies, then make external comparisons with the sport psychology consultant's philosophy.

Assessment

For both coaches and athletes, success in aligning philosophies with actual practices depends heavily on securing guiding information and quality feedback. This process begins with assessing current philosophies, comparing and contrasting them for compatibility (or lack of it). Another important consideration deals with the outcomes that these aligned or misaligned philosophies produce. Finally, this reflective cycle continues to a phase of contemplating different (yet feasible) scenarios of how things could be different and *why* a coach or athlete might do things differently. Thus, the coaches and athletes complete the assessment cycle by designing future philosophies. All these steps are discussed in detail.

Evaluating Current Philosophy: Why Are You Doing What You're Doing?

Given the complexity of the philosophy underpinning sport psychology services or principles in the environment, assessing what currently works and what to improve and how is not an easy task. However, a few evaluation tools can help you gain a working insight. It starts by knowing what your own philosophy is (the self-exploration project described earlier). In the next step, compare and contrast your wider coaching, training, and performance philosophies with what you observe about the sport psychology principles in your environment (as well as the services of a sport psychology consultant, if present). Are yours and others' philosophies aligned and integrated with each other? What are the signs they are, and what are the signs they aren't? How (or when) will you know that something different is needed? High-level coaches and athletes can observe a sport psychology consultant or others who play a role in what psychological principles are applied (e.g., program leaders) during their day-to-day operations. What you see and hear and how you react internally (how it feels) are your starting points as information gathering that you will analyze in the next step. Based on your casual (or structured) observations, you may decide to analyze this information for how athletes or coaches are responding to the sport psychology consultant's (or other individual's) efforts in what they say and how they say it, how feedback is provided, and what type of information they share and how (their knowledge).

For instance, what can coaches deduce when they have well-rounded athletes who do not perform to their full potential? How about in the opposite case, when athletes achieve performance goals but tend to be miserable and lack well-roundedness as individuals (Baltzell, 2011)? In the former case, is it partly because the values and practices of a person-centered approach (e.g., autonomy) are not in balance with values and practices of promoting performance excellence (e.g., organizationally imposed discipline and athletes reaching high level of self-discipline)? Does the situation indicate an overemphasis on personal growth and self-exploration at the cost of mental performance enhancement? Are sport psychology services not integrated enough with other sport science interventions? (See chapters 1 and 3.) Has too much one-on-one work versus team sessions led to an imbalance in personal and public accountability? These questions tap into the various elements of the philosophy behind psychological principles and the day-to-day practices that are based on it.

Other helpful questions for a coach to ask at any stage of collaboration with a sport psychology consultant, coach, or other practitioner who uses ideas from sport psychology include the following:

- What is your philosophy of success, failure, growth, or selection in sport?
- What are your typical ways of collaborating (or not) with the rest of the sport science staff?

If you are the coach, the next step in assessment is to continually monitor these points over time, record answers to your questions, and look for stable patterns. These patterns can confirm or refute the desired fit into the team operations and your own assessment of whether the mental practice objectives are achieved. You can also reflect on whether sport psychology consulting work is compatible with the wider coaching philosophies (for athletes, training and performing philosophies). Again, the basis for your evaluation will be what you see, hear, and know about sport psychology principles or services. Then, you should compare and contrast these insights with your own goals. Consider a comparing and contrasting analysis based on these questions:

- Is what you are experiencing best suited to your goals, needs, and how you learn?
- What are the signs it is a good fit?
- What are the signs that it is not a good fit?
- Would something different be a better fit?
- How would you describe something different that is needed?

Additional questions are useful in examining the current status quo. Coaches can ask, *If some features of the context change, how would things be different? Or perhaps things are right given the current context? Is this just a transition phase? Could this be a plateau?*

In most cases when an expert sport psychology consultant is involved, the sport psychology consultant routinely seeks feedback from coaches and athletes as part of their professional and ethical standards of practice (e.g., Haberl & McCann, 2012). This process naturally adds to your own assessment process where feedback, improvement, and accountability are essential in setting and reaching increasingly challenging goals.

Evaluating Future Philosophy: Why Might You Do Things Differently?

In the ever-changing world of elite sport, beyond solid grounding in the present, an increased need also exists to foresee upcoming challenges and opportunities. As a high-level coach or athlete, how can you identify the philosophy that you might need in the future to underpin sport psychology principles or services in your environment? Clearly, your ability to recognize trends in technology development, generational changes, the evolution of the sport, and the generation of revenues is as important as ever. Coaches' context-specific knowledge, well-calibrated professional judgment, and decision-making skills, as well as their adaptability and flexibility, are essential contributors to success in their work (Collins & Collins, 2016; see also chapter 2). Being engaged in continued education (e.g., in coaching, sport sciences, or other related fields); inviting experts in different areas to implement cutting-edge programs (e.g., nutrition, sleep and recovery); and attending conferences, summits, and think tanks can be useful in growing awareness about new trends and tools. In addition, discussing issues with other coaches and mentoring younger coaches are good opportunities to exercise professional judgment and decision making, allowing for self-awareness about how they select and prioritize information, how they think, and how they arrive at a given decision. For example, sport psychology consultants have identified new aspects in their own work that might be relevant to coaches too (Poczwardowski et al., 2020). These aspects are intensified gender dynamics (fit of female versus male sport psychology consultants into different sports) and the unique learning needs and communication preferences of a modern athlete, which places a great emphasis on the use of technology. Consequently, keeping the latter in mind, how will coaches set proportions for relying on available technology to train an athlete's mind (e.g., phone apps for mindfulness, concentration, anxiety management) versus tele- or virtual consulting versus in-person consulting? How will athletes protect their self-reliance and independence from ever-increasing technology in both sport and life?

In 2020, challenges related to the COVID-19 pandemic intensified the need for engaging in reflection about the future with a leading question about how things will be different in the new normal—or, more precisely, the new next. From a standpoint of both coach and athlete, another important question is *How would I want things to be different?* Prospective hindsight can be a helpful tool. It is based on a series of questions such as the following:

- If we completely succeed, how will this have happened?
- If we totally fail, how will this have happened?
- If our ability to control distractions involving worry about health and safety (our own and our families, athletes, coaches, teammates), financial well-being, fan support, cancellations of events, and so on, will be ultimately tested, what psychological principles will work best?
- What sport psychology service philosophies would seem to be the best fit for such a distraction control program?

Naturally, going through the alignment assessment of the current services (or the general sport psychology principles applied) will yield a process in which most tools can be used in prospective reflection.

Optimization

At this stage as a coach or an athlete, you are now aware of what your own philosophies consist of and you have some knowledge of the mainstream sport psychology philosophies. Further, you now know more about what works and what doesn't, and you are more aware of a few current trends that point at somewhat different challenges and opportunities in the future. This important question arises: *How do I align or integrate my needs with the philosophies that underpin sport psychology principles or services in my environment?* Another related question to ask is *How did this philosophy evolve to match my needs, and how can I make space for reasonable changes to fit into the ever-changing world and sport contexts?*

Aligning Philosophy: Fitting Principles of Sport Psychology to Your Needs

With regard to the external alignment, high-level coaches and athletes can plan and engage in a number of activities already covered earlier in the chapter. Once again, the key question is *Why are we doing what we're doing?*

The inner alignment is equally complex. Because it involves your convictions and beliefs, it requires introspective skills and self-discipline in pursuing the breadth and depth of your thinking. Collins and colleagues have published an excellent body of work on such processes for coaches (e.g., Collins & Collins, 2016; Collins et al., 2015; Nash et al., 2012; Webb et al., 2016; see also chapter 2). One step of this process involves what the coach or athlete knows about sport psychology principles (either as part of a sport psychology consultant's services or their independently developed knowledge of sport psychology principles). These vital blocks of knowledge are a starting point to a more complex process of professional judgment and decision making. This complexity largely depends on the context, its features, and its ever-changing dynamics.

One difficulty in seeking inner philosophical alignment lies in the need to consider interactions among many factors. Consequently, based on their knowledge of sport psychology principles, coaches and athletes examine what is effective and what is not effective in pursuing their goals. At the same time, they are reflecting on how this result came to be and why. For example, a coach may know that an athlete's focus during practice is helped by increasing awareness of practice goals prior to the training session, through activating the bigger picture in which these goals sit (e.g., long-term commitments), and through developing and maintaining the coach–athlete relationship with equal attention to both on- and off-field matters. Specifically, on periodic reflection a coach is happy to note that one athlete, despite current issues with a romantic partner, can effectively and consistently focus on training drills; this conclusion is reflected through observations of athlete practice behavior and documentation of the athlete reaching their strength and conditioning goals. Useful questions now are as follows: *How did I help the athlete shift focus to the task at hand? Is it because of the locker room chats about the training before the athletes are headed to the gym? Is it because of last week's team discussion of how the vision for this season is present in the team's day-to-day actions? Or because I went out for lunch with the athlete after hearing about the issues with the partner two weeks ago?* In other words, questions revealing the *hows* of operating (coaching) become an overall self-reflective approach. Similarly, going even deeper, a coach's reflection can be guided through these questions: *What are my reasons for having these brief chats with the athletes? Why do I plan team meetings to revisit team vision and mission statements periodically? What are my values attached to coaching work that are served by my inviting athletes for lunches to allow them space to talk about personal matters?* Once again, clearly *Why am I doing what I am doing?* is the underlying question that leads the coach to continually work toward internal alignment, and this alignment is evident in an increased coaching coherence.

For athletes, actions aimed at aligning their own needs and philosophy with the sport psychology principles will be similar. The athlete's own attempts, both skilled and intuitive, are critical in growing independence, accountability, and overall expertise as a high-level athlete. Additionally, when athletes invite others to provide input on their process and insights—for example, during meetings reviewing an individual performance plan—athletes gain support and confirmation of their thinking or receive suggestions from alternative viewpoints. This combination stimulates growth and learning. Note that coaches and sport scientists (including sport psychology consultants) have ways to quantify athlete progress and are trained (or self-educated) to invite and value athlete input. Thus, in this discussion step that is based on quantification, the athlete's perceptions are compared in collaboration with a high-performance support team (conducting a so-called gap analysis) in order to stimulate honest insights about how things are going. This is a vital step in designing improved action plans. As a result, everyone is on the same page (external alignment), and the athlete has an opportunity to test and adjust (if needed) their internal alignment.

Changes in Philosophy: Finding Principles that Work Better for You

Peoples' needs and philosophies evolve. As experience accumulates, views on failing and succeeding are refined, beliefs about how life and sport interact are continually tested, knowledge about sport psychology grows, and input from experts shapes all levels of philosophy. A growth mindset (Dweck, 2006) is a great tool for those who aim high with their goals in numerous performance domains. Openness to learning through your own and others' experiences, sustained motivation and effort, seeking out challenges, and thriving on opportunities are key examples of how a growth mindset (as opposed to a fixed mindset) shows up in daily actions.

For coaches, growth mindset as a concept overlaps with a well-described approach to successful coaching labeled as pursuing a developmental focus (Collins et al., 2015). Coaches with developmental focus have a higher need for self-generated challenge and for embracing challenges in general, and they openly seek critiques afforded by others (coaches, athletes, managers, owners, media). They also engage in deeper (not surface) assessment and self-examination. Other approaches such as brainstorming, team retreats, and learning about the practices of others are examples of deliberate strategies to continually be on the leading edge. The process of shifting from what one *should* do to what one *could* do is yet another tool in ongoing growth; it aims to develop high-level expertise reflected in dynamically acquired contextual knowledge. Taken together, all these practices aim to develop flexible, adaptable, and creative coaching (Collins & Collins, 2016).

Athletes go through similar evolution paths in their performance philosophy. They benefit greatly from coaches who model these growth mindsets and teach athletes how to use various tools to promote continuous improvement in physical, technical, tactical, and psychological preparation, performance, and recovery.

Sarah Sachs/Arizona Diamondbacks/Getty Images

Coaches with a developmental focus engage in brainstorming sessions, team retreats, and critiques by others.

Success Story: An Immersion Approach for Developing and Maintaining Philosophical Alignment With Paralympic Teams

For the past six years, I have been a part of an interdisciplinary support team (IST) for three U.S. Paralympic teams in individual sports, which resulted in a very immersive engagement consisting of in-person meetings, group and individual telesessions, travel to multiple events, prolonged engagement at sport camps, and more. I frequently found myself involved in decisions about the topics of team sessions, supporting adherence to dietary recommendations, and collaborating on periodizing mental skills training. This immersive approach required me to continually and patiently communicate to make sure everyone involved was on the same page. Comparing and contrasting values and beliefs, action planning, problem solving, and evaluating allowed for a wider (systemic) external alignment of philosophies of all involved. This alignment was further enhanced by multiple retakes in assessment and optimization through informal postsession, informal postcompetition, and formal postseason evaluations. For instance, this alignment featured the personal accountability of athletes, high levels of autonomy in athlete decision making, and focus on long-term growth as an athlete and person.

Concurrently, the team embraced the need for high-level mental performance as a natural component of their sport. Internal alignment between the athletes' sport and life philosophies and the mission and vision of the team as a whole included the sport psychology consultant and their services. This alignment was expressed as a pervasive and widely accepted belief in investing into the process as a way to perform optimally and a belief in the overall emphasis on learning and growing both on and off the field. Consequently, acquiring, practicing, applying, refining, and performing mental skills became markers of success of a well-designed sport camp, World Cup, and summer training for individual athletes. Additionally, personal excellence outside of sport (academics; professional pursuits such as motivational talks and lectures or job responsibilities; support of a spouse during a time of distress) were highly valued and expected attributes of our working together. Throughout the process, the systemic approach of getting on the same page has been essential to the overall success of the collaboration.

Conclusion

With a focus on high-level coaches and athletes, this chapter has outlined a rationale for a structured approach to understanding, refining, and applying the philosophy underlying sport psychology services (if a consultant is part of the preparation and performance system) and psychological principles more broadly, a number of which are presented in the chapters that follow. Framing the discussion were guiding questions, a detailed presentation of elements of professional philosophy, assessment tools, and selected strategies for optimizing both internal alignment (within the coach and athlete themselves) and external alignment (between the coach or athlete and others in their environments, including a sport psychology consultant). The chapter emphasized a coach's and athlete's active and engaged role in deciding what psychological content (knowledge, tools) should be used, what benefits might arise from using the services of different sport psychology consultants, and how to apply different psychological principles in practice and competition. In today's increasingly demanding sport environments, fixed and rigid approaches are less effective in meeting the goals of high-level coaches and elite athletes. Instead, flexibility, adaptability, and creativity are at the forefront of essential skills. The ultimate aim is to help athletes and coaches become expert users of sport psychology.

PART II | ENHANCING ATHLETES' PERFORMANCE MINDSET

5 | Motivation

David Shearer
University of South Wales

Motivation is a keystone of human behavior. In simple terms, without motivation, you would not do anything at all. If you lacked motivation, you wouldn't swing your legs out from under the covers onto the cold bedroom floor when you awoke in the morning. You wouldn't get dressed, eat breakfast, leave your home, or take part in sport. Literally everything you do is driven by a specific motive or a wider motivation. Motivation is fundamental to what makes you human; most likely, it is to some extent embedded in your DNA (Schaller et al., 2017).

Relevance

Athletes, coaches, psychology specialists, and other support practitioners have a number of specific reasons why they should understand how to develop, maximize, and sustain motivation and embed this knowledge into their sport programs. First, motivation is relevant and important at all levels of sport—from early skill development in children to competing at an elite level to the lifelong participation in a post-athletic career. Second, whether consciously or subconsciously, the type and amount of motivation people have, alongside contextual and environmental factors, drives all sport behavior. For example, if a promising young athlete gets injured, they might be highly motivated to return to play as quickly as possible and therefore engage fully with the rehabilitation process because competing in the Olympics is their lifelong dream. An older athlete with a similar injury might view it as a cue to prepare for retirement and therefore be less moti-

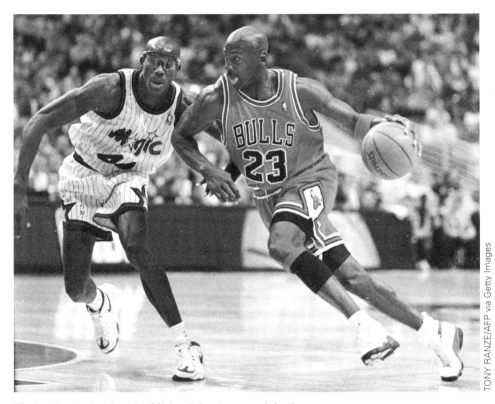

TONY RANZE/AFP via Getty Images

Motivation helped make Michael Jordan a serial winner.

vated to do their rehabilitation, knowing realistically they likely do not have another Olympics in them. When athletes and coaches understand these differences, they may be able to maximize performance. Third, motivation is central to what makes some athletes want to be serial winners—those who will win at all costs (e.g., Michael Jordan; watch *The Last Dance* series about him)—and others want to be immersed in the process, journey, and flow of what they do rather than focus on the outcome (e.g., Alex Honnold; watch the *Free Solo* film about him). Understanding what makes athletes tick helps coaches and trainers tailor their approach and evaluate the emotions surrounding performance. Fourth, motivation is transitory. Even for the most committed athletes, motivation ebbs and flows daily. Understanding this quality of motivation is central to effective athletic programs. Finally, one person's motivation and subsequent behaviors influence that of others. Specifically, how members of teams transmit their motivations through displays of emotion and behaviors can both consciously and subconsciously affect the motivations and behaviors of other team members. Understanding this fact can help people create a positive motivational environment for everyone.

The types of scenarios in which motivation affects behavior are particularly varied, but you may have encountered some of the following:

- Some athletes in a group always appear driven and motivated. For others, motivation is transient.
- Some athletes never miss practice, while others are regular absentees.
- Some athletes stay for extra practice after the formal training is finished, while others leave as soon as possible.
- Seemingly excellent, even world-class athletes sometimes fail to bring their A game in competition.
- Athletes look to their coaches and trainers to check their responses when the athletes make mistakes.
- Teams exhibit group rebellion or dissatisfaction when a coach prescribes a training session.

These common scenarios occur in all sports. At the heart of each is motivation, which is further influenced by the personalities of the athletes and coaches, the interactions between all members of the group, the underlying philosophy of the training environment, the level of parental support, the current position in the training or competition cycle, and more. Academic papers on motivation paint a complex picture. This chapter serves as a navigational guide for athletes, coaches, and practitioners to understand motivational issues in the sport environment, identify issues as they arise, and enact practical solutions to help generate positive motivation.

What We Know

Theories of motivation are complex not because any one theory is particularly hard to understand but because each theory takes a slightly different perspective. In addition, motivation is inextricably linked with so many other situational, contextual, environmental, social, and psychological factors. Therefore, it is impossible to name one theory as the guiding light for all athletes, coaches, and practitioners to follow. This section offers the most practically useful theories to guide your work in athletic environments. It covers three individual-focused theories (attribution theory, self-determination theory, and achievement goal theory) and one theory that more widely examines the athletic environment (i.e., motivational climate). All these theories are well supported in the academic literature.

Attribution Theory

Attribution theory (Weiner, 1972) accounts for how people explain their behavior to themselves, the outcomes associated with their behavior, and the behavior of others or events they experience. To maintain emotional equilibrium, people act as so-called naive scientists and make mental shortcuts to explain what happens around them. For example, a tennis player who wins a series of matches might explain this streak in a number of ways.

They might tell themselves it reflects a large increase in their capability to perform and focus during important matches. They could also explain it as a function of the quality of their opposition; had they been playing better players they would have been less successful. Both explanations might be true, but they affect the athlete's motivation in different ways. The first attribution (performance due to increased capability and focus)

- has internal causality (is caused by their effort or as a function of internal factors, such as height),
- is unstable (can be changed over time, which is good in this instance), and
- is under the athlete's control (they can choose to train hard and improve).

In contrast, the second attribution (performance due to the quality of the opponent)

- has external causality (is all down to their opponent's abilities),
- is unstable (the other athlete's performance is hard to predict), and
- is (mostly) uncontrollable (they can't control how good their opposition is).

For long-term commitment and progress, it is usually better for athletes to attribute their performances to internal, unstable (i.e., it can change), and controllable factors. However, it is even more important that the attributions are realistic and as objective as possible. So, in the previous tennis example, if the opponent *were* objectively (as opposed to perceptually) too easy, it could easily blunt an athlete's development if they attribute their success to their own ability or effort. Table 5.1 presents a matrix of attributions this tennis player might have.

TABLE 5.1 Sample Attributions Made by an Elite Tennis Player

	Internal		External	
	Stable	**Unstable**	**Stable**	**Unstable**
Controllable*	"I won because I played to my potential and focused as well as I always do."	"I won because I'm stronger from all the strength training."	"I lost because my tennis rackets from my sponsor don't suit me."	"I won because my coach encouraged me for once."
Uncontrollable	"I lost because my arms are too short to return my opponent's shots."	"I lost because I'm growing too old."	"I won because the newly introduced rules match my style of play."	"I only won because all my opponents were weaker than me."

*Even though one can roughly place factors and events into attribution boxes, crossover always exists. For any attribution type, there exists something you can control (e.g., your response).

Self-Determination Theory (SDT)

While attribution theory is a simple guide to understand how your view of a situation affects your motivation, it doesn't take into account the countless nuances surrounding motivation in sport. In contrast, self-determination theory (SDT) is probably the most widely used, accepted, and practically helpful motivation theory applied in sport (Deci & Ryan, 2000). It is positivistic and growth focused, assuming humans generally want to challenge and improve themselves to live a fulfilled life. Thus, it is well-matched with competitive sport. SDT is known as a metatheory because it comprises six mini theories (see Ryan & Deci, 2017). For simplicity, these mini theories are not covered separately; instead, this section discusses the general ideas of SDT in relation to sport.

Practitioners most often refer to these two components of SDT: the basic psychological needs of humans and the continuum of motivational orientations. The latter spans a spectrum from a complete lack of motivation (amotivation) through four externally driven motives (extrinsic motivation) to motivation focused on internal factors (intrinsic motivation).

Basic Psychological Needs

According to SDT, competence, autonomy, and relatedness are the three psychological needs that are essential for motivation. Satisfying these three basic needs increases the likelihood that an athlete's or coach's motivation will be productive in terms of training and competition behaviors.

Competence should be familiar to all athletes and coaches. When someone becomes involved in competitive sport, they usually want to improve their current performance standard in some way. The feelings experienced when performance improves are universally human; broadly, they are feelings of satisfaction. However, the challenge is to create environments that allow development or demonstration of competence. For example, a team athlete who feels most competent playing a specific positional role (e.g., outside half in rugby) will likely feel less motivated when continually asked to play elsewhere (e.g., fullback) where they are less competent.

Autonomy is the state of being both independent and self-governing. This basic need is often hardest for coaches to balance when delivering coaching sessions and training. SDT suggests that for optimal motivation, athletes (and coaches) have a need to forge their own path and make decisions for themselves that influence how they achieve their goals; the athlete should be self-determined. Sometimes coaches mistakenly assume that self-determination means they should let athletes do what they want, let them write the program, let them dictate the length of training sessions, and the like, so this thought often is met with significant resistance. However, SDT does not suggest coaches hand the reins to athletes; it is more about how motivation and subsequent behavior are maximized when athletes enter into an activity of their own free will. For example, two swim coaches who set the exact same training session can affect autonomy differently depending on the message attached to that session. Coach A may dictate a performance standard they expect, while coach B may collaborate with the athlete to set performance targets for the session. The latter approach maximizes autonomy and subsequent motivation, but it also requires a coach–athlete relationship with strong communication, trust, and understanding. Difficulties can arise when what an athlete wants to do doesn't match the goals they need to achieve.

Relatedness is the need for social bonds. Evidence indicates that early success of the human species was through success in forming large and complex social networks (Hare, 2017). The need to feel close to other people is probably innate. Therefore, in sport environments it is important to consider the required social elements. For most athletes and coaches, motivation will be suboptimal unless opportunity exists to relate with others in the group. Relatedness has implications for many group processes, including leadership, cohesion, trust, and communication.

In addition to the basic needs of SDT, other basic needs are the foundations of athlete and coach well-being and subsequent motivation. Maslow (1943) outlined a hierarchy of needs, the foundations of which were physiological needs (food, water, warmth, sleep) and safety. While it should be obvious, a safe home and training environment, correct recovery protocols, and nutrition are paramount to motivation. An athlete cannot be their best unless these needs are satisfied.

SDT Motivation Continuum

As noted earlier, SDT proposes a range of motivation types that begins with amotivation and ends with intrinsic motivation (figure 5.1). *Amotivation* refers to a complete absence of motivation typified by a lack of competence and any care for the activity in question. This state is not common in sport environments but might be encountered in some situations, such as burnout, in which athletes are exhausted to the point that their motivation completely breaks down (Cresswell & Eklund, 2005). *Extrinsic motivation* refers to behavior motivated by factors external to the athlete, coach, or practitioner. Four types of extrinsic motivation are on the continuum; they become increasingly internalized from external to integrated (see figure 5.1). Behavior associated with extrinsic motivation might include playing sport to simply earn money (external) or because an athlete believes their parents have invested a lot of money in their sport and they want to keep their parents happy (introjection). *Intrinsic motivation* is often considered the most desirable form of motivation. It reflects behaviors driven entirely by internal factors, such as enjoyment and self-fulfillment. While intrinsic motivation is mostly desirable, because of

Motivation type	Amotivation	Extrinsic motivation					Intrinsic motivation
Type of regulation	Non-regulation	External	Introjection	Identified	Integrated		Intrinsic
Internalization	No	No	Partial	Almost full	Full		Not required
Defining characteristics	Lack of • competence • contingency • intention • activity value	Presence of external • constraints • rewards • compliance • punishments	Focus on approval (i.e., self or others) • ego involve-ment • internal rewards and punishment	• Activity valued • Personally important • Consciously pursued	• Synthesis of identified regu-lations to self • Awareness • Congruence		Action is based on interest and inherent satis-faction
Location on the autonomy continuum		◄──►					
		Controlled motivation		Autonomous motivation			
Perceived locus of causality	Impersonal	External	Somewhat external	Somewhat internal	Internal		Internal

FIGURE 5.1 Schematic overview of the self-determination continuum outlining the types of motivation advanced within SDT and related processes.

Adapted by permission from M. Standage and R.M. Ryan, "Self-Determination Theory and Exercise Motivation: Facilitating Self-Regulatory Processes to Support and Maintain Health and Well-Being," in *Advances in Motivation in Sport and Exercise,* 3rd ed., edited by G.C. Roberts and D.C. Treasure (Champaign, IL: Human Kinetics, 2012), 242. Based on Ryan and Deci (2000).

the interplay between the basic needs, most people sit somewhere on the continuum between extrinsic and intrinsic motivation; both carry benefits. Indeed, most top athletes are characterized by an optimal blend of internal and external motivation that suits their bespoke profile, context, and goals. Optimizing this blend is the challenge.

Most elite athletes have a variety of motivational types that occur simultaneously within the same athletic environment. For example, an athlete may only commit to training because they understand the value of doing it without necessarily enjoying it. The same athlete can be 100 percent intrinsically motivated to compete in their sport. Regardless of success, they love competition and the sense of development they get when they test their skills. Likewise, a coach may coach athletes in competition purely so that they can pay their mortgage, and they are happiest immersing themselves in the fundamentals of developing athletes in training. The model should therefore be used pragmatically to address the multitude of contexts encountered in the environment.

Achievement Goal Theory

While SDT provides a good account of how psychologists understand most aspects of motivation, it doesn't explicitly explain the relationship between perceived competence and the goals people set; this relationship is important in competitive sport. Indeed, achievement and demonstration of competence (ability) are integral to why athletes participate. Achievement goal theory provides a framework you can use to enhance this natural tendency in athletes and coaches and to create performance environments that encourage all to flourish.

Achievement goal theory (Nicholls 1984) focuses on how your definition of success (or failure) leads to judgments about how competent you are at a task. The theory outlines two ways in which individuals make their judgments of competence.* The first is how well the individual felt they had completed the task based on the standards they set for themselves regarding the demands of the task or based on previous best performances (task- or self-focused). These judgments are self-referenced, self-determined, and focus on elements of competence entirely within the control of the performer. Athletes and coaches who judge their competence this way most often set personal task (skill improvement) or performance (e.g., a personal best) goals. The second judgment is made by drawing comparison to others who are also performing the same or similar skills or tasks (ego-focused). Athletes and coaches who judge their competence in this way most often set outcome (e.g., want to win) or other-referenced goals (e.g., want to beat their nearest rival). Both types of goals can occur at three levels: An athlete's goals might change moment by moment (goal state) but are also a function of their personality (goal orientation) and the context or situation in which they find themselves (goal climate). For example, an athlete's goal orientation might be predominantly based on their tendency to judge their competency on task-based criteria. However, this might change if the goal climate changes as a function of a new coach who emphasizes winning more than development, forcing the athlete to adopt an ego-oriented view of competence.

Your perception of competence can also be positive or negative (termed *valence*), leading you to approach or avoid certain scenarios. For example, in competition, an athlete with a positive view of their competence is more likely to view that situation as a positive challenge. In contrast, an athlete with negative competence is likely to avoid the same situation, attending mostly to the potential for threat or ego-damage. These two perspectives on competence affect the goals athletes set for themselves, such that athletes and coaches with high levels of avoidance motivation may either set goals too easy (i.e., they know they will win) or too hard (i.e., they would never be expected to win).

*More recently, Elliot et al. (2011) further split the types of competence evaluations by distinguishing between pure task and mastery evaluations and self-based evaluations using factors such as personal bests.

Success Story 1: "Forgetting" How to Shoot

When I was working with an international wheelchair basketball team years ago, one of the young contenders for the Paralympic squad approached me during lunch break. He started the conversation with a simple statement: "I've forgotten how to shoot." When I asked what he meant, he recounted how he had arrived at camp at the beginning of the week, and in the first scrimmage had missed two early opportunities for what he considered an easy lay-up shot. Given the pressure for places on the team, his focus changed from one of individual improvement (task approach) to one in which he was obsessing over avoiding looking like a poor shooter in front of the selectors. Instead of getting in positions where he could make a cut into the D to score, he worked on distributing the ball. Then after each practice he stayed behind to try and "sort his lay-ups out." He told me that instead of just taking the shot automatically, he was trying to ensure every component of the shot was just right. In other words, he was reinvesting in the rules he learned the skill by and was forgetting that it was already automated. After working through the pragmatics of holding a belief that he "must not" demonstrate inadequacy in front of the selectors, I asked him to choose one word that represented a successful shot to him; he chose *height*. I asked him to take some shots while repeating that word to himself and in a blink of an eye, he'd remembered how to shoot. Overall, this case highlights the role the current situation has on our evaluation of competence and how this can change our motivational focus. In this case, the athlete moved from a mostly intrinsic focus toward more external-focused motives (i.e., to satisfy the selectors) and behaviors consistent with a need to avoid failure.

Motivational Climate

The notion of motivational climate is related to achievement goal theory. Just as athletes have preferred ways to judge their competence, all coaches, parents, practitioners, and increasingly fans also have their dominant ways to judge their own, the team's, and the athlete's competence. These preferences inevitably trickle down to the athletes, but they often affect the philosophy and behavior of everyone in the athlete's support group. For example, coach A might embrace a task-focused approach in how they deliver training sessions and review competition performances with their athletes. This climate will more likely foster an athlete's intrinsic motivation and encourage them to make judgments about their competence that are mostly self-referenced. On the flip side, coach B, who judges their athletes against the competence of other athletes or teams, is more likely to emphasize the importance of winning. In this climate, athletes might feel compelled to adopt a similar perspective in order to be selected or considered worthy of attention. Similar effects can occur through the transmitted philosophies of parents, sibling, and guardians. Recent research (Hogue et al., 2017) shows that ego-involved motivational climates in youth sport can elicit physiological and psychological stress states in youth athletes. Although not all references to performance and winning are bad, the balance should be in favor of a task-focused motivational climate.

Assessment

Assessment is a critical part of developing tailored interventions for any psychological issue. All the theories discussed so far provide a framework for how to measure motivation in performance environments. This section outlines methods of assessment that allow for the development of a complete picture of motivation in athletes. Athletes and coaches can choose to implement these methods themselves or discuss them with a sport psychology consultant.

One approach to assessment is to begin informally, using live observations and conversations with as many relevant people in the athletic environment as possible. This initial approach works better than abruptly asking athletes, coaches, and practitioners to complete a questionnaire; the latter reinforces unhelpful stereotypes about psychology and can damage rapport. Moreover, observation and conversation (or reflection) are key tools athletes and coaches can use to assess the nature of their own and each other's motivation.

For example, watching video footage of an athlete in training can inform the athlete and coach about current motivational focus and the motivational climate created. The athlete who celebrates loudly both in their own success and in their teammates' failures is likely to have more of a performance or ego focus. In contrast, the athlete who stays after practice to fine-tune technical skills when no one is watching is likely to be more task-focused. Similarly, it is possible to observe the extent to which the coach provides autonomy to their athlete, seeks to develop their competence, or works hard to develop a strong relationship with them. In this regard, the theories discussed in the previous section can serve as a framework for observations. From an informal conversation perspective, these short interactions are a great way to build an understanding of athletes', coaches', and practitioners' goal perspectives, their plans and ambitions, their key drivers (e.g., to make my dad happy), and to understand how they prepare for and reflect on competitions.

Observations and interviews are good methods for initially developing a rich understanding of an individual, but they are inherently subjective and provide only part of the picture. A bias may exist that affects the judgment and conclusions made following observation or interviews. Adding the use of questionnaires can help to manage this bias. However, it is important that psychometric measures be scientifically validated as much as possible. They should not be changed or adapted for use in a particular sport or setting; doing so affects their accuracy in measurement. The following sections identify three measures based on SDT and achievement goal theory. Athletes and coaches may find them useful for confirming issues with motivation or measuring changes in motivation in response to a particular intervention. Beyond this chapter, a review by Clancy and colleagues (2017) has provided comprehensive coverage of the most worthwhile psychometric measures of motivation that have been used in a sport setting.

Sport Motivation Scale II (SMS-II)

The original Sport Motivation Scale (Pelletier et al., 1995) has undergone a number of revisions by both the original authors and others (e.g., Mallett et al., 2007). The most recent iteration, the Sport Motivation Scale II (SMS-II) (Pelletier et al., 2013), measures all elements of the motivational continuum as prescribed by SDT, and it is robust and short enough to be used in practical settings (see Clancy et al., 2017).

The SMS-II is made up of 18 statements. These statements are separated into six factor groupings with three questions in each that measure each of the motivational types proposed in SDT. Each statement is answered on a Likert scale ranging from 1 (does not correspond at all) to 7 (corresponds completely) so that athletes can answer and coaches can interpret the degree to which the statements reflect motivation. Each statement is preceded by the stem *I practice my sport* . . . . Comparing scores on different subscales identifies how athletes are primarily motivated in their sport. Composite scores can be created to reflect, for example, a total extrinsic motivation score (add the average of external, introjected, and identified together), or they can be used to create a weighted algorithm for an overall self-determined score (see Gillet et al., 2010).

Perception of Success Questionnaire (POSQ)

The Perception of Success Questionnaire (POSQ) (Roberts et al., 1998) measures achievement goals from task and ego perspectives; it has six questions for each subscale. The POSQ is simple, but it does not cover the full spectrum of achievement goal theory. To cover all bases, more recent research introduced the Achievement Goal Questionnaire for Sport (Mascret et al., 2015), which measures both the type of goal (task, self, other/ego) and the valence (approach versus avoidance). However, unless the situation dictates that this approach is the only viable method of assessment (an unlikely scenario), it is best to keep the questionnaires simple and complement the assessment with conversations, observations, athlete diaries, and the like.

Perceived Motivational Climate in Sport Questionnaire–2

The Perceived Motivational Climate in Sport Questionnaire–2 (Newton et al., 2000) measures the athlete's perception of the motivational climate that the coach is trying to create. This questionnaire might be particularly useful for head coaches if they are working to make the other coaches more aware of how athletes perceive their coaching environment.

Optimization

Understanding exactly how athletes or coaches become motivated is a complex topic. Happily, from a practical perspective, the application of the theory is mostly common sense. I generally use the frameworks of SDT or achievement goal theory to guide my interventions. Depending on the issue, interventions mostly revolve around changing behaviors and attitudes of specific people in the athletic environment. However, given the interpersonal nature of motivations, in most cases interventions are focused on more than one person. For example, while an athlete lacking motivation to train may need to adjust their view of competence (e.g., from other- to self-referenced), their current view might be a function of the environment created by the coach. A coach who emphasizes results over performance may cause an athlete to question their competence. Similarly, a parent who uses guilt to coerce motivation takes away some of the athlete's autonomy. This section will consider some common and effective ways athletes, coaches, and sport psychology consultants can optimize motivation.

Education and Awareness

Before change can occur, everyone involved needs to be ready and motivated for it. The first step toward change includes education and increased aware- ness about the current motivation issues identified during any assessment. Often, those who are responsible for developing motivation (e.g., athlete, coach, parents) are unaware of their contribution to a problem and how their attitudes affect their own or others' motivation. For an example of this type of situation, see Success Story 2: Weight Loss and Shaming Don't Mix.

Increasing a person's self-awareness about how their behavior and atti- tude affect the motivation of others requires presenting evidence of that behavior or attitude. This evidence can be taken from a range of measures. Generally, a good way to help raise awareness is to observe how specific people behave and then provide feedback (as outlined in the Assessment section). For example, in Success Story 2: Weight Loss and Shaming Don't Mix, the author observed the event unfolding and then approached the coach privately to discuss what had happened. A sensible approach is to ask what they wanted to achieve, how effective they thought their strategy was, and whether they have alternative, more helpful ways to handle similar situations in the future. Athletes and coaches might find it helpful to explain how the other person's behavior made them feel (e.g., annoyed) and why (e.g., it undermines the team's values). This approach provides the coach or athlete agency in their own reeducation; keeping with SDT, having this autonomy likely encourages motivation to change. If the other person does not believe they behaved as others observed or doesn't see a problem with how they behaved, it might be possible to demonstrate the observation with existing video footage filmed with the person's permission. Similarly, feedback from others in the athletic environment (e.g., a sport psychology consultant) can help drive the message home. This approach can stimulate tough conversations, but you can handle resistance by communicating the rationale beforehand and keeping the goal in mind. When communicating your observations, always remember to critique behaviors and not the person (e.g., "Your behavior yesterday went against everything we are working for together as a team").

Success Story 2:
Weight Loss and Shaming Don't Mix

Some years ago, I was working with an elite international team. One of the players was overweight beyond the point where he could be effective in his position and to the extent that he would likely be dropped from the squad. I had been working closely with the player alongside a sport nutritionist to help develop control over his eating behaviors and guide him to make healthy choices. I was mostly using a motivational interviewing approach to help him understand how his current behavior choices matched his ambitions to play internationally (which he rated as highly important). The situation was improving slowly, and he was losing some weight. However, from the coach's perspective, it wasn't happening fast enough. During lunchtime at a training camp, the coach walked past the player in question, who was eating a salad. In front of every other player in the dining hall, the coach said, "Who are you kidding?" I later found out that the player subsequently left the dining hall, returned to his room, and ate six chocolate bars back-to-back. When questioned, the athlete reported thinking *Why do I even bother trying* and feeling hopeless to the point of abandoning his weight loss goals altogether. Following the event, I discussed with the coach his approach to dealing with what he considered a frustrating situation. I tried to raise his awareness of how shaming was a high-risk strategy. I explained that it created a climate of fear among players that may result in a breakdown of relationships and could also be considered bullying. Further, in this case it also resulted in a destructive, not productive, response from the athlete. At the next practice session, the coach apologized to the player and allowed me to deal with the athlete's motivation to achieve his weight loss goals in the future. This scenario highlights how one comment can dramatically change the motivational climate on a team. It might be momentary, but if this type of communication is commonplace, it creates a sustained and unproductive climate in which to develop athletes. By educating the coach to understand how one flippant comment can negatively impact motivation, it raised his awareness of suitable communication strategies for future interactions with athletes. This made my job as sport psychology consultant that much easier, as the coach and I were now pulling in the same direction.

Goal Setting

Goal setting is the most fundamental, simple, and effective motivational intervention an athlete or coach can implement to change behavior, develop skills, and improve performance. It increases focus and attention to performance-relevant factors, increases effort and determination in the face of setbacks, and helps the user find or learn ways to realize success. Despite this fact, many athletes and coaches do not have a clear goal-setting plan. When they do have a plan, it is often poorly crafted or set by someone else. (Remember, lack of autonomy often leads to diminished buy-in.) The general guidelines for setting goals have been driven by the SMART mnemonic, whereby goals should be specific, measurable, attainable, realistic, and time bound (Doran, 1981). Since their initial creation, these guidelines have been corrupted to some degree; other elements have been added and names have been changed, ultimately causing confusion for those people who want to use them. Weinberg and Butt (2015) have moved away from this mnemonic; instead, they explicitly state that goals should be

1. specific and measurable,
2. realistic and challenging,
3. short and long term,
4. set for practice and competition,
5. underpinned by a plan of how to achieve them,
6. set for the individual and team (where relevant), and
7. reevaluated regularly.

A valuable addition to this list would be that goals have to be meaningful for the athlete or coach. Reflecting the discussion on SDT, allowing autonomy in goal choice can contribute to meaningfulness. Indeed, a number of studies have shown that goals are more effective when autonomy is promoted (Smith et al., 2007). Studies have also highlighted that when coaches employ controlling motivational strategies, they can have negative consequences on athletes' well-being (Bartholomew et al., 2009; Smith et al., 2010). To reiterate, it does not necessarily mean that coaches and practitioners should give free reign to athletes to set whatever goals they like or vice versa. Instead, they should try to make goal setting a collaborative process that entails discussions with all relevant support staff (including parents of young athletes if applicable). Indeed, in a primer for coaches on how to set goals, Weinberg (2010) outlined a case study that had collaborative goal setting as a central component. Collaboration is important for many reasons. First, it can keep athletes, coaches, and support staff honest. Second, it helps athletes feel supported. Third, it ensures athletes, coaches, and support practitioners aren't under- or overselling their abilities. (However, it does rely on how accurately everyone involved can judge ability.) Finally, it is a great way for an athlete to understand themselves better and for everyone involved to see the world from their own and each other's perspective. Most of all, everyone involved is more engaged in their own development and behavior change.

Individual Athlete Plans (IAPs)

It is common practice in elite sport to develop individual athlete plans (IAPs) for every athlete embedded in a performance environment. These plans set out an athlete's goals and the projected plans for their attainment. It seems that no common standard exists for how these IAPs are formulated; most sports develop their own to suit their needs. Fundamentally, though, most effective IAPs have a common primary focus: how to best move an athlete from their current performance standard to that of a higher level (or sometimes as a pathway toward career termination). At some level, this aim involves behavior or attitude change on the part of the athlete, so providing the right conditions or climate to foster motivation is key. In terms of how the IAP is developed and subsequently used, both good and bad examples exist.

Demotivation through using IAPs tends to occur because of the potential conflict between the athlete's focus on enhanced performance and a coach's or system's potential use of IAPs to make decisions on selection or future investment. If the emphasis of the IAP leans too heavily toward selection, it can become a punitive tool. This emphasis is most often terrible for motivation on many levels, but in terms of SDT and goal achievement, athletes often end up questioning their competence and ability all the time. This questioning can lead to heightened states of anxiety, which threaten the athlete's well-being and undoubtedly affect performance. In addition, when athletes understand that a coach or performance director is emphasizing their power to effectively end their career, it places a barrier of mistrust between them. In other words, any hope of the athlete experiencing relatedness with the coaching team is unlikely, and the athlete is much more likely to take an at-all-costs approach to their own development.

In contrast, a good IAP process is grounded in the autonomy given to the athlete to collaborate with coaches in its development. Following an SDT approach, when athletes feel they have some level of autonomy in how the IAP is developed, they are more likely to engage with it. This is easier said than done; often an imbalance of power exists between coaches and athletes due to differences in age and perceived expertise. However, it can be mitigated if the process involves other coaches and (where relevant) sport science practitioners. Despite all these facts, given the competitive nature of funding in elite sport, it is difficult to completely remove every element of fear concerning the IAP as a selection tool. However, it should never be the only method of making these decisions. It should ideally focus on processes of improvement rather than performances per se, and it should never be inappropriately used as explicit leverage in an attempt to increase motivation. With this approach, the athlete should feel that their place on the team and their performance is something they have control over, and they will more likely give 100 percent of their effort to each part of the IAP.

Managing Attributions

As another practical consideration, athletes and coaches will find it useful to become sensitive to their own and others' attribution styles. This information is displayed most clearly in the language used to describe events and outcomes. First, it helps educate other athletes and coaches on the effect their attributions can have on motivation toward their goals. An explanation of the various attributional styles with illustrative examples can help individuals think more carefully when attributing reasons for success or poor performance. As covered earlier, it is generally better to make attributions to factors that are internal (a direct result of the individual), unstable (it can change), and controllable (the person can effect the change). This type of attribution can empower the athlete and coach to stay focused and motivated to improve. However, it is important to note that it isn't always this simple. As described earlier, it is essential that attributions be realistic; don't pretend you have control over something if you really don't. Once athletes and coaches are aware of different types of attributions, it will likely be necessary to challenge attributions when they arise in conversation. So, if another athlete blames the referee for a recent bad performance, you can actively challenge them to seek an alternative viewpoint. Keep in mind that the more quickly and more often you encourage an alternative, the faster the appropriate habit of attribution is built. Most people are very good at recognizing attribution errors when they are calm, but they are less so when high emotion is present. However, given that in-competition attributions can affect momentary motivational states, it is useful to work systematically toward correct attributions when the heat is on.

Conclusion

Motivation is critical for long-term athletic development and performance. This importance has resulted in an abundance of theories and research that can often be confusing on a practical level. Indeed, many theories have crossovers in what they predict and the consequent methods best used to develop motivation. This chapter emphasized the most practically useful theories, assessments, and interventions, and it focused mostly on the components of each theory that apply to athletic development. In short, the chapter prepared you to approach motivational issues in your sport with greater confidence.

6 Confidence

Denis Hauw
University of Lausanne

In the world of sport, confidence is a powerful component of high-level performance. Confident athletes do not let worries overwhelm them; they have become mentally strong and have acquired an almost limitless sense of possibility. These effects illustrate why confidence is one of the most important mental dispositions for sport achievement (Vealey, 1986). However, they may also mask the complexity of what confidence is. Indeed, confidence is multifaceted; it can be related to and lodged in a number of factors, including the self, coaches and managers, the team or training partners, movements and training effects, sport facilities, and the field or sport environment. In addition, confidence is not always stable; it can decrease in a wide range of situations. Confidence is both dynamic and situated, and fine adjustments are not always easy to achieve. Knowledge and competencies in determining how the varieties of confidence are formed and regulated are essential not only for sport psychology consultants but also for coaches (who must manage teams) and for high-level athletes (who need to develop and self-regulate).

This chapter provides experience- and research-based insights and resources to help you create a confidence-building program in the sport realm. This program can be integrated into athletes' personal self-development practices or those provided by coaches, managers, and sport psychology consultants. The first section is an examination of the relevance of confidence in sport. The following section covers the zones of action of this concept in training, management, and performing, and it provides a condensed overview of the research findings. Next, assessment issues, including tools and practical indicators, are considered. Finally, the chapter concludes with methods for improvement, suggesting what should be included in mental preparation and the key points for managing confidence in the environment of practice.

Relevance

What does *confidence* mean? This multifaceted construct is related to the belief of efficacy—the belief that an individual can accomplish a goal with their own resources emerging from a complex mixture of self-appraisal and self-persuasion.

When confidence is high, it permeates an athlete's activity, targeting cognitive, emotional, embodied, and situated dimensions. In other words,

a. negative thoughts (e.g., *This fight is already lost because this boxer has won all their previous fights*) are less likely to occur;

b. general feelings of happiness, ease, calmness, or well-being pervade the athlete despite their fear of failure (e.g., when a kicker is ready to shoot a penalty);

c. the body responds and behaviors emerge in situations with a high degree of comfort and technical ability, as if the athlete is in the right place, making good decisions and without hesitation;

d. presence in situations is strong (e.g., an athlete dominates areas of sport such as call rooms or tracks and in standoffs with opponents); and

e. distraction control is in place, protecting the athlete from losing focus when negative experiences (e.g., an opponent's remarks or press allegations) occur.

However, confidence does not protect against unfounded expectations of success, a loss in critical thinking (cf. group think; Tasa & Whyte, 2005), or a form of dangerous negligence when performing. Imagine an overconfident team competing against a lower-ranking team in a knockout competition. The high-ranking team may underestimate the confidence of their opponent and the challenge facing them (see Success Story 1: Do You Believe You Can Win?). Hence, if confidence leads to appropriate training and determination, its value is linked to self-control and conscientiousness.

Team confidence also needs to be considered. Indeed, different types of team confidence exist and can vary within groups. Obviously, team confidence is influenced by significant teammates (particularly those who are able to inspire confidence in others) and coaches who generate climates of confidence. Another remarkable point about team confidence is the nature of shared beliefs. Interindividual synchrony in both cognitive and bodily or behavioral processes creates a collective confidence among teams. Rituals

Success Story 1: Do You Believe You Can Win?

Beliefs about winning can help athletes reverse the outcome of a competition. Use the following authentic stories to feed your own confidence.

- On June 11, 1989, 17-year-old Michael Chang beat Stefan Edberg to win the French Open, becoming the youngest player to win a Grand Slam title in tennis. Six days earlier, Michael Chang defeated Ivan Lendl, who was ranked number 1 in the world. One of the most famous moments in the match was his underhanded serve to Lendl. An underhanded serve was unusual and daring, but it was clever in the context. Chang said he made the serve because he believed in himself and this was one of the solutions he had found. He dared to do it because, despite his extreme exhaustion, he couldn't bear leaving behind the image of a player who had played a good match against the world number 1 but failed. This feeling motivated him to not give up until the last point. Chang said, "This has helped me in my career and in my life. Believe in yourself. Never give up."

- In 2015, jockey Michelle Payne became the first woman to win Australia's most famous horse race, the Melbourne Cup. She rode a horse with long odds of 100–1. She said she had dreamed of being a winning jockey as a child and announced she would one day win the Melbourne Cup. She also said she was always supported by her family in her project to win this race. In a sport managed exclusively by males, it was not always easy to stay confident, but as she said, "I just want to say, everyone else can get stuffed, because they think women aren't strong enough and we just beat the world."

- The Champions League in soccer has mainly been won by big teams such as Real Madrid or Bayern Munich. In 2004, the Champions League was won by the Portuguese team FC Porto, led by their young coach José Mourinho. "We have everything to win and nothing to lose," said the coach. In addition, the players said, "We knew each other by heart. Every player knew what the others were going to do and when they were going to do it. . . . Sometimes we didn't even talk on the field, we were confident of what the other one was going to do. All we needed was a look, a glance." This excerpt illustrates the extent to which the team confidence that Mourinho built among the players was linked to the fluency of their behavioral coordination on the field.

- At the 2014 European Athletics Championship, the French team won the women's 4 × 400 m relay final after an incredible race. Floria Guei ran the last leg of the race, and it was the performance of a lifetime. Frankly not favorites, the French runners had nevertheless built their success on a collective belief in possibility in the first legs, even though the British and Ukrainian athletes had taken control of the race. When Floria Guei took the baton, inspired by her team's belief, she unleashed her capacities and the power of her belief in herself and surged forward for a phenomenal finish, beating her competition by a breath.

Kai Schwoerer/Getty Images

FIGURE 6.1   For New Zealand rugby players, doing the haka reinforces collective confidence.

such as the haka, a Maori posture dance in New Zealand (figure 6.1), are useful. During the ritual, behaviors and minds synchronize, creating affective rewards such as feelings of solidarity, connectedness, and cooperative motivation, which support collective confidence (Collins, 2005). Think about a soccer player making an instinctive blind pass to a teammate. The confidence of the passing player that the teammate can receive it is fundamental to taking this action. Of course, the player also could try it without being completely sure of success. However, trying and succeeding creates a feeling of confidence that unites the behavior, emotions, and thoughts for future actions.

To summarize, confidence covers a wide range of cognitions, emotions, and behaviors. It is adaptable and can be built. It is also an interpersonal, social, and cultural construct that is linked to life stories. Confidence is like a shield that can be used in difficult situations to protect athletes from excesses and enable them to keep a cool head when managing challenging situations. With confidence then, athletes should be able to climb onto their own shoulders.

What We Know

Almost everyone has experienced the effect of a temporary loss of self-confidence. This erosion in confidence has a significant correlation with performance in sport (Hays et al., 2009).

Factors That Erode Confidence in Sport

Hays and colleagues (2009) identified seven factors that erode confidence in relation to sport. The first factor is defined by the level of performance. When a heptathlete underperforms in the hurdles and long jump at the beginning of an event, it is harder for them to face the high jump and the following events. This factor is identifiable for any type of performance, from those that are very brief to those spanning many days with qualification rounds before the final. Confidence follows the stream of performances in the events. Confidence is dynamic, and its evolution has a wide temporal horizon. This dynamic fills the competitive life stories of an athlete and provides a narrative foundation for their self-confidence.

The second factor is the physical state of the athlete. After an injury, debilitating effects immediately ensue, often reducing the possibilities of enacting a performance. Also, chronic backache, joint pain, and muscle soreness are frequent in sport, and they may affect athlete confidence. In contrast, though also somewhat complementary, consider someone who works out in a gym. Bodybuilding creates a feeling of self-confidence because it enhances the physical state, shaping the body to correspond to the norms of social efficacy. Confidence is thus deposited in the body and its efficacy.

The third factor is the subjective assessment of training sessions. Athletes tend to connect the assessment of precompetitive training sessions to predictions about competitive performances. Some athletes prefer perfect training sessions and a perfect competitive warm-up in order to be fully confident for competition. Others are comfortable with minor problems and look for key points they can adjust for their competitive performance. This interaction between training assessment and the belief in success in competition or in the following events varies depending on the athlete.

The fourth factor is linked to coaches' activity. When coaches display doubts about performance, athletes are affected. This connection between coach activity and athlete self-efficacy suggests that individual confidence is thus social because coaches and close relatives participate in developing athletes' efficacy beliefs.

The fifth factor is pressure from the social environment. Federations have expectations for their athletes, but they do not always measure the pressure they exert. The media, too, creates pressure. Social networks especially amplify this phenomenon. Unfortunately, even if an athlete closes off all communication during competition, pressure can remain intense and affect confidence by creating the fear of disappointing others.

The sixth factor is specifically linked to mental preparation. For example, when unprepared for the challenges encountered in competition or with little experience participating in international events, athletes may lack the mental strategies needed to self-regulate these types of constraints. Athletes can learn these strategies through psychological training.

Finally, the seventh factor is made up of all the specific situations that are unpredictable. For example, the semifinal match of the 1995 Rugby World Cup was delayed because of weather conditions. The players had to wait for several hours in their locker rooms before the field became accessible. During this long and uncertain waiting period, confidence had ample time to fluctuate.

Some Roots and Sources of Confidence

Reflecting on these seven factors, consider where your confidence is and what it is rooted in. At first, it is common to consider confidence a personal attribute. Trait confidence has even been described as a facet of personality (Vealey, 1986)—a relatively stable personal disposition to act, think, and be emotionally affected in such a way that goals seem obtainable despite challenging circumstances. Certainly, athletes with high trait confidence will feel comfortable in circumstances such as competition, training, career management, and media communications. Athletes likely can distinguish differences in levels of confidence between their teammates. Further, many are convinced that having confidence is beneficial. However, it is not so uncommon to find elite athletes with relatively low trait confidence. Thus, they are likely to doubt their overall potential to perform well, their success when in adverse situations, or their ability to achieve in a specific competition.

Developing confidence is a big undertaking, and many environmental elements are involved. For example, a coach's doubts can have a debilitating effect on an athlete. Fortunately, in most situations, coaches bolster confidence. Their many discussions, meetings, and other coaching practices (e.g., spotting a gymnast's flight or having a quiet word in warm-up) likewise support confidence.

Athletes also find many resources in the environment. Examples of material resources might be some of the things they put in their bags, such as soft toys or ritual objects. These things, too, support confidence during competition. All these examples show that although confidence is a personal attribute, it emerges in situations from a distributed network composing the athlete's environment. Spectators, crowds, and the media are also part of the social environment.

Other factors athletes report for locating and containing their confidence are religion, culture, philosophy, and politics. Take the example of the two-time world champion Brazilian surfer Gabriel Medina. In an interview, he said, "I believe in God. I pray for His support and He blesses me when I go into the water. Prayer energizes me. I feel confident and know that God is with me and that I'm going to give my best . . . Before getting into the water, I put myself completely in God's hands. This phase is important because it sharpens my concentration and makes me able to go beyond myself. So my confidence is immense" (Michel, 2019, p. 21). Another example involves a study of the sociocultural influences that feed the success beliefs of some African-American athletes (Galli & Vealey, 2008). The authors of this study cite the case of an athlete who mentioned that his ethnic origin was associated with the idea of success and overcoming obstacles and that it helped to feed his confidence because he embodied these ideas in his daily practice of sport.

Consider also the dynamic nature of confidence. Narratives that encompass athletes' life stories form a key component of confidence (e.g., Warnick et al., 2016). Triggering situations activate memories, and they may cause confidence to fluctuate because they are linked to meaningful past events. The memory of a previous unsuccessful standoff can convince an athlete that success is impossible. In contrast, when an athlete reaches their personal best, it may become the expected outcome for all successive seasons.

In summary, many beliefs help athletes fashion their confidence, and cultural differences and social influences are key points for understanding where confidence is located and what it is rooted in.

Confidence for Growth and Performance

Confidence is also required for athletes to grow and perform at their best. This fact is evident in various sport situations, such as everyday training, high-level competition, performing in collective environments, and managing sport injuries. The following text explores each of these situations.

A certain level of confidence is required for everyday training because it provides a positive attitude associated with satisfaction. Confidence also affects attitudes about involvement in tasks, prompting a focus on solutions in spite of perceived incompetence (e.g., Bandura & Wood, 1989). Confidence is especially needed when coaches provide challenging training situations. When faced with problems, athletes can show striking differences. For example, some withdraw, and others push past their limits. Confidence may come into play in these situations; studies have shown that athletes with a strong belief in their efficacy display maximal effort and persistence in reaching goals (Bandura, 1986). Finally, from a long-term perspective, training can conflict with other activities, and performance may stagnate for a period. Again, confidence in long-term success powers the commitment of youth to reach master levels of performance (Larson et al., 2019).

As well as in training, confidence is crucial during competition. For example, the precompetitive anxiety generated by expectations and uncertainty can be partially compensated by confidence (e.g., Mellalieu et al., 2009). It is natural for confidence to fluctuate before and during competition. This instability has sometimes been linked to gender differences; female athletes were found to be more likely threatened by external information such as the perception of their opponent's level of play (Vealey et al., 1998).

Confidence for Rehabilitation, Readiness, and Responding to Stressors

To manage sport injuries, one of the key psychological points is the regulation of the emotional waves that wash over athletes from the time they leave the field until their return. Confidence in rehabilitation changes at various speeds, although the general trend is toward acceleration over the course of the rehabilitation process. This change indicates a decrease in pain and an increase in the perception of the injured body's functionality (Chmielewski et al., 2011). Athletes with high confidence overcome this challenge more easily than others. Psychological readiness has been used to characterize the "psychological resources that facilitate a safe, productive and enjoyable return to sport" (Brewer & Redmond, 2017, p. 139). Confidence is a key component of psychological readiness, not only in the recovery of the injured body parts but also in the capability to perform successfully.

To conclude, confidence is a powerful tool for dealing with the sport life course and life stories. Studies have shown that confidence protects the world's best athletes from the potentially negative effects of stressors (Fletcher & Sarkar, 2012). Confidence thus participates in optimal sport performance and positive individual and collective development.

Bringing It All Together: Bandura's Model of Self-Efficacy

Capturing many of the messages presented earlier and connecting with the later section on the optimization of confidence, it is useful to now consider one of the best-known psychosocial models of confidence: Bandura's self-efficacy theory (Bandura, 1997). Within this theory, confidence is tied to the concept of *self-efficacy*—the belief in one's competence to perform. This belief, best thought of as situation-specific confidence, transforms the way people look at and act in the world. People with high self-efficacy perceive tasks as challenging but under control rather than as threatening and unrealizable. This attribute has two consequences. It increases interest in the task, and it reduces stress and depression. This belief also prompts people to set stimulating goals and maintain high involvement, especially in cases of difficulties. Indeed, people with high self-efficacy are able to stay focused and look for solutions in such situations. Self-efficacy reinforces persistence, and failure is attributed to insufficient effort; both favor the development of successful attitudes.

Bandura identified four main factors that affect self-efficacy (Bandura, 1986). The first is the experience of success. Confidence is based on previous successes, and the best way to improve confidence is to succeed. The wording *experience of* implies that a cognitive-emotional appraisal is linked to the way the person attributes success or failure. For instance, even if an athlete loses a competition, they can try to identify the positive points that balance the experience of failure, thus generating positive rewards (Carver

& Scheier, 1998). Indeed, the influence of past performance experiences on self-efficacy beliefs depends on various cognitive processes, such as the perceived difficulty of the performance, the effort expended, the amount of guidance received, the importance of this experience, and the personal conception of what ability is.

The second factor of Bandura's model is the experience of seeing others succeeding in a shared task. Vicarious experience is related to observational learning. Seeing teammates succeeding in a task brings forth the belief that the athlete can also do it—even if the athlete has never tried it. This has a big effect on confidence.

The third factor is verbal persuasion. Many coaches can be particularly persuasive through their attitudes, spoken words, and behavioral incentives. Many incredible (and sometimes funny) examples can be found on the Internet.

The fourth and final factor is the physical or emotional state. Imagine an athlete who is particularly tired after a long portion of ascent in a trail race. Before them is a short descent and then a very sharp ascent. The athlete's confidence is probably reduced by feelings of exhaustion. This phenomenon probably explains many cases of withdrawal from trail races.

Collective Confidence

Of final note in this section, it is important to recognize that team confidence is an essential factor in team success, especially when the game is close and both pressure and stakes are high. Collective efficacy is "a group's shared belief in its conjoint capability to organize and execute the courses of action required to produce given levels of attainment" (Bandura, 1997, p. 477). Zaccaro et al. (1995) defined collective efficacy as "a sense of collective competence shared among individuals when allocating, coordinating, and integrating their resources in a successful concerted response to specific situational demands" (p. 309). Collective efficacy is not limited to team sports. Individual elite athletes work with a team around them that may include the coach, a manager, physicians, and physical and mental coaches. All contribute to the collective confidence that adds to the athletes' personal confidence. Nevertheless, it is particularly important for team sport, where tight interdependence is needed for success. Like individual confidence, team confidence is dynamic and linked to the events that mark a season, tournament, race, or match.

To better understand the dynamics, Fransen et al. (2017) have distinguished confidence in collective efficacy with a focus on group processes (*We can work like this*) and confidence in the team outcomes (*We can achieve this target*). These two types of team confidence are important predictors of team functioning regarding effort, cohesiveness, resilience, and ultimately success. For example, Zaccaro et al. (1995) proposed that group qualities, especially cohesion, contribute to a team's sense of efficacy.

However, team confidence is not always the same among members; it may be unevenly dispersed. Fortunately, the same degree of shared beliefs about collective efficacy is not necessarily needed. For example, a distributed network of beliefs about confidence regarding positions on the team may better represent the ecology of team functioning, and various types of dispersion of these beliefs can be managed (e.g., DeRue et al., 2010). Another point is that efficacy of work and performances in the collective environment depends on both individual and collective efficacy. Finally, if the same four incentives Bandura (1986) identified for individual efficacy can affect collective efficacy, the experiences of past performances determine cohesion and team confidence (Heuzé et al., 2006).

Assessment

Many instruments have been developed to assess confidence. A number of them are open access. This section introduces and briefly describes some of them.

At the individual level, two popular instruments exist: Vealey's (1986) Sport Confidence and Competitive Orientation measure and the self-confidence subscale of the Competitive Sport Anxiety Inventory-2 (CSAI-2: Martens et al., 1990). The first focuses on trait and state perception regarding success in sport, and the second focuses on the perception of success in competition. General self-confidence can also be characterized using a personality questionnaire that includes this facet in the general traits of emotional stability (e.g., the revised NEO personality inventory and other personality inventories). In this case, the benefit is to combine this facet with other personality dispositions, such as enthusiasm, self-discipline, or openness to experience, to gain a comprehensive understanding of athletes' psychological functioning, how they manage themselves in professional environments, and their personal development (e.g., Gardner & Moore, 2006; Hauw et al., 2021).

To assess team confidence across sports, two reliable and valid questionnaires are recommended: the Collective Efficacy Questionnaire for Sports (CEQS) (Short et al., 2005), which measures team efficacy processes and outcomes, and the Observational Collective Efficacy Scale for Sports (OCESS) (Fransen et al., 2014). The CEQS assesses team confidence in terms of the upcoming game or competition using a five-factor model (*ability*, *effort*, *persistence*, *preparation*, *unity*). Keep in mind that in this questionnaire, ability specifically does not measure the process inside a team but rather the outcome in comparison to other teams. The OCESS includes these five items:

- React enthusiastically when making a point
- Have leader figures on the team who believe that we will win this game
- Have players both in the game and on the bench who cheer enthusiastically

- Encourage each other during the game
- Communicate tactically a lot during the game

All these instruments offer effective and validated tools to evaluate different elements of confidence. At a basic level, however, simple scales of *How confident are you that...,* scored 1 to 10, can offer good insights into how athletes view their self-efficacy on key aspects of their performance.

According to coaches and sport psychology consultants, confidence should be regularly assessed. Because of its dynamic nature, it should be assessed in the context of specific situations (e.g., a first selection), the phase in the season (e.g., interseason, midseason, final phases), when a newcomer enters the group, or over the course of a career (see Success Story 2: Checklist for Strong Team Confidence). It is one of the key indicators that should be managed for both performances and development. Tools are important for detecting fluctuations, but situated observations must complete them. For example, behaviors such as avoidance, decreased involvement while the season is in full swing, or a rise in defeatist attitudes should alert coaches. Other emotional signs, such as crying, vomiting, or trembling, may also be identified and linked to problems with self-confidence. Lastly, in discussions with athletes, coaches can collect relevant information on athletes' mental state and the level, strength, and generality of their confidence.

To summarize, confidence assessment is grounded in a joint approach; it is observed as part of the sport psychology consultant's or coach's everyday concerns and documented regularly using reliable instruments.

Optimization

Working on confidence is as multifaceted as confidence itself. Building confidence is based on repeated self-observation, self-analysis of the correct or best part of an athlete's own past performances or sport activity, and using it as a model for the athlete's future; generally it is called self-modeling (e.g., Dowrick, 1999).

Using Bandura's Model to Optimize Confidence

A simple approach for determining the various directions of self-modeling work is to use the four incentives that Bandura (1986) identified to optimize confidence.

First, feed your confidence with your positive experiences of high achievement. Try to detail the positive elements over a period of time in your career. For example, list the positive aspects of a part of a season, such as what you learned, what you improved, and what the works in progress are. Gradually, you will begin to see something good in what you are examining (e.g., a competition, a period of training, or the whole past season). People tend to remember the negative aspects. This human tendency is understandable because people are affected by failures, injuries, and important negative experiences. Giving yourself credit where it's due is sometimes hard work!

Second, use observational learning to feed your confidence. Observing others or yourself when performing well has a positive effect on confidence. Video observation is well-suited for this task. Research has shown that watching positive multilevel footage (video of positive team and individual behaviors) enhances team efficacy (Bruton et al., 2019). It is also true for self-efficacy. Thus, preparing for or debriefing performances using positive behavior footage is recommended as you work to build confidence. Athletes can use this method themselves, and coaches can use it with their teams.

Third, feed confidence with positive feedback. The clever use of positive feedback is well-suited for building confidence at the right moment, such as just before a challenging event. It should be used in a favorable way to maintain the effect, and it should be self-referenced and not based on comparisons with others—even when the challenge is the opponent. Some athletes find it difficult to deal with coaches who preclude frequent positive feedback. As an athlete, you have alternative solutions. One is to use self-talk to convince yourself of your efficacy, reduce negative thoughts, self-regulate activity, and bolster mental strength—all without extrinsic feedback. Imagery is also a helpful tool for building self-efficacy, but it requires caution. You may get stuck in a cycle of endlessly imagining your performance and even lose sleep during periods of competition. Another solution is to accept the situation as you continue to offer yourself encouragement using the self-modeling introduced earlier or using all the affordances available in your social environment (e.g., close relatives, social media). Acceptance is explained in more detail later in the chapter.

Fourth, work on your body and emotions to affect your confidence. In other words, be physically well-prepared for events, and learn how to regulate your emotions. To be well-prepared physically means taking charge of your physical resources and the development of your relative weaknesses. For example, a tall, imposing, and talented rugby player thought he was too timid on the field. Adding boxing sessions to his training program helped him improve his aggressiveness, and when he saw the gains in matches, his confidence increased. Learning to self-regulate emotions means developing coping strategies for when stressful events threaten to overwhelm your feelings. Typically, strategies for efficient coping include distracting yourself with music, exercising self-control, and turning to social supports.

Important Extras to Optimize Confidence

In addition to Bandura's four basic principles for building confidence, three key points for autonomous work on confidence may be added.

The first point is to feel comfortable with the idea that you can lose confidence in certain situations. Variability in confidence is quite common, and strength is seen in the ability to regulate this variability. Along the same lines, it is not unusual to feel a loss of confidence over the course of a career. Pathways of careers in sport look like long, winding roads, and confidence is sensitive to the setbacks and concerns that are par for the course (of life). If you can keep this fact in mind, you will remember that low-confidence situations are not unusual and that you are not alone. In turn, this awareness can help you start the work of relativizing the situation.

A second key point is to make a detailed analysis of the situated and dynamic properties of your own confidence. Of course, you can characterize yourself according to the general trait of confidence that tends to either crumble or remain strong when facing critical situations. However, your performances, behaviors, emotions, thoughts, and therefore feelings of confidence always emerge during interaction with situations. Detailing how your confidence is expressed in the present and along your pathway is therefore a big undertaking. Examine in detail (a) the performance level you can reasonably imagine now and at different past and future times, (b) the strength of your confidence as a timely certainty, and (c) its generality regarding the number and variety of domains, situations, or people that act as affordances or constraints. Doing this examination is an active way to build your self-confidence by anticipating the future, better understanding the past, and making sense of the situations you experience.

It is quite common for an athlete's confidence to vary throughout a season or career.

A third key point is to build a flexible mind—one that is not blocked or that is preoccupied with negative emotions. A flexible mind means having the capacity to use positive experience for your own concerns, the capacity to accept negative aspects as normal and as challenges for future development, and the capacity to develop presence in a situation. Rather than struggling and trying to control stressful situations that decrease your confidence, accepting these situations as normal facets of life in sport will help you in working on your confidence (Gardner & Moore, 2006). To illustrate this point, imagine you are a fish swimming along the shore where fishermen are trying to catch you. You have four possibilities: fight, flight, freeze, or accept. First, you could risk getting caught and fight the fishermen; you fight, resist, dive, jump, and sometimes manage to come off the hook—or not. Another solution is flight toward other parts of the sea. Another is to become immobile (freeze) until the fishermen go home. The fourth solution is to look carefully at the fish-hooks and don't get caught. Continue swimming between them, seeing the dangers but remaining confident because you know the problems are there but also that you are able to avoid them. This attitude of acceptance means refusing to engage in immediate reactive behaviors but instead keeping in mind a commitment to personal values that direct you to more thoughtful behavior. Personal values are important in your sport practice as well as in the directions you pursue. Values are not the goals; they are the reasons why you set the goals. For example, you want to be an Olympic champion to be a model for youth and to have a successful pathway. You have the values, and committing to them will transform your relationship to the stressful events that made you lose confidence when you were only focused on your goal. The work of acceptance can be developed individually. Many Internet and print resources are available to help with this work. A sport psychology consultant trained in this area is also a helpful resource.

Role of Coaches and Sport Psychology Consultants in Optimizing Confidence

For coaches, the basics for confidence include these abilities: (a) to create a motivational climate where fear of failure and anxiety are minimized, (b) to encourage positive self-talk and self-modeling, (c) to use instructions and drills to ensure that performances improve and do not stagnate or decrease, and (d) to use rewarding statements as well as verbal persuasion.

Athletes' confidence in their coaches is also grounded on their efficacy, which has been defined with five dimensions: motivation, technique, game, game strategy, and character building efficacy (Feltz et al., 1999). The athlete's confidence may vary for the same coach within these dimensions, and it may do so quickly, such as in the course of weeks, days, or even a game. Consequently, working continuously on self-confidence, team confidence, and coach confidence is recommended.

Success Story 2:
Checklist for Strong Team Confidence

- Team composition is a crucial point. Team confidence requires team cohesion. The difficulty is finding the right balance between performance levels and functional relationships.

- Past group and individual experiences should be considered when, for example, you bring new members into a team. Team confidence is grounded in the compatibility between the members' narratives.

- The lead players must be chosen with attention, and their roles must be accurately defined.

- Coaches' activities generate important resources for team confidence. Climate of confidence and leadership are particularly triggered by upward and downward spirals of team confidence.

- Team-building focused on shared goals is the traditional foundation for team confidence.

- Conflict-management meetings are useful when the team is splintered and team confidence is blocked by the unspoken. Nip conflicts in the bud by ensuring constant and proactive communication.

- Build team confidence early in the season. Team efficacy beliefs at the beginning of the season predict later team efficacy and overall performance at the end of the season. If sport teams develop persistent efficacy beliefs relatively early, it has a positive influence on subsequent performance.

- Management of team activity and achieving goals in training and competition are the basis for developing shared beliefs in success. In training situations, success based on indicators (e.g., distances covered, number of decisive passes, number of shots) might be used to work on team confidence. For example, comparing and enhancing indicator scores is a resource for increasing team confidence along with the increasing levels of performance. In the same vein, comparing team indicators across competitions in relation to the goal set is also a good idea.

- Use imagery and observational learning for building and regulating team confidence. Design observational learning interventions that contain positive images of the team performing and images of the individual player performing. In addition, ask players to imagine achieving the same successful cooperative actions in the future. When players are away from training camp, you can send video footage to use this method. It is also a good way to prepare or maintain contact between players on a national team because those players do not spend much time together.

- Regular personal interviews help increase awareness of group narratives and identify erosion of confidence in individual players or subgroups of players.

The key recommendation for coaches is to interact with the athletes. As a coach, be out there among the athletes, and regularly assess the situation. Building confidence is a collective project. Therefore, identify leaders, ask them to participate in the project, and regulate with them. The coaches' work on confidence will help reveal their athletes' potential as well as their own confidence. Mutual development is crucial.

Additional processes might be used in the regulation of individual cases. For example, sometimes coaches do not understand why their athletes have low confidence in their competence despite their physical ability or their self-evaluation of resources. Beliefs block the activity or inhibit the movements. The fight, flight, or freeze attitudes might be efficient in the short run, but they usually displace the problem without solving it. Indeed, some athletes have irrational beliefs—misattributions of success that, processed in the athletes' mind, generate inefficient cognitive schemas that explain this kind of low confidence. To modify these schemas, cognitive and behavioral interventions as well as acceptance approaches are needed. Sport psychology consultants can be helpful in these situations.

Conclusion

This chapter considered confidence over a wide spectrum of embodied, cognitive, social, and material factors that are involved in its formation, development, and regulation. Work on confidence is needed because many athletes misrepresent their true capacity. Efficacy may thus be enhanced, helping achieve the self set or team set of sport outcomes. Significantly, working on confidence in the course of life in sport, which inexorably is marked by failures and setbacks, might be considered as transferable to life in general. Indeed, Bandura (1997) suggested that athletes may develop a resilient sense of self-efficacy that is useful for sport competition and, more generally, for life.

7 | Imagery and Mental Practice

Geoff P. Lovell
University of the Sunshine Coast

John K. Parker
Hartpury University

Imagine this scene: You're sitting in deep, soft powder snow high in the Rocky Mountains. You're alone. The sky is blue, and the air is cold and clean. You breathe in deeply, and it's absolutely silent. You can feel the texture of the perfect snow all around you. The tip of your snowboard is just poking through it. You check the bindings for the third time. As you stand to take one last look down the route before you start, you feel the pounding of your heart and the rush of adrenaline.

You're not actually in the Rocky Mountains, but the scene feels real. In fact, you are using a key psychological strategy for sport performance called mental imagery (MI).

In general, most people have limited knowledge of MI. For example, when the authors of this chapter are introduced to organizations as sport psychology practitioners, usually the first response is a question such as "Is it true you can read people's minds?" After explaining that we don't possess that type of superpower, the second comment is often something like "Sport psychology means you motivate people and do visualization." While some glimmers of truth exist in that statement, it demonstrates how MI is widely known by the general public and sports people alike, but also how poorly the concept is generally understood. For example, the term *visualization* offers too narrow an interpretation of the term *MI* that is used throughout this chapter. *Visu-alization* implies that engaging in this strategy involves only *seeing*. However, if you imagine one of your most poignant sport experiences (e.g., making that perfect tee shot in golf or that buzzer-beating three-point shot in basketball, standing on the podium and receiving a medal), you will probably be doing more than just seeing. Most likely you'll experience the emotions associated with the performance; you might even feel the hairs on your arms and legs stand up. Your muscles will probably feel as if you're actually moving, and you may even notice your muscles twitch. You might hear the crowd roar, and you may relive certain associated smells (e.g., the aroma of the warm-up room). In other words, MI is more than seeing; when it is done well, it uses all the senses.

Krzysztof Tkacz/fotolia.com

Mental imagery can make you feel as if you are snowboarding in the Rocky Mountains.

Another common limitation in people's understanding of MI is why they should do it. Most coaches and athletes, as well as many strength and conditioning instructors and physical trainers among others, will have at some point in their careers watched presentations or read about how they should be using MI. However, people are somewhat unclear of why and for what they should be using MI.

Relevance

While MI has been defined in various ways, for the purposes of this chapter, it is defined as the deliberate construction of an image from information stored in memory, consisting of quasi-sensorial, quasi-affective, and quasi-perceptual components (Morris et al., 2005). Furthermore, the general intention for MI is to create representative, vivid, and sensory-rich images that reinforce the desired performance outcomes or optimize psychological functions (Cumming & Williams, 2013). More succinctly, MI is a multisensory experience that occurs without the need of actual perception (Murphy et al., 2008). A related mental strategy with subtle yet important differences is mental practice (MP), also commonly called mental rehearsal. MP is the use of MI to cognitively practice a skill, either physical or mental, without overt physical movement. MP is routinely used to enhance performance in sport and other performance domains (e.g., performing arts).

Somewhat confusing is that MP is also often termed MI. More accurately, MI can be considered an umbrella term with MP as a subcategory. The following examples may better explain the relationship and difference between MI and MP. Consider that you're training to run a marathon. Now imagine this scene:

> You're finishing the London Marathon; you have less than half a mile to go as you head down the Mall in front of thousands of people packed in front of the international icon that is Buckingham Palace. Your watch reads 2 hours, 26 minutes, and 3 seconds. Despite the burning sensation in your legs and the sting of the sweat in your eyes, you're going to make that lifetime goal of getting under two and one-half hours for the marathon—and what a place to do it.

Mentally imagining yourself achieving your goal is likely to boost your confidence and increase your motivation. Indeed, if you are lying in a warm bed on a cold winter morning, having just been awakened by the alarm to get you up and out for a long morning training run even though it's still dark outside, a good dose of MI may be exactly the motivation you need to break the grasp of your warm slumber. The strategy you just employed was MI; you created a multisensory experience without actual perception.

Now consider that you're a college football team's starting quarterback and you're mentally preparing for your bowl game. The coach and support team have analyzed the opposing team's previous games and accordingly designed a number of new plays for your team. To help you learn these new sequences of plays and calls, you mentally practice receiving the ball and making the new play sequences. This time, imagine the following:

> You are making the call in the huddle, walking forward to the starting position, and standing behind the line of scrimmage. The snap is called, you receive the ball, you fake a handoff to your running back, then you drop back three steps, spot an open receiver downfield, and make the long pass.

In this example you're mentally practicing the new play sequences in the same way a gymnast might mentally practice learning a new bar dismount. Although you're still using MI, because the aim is to practice a particular skill and very little actual movement is involved, it is MP.

Regarding the relevance of MI for sport, research has further shown that athletes use MI in several ways to support peak performances (e.g., Weinberg, 2008). Research has also identified that MI can serve both cognitive and motivational functions (Paivio, 1985) and elicit a positive influence on athletic performance (Weinberg, 2008). Studies have also demonstrated that MI can enhance learning of motor skills (Schuster et al., 2011), control anxiety levels (Vadocz et al., 1997), improve the interpretation of symptoms contributing to competition anxiety (Sheard & Golby, 2006), and increase intrinsic motivation (Martin & Hall, 1995). Research also shows that MI is reliably associated with increased muscular strength when used as an adjunct to strength training programs (Tod et al., 2015). Furthermore, research shows that MI can enhance and expedite injury rehabilitation outcomes through mechanisms including decreasing pain, promoting healing, and enhancing motivation and adherence to the rehabilitation process (Arvinen-Barrow et al., 2013; Brewer & Redmond, 2017).

A substantial body of reliable research literature evidences the utility of MI in facilitating a range of important athletic functions and outcomes. It should be clear that whether you are a sport psychology consultant, coach, physical therapist, strength coach, or athlete, MI and MP are relevant for whatever you are trying to achieve in sport. Based on this relevance of MI for sport while also acknowledging that too frequently athletes, coaches, and support staff fall short of taking full advantage of this important performance strategy, this chapter aims to stimulate your application of MI.

Next, the chapter presents an overview of pertinent constructs that underpin practice in this area. It briefly describes some methods and tools to assess how well an athlete can make (and is making) use of MI, along with how well support staff are facilitating athletes' application of MI. Finally, the chapter examines practical examples of how to make use of MI and MP to achieve some specific functions and outcomes that support athletic performance and achievement. The chapter also highlights some key considerations for the application of MI.

Success Story: Mental Imagery and Pacing

Sarah was a 400-meter freestyle swimmer, a particularly difficult event in terms of pacing. To enhance Sarah's pacing, with the help of a sport psychology consultant and in conjunction with her coach, she developed a race plan that segmented the event into different phases; each phase had appropriate target pacing intensities and nonverbal triggers to support optimal technique execution and defend against intrusive negative thoughts and images. Sarah used her race plan to great effect during training and low-level competitions. However, at major competitions, Sarah tended to forget to use her routines, resulting in poor pacing and, in turn, poor performances. To resolve the inconsistent application of her pacing strategy, a program of MI and MP was developed to help desensitize Sarah to the distractions of major competitions and to reinforce the use of her race plan. As part of her mental training, with the use of video and audio from major meets to help her generate vivid and realistic images, Sarah would mentally image competing at major championships while successfully using her race routine. Sarah also employed MI during physical training sessions; her coach instructed her to imagine the racing environment while also reinforcing her race plan. The result was that Sarah's pacing dramatically improved as she routinely and effectively used her race plan in major competitions. The outcome was that she became better able to race to her full potential.

What We Know

For additional coverage of MI, several excellent frameworks and models are available to guide MI and MP program design (e.g., Martin et al., 1999; Cumming & Williams, 2013). Also available are useful reviews on the relationship between MI, motor learning, and sport performance (e.g., Slimani et al., 2016).

Use of Mental Imagery (MI)

MI serves five cognitive and motivational functions (Paivio, 1985; Hall et al.,1998); they are outlined in table 7.1 and described next.

Cognitive specific (CS) MI involves the rehearsal of physical skills, such as the placement of one's arms during a golf swing. Cognitive general (CG) MI contains mental rehearsal of strategies and game plans. Motivational specific (MS) MI is focused on goals people aspire to achieve, such as imagining a podium finish and being congratulated by others. Motivational general-mastery (MG-M) MI involves content that concerns overcoming challenges and obstacles encountered during a sport event, such as remaining focused and confident. Motivational general-arousal (MG-A) MI represents emotions experienced when participating in sport, such as anxiety and arousal, along with exertion and discomfort.

Research suggests that the content of a mental image should reflect what function that image serves (Martin et al., 1999). Therefore, the research-provided guidance to optimize the benefits of MI and thus help achieve the intended outcome has been to match the demands of the situation (e.g., competition) with the most pertinent MI function (e.g., CG). An example is a training session during which the athlete uses MI to practice new tactics. The use of the CG MI should accelerate learning of the new game plan.

In terms of various practical guidelines available to aid MI use, PETTLEP (Holmes & Collins, 2001) has been shown to be an effective model. PETTLEP is an acronym; each letter represents an important factor to consider when designing imagery interventions.

TABLE 7.1   Five Functions of Mental Imagery

Mental imagery function	Content
Cognitive specific (CS)	Rehearsal of specific physical skills
Cognitive general (CG)	Rehearsal of strategies and game plans
Motivational specific (MS)	Imagery focused on goals people aspire to achieve
Motivational general-mastery (MG-M)	Imagery that concerns overcoming challenges and obstacles encountered during a sport event
Motivational general-arousal (MG-A)	Imagery regarding the feelings experienced when participating in sport

From Hall et al. (1998).

Physical and **E**nvironment: All relevant physical and environmental characteristics of the activity are imagined.

Task and **T**iming: The image accurately represents all steps of the task and in real time.

Learning: The image is updated based on learning and experience.

Emotion: Images include emotions associated with the activity being imagined.

Perspective: The imagery is from an internal, first-person perspective.

Using this framework, MI and MP interventions can be designed and implemented in a logical and effective fashion (see Wakefield & Smith, 2012).

Mental Imagery (MI) Ability

MI ability has been defined as "an individual's capability of forming vivid, controllable images and retaining them for sufficient time to effect the desired imagery rehearsal" (Morris, 1997, p. 37). The controllability aspect of the rehearsal process represents how effectively mental images can be manipulated, while an image's vividness is a measure of its clarity and realism. These features of imagery ability are evidently associated with age (Parker & Lovell, 2009; 2012) and are important determinants in how well athletes can use MI (Martin et al., 1999; Parker et al., 2021). Of the various modalities people can image in, visual (seeing with the mind's eye) and kinesthetic (feeling movements in the mind's eye) imagery ability have received the most research attention (see Weinberg, 2008).

A viable means of improving MI ability is a technique known as layered stimulus response training (LSRT) (see Cumming et al., 2016). LSRT was developed by adopting principles from Lang's (1979) bioinformational theory that specific images are memorial propositional structures stored in long-term memory and contain three classes of information: stimulus propositions, response propositions, and meaning propositions. *Stimulus propositions* provide the basic constituent elements of a scene (e.g., the running lane or a golf fairway). *Response propositions* describe the likely interaction effects with a given stimulus (e.g., sensation of gentle contact between foot and ground). *Meaning propositions* evaluate the strength of the relationship between the stimulus and response propositions (e.g., feelings of satisfaction from executing good running technique). Cognitive processing translates these structures into a code the mind understands, resulting in the experience of a mental image. A key element of Lang's bioinformational theory stipulates that MI, which effectively links response and meaning propositions with stimulus propositions, will produce superior performance benefits. Therefore, practitioners adopting LSRT should aim to layer images using an athlete's self-generated stimulus, response, and meaning propositions. Images progressively develop in complexity as each layer adds to the next, creating imagery that approximates actual perception as closely as possible. The effectiveness of LSRT has been demonstrated to improve motor performance and both visual and kinesthetic MI ability (e.g., Marshall & Wright, 2016; Williams et al., 2013). Given that improvements in MI ability have been demonstrated when applying the LSRT technique, practitioners should consider adopting it to enhance the effectiveness of imagery interventions.

Involuntary Mental Imagery (MI)

The majority of MI research in sport has focused on deliberate imagery use, with imagery interventions predicated on the view that athletes use MI in a solely systematic and focused way. Although evidence indicates that athletes predominantly use MI in this manner, a broader appreciation of their image ideation is warranted because individuals often report also experiencing spontaneously occurring mental images. Evidence suggests that depending on the situation, spontaneous MI can be either unintentionally facilitative or debilitative; outcomes depend on how the individual interprets the imaged content. Spontaneous images are characteristically positive or neutral in valence (how the image is experienced on a continuum from pleasant to unpleasant or from attractive to aversive), which is substantially different from intrusive images. Intrusive images are predominantly visual, vivid, difficult to control, and capable of evoking strong physiological and emotional reactions (Brewin et al., 2010). Parker and colleagues (2015) have investigated the extent to which intrusive visual MI is experienced in athletic samples. In a sample of university undergraduate students participating competitively in a variety of sports, 37.8 percent experienced low levels of trait intrusive visual MI; a further 13.4 percent recorded high levels of intrusive visual MI.

MI has been found to amplify emotional states compared with verbalizing the same imagery content. Indeed, Vadocz and colleagues (1997) suggested that athletes susceptible to experiencing high levels of cognitive state anxiety should be advised not to engage in motivational general-arousal imagery. Exploring whether a similar pattern emerges in athletes when experiencing involuntary imagery types, Parker and colleagues (2017) demonstrated that only intrusive visual MI related significantly to athletes' state negative affect. Although collecting data in a noncompetitive setting limited the generalizability of their findings, these authors highlighted that future investigations should consider whether intrusive visual MI contributes to the mood state–performance relationship that is associated with optimizing sport performance. Although speculative, based on the results of Parker and colleagues (2017), the presence of intrusive visual MI would hinder rather than help athletes achieve a desired mood state prior to competitive performances.

Acknowledging that examining the predictors of intrusive visual imagery is still in its infancy, Bierton and colleagues (2019) provided some much-needed research in this area. Specifically, they investigated whether dysfunctional metacognitive beliefs, judgments, and thought-monitoring tendencies predicted athletes' trait intrusive visual imagery. Broadly, metacognition encompasses the way individuals monitor and control their own thinking (Norman et al., 2019), and it has been shown to influence the effectiveness of cognitive processes (Wells & Cartwright-Hatton, 2004). The results of the 2019 study by Bierton and colleagues indicated that two dysfunctional meta-cognitive beliefs—higher levels of negative beliefs about the controllability of thoughts and their danger, and the perceived need to control thoughts—were significant predictors of intrusive visual imagery. An additional purpose of that study was to establish whether performance context (training v. competition) related to differences in intrusive visual MI and metacognitive beliefs. Athletes reported significantly lower intrusive visual imagery before competing than before training and experienced fewer metacognitive beliefs prior to competing. Bierton and colleagues suggested that the results show athletes were exerting greater monitoring over their thoughts in the lead-up to competition in an attempt to minimize disruption from intrusive mental images while competing. Although still a nascent area of research, these investigations have established that athletes experience a variety of types of involuntary imagery, with intrusive imagery occurring more frequently in training than in competition and the presence of dysfunctional metacognitive beliefs influential in predisposing athletes to intrusive imagery.

Summary

It is evident that a number of constructs exist that can influence whether the athlete can successfully employ MI and positively contribute to their performance-enhancing armory. Failure to adequately consider these constructs can lead athletes to interpret MI as something that takes up valuable time that could be spent more productively on areas they believe will yield more tangible improvements. In short, to optimally apply MI, the key is to robustly align the purpose of the prescribed MI with desired performance outcomes while considering a range of important constructs, including MI ability and controllability. Clearly articulating to the performer *why* you are using MI, along with *how* and *when* you will use it to effectively enhance performance, is extremely important in enabling them to actually use this powerful performance-enhancing mental strategy. Furthermore, clarity about *why*, *how*, and *when* is likely a key ingredient in ensuring that sport psychology consultants, coaches, and athletes are effectively applying MI; as such, they are more likely to achieve positive performance outcomes associated with its application.

Assessment

Reflecting the multifaceted nature of MI, a number of different tools and approaches exist to assess it. Various validated and reliable questionnaires are available to assess different aspects, such as MI use (e.g., Sport Imagery

Questionnaire [Hall et al., 1998]), abilities to form and manipulate mental images (e.g., Movement Imagery Questionnaire-R [Hall & Martin, 1997] and the Sport Imagery Ability Questionnaire [Williams & Cumming, 2011]), and predispositions to experience intrusive mental images (e.g., Intrusive Visual Imagery Questionnaire [McCarthy-Jones et al., 2012]). These questionnaires are relatively straightforward to use, do not require extensive training, are supported by test manuals, and can be purchased from their authors. Use of the Sport Imagery Ability Questionnaire is free (https://www.researchgate.net/publication/274953600_The_Sport_Imagery_Ability_Questionnaire_Manual).

For more qualitative approaches, asking athletes or performers whether they use MI as part of their training and competition can be especially informative. Ideally, this type of questioning should be conducted during training and as close as possible to performance contexts. It is possible that athletes will report myriad elaborate reasons why they use MI despite the fact that they actually almost never indulge in the mental strategy. Therefore, asking athletes about what they are actually doing in real time during training and competition, in addition to observing them, can provide more valid information than may be obtained merely through standard interviews. A further questioning approach that is informative is to ask athletes why they use the MI they report engaging in. If athletes struggle to give an answer deeper than "My coach told me to," it is highly likely that they're not using MI regularly or effectively.

A further approach to assess how well athletes are taking advantage of MI is to consider the role of the instructor, be it the coach, physical trainer, or sport psychology consultant (even if one of these roles is you). If you adopt a team responsibility approach, gaining an appreciation of how actively, how frequently, how structured, and how knowingly instructors stimulate and reinforce MI is likely key in understanding how well the strategy is being used. Examples of useful things to watch out for may include whether training sessions specific to MI exist, the coach overtly instructs athletes to use MI during training and competition, the physical trainer instructs MI as part of rehabilitation processes, or props are used in the training environment to help replicate the competition environment. Examples of props include recordings of crowd noise to help replicate images of competition or a racket to hold while mentally imaging a tennis serve. Furthermore, assess whether staff in these roles explain *why* they are instructing MI, *how* they are instructing the athletes to use it, and *when* they are instructing athletes to use it.

Optimization

This section examines some practical examples of how MI and MP can be applied to achieve some specific functions and outcomes that support athletic performance and achievement. Using the five functions of MI described by

Hall et al. (1998), this section also describes a *why*, *how*, and *when* of MI for each example. Obviously, it is not possible to include descriptions of MI interventions for every possible performance determining context. Instead, the aim is to provide some sample approaches on which you can build so that you can design your own effective MI interventions specific to your particular performance challenges.

Learning New Movements (Physical Skills)

Consider an example of a gymnast learning a new dismount move on the high bars. Research has demonstrated that MI in the form of MP enhances the acquisition, retention, and transfer of physical skills, especially when individualized and conducted after or in association with physical practice (e.g., Schuster et al., 2011). Supporting the gymnast to engage in MI of the new dismount should enhance acquisition of the new movement. So, in this situation the *why* of MI would be to enhance learning. The *how* would involve the gymnast physically performing repetitions of the new dismount (or parts of the technique if they have not yet mastered the complete move). The athlete would then mentally practice the new dismount. If the gymnast was still physically practicing the subelements of the new move, MP would provide the opportunity to not only develop physical competence of the individual elements, but it would also provide the gymnast with the ability to practice combining those elements into one complete movement. If the gymnast was in the early stages of skill acquisition for the new move and having difficultly conceptualizing the new movement, watching the skill being completed either in person or on video would help the gymnast construct their mental image, called a combination of MP with self-modeling. The *when* of MI in this example would be during the skill development phase of training, in the gymnasium, interspersed throughout the physical practice trials. This scenario would be an example of using cognitive specific (CS) MI.

Learning New Game Plays

Recall the example at the start of the chapter about the college quarterback using MI as MP to learn new sequences of plays and calls. This example is similar to the previous in that we're using MI to learn a skill. In this situation, however, the skill is more cognitive than motor. In this example the *why* would again be to enhance acquisition of the information, especially how quickly it will be learned. MP helps the learning of cognitive skills through enhancing the performer's understanding of the task, helping them attend to the more important and pertinent performance cues. With regard to the *how*, MP could again be interspersed with physical practice on the field. Other MI activities could be based on further supporting development of the quarterback's understanding of the new plays. It could include drawing the plays on a whiteboard or explaining the plays to other team members.

Athletes such as quarterbacks can use mental practice to learn new sequences of plays and calls.

A further optimization of this situation could be based on the specificity of learning hypothesis, which states that practice conditions should be as similar as possible to test conditions, or in this context, the competition environment (Schmidt & Wrisberg, 2004). Therefore, if the quarterback can imagine themselves in the actual competitive environment (sounds, sights, smells, and even emotions) as they practice and MP the new plays, they will be more likely to effectively retrieve (remember) the new plays in the forthcoming bowl game. Using props, such as recordings of crowd noise, and wearing competition gear (in this case, the helmet) can help make the images of the competition environment more realistic. The *when* for this example would be centered on training times. This scenario is an example of using cognitive general (CG) MI.

Enhancing Motivation

MI has been shown to have motivational functions (e.g., Munroe-Chandler & Gammage, 2005; Paivio, 1985). Many theoretical frameworks center on motivation in sport and performance contexts. Self-determination theory (SDT; see also chapter 5) is a particularly applicable and useful perspective for this example of how MI can enhance motivation (Deci & Ryan, 2012). Briefly, self-determination theory posits that motivation is increased when three basic psychological needs are satisfied: autonomy, competence, and relatedness. The inherent need for autonomy is fulfilled when people perceive that they are the origin of their choices and decisions and that they are acting in accordance with their integrated sense of self. Competence concerns an individual's need to feel a sense of mastery through effective interaction within their environment. The third need, relatedness, corresponds to feeling securely attached to and being respected by significant others. Therefore, encouraging and supporting athletes to create mental images where they are autonomous, competent, and related should increase motivation. In the example at the start of this chapter about the athlete imagining they were successfully completing the London Marathon, MI should increase their motivation through increasing their perception of competency. Furthermore, the autonomous nature of MI may also enhance motivation through increasing the athlete's mindfulness of their autonomy. An additional explanation of how MI can enhance motivation is that engaging in images of their goals reminds and reinforces the athlete of their primary goals, triggering access (or saliency) of that target and associated behaviors. The result of the increased satisfaction of these basic psychological needs, along with enhanced goal saliency, would be an increase in motivation for the desired goal. In this marathon running example, the increased motivation resulting from the MI of achieving success should help the athlete effectively engage in purposeful training behaviors with direction and intensity.

With regard to *why* the MI, the answer for this example would be to increase motivation and productive training behaviors. The *how* would be through MI of desired goal outcomes. The *when* would be times the athlete is most at risk of insufficient motivation; for this specific example, it would be when trying to get out of bed for early morning training. This situation is an example of motivational specific (MS) MI.

Increasing Self-Efficacy

Self-confidence—more accurately self-efficacy—is well recognized as strongly associated with achievement and lower levels of performance anxiety (see chapters 5 and 6). According to Bandura (1982), self-efficacy is a personal judgment of "how well one can execute courses of action required to deal with prospective situations" (p. 122). As such, increasing self-efficacy is a common goal of sport psychology interventions. According to Bandura, performance accomplishment is a key source of self-efficacy. Therefore, encouraging an athlete to relive their training and performance accomplishments through MI should reinforce such achievements and thus increase their self-efficacy. Consider the example of a young golfer with lower than expected self-efficacy. Their precompetition self-efficacy should increase if they devise a structured preperformance MI program in which they recall through MI a series of preselected successful first tee shots from previous competitions. An additional approach could be based on the daily performance environment. Following each training session, be it skills-based or strength and conditioning, the performer could systematically mentally image five aspects of that training or practice session that they success-fully executed. Inspecting the achievements of the training session should reinforce and remind the athlete of the accomplishments, thus increasing their self-efficacy. In this example the *why* of MI would be to increase self-efficacy, the *how* would be through revisiting previous achievements, and the *when* could be in training or competition depending on the specific aim of the intervention. This example could be considered as motivational general-mastery (MG-M) MI.

Practice and Reinforcement of In-Performance Mental Strategies

MI should be integrated with other mental performance strategies. For example, MI can be incorporated into preperformance routines, and MI can be used to practice such preperformance routines as well as other in-performance mental strategies. Consider this example of an archer who already has developed precompetition and in-match routines along with mental checklists to help them maintain concentration. Without doubt, mental routines and checklists can be very effective in supporting performance. However, a frequent challenge for athletes is to remember to actually use the routines in the competitive arena. It can be especially challenging if the sport involves high volumes of training with only few competitions (e.g., swimming) and therefore little opportunity to practice using the checklists and routines in competitive environments. For this example, the *why* of MI could be to increase the likelihood using the checklist- and routines-based mental strategy in competition by using the strategies in competition for MP. The *how* could involve the archer imagining they are in competition situations, ideally experiencing associated challenging emotions and cognitions, being aware of losing concentration, then actively using the routines and checklist to regain concentration. The *when* could be during physical training sessions as well as in MI-specific training sessions. While the focus of this example is cognitive general (CG) MI, with minor adaptations this example could also include motivational general-mastery (MG-M; overcoming challenges and obstacles encountered during a sporting event) and motivational general-arousal (MG-A; regarding feelings experienced while participating in sport).

Recovering From Injury

High rates of injuries are still associated with competitive sport performance and training; strong evidence suggests that physical and psychosocial factors influence recovery from such injuries. MI, a psychosocial factor, appears to be useful at all stages of the recovery journey, aiding physical recovery and return to competition (see Miller & Munroe-Chandler, 2019). Consider an example of an injured rugby player. The player will need to contend with many challenges to attain full recovery and return to competitive play. These challenges include pain, physical healing, motivation, self-efficacy, anxiety, and deterioration of physical skills. You have already considered how many of these challenges can be approached through MI in the previous examples. Clearly the *why* of MI for injury recovery can include numerous factors. Two *whys* are MI to reduce pain and MI to increase healing. One can apply many different approaches to *how* MI can be used for pain management and healing outcomes. For pain management, most approaches involve images associated with feeling safe and secure, and representations of the pain leaving the body or injured body part. For healing MI, in general the athlete imagines positive healing processes (e.g., the swelling reducing, the tissues repairing, and function returning). Regarding the *when* for injury recovery MI, the options are extensive; the key is to systematically program and schedule the activity.

Conclusion

Practitioners, coaches, athletes, and others who serve in a performance context should adhere to the take-home messages and considerations covered in this chapter. Make use of MI; it is useful only if athletes use it! Don't assume that all athletes can perform MI well; consider it a skill that should be developed alongside all the other athletic skills that are systematically instructed during athlete development programs. Several different frameworks can be used to enhance MI ability, such as layered stimulus response training (LSRT). It is important to integrate MI with other mental performance strategies as you proactively and routinely support athlete use of MI in training and competition settings. For example, coaches should provide instruction to athletes during training to use MI in the same way they provide instruction about physical skills and effort. Physical trainers should program and schedule MI into the training and recovery programs. Sport psychology consultants must make sure everyone on the support team is encouraging MI. Be completely clear what you are using MI for and what you are aiming to achieve by using it; consider the MI questions of *why*, *how*, and *when*. It is especially important that the athlete knows the *why* of their use of MI.

While the usefulness of MI and MP is clear, they are not a panacea; for some athletes and performers, they may even be detrimental. Consider how controllable each athlete's MI is, and to what extent they are troubled by intrusive mental images. For athletes who suffer from debilitating precompetitive anxiety and experience uncontrolled intrusive negative MI, encouraging them to engage in imagery prior to competition is likely to be detrimental to their performances. Imaging unsuccessful performances prior to competition is unlikely to be helpful. In these situations, other performance strategies are likely to have a better fit.

8 | Self-Regulation

Tynke Toering

Hanze University of Applied Sciences

Self-regulation is the capacity to change or maintain behavior and adapt to the environment in an optimal way. It is essential for athletes and coaches because it contributes to athletic performance, is related to the athlete lifestyle, and enables athletes to take charge of their development. To reach excellence in sport, athletes must explore a variety of self-regulation strategies and find the ones that are optimal for learning and performance. This chapter starts with a summary of what we know about self-regulation of performance and self-regulation of learning in sport. These research findings are then applied in the context of both performance and learning; first the focus is on assessment of self-regulation, then it moves to recommendations for elite athletes and coaches to optimize self-regulation.

Relevance

Given that performing well when it counts is important in the careers of talented and senior elite athletes, paying attention to athletes' self-regulation capacities is essential. At events such as the Olympic Games, athletes ideally have enough mental capacity to deal with the challenges that inevitably come with taking part in such a competition (e.g., being the favorite) rather than waste energy on things for which they could have been prepared (e.g., what the venue looks like and how much time they need to get from the warm-up area to the performance arena). To reach this capacity, athletes should know how they tend to respond to challenges or pressure and develop self-regulation skills to optimally handle the situation. For example, for a gymnast who performs in the beam final, it may be best to not know how competitors performed so that they can focus on their own routine. For a speedskater racing in the final pair of the 5K, it could be critical to know other skaters' times to decide on tactics for their own race. Complicating matters more, each athlete responds differently. This tendency has consequences for the factors an athlete may need to have control over beforehand.

On the road to excellence, self-regulation is key for maintaining a performance lifestyle and for taking charge of one's learning process. The latter enables athletes to develop their own set of skills and strategies and, as such, become more flexible when they must perform. For example, a striker in soccer who wants to increase efficiency in front of the goal may decide that after training, they will practice receiving the ball with their back to the goal, turning, and shooting 20 balls in the left lower corner and 20 balls in the right lower corner of the goal; they studied the game and found out that such shots are most likely to be scored. Doing this drill from several angles and distances will increase the athlete's range of potential actions. Studying one's performance and transforming these thoughts into action will increase athletes' possibilities and help them own their development. In essence, self-regulation of learning contributes to a more effective development process and performance.

What We Know

This section considers some key themes relating to what we know about self-regulation of performance and learning. The main body of self-regulation research literature relevant for elite sport performance is based on theories and models of generic self-regulation. Some of these sources and associated sport-specific findings are briefly presented. In addition, this section presents research literature on self-regulation of learning (SRL) relevant for elite sport.

Self-Regulation of Performance

The term *self-regulation* can be defined as the capacity to alter one's responses to achieve a desired state or outcome that would not occur naturally (e.g., Vohs & Baumeister, 2016; De Ridder et al., 2012). For example, a soccer player responds positively after missing a penalty kick in a match. A large body of literature also indicates that self-regulation is positively associated with a healthy and successful life, and it is negatively associated with issues such as aggression and addiction (e.g., Hagger et al., 2010; Vohs & Baumeister, 2016).

People often use the terms *self-regulation* and *self-control* interchangeably; this chapter does so too. A main concept within generic self-regulation is trait self-control, and a central model is the strength model of self-control. They are discussed next.

Trait Self-Control

A *trait* is a relatively stable attribute of an individual. Research investigating the relationship between self-reported trait self-control and behavior showed that trait self-control is primarily associated with the ability to form good habits and break bad habits (De Ridder et al., 2012). Individuals who score high in trait self-control tend to make decisions that are beneficial for a healthy and successful life; they structure their lives in such a way that they minimize the extent to which they get into tempting situations (Hofmann et al., 2012). Athletes with high trait self-control structure their lives in accordance with their long-term athletic goals by controlling the variables they can control (e.g., not buying junk food because then they do not need to resist the temptation) and by developing strategies to control their behaviors, specifically in challenging situations (e.g., taking a step back and focusing on the basics when training or competing).

A study on professional soccer players found that self-control variables were associated with players' daily activities (lifestyle) and performance level, namely, those relating to restraint (capacity to work toward long-term goals and structure life accordingly) and impulse control (capacity for behavioral and emotional control; Toering & Jordet, 2015). For example, players scoring high in restraint spent more time in daily practice and less time in front of the television. In terms of performance, impulse control was positively related to whether players had represented their country at the senior level. Team restraint scores were highly correlated with their league result at the end of the season. In addition, based on scores found in a meta-analysis using the same questionnaire, professional soccer players scored significantly higher on trait self-control than the general population (De Ridder et al., 2012). These findings suggest that trait self-control helps athletes prepare for performance and tolerate adverse conditions, such as pressure, performance slumps, and injuries (Toering & Jordet, 2015). Research focusing on the well-being of elite youth athletes has proposed that a combination of trait self-control and favorable types of motivation (the more intrinsic, the better) are associated with lower levels of perceived exhaustion, which has implications for burnout prevention (e.g., Jordalen et al., 2016, 2020). For young athletes it may therefore be beneficial to develop self-control skills and focus on the enjoyment they find in doing their sport to tolerate the demands of the pathway to the top. Thus, the development of self-control skills and a constructive motivational climate by coaches, such as a mastery climate (e.g., Roberts et al., 2007), may contribute to athlete well-being and, in conjunction with it, to performance and perseverance. The momentary availability of self-control could greatly affect elite performance too. The next section discusses findings based on the strength model of self-control.

Strength Model of Self-Control

One of the main self-regulation models used in sport psychology is the strength model of self-control (e.g., Hagger et al., 2010), which suggests that self-control strength is a limited, generic resource that does not depend on the modality of self-control that is used (e.g., emotional control, cognitive control). The model indicates that performance decreases when individuals have used too much of their momentarily available self-control strength, which is indeed confirmed by many studies using this model (Baumeister & Tierney, 2012). Applied to an example in sport, it means a tennis player who loses their temper may waste valuable mental resources by reacting negatively to the chair umpire instead of focusing on their play for the next point.

Laboratory studies examining self-control in sport have indicated that performance decreases when athletes' resources for self-control are drained (e.g., Dorris et al., 2012; Englert & Wolff, 2015; Wagstaff, 2014). For instance, sprint start reaction time was compared between athletes in conditions of fully available self-control and athletes in conditions in which part of those resources had already been used. Results showed that athletes started more slowly when their self-control strength was no longer fully available compared to when their self-control strength was fully available (Englert & Bertrams, 2014). Related research has examined the relationship between self-control and performance under pressure in sport. These findings indicated that decreased self-control strength is associated with decreased performance

Decreased self-control strength is associated with decreased performance under pressure, such as when taking a penalty kick.

under pressure (e.g., Englert, Bertrams, et al., 2015; Englert, Zwemmer, et al., 2015). For example, studies of basketball and dart players who were anxious to perform well showed that they scored fewer basketball free throws and performed worse in a dart throwing task when they had already used part of their available self-control in a previous task (Englert & Bertrams, 2012). In addition, the combination of anxiety and decreased available self-control strength was found to be associated with decreased attentional control (e.g., Farley et al., 2013). Thus, momentary available self-control strength seems to be important to prevent performance decrements under pressure.

Research in real-life elite sport performance settings has also revealed that the failure to self-regulate harms performance under pressure. As an example, self-regulation failure during important soccer penalty shootouts was found to negatively affect performance (e.g., Jordet et al., 2009). Players missing a penalty shot tended to use less time to take the shot after the referee blew the whistle and were more likely to turn their body and face away from the goalkeeper after they placed the ball on the penalty mark. The researchers suggested that this desire to escape the pressurized situation was related to poor performance. Moreover, high-status players tended to perform worse in important penalty shootouts (Jordet, 2009), indicating that increases in perceived pressure may increase the likelihood of self-regulation failure. The momentary available self-regulation strength appears to have great influence on performance, particularly performance under pressure. Given that self-regulation capacities are limited, preparation seems key to making sure that enough mental resources are available for performance. Self-regulation has also been investigated in the specific context of learning and development. The following section provides a brief overview of self-regulation of learning (SRL) literature in sport.

Self-Regulation of Learning (SRL)

The term *self-regulation of learning (SRL)* has been defined as being proactive in one's learning process by using metacognitive, motivational, or behavioral strategies; being responsive to self-oriented feedback related to learning effectiveness; and being self-motivated to learn and develop (Zimmerman, 2006). Simply put, self-regulated learners take charge of their learning process by thinking about their own thinking (e.g., planning, evaluation, and reflection), being self-motivated (e.g., high standards, maximum effort, high self-efficacy), and acting proactively to attain their goals (e.g., effective learning strategies). SRL processes are expected to help people learn more effectively rather than to immediately produce higher performance levels (Zimmerman, 2006).

Expert learners have been described as strategic strategy users who match task demands with their own personal resources and constraints (Ertmer & Newby, 1996). For example, a soccer player who sees the opportunity to give a cross pass, who is in a situation where they are forced to give that pass with their left foot, but who knows that they will not be able to give a quality cross pass with their left foot, may decide not to go for the cross pass. Expert learners are aware of their knowledge and skills (or lack thereof) and employ effective strategies to apply (or learn) them. So, the soccer player mentioned earlier may decide to go practice cross passes with the left foot. As such, expert learners are regarded as self-regulated. However, self-regulated learners are not involved in their individual learning process by themselves; they seek help when they need it (Hadwin et al., 2011; Karabenick & Newman, 2009).

Zimmerman's (2006) sociocognitive model describes SRL as a cyclical process including a forethought (before task), performance (during task), and self-reflection phase (after task). According to Ertmer and Newby (1996), expert learners use reflection in and on action to self-regulate the learning process during, before, and after performance. For instance, a gymnast who is practicing a complex routine (e.g., doing two or three flight elements directly after each other on the horizontal bar) may decide that they need to take one step back when they do not immediately succeed, because they know that by doing so, they will then be able to take two steps forward. Another gymnast practicing the same routine may decide to keep pushing because they know from previous experience that they will get it soon if they keep pushing.

A large body of research on talent identification and development (TID) has highlighted the importance of SRL processes in sport (e.g., Baker & Young, 2014; Toering et al., 2012). A recent review on SRL in practice concluded that the best athletes make use of SRL processes, it is possible to train SRL processes, and SRL processes are associated with other psychological and environmental factors, such as the presence of observable models and the role of coaches (McCardle et al., 2019). SRL processes are positively related to sport performance level (e.g., Bartulovic et al., 2017; Erikstad et al., 2018; Toering et al., 2009), training volume (Elferink-Gemser et al., 2015), and the quality of practice strategies employed (e.g., Massey et al., 2015). For example, it has been shown that experts demonstrated better structure in practice, employed more SRL strategies, and evaluated practice more than nonexperts or novices in volleyball (Kitsantas & Zimmerman, 2002).

Self-Regulated Learning and Practice

SRL seems to be a key process in athlete development through its relationship with practice quality and learning effectiveness (e.g., Toering et al., 2013). However, how exactly SRL is linked to practice quality and development potential remains unclear. One of the few studies investigating the link between SRL processes and deliberate practice indicated that self-monitoring, and to a lesser extent planning and effort, were instrumental processes related to deliberate practice amounts (Bartulovic et al., 2018). However, these effects were small.

Two studies have investigated how athletes apply SRL processes in practice. Young and Starkes (2006) had swim coaches and swimmers rate the swimmers' self-regulated practice behaviors in a series of nine practice sessions. These ratings were then compared with video observation data, where swimmers who the coaches rated as well self-regulated were compared with the ones rated as poorly self-regulated. Results based on video observations showed that poorly self-regulated swimmers indeed showed more nonregulative behaviors, such as missed swim volume during warm-up (relative to a coach's prescription). Furthermore, swimmers tended to underestimate the amount of nonregulation they showed in practice (e.g., overestimation of actual swim volume compared to prescribed volume). Toering and colleagues (2011) interviewed expert youth soccer coaches to gather practice behaviors that the coaches regarded as self-regulated and nonregulated. Coaches indicated that they mainly regarded behaviors such as asking questions, coaching of teammates, and behaviors referring to focused practice as expressions of SRL. These behaviors were observed during practice and then linked to players' self-reported scores on an SRL questionnaire. SRL as reported by the players was associated with observed practice behaviors referring to providing and receiving information (e.g.,

Majdi Fathi/NurPhoto via Getty Images

Research indicates that self-regulated learning is reflected in taking responsibility for one's learning during practice.

coaching others and asking questions), as well as being focused during prac-tice. Overall findings indicated that SRL is reflected in taking responsibility for one's learning during practice.

Self-Regulated Learning and Learning Outcomes

SRL has often been examined in association with motivation, performance level, and practice strategies, but how SRL exactly contributes to learning and development in elite athletes is still largely unclear. Central aspects are the athlete's self-knowledge, knowledge of the sport, and self-knowledge within the sport context. As described earlier, SRL involves applying relevant knowledge of cognitive, motivational, and behavioral learning strategies (Ertmer & Newby, 1996). Without such knowledge, it will be difficult to find out what variables athletes should self-monitor, what information they need to reflect on, and how they should interpret or evaluate their actions. In fact, athletes would have a lot of disjointed information but little idea of how to connect the dots. Therefore, to optimally make use of SRL, athletes must increase self-knowledge, knowledge of the sport, and self-knowledge within the sport context.

One way to increase that knowledge is to leave their comfort zone, which forces athletes to come up with new learning or performance strate-gies (Phillips et al., 2010). This approach suggests that one needs to make mistakes in order to know where the bar is and make adjustments to get it right. When pushed out of their comfort zone, athletes can discover their limits and become aware of how they deal with situations in which they meet their limits. As discussed earlier, performance is likely to decrease in such challenging situations. In these situations, self-monitoring and reflec-tion could help athletes increase their self-knowledge and situation-specific self-knowledge, which in turn may help to find self-regulated learning and performance strategies. For example, a young team sport athlete who has to play in a different position than usual may find ways to learn about specific game situations, how to effectively deal with these situations, and how this knowledge can help them become a better athlete.

The role of the coach is particularly important when it comes to situation-specific self-knowledge. The coach should identify optimal learning situa-tions; they should first have an honest conversation with the athlete to show where the bar is, notice when the athlete is ready to learn, then provide tailored guidance, and finally make sure a good balance exists between cognitive load and relaxation to create optimal learning conditions.

In summary, research shows that generic self-regulation and self-control skills help elite athletes structure their lives to facilitate performance, con-tribute to performance directly, seem particularly valuable under pressure, serve as a buffer for elite athletes in adverse conditions, and may in combination with intrinsic motivation help protect against burnout. Furthermore, SRL processes have been found to be related to performance level in elite youth athletes, characteristics of practice, and practice quality. As such, it is clear that athletes may benefit from working on their SRL skills. To develop these skills, athletes must focus on their self-knowledge, sport knowledge, and self-knowledge in the sport context. The following section provides guidance on how to assess self-regulation and SRL.

Assessment

Athletes must try to find out how they usually behave in practice and competition and how they tend to respond to challenging situations. Based on this knowledge, they can develop self-regulation strategies, ideally making use of a psychological skill set. Sample questions to ask with respect to pressure are as follows:

- In which situations do I feel anxiety?
- How do I typically respond—physically, technically, tactically, mentally—in these situations?
- Which self-regulation strategies (if any) do I use in these situations?
- Are these strategies effective?

A simple way an athlete can assess the answers is to draw an inverted-U curve and write down which situations make them feel too relaxed, optimally stressed, and too stressed to perform well in their sport (figure 8.1).

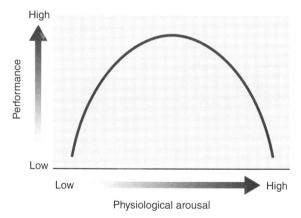

FIGURE 8.1 The inverted-U relationship between stress and performance (c.f., Landers & Arent, 2010).

Reprinted by permission from R.S. Weinberg and D. Gould, *Foundations of Sport and Exercise Psychology,* 6th ed. (Champaign, IL: Human Kinetics, 2019), 87.

Once the athlete writes the answers, they reflect on why it is the way it is. Based on that information, the athlete can develop self-regulation strategies. Generally, when athletes study their behavioral patterns during performance (particularly in high-pressure situations), reflect on these patterns, ask for feedback from people in their support system, and develop strategies that help them self-regulate, more momentary self-regulation strength is available for optimizing performance when it counts most.

An example for athletes of how to assess their SRL is by keeping track of the SRL process related to practice. They can track the process by goal setting and through asking oneself a few questions after each practice session (figure 8.2). Having only a few goals or even one for each practice session ensures that they don't get lost in the shuffle. Depending on personal preferences, it may be helpful to set weekly goals, monthly goals, and goals for the competitive season. When it comes to goal setting, athletes should have goals for practice and competition as well as process, performance, and result goals. Goals can be connected to each other and to the monitoring process shown in figure 8.2. After practice sessions, the athlete can answer the other questions. Depending on individual preferences, using some type of log may be an effective tool. A meta-analysis indicated that this approach may be most effective when outcomes are reported and the information is physically recorded (Harkin et al., 2016).

To assess athletes' generic capacity to self-regulate, coaches are advised to observe athletes' behavioral patterns. Looking at lifestyle, work ethic, and perseverance in adverse conditions may provide the coach some indications of trait self-control. This information needs to be triangulated; for example, the coach can have a conversation with the athlete or parents as well as other relevant people. To assess athletes' momentary self-control strength, it makes sense to observe and compare how the athlete usually behaves and whether or how this behavior differs from behavior in high-pressure situations. Answer these questions: *What situations does the athlete perceive as pressurized? How come? Does it affect momentary self-control strength? In what way does it affect performance? What can the coach do to help the athlete?* These approaches imply that coaches increase and update their knowledge on psychological skills in sport and how those skills can be measured and observed.

A coach can assess the extent to which an athlete self-regulates their learning by first providing them with tools (such as one presented in figure 8.2) and then regularly discussing the athlete's responses after practice sessions. By also keeping track of each practice session, a coach can connect their own observations to the athlete's answers. Another way of examining an athlete's SRL is to systematically observe practice behaviors evidently related to SRL, such as approaching the coach to ask a question or coaching

SRL in practice

My goals for this practice session:

Practice intensity (Physically how hard was the training?)

0	1	2	3	4	5	6	7	8	9	10
Easy										Hard

Practice resistance (How difficult was the session? How much was I challenged?)

0	1	2	3	4	5	6	7	8	9	10
Little										Much

Practice focus (How "present" was I during each exercise?)

0	10	20	30	40	50	60	70	80	90	100%

Practice benefit (How useful was this practice session for my development and learning?)

0	1	2	3	4	5	6	7	8	9	10
Little										Much

Two positive things I take with me from this practice session:

Two things I need to improve next time:

Will I practice on my own?

If yes, what activity and for how long?

FIGURE 8.2 Keeping track of SRL in each practice session.

one's teammates and completing the warm-up (Toering et al., 2012; Young & Starkes, 2006). These behaviors may differ slightly according to the sport.

Optimization

Based on what is known, the obvious advice to athletes is to make sure that they are optimally prepared to perform; in other words, they should be in control of the things they can control. Several examples of interviews with world-class athletes indicate how they were mentally prepared for many details, such as exactly what the performance arena would look like, how much time they needed to get from one area (e.g., warm-up) to another (e.g., competition area), what the physical requirements were likely to be as a consequence of climate, what the technical requirements were likely to be in terms of track and terrain, who their competitors were and how they would deal with them, and lessons learned from previous experiences in similar championships. Knowing what to expect will help athletes handle the unexpected things that undoubtedly come up in and around competition. Athletes increase their momentary self-regulation strength by not having to spend energy on finding out about things during or close to competition that they could have known beforehand. This preparation contributes to optimal performance.

In addition to proper psychological preparation, it is important to optimally prepare in all other performance domains, such as the physical, tactical, and technical domains. Specifically relevant for self-regulation, athletes would benefit from making sure that they develop a toolbox of skills that enable them to optimally deal with whatever demanding situation they meet during performance. They can deploy several psychological skills to address these challenges (e.g., Gould et al., 2002; Hardy et al., 2010; Orlick & Partington, 1988). One example is the Psychological Characteristics of Developing Excellence (PCDEs), which are also described more specifically in chapter 17. Athletes who possess such a hand of cards will be more flexible when meeting performance challenges; in other words, more self-control strength will remain available for optimal performance.

A study on coach perspectives on self-control, grit, and resilience showed that different coaches tend to define these characteristics in different ways (Tedesqui & Young, 2020). It is likely the same for athletes. The importance of having a shared mental model (SMM) has been investigated in sport (e.g., Giske et al., 2015), and this fact is equally relevant when it comes to working on psychological performance skills.

In 2013, I (the author of this chapter) collaborated with Geir Jordet to develop a soccer-specific screening instrument based on a combination of research findings and practical experience in professional soccer. For each of the factors of the so-called 11-model (Jordet, 2016), we created a practical set of items. The items can be used as a self-report tool and a behavioral observation checklist for coaches, but the model is mainly intended to facilitate communication and lead to self-insight. Different versions of such a tool should be employed in different age groups because athletes vary in their levels of understanding and maturity and because different behaviors may be relevant at different ages and performance levels. Different sports may also have slightly different items; context is essential (Mischel et al., 2011).

The following success story relates to the *coping with adversity* items (figure 8.3) and provides an example of how an athlete, together with a sport psychology consultant or coach, may use a screening tool for performance behaviors to improve their communication, keep track of the athlete's performance behaviors, and develop strategies to improve self-regulation.

A player and coach can also use the mental screening tool together. In addition to the player's own ratings, the coach may indicate how they rate the player on each item. The items on which players score very low or very high, as well as those on which player and coach disagree, warrant a discussion. Screening such a broad spectrum of sport-specific performance behaviors and psychological skills can help coaches gain knowledge about areas that they would not naturally talk about with players but that do affect performance. Thus, in addition to developing a SMM on players' psychological characteristics, this approach helps coaches cover a broad range of mental factors that influence athletes' performance.

Coaches must help athletes develop their self-regulation skill set. As indicated earlier, planning, preparation, and developing a psychological skill set are essential. Related to skill development, coaches need to pay attention to cognitive load when planning their programs. Collins and colleagues (2018) present an excellent paper on self-regulation and periodization in action sports (Collins et al., 2018). (These ideas are also featured in chapter 15.) The authors explain how risk is common in action sports and that the challenges are increased when competition is added, which means psychological load increases. They describe a process of emotional periodization, which is referred to as a deliberate and carefully planned variation in mental challenge and load, including the push-hard-and-recover training cycles typical of park and pipe sports (e.g., snowboard slopestyle and freeski halfpipe) and individual factors such as perceived anxiety. Athletes carefully plan periods of learning new tricks in optimal conditions, and they make sure to achieve sufficient repetitions before taking a new trick to specific competitions. This approach requires that coaches be astutely aware of the need to time when to push and when to hold off; they must be well able to read their athletes' mood in several ways and to affect their athletes' mood in several ways. It indicates the need for coaches to have up-to-date psychological knowledge, know how it can be applied, and know their athletes well.

Coaches can influence SRL in their athletes by creating practice sessions that emphasize SRL and give athletes the opportunity to practice self-regulation. Naturally, coaches will provide more guidance to very young

Success Story: Improving Performance Using a Mental Screening Tool

Figure 8.3 shows a 16-year-old male player's scores on the items. Based on the player's scores, it could be concluded some issues existed related to coping with adversity on the field and related to the resilience items 12 to 15. In conversations, the player indicated focus difficulties when making mistakes. The player said, "I become angry at myself and then pay attention to things I should not be preoccupied with, such as the referee and spectators. My teammates try to get me back on track, but I do not like it when they do that because I already know what I should do." When asked, the player indicated that after making mistakes, he seemed absent for a few seconds. These few seconds can be important in terms of repositioning or when the team quickly recovers the ball. Furthermore, when teammates tried to encourage the player to get back in the game, he tended to respond negatively. When asked about the latter responses, he referred to shouting negative things and making negative gestures. As a response to his own mistakes, the player often responded negatively when teammates made mistakes too.

Why did the player respond so negatively to others? It turned out that he was focused on performing well much more than on enjoying the game. Being on a selection team meant a lot to him, and having such high expectations of his own performance created a sole focus on mistakes. This focus cost the athlete enjoyment and momentary self-regulation strength, and it had a clear negative effect on performance.

To work on these issues, the player started keeping a log, which included short descriptions of practice sessions and how the rest of the day went. In order to learn to identify potential behavioral patterns, the player noted the moments he lost focus because of making mistakes. The player also worked on self-talk in the sense that he made sure to take a moment for himself before practice and games, remind himself of why he loved the sport so much, and focus on practice or the game at hand. He also started using a specific word to remind himself to get back in the game when a mistake occurred. He completed the screening every other week, and scores improved. This way of working helped the player to get more control over his behavior, and he kept making progress.

Coping with adversity

I am a player who...		Never	Sometimes	Often	Very often	Always
Coping with adversity on the field	does not let my game be negatively affected when I make mistakes that, for example, lead to a goal against us.	X				
	does not let my game be negatively affected when I make several passing errors.	X				
	does not let my game be negatively affected when I have several bad games in a row.			X		
	continues to work hard and focus during practice, even when the level is too high for me and I don't play particularly well.				X	
	is able to continue to focus and play even when I have small pains and nuisances (only ones that will not lead to more serious injuries).				X	
	works hard with myself in training to quickly recover after illness and injury.				X	
Coping with limited playing time	works really hard with myself, focusing on that over which I have control, when I am on the bench.			X		
	works really hard with myself, focusing on that over which I have control, when I am on the bench even when I feel the coach is not treating me fairly.			X		
	maintains my performance even during periods when the coach's feedback and support are missing.			X		
Coping with adversity off the field	maintains my performance even when I struggle at home.				X	
	maintains my performance even when I struggle with issues unrelated to sport.				X	
General resilience	takes charge of what I can control during periods of adversity and is less preoccupied with what is outside my control.	X				
	focuses on myself and what I can do during periods of adversity and avoids blaming others.	X				
	uses adversity to motivate me to give more energy, focus better, and work harder.		X			
	takes responsibility and contributes positively to my teammates when the team loses a lot or is badly positioned in the league table.		X			
	seeks out coaches and other staff for help when I struggle.				X	
	seeks out people outside the sport when I struggle, those who can help me work harder on myself and focus more on what I can control.			X		
	avoids listening to those who, when I struggle, give me a wrong focus by letting me blame others, think about things I cannot control, and ignore things I can control.				X	

FIGURE 8.3 Screening tool scores.

athletes compared to senior elites. In very young athletes, coaches may start with goal setting; they can help athletes set a simple goal for an exercise and afterward evaluate in a simple way, such as using colored smiley faces in a traffic light system. They could then shortly discuss with the group why they judged their goal accomplishment the way they did—all in a way that is suitable for the age group. Coaches observe how athletes respond and whether their responses become richer over time. An important notion when coaches want athletes to start self-regulating their learning is that the coaches clearly explain *why* athletes do the exercise they do. Sharing this reasoning will help athletes develop their sport-specific knowledge and enable them to connect with perceptions of their own performance. When athletes are older, coaches may provide the goal that should be reached with an exercise and have the athletes themselves develop the exercise (with the coach providing guidance in the process by asking questions). Another option is the use of peer-to-peer feedback, where athletes must mention two things their peer did well and one thing to improve and explain why. Furthermore, in older age groups, coaches may have athletes design a whole session based on athletes' strengths and weaknesses that the athletes have listed. Coaches can again provide guidance in the process where necessary. These examples are just a few. Coaches can use a wide variety of approaches to their session design to emphasize SRL, specifically focusing on the phases of SRL and reflection.

A prerequisite for using any of these approaches is that coaches develop a trusting relationship with their athletes (e.g., Jowett & Arthur, 2019). For instance, it has been shown that approachable and trustworthy coaches who show concern for their players positively stimulate self-determined motivation in soccer (Adie et al., 2012; Taylor & Bruner, 2012). This point is also emphasized in the action sports example from Collins and colleagues (2018); if a trusting relationship is absent, it will be impossible for a coach to optimally read the athlete, and the athlete may be less willing to act on the coach's advice or feedback.

Conclusion

Self-regulation capacities are essential for performing well when it counts. Self-regulation requires athletes to know how they respond to adverse conditions and develop self-regulation skills to optimally deal with such situations. It requires athletes to focus on controlling the controllable aspects related to performance. Athletes' lifestyle and responsibility for their learning process are also essential on the pathway to excellence. While a performance lifestyle seems to be a necessary requirement for becoming a senior elite athlete, studying one's performance and transforming these observations into practice and performance strategies can contribute to an athlete's flexibility. The latter may lead to greater development potential.

9 Concentration, Focus, and Attention

John Toner
University of Hull

The study of attention has a long and rich history in the field of psychology. Researchers have invoked this construct to account for a range of cognitive phenomena such as selectivity of information processing, intensity of focus, and the allocation of limited mental resources to cope with ongoing task demands (Moran & Toner, 2017, 2018). In exploring the role that concentration and attentional control play in the maintenance of performance proficiency, this chapter addresses the following questions:

1. What exactly is *concentration,* and how is it related to the broader psychological construct of attention?
2. What theoretical frameworks best help you to understand concentration and attentional processes?
3. What factors cause skilled performers to lose their concentration? (Bear in mind that it is not *lost* in the sense that it has been misplaced; rather, it is *directed* toward something irrelevant to the task at hand.)
4. How might coaches and practitioners assess concentration and, more broadly, attentional focus?
5. What practical techniques might coaches use to improve their athletes' concentration skills and attentional control?

The purpose of this chapter is to answer these questions using the principles and findings of cognitive psychology, a discipline that studies how the mind works in acquiring, storing, and using knowledge (Eysenck & Keane, 2015).

Relevance

Athletes are confronted by an extraordinary array of information and stimuli as they plan and execute complex tasks, often under severe time constraints. Effective performance requires them to make decisions about what stimuli to prioritize and what to ignore; for example, a penalty kicker in soccer must maintain their focus on the area of the goal they intend to place the ball while ignoring the baying crowd imploring them to miss. Not only are they faced with the problem of deciding which environmental stimuli to process, they must also process thoughts and feelings that arise in the conscious mind. It is of little surprise, then, that athletes are capable of processing only a fraction of the information available to their senses, thoughts, memories, and imagination. In cognitive sport psychology (the study of mental processes in athletes), the attentional process of *concentration*—the ability to focus effectively on the task at hand while ignoring distractions (Moran, 1996)—has been acknowledged as a crucial element of successful performance. For Dan Carter, a World Cup winner with New Zealand and widely regarded as the greatest out-half in the history of rugby union, concentration is a vital prerequisite of successful performance. According to Carter, "You have a mindset of just nailing each task, staying in the moment, and it has really helped myself and this team . . . It is quite easy to start thinking about the result and what potentially could happen, but you soon lose track" (Sky Sports, 2015).

By contrast, an inability to focus effectively can prove the difference between success and failure in competitive sport. For example, consider

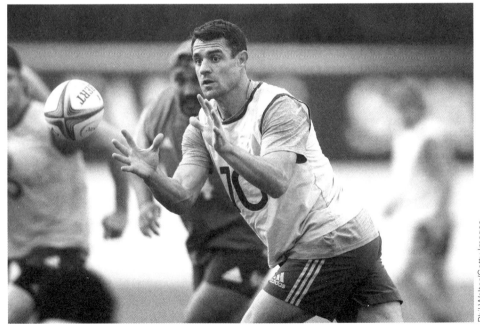

Concentration was a crucial element to the success of New Zealand rugby star Dan Carter.

Phil Walter/Getty Images

the case of Andy Murray, who blamed a lapse in concentration for his defeat to Novak Djokovic in the 2015 Australian Open tennis final: "The third set was frustrating because I got a bit distracted when he fell on the ground after a couple of shots . . . it appeared that he was cramping and then I let it distract me a little bit" (Newman, 2015). Elite-level coaches are well aware that athletes are susceptible to a whole host of distractions during competitive performance, and they purposefully design training activities to teach performers how to improve their concentration when executing complex skills in high-pressure situations. The tendency to become distracted by task-irrelevant stimuli (to put it differently, the inability to maintain focus on an intentional goal) is often cited as one of the main causes of performance breakdown, otherwise known as choking under pressure. Elite sport is replete with examples of performers suffering momentary losses of concentration that prove the difference between success and failure. The American golfer Scott Hoch's extraordinary missed putt from 2 feet (0.6 m), which would have won the 1989 U.S. Masters, is perhaps one of the best-known chokes in the history of sport. Such high-profile mistakes or errors tend to captivate the public consciousness and give rise to a number of intriguing questions for practitioners and coaches alike. Namely, how do coaches help their athletes maintain concentration and exert attentional control in situations that are of huge personal significance to the athlete and that represent the culmination of countless hours of preparation and hard work?

What We Know

In psychology, the term *attention* refers to a brain-based cognitive system that serves the selection of some stimuli for further processing while inhibiting that of other stimuli. More precisely, paying attention is the process of "focusing on specific features, objects or locations or on certain thoughts or activities" (Goldstein, 2011, p. 391). Attention is considered to be a multidimensional construct involving at least three different cognitive processes. The first process is called *concentration,* or effortful awareness, and it refers to an individual's conscious decision to invest mental effort on what is most important in any given situation. The second process is *selective attention,* or the ability to zoom in on task-relevant information while ignoring distractions. The third dimension is *divided attention,* or the ability to coordinate two or more actions at the same time in an equally effective manner. For example, consider how the expert basketball player has little difficulty dribbling the ball and simultaneously identifying a teammate well positioned to receive a pass (Moran & Toner, 2018). Influential theories of attention in the mainstream psychology literature include Kahneman's capacity theory, Posner's spotlight metaphor, and the memory representation approach. Space constraints preclude a detailed examination of each of these theories; some of the key principles and ideas associated with these frameworks are explained next.

First, Kahneman's (1973) capacity model, or resource theory of attention, sought to elucidate the mechanisms underpinning divided attention, or people's ability to perform two or more tasks concurrently. A key principle of this theory is that practice affects attentional capacity (one's pool or reservoir of mental energy). As such, tasks that are highly practiced require less mental effort than novel ones and therefore free up attentional resources (spare mental capacity) that can be directed elsewhere. For example, skilled performers can direct attention away from the mechanical details of their action and toward the strategic aspects of performance. According to Kahneman (1973), the way in which a performer allocates their attentional capacity is determined by a combination of factors, such as momentary intentions (factors that are deemed important at the time; e.g., the decision to pay attention to whoever is speaking to you at a party) and enduring dispositions (factors that are always important to you; e.g., hearing the sound of your own name being spoken). A strength of this model is that it helps explain how extensive practice can reduce the attentional demands of any task. A weakness of the model concerns the difficulty of measuring capacity independently.

The second influential theory, Posner's (1980) spotlight metaphor of attention, argues that selective attention resembles a mental light beam (like the head-mounted torch that miners, divers, and spelunkers wear in dark environments). This spotlight illuminates targets located either in the external world around you or in the internal world of your subjective experiences. A strength of the spotlight metaphor is how it shows that concentration is never really lost but merely diverted to some target that is irrelevant to the task at hand. The spotlight metaphor undoubtedly has intuitive appeal, but it has failed to explain the mechanisms responsible for the executive control of one's attentional focus. A criticism often leveled at the metaphor is the issue of what lies *outside* the beam of concentration. Thus, it ignores the possibility that unconscious factors (e.g., ironic or counterintentional processes; see Wegner, 1994) can affect people's attentional processes. (For a more extensive critique, see Moran & Toner, 2018.)

In the third influential theory, the memory representation approach, much contemporary thinking about attention has been influenced by cognitive neuroscience; the theory claims that memory representations determine the stimuli to which people pay attention (Reinhart et al., 2016). According to this perspective, working memory representations (i.e., a cognitive system that allows you to hold and manipulate information in your mind as you perform a task) play an important role in controlling attention when you start to look for something new amidst an array of stimuli. Once a target item has been selected, the target representation is no longer maintained in working memory; long-term memory representations of the identified item take over the control of attentional selection. Support for this proposal has come from electrophysiological studies using event-related potentials (ERPs) to measure memory representations as participants learn to search for specific target objects (see Woodman et al., 2013).

All three theories have shed light on how individuals might select target features of a display for processing, but they don't necessarily help explain how expert athletes lose concentration or become distracted during performance. Addressing this issue will be important for gaining a better understanding of the ephemeral nature of concentration.

Distractions and Their Effect on Performance

Concentration is rarely lost in the strictest sense. Rather, your mental beam is diverted to stimuli that are irrelevant to the task at hand or beyond your ability to control. In sport, this mental spotlight may be diverted by a host of different *internal* (e.g., self-generated concerns such as worries about how the athlete might be perceived if they perform poorly) and *external* (e.g., crowd noise or behavior of an opponent) distractions that the performer may experience or encounter during competitive performance. An oft-cited example of a performer falling prey to an internal distraction is the case of golfer Doug Sanders, who missed a putt of under 2 1/2 feet (about 76cm) that prevented him from winning the 1970 British Open championship at St. Andrews, Scotland. This extraordinary lapse of concentration was prompted by Sanders projecting himself into the future rather than focusing on the task at hand: "I had the victory speech prepared before the battle was over . . . I would give up every victory I had to have won that title. It's amazing how many different things to my normal routine I did on the 18th" (Moran, 2005, p. 21).

Both external and internal distractions are often cited as primary mechanisms underpinning the fascinating phenomenon known as choking in sport. *Choking* is a sudden and significant breakdown in performance proficiency

R & A Championships/Getty Images

A lapse of concentration prevented Doug Sanders from winning the 1970 British Open.

in situations that are personally meaningful to the performer (Hill et al., 2011). It is characterized by an inability to control one's mental spotlight. An exploration of this phenomenon can shed considerable light on some of the internal and external distractions that disrupt attentional control in skilled performers. Researchers generally draw on one of two competing theoretical accounts when seeking to explain the attentional mechanisms responsible for instances of choking, namely, distraction or self-focus models.

Distraction models, such as attentional control theory (ACT) (Derakshan & Eysenck, 2009), postulate that performance anxiety hinders efficient attention by disrupting the balance between the top–down attentional system (one influenced by a person's current goals and expectations) and the bottom–up attentional system (a stimulus-driven system initiated by salient environmental events). According to ACT, anxiety may disrupt performance by impairing *attentional inhibition* (the ability, under normal circumstances, to suppress task-irrelevant cognitive processing and ignore salient yet irrelevant features of a situation) and by hampering *attentional shifting* (the process by which people can usually switch their attention in response to changing task requirements). In other words, anxiety often results in athletes fixating on some perceived threat. This anxiety consumes their attentional resources and prevents them from shifting their focus to the strategic demands of a performance situation.

While distraction models of choking tend to emphasize the importance of external distractions, *self-focus* models propose that anxiety increases athletes' level of self-consciousness and causes them to turn their attention inward. It is viewed as a form of paralysis by analysis, whereby athletes become overly concerned with the mechanical details of their action; as a result, they break down whole movements into component parts in order to regain control over performance. Two self-focus theories of choking are particularly prominent in the literature: the conscious processing hypothesis (CPH) (Masters, 1992) and the explicit monitoring hypothesis (EMH) (Beilock & Carr, 2001). The EMH postulates that athletic performance is disrupted when performers monitor their step-by-step execution of the skill, whereas the CPH hypothesizes that disruption is caused by athletes consciously controlling or manipulating their technique during skill execution. A wide range of evidence points to the detrimental effects of skill-focused attention on skilled performance (e.g., Beilock & Carr, 2001), and it is often cited in support of claims that self-focus is directly responsible for choking episodes. However, in one of the few empirical studies to test the predictions of distraction and self-focus models, Englert and Oudejans (2014) found that the self-reported level of distraction—not self-reported skill focus—was what mediated the anxiety–performance relationship among a group of tennis players. In other words, a focus on thoughts unrelated to a task can prove more detrimental to performance efficiency than a detailed focus on one's bodily movements.

Considering other research, the findings from a number of qualitative studies that have explored skilled performers' experiences of choking show

how attentional disruption is often characterized by external distractions. Using a verbal report protocol to explore which focus of attention occurs more often when expert athletes perform under pressure (thinking about skill execution or worrying about performance), Oudejans and colleagues (2011) found that these athletes were far more likely to focus on external factors than on technical elements of performance. Findings from a number of other qualitative explorations of athletes' experiences of choking under pressure have shown that experts are vulnerable to a host of external distractions. These distractions may involve self-presentational concerns, such as worries about receiving a negative evaluation from friends, family, coaches, or the media (e.g., Gucciardi et al., 2010; Hill et al., 2010; Hill et al., 2011). For one golfer in a study by Hill and colleagues (2010), it meant that he was not thinking about his shot or his swing but instead was "Just thinking about what they [the spectators] are thinking. What are they going to say if I hit a bad shot . . . so I rush the shot, in order to get away from them" (p. 226).

These studies have shown that athletes who are susceptible to choking have a bias for threat-related information (e.g., focusing thoughts on the consequences of failure). This evidence supports the main predictions of Eysenck and Wilson's (2016) extension of the ACT, namely, the attentional control theory: sport (ACTS). According to the ACTS, pressure will prove deleterious to performance if it results in performers focusing on threat-related information, such as concerns about how a poor performance might cost them a place on the team. Athletes who lack these biases should outperform those who possess them because they are less likely to believe that losing in high-pressure environments will have high costs. Significantly, the ACTS predicts that training with anxiety gets the athlete acclimated to the processes involved in performing under pressure and that investing additional mental resources in a task can counter the potentially deleterious consequences of anxiety. In addition, increasing the effort devoted to performance appears to be precisely what happens when athletes produce clutch performances in extremely high-stakes situations.

Attentional Control and Clutch

While the choking phenomenon sheds light on the various factors that can disrupt attentional control, investigating the phenomenon known as clutch can help you understand how athletes might exert control over their attentional processes in response to perceived pressure. A clutch performance occurs when a participant in a competitive sport succeeds at a point in competition in which success or failure has a significant effect on the outcome of the contest (Hibbs, 2010). For example, rugby player Jonny Wilkinson scored a winning drop goal with 26 seconds remaining in the 2003 Rugby World Cup final. While choking often is characterized by a total loss of control over strategic focus (e.g., Jean Van de Velde's insistence on taking on a series of increasingly risky shots on his way to squandering a three-shot lead on the final hole of the 1999 British Open championship) or one's ability to smoothly and efficiently execute fine motor patterns, clutch performances are characterized by the ability to strategically allocate and redirect attentional resources in response to situational demands. From an attentional perspective, clutch is an intriguing performance state because it appears to involve deliberate attempts on the performer's behalf to redirect their attentional resources in response to increases in perceived pressure. These findings suggest that contrary to conventional wisdom, consciously attending to behavioral routines can improve performance proficiency.

Sport is often at its most compelling when athletes and teams produce moments of brilliance at a point in a contest when an error or mistake would lead to certain defeat. For example, Tiger Woods is renowned for his extraordinary ability to hole clutch putts at crucial moments during the final round of major golf championships. While it is a fascinating phenomenon, researchers have only recently begun to explore the attentional mechanisms that underpin this performance state. In one such study, Swann and colleagues (2017) interviewed 26 participants from a range of sports about a recent excellent performance (e.g., where they had placed highly in competitive events). Although flow and clutch states were found to share a number of the same characteristics (e.g., confidence, perceptions of control), clutch states possessed a number of characteristics that were absent in flow states, such as an increase in maximal effort (rather than the feelings of effortlessness typical of flow states) and the use of conscious processing (rather than being fully automatic). In short, while flow experiences broadly involved athletes *letting* it happen, clutch experiences broadly involved athletes *making* it happen. These findings suggest that clutch might be a distinct state underlying excellent performance in sport and that certain strategies may be useful to performers seeking to induce it. For example, athletes reported the use of fixed goals, which include specific and challenging objectives, during clutch states; a triathlete reported that getting to the finish line before anyone else constituted his main goal (Swann et al., 2017). Setting these goals helped athletes to increase their effort, intensity, and concentration, thereby allowing them to maintain performance proficiency in a clutch situation. These findings offer encouragement that performers might be trained to manipulate their attentional focus so that they may flexibly adjust their behavior in response to situational demands. More attention is devoted to this topic later in the chapter. The next section offers a number of useful methods for coaches and athletes to gauge a performer's ability to adopt and maintain a task-relevant focus of attention during performance.

Assessment

Assessing concentration (and attentional processes more generally) is far from straightforward. In fact, researchers have yet to identify a truly reliable means of assessing an athlete's ability to concentrate in real-life sport situations. It is entirely understandable given that concentration is a hypothetical construct and therefore unobservable, and it undoubtedly limits people's ability to understand concentration as a process. Attentional processes can, however, be measured indirectly; this section considers a number of these methods and how they might be employed to identify what athletes are focusing on as they plan, execute, and reflect on motor performance. The following text explores two such methods: psychometric approaches and the use of think-aloud protocols.

Consider some psychometric approaches that researchers have used to measure individual differences in attentional processes in athletes. The Test of Attentional and Interpersonal Style (TAIS) (Nideffer, 1976) is a paper-and-pencil test that has been deployed as a screening device in a number of high-performance settings (Nideffer et al., 2001). Nideffer (1976) posited that people's attentional focus varies along these two independent dimensions:

1. *Width*: A broad focus where one is aware of many stimulus features and a narrow focus where one focuses exclusively on a limited range of stimuli
2. *Direction*: Internal or external

These dimensions of width and direction can be combined factorially to yield four hypothetical attentional styles (e.g., a narrow external attentional focus such as when a basketball player focuses on the rim of the basket prior to releasing a free throw). Despite its intuitive appeal and widespread popularity, the TAIS has a number of flaws, including its lack of predictive validity (Boutcher, 2008)—and its inability to identify different attentional styles between performers of different levels.

Perhaps a more promising psychometric tool is Hatzigeorgiadis and Biddle's (2000) Thought Occurrence Questionnaire for Sport (TOQS), which sets out to measure cognitive interference (task-irrelevant, self-preoccupied thinking) in athletes. This 17-item test allows coaches to determine the extent to which their athletes experience performance anxiety, situation-irrelevant thoughts, and thoughts of escape, and how these thoughts affect subsequent effort.

Coaches might also wish to consider the use of think-aloud (TA) protocols to determine what their athletes are attending to during the various phases of skill execution. This approach requires performers to verbalize their thoughts as they perform a task (see Eccles & Arsal, 2017, for a critical review of this method); researchers wishing to capture the in-event cognitions that skilled performers experience as they tackle complex tasks in both naturalistic (see Whitehead et al., 2015) and laboratory settings (Arsal et al., 2016) have used this approach with increased frequency. When using this approach, coaches would ask athletes to perform a task and "talk aloud everything that they say to themselves silently … acting as if they are alone in the room speaking to themselves" (Eccles & Arsal, 2017, p. 519).

One way that coaches might effectively employ this method is to require their athletes to verbalize their thoughts as they perform tasks of varying difficulty. This approach can allow coaches to determine whether their athletes distribute their attentional resources in a context-sensitive manner. To illustrate using the TA approach, Arsal and colleagues (2016) found that skilled golfers had a greater number of higher-order strategy thoughts (e.g., considering the direction in which previous putts have been missed and altering their aim for subsequent attempts) than their recreational counterparts, and this difference was pronounced when a putting task became more challenging in nature. This approach can help athletes to gain important insights into their ability to manipulate their mental spotlight. For example, TA can be used to determine whether or not they increase the attentional resources (e.g., planning, reflection) they devote to task execution when faced with challenging or unpredictable conditions. More specifically, one might use this approach to determine whether the behavioral steps of the preperformance routine are executed in a consistent manner when performing under conditions of mental stress or physical fatigue. The TA approach could also be used to assess an athlete's postperformance routine and the strategies they employ to cope with or move on from poor task execution.

In a similar vein, verbalizing one's thought patterns during skill execution might also help athletes to identify the core action components of their behavioral repertoires; *core action components* are actions that, when executed in a less optimal manner, prove deleterious to performance (see Bortoli et al., 2012). This technique requires coaches and athletes to work in concert in seeking to differentiate functional thoughts from those that prove deleterious to performance proficiency. Bortoli and colleagues (2012) found that a focus on core action components such as body stability, grip, and trigger helped elite shooters to effectively cope with the dysfunctional effects of competitive stress. These authors argue that it will take a minimal amount of conscious control to supervise these movement components when optimal performance conditions occur, but performers will need to devote increased attention to these components when they encounter stress, fatigue, or other challenging or unpredictable situations.

Athletes and coaches need to follow a number of steps in seeking to identify these core components. In Bortoli and colleagues' (2012) study, elite shooters were asked to describe their usual optimal sequence (chain of actions) from start to follow-through as they executed the skill. Next, shooters identified from their chain of actions those core components deemed fundamental to optimal performance. To aid this process, athletes were asked the question *What are the actions that, when executed in a less-than-accurate manner, cause your shooting scores to drop from optimal to suboptimal level?* A final step in this process was to assess the efficacy of these core components under conditions of physical and mental fatigue. The next section returns to this point and considers how coaches might create such conditions.

Optimization

The following text draws on more recent empirical literature to explore whether attentional control can be developed and improved in athletes. In doing so, it outlines a range of approaches that athletes can use—and coaches can coach—to switch their focus or redistribute patterns of attention when they start to experience internal or external distractions. The text draws on a range of studies that have shown how attentional control may be improved through the strategic use of self-talk and by practicing under high-pressure conditions.

Self-Talk

Perhaps one of the most effective ways of improving attentional control is to encourage athletes to adopt a preperformance routine that incorporates the use of motivational and instructional self-talk. Much research has been devoted to exploring the relationship between attention and this cognitive strategy in skilled performance. The term *self-talk* has been defined as "verbalizations or statements addressed to the self" (Hardy, 2006), and it can involve the use of either out-loud or inner verbalizations that serve instructional or motivational functions (see review by Van Raalte et al., 2016). It is not uncommon for elite athletes to talk to themselves either silently or out loud when they compete, often in an effort to maintain focus or to increase the effort they devote to the task. Covert self-talk may involve praise (e.g., "I nailed it! That's brilliant!"), criticism ("You fool. How could you make such a basic mistake?"), or instruction ("Swing smoothly"). In a meta-analytic review of the effectiveness of self-talk interventions, Hatzigeorgiadis and colleagues (2011) found that for the performance of fine motor tasks, instructional self-talk was more effective than motivational self-talk. For example, technically demanding tasks that require the precise execution of specific movement patterns (e.g., free throw in basketball; see Abdoli et al., 2018) may benefit more from instructional self-talk (e.g., "ring front, elbow, wrist") than motivational self-talk (e.g., "give it your all"), which seems to be more effective in tasks requiring strength or endurance or when one wants to psych up for competition. Overall, some intriguing evidence suggests that self-talk strategies can help athletes maintain performance proficiency when subject to external distractions (see Galanis et al., 2018).

As another specific consideration, athletes can be encouraged to use what Van Raalte and colleagues (2016) have called System 2 self-talk. While System 1 self-talk involves the use of rapid or autonomous processes (e.g., expressed as an automatic reaction such as when the athlete exclaims, "I'm terrible today!" after making another error), System 2 draws on working memory processes to consciously plan and deliberate on a course of action. The latter form of self-talk might include the use of specific instructions (suggested by coaches or identified by athletes during the course of their practice) that seek to direct the athlete's attention away from the task-irrelevant focus (e.g., self-presentational concerns) and toward a core action component that is highly practiced and requires minimal supervision (e.g., a skilled shooter focusing on stabilizing the body during task execution; see Bortoli et al., 2012). It may also promote the adoption of a challenge state, an approach that may prove particularly beneficial for those athletes who are prone to processing threat-related biases during performance.

Success Story:
Alleviating Choking Under Pressure

My own (the author's) experience working with athletes has shown how self-talk can prove particularly effective in helping them to exert attentional control and to combat the potentially deleterious consequences of performance pressure. In one case, I worked closely with a highly skilled amateur golfer by helping him to use self-talk in order to redirect his focus of attention when he found himself subject to distractions during performance. The principal goal of the intervention was to help the athlete combat a series of choking episodes he had experienced in high-profile amateur events. More specifically, the performer found that having played his way into contention, he had a tendency to catastrophize and fixate on the consequences of a poor performance (e.g., the negative comments he might receive from teammates or friends and the likelihood of him being dropped from the national panel). Negative appraisals were accompanied by an increase in physiological arousal and occasionally by a sense of panic. A consequence of this tendency was that he often sought to remove himself from the situation by rushing shots and failing to complete some important elements of his preshot routine. In the postperformance phase of the routine, he would continue to ruminate on the poor performance as he started to prepare for an upcoming shot. We sought to prevent these external distractions and redirect his focus of attention by using various forms of instructional and motivational self-talk. For example, instructional self-talk included the use of the covert phrase "take dead aim" to encourage the athlete to adopt a visual attentional focus on the target immediately prior to task execution. He was also encouraged to utter various motivational self-talk cues (e.g., "I can finish strongly in this round") when he recognized that he was beginning to experience negative thoughts. Another strategy involved reminding himself of the need to slow down (e.g., his walking pace, breathing rate) and to focus on completing each step of his preperformance behavioral routine by repeating the word *process* prior to task execution. The final strategy involved encouraging the golfer to use the postperformance routine to converse with his caddie or playing partner, thus discouraging excessive rumination on poor task execution. Together, these approaches improved the athlete's ability to maintain concentration in high-pressure conditions and reduced his tendency to experience performance breakdown in clutch situations.

Simulating Pressure, Stress, and Mindful Awareness

Simulating pressure in training contexts is another potential means of improving an athlete's attentional control. This approach aims to get athletes acclimated to the range of negative emotions and cognitions that might be evoked during competition and to help them identify various strategies to maintain concentration under such conditions. Some empirical evidence suggests that this approach can prove beneficial to performance. In a series of studies by Oudejans and Pijpers (2009, 2010), participants who trained with anxiety (being told that their performance was being recorded and that experts would watch the recordings in order to evaluate their technique) maintained performance proficiency in a high-pressure posttest, whereas the performance of control group participants deteriorated. However, the use of appropriate stressors might play a particularly important role in optimizing these training conditions. For example, Stoker and colleagues (2019) found that the introduction of judgment, or *forfeit consequence* stressors, created debilitative anxiety among elite shooters while the use of *demand* stressors (e.g., environmental manipulations, such as the use of a noise distraction in the form of a repetitive beep) had no such effect.

In seeking to simulate pressure, coaches might want to work with their athletes to identify the stressors they face during competition and the extent to which these stressors are meaningful to them. Coaches can then subsequently expose the athletes to stressors of a similar intensity during practice (Stoker et al., 2016). In addition, coaches should aim to re-create, as accurately as possible, the range of mental and bodily states that occur during competition. For example, athletes could be asked to execute tasks under conditions of physical fatigue, muscular tension, or temporal constraints. Ultimately, the aim should be to present athletes with what Bortoli and colleagues (2012) refer to as "dysfunctional conditions of competitive stress," when it is not possible to execute skill in an optimal or automatic manner. This challenge will also provide athletes with an opportunity to mindfully accept conditions of mental and physical distress and learn to refocus attention on core action components.

Related to the role that mindful awareness might play in helping athletes to establish attentional control, it has been speculated that mindfulness training may have the power to improve attentional switching; in other words, it may help the performer identify an inappropriate thought, allow them to accept that such negative thoughts, emotions, or bodily states arise on occasion, and provide them with the ability to switch to a more appropriate and task-relevant focus. Athletes can participate in a variety of mindfulness programs and use apps (e.g., Headspace) as part of their preparation strategies for competitive performance, and a growing body of evidence supports the use of such training. To illustrate, Bu and colleagues (2019) found that a mindfulness training intervention improved levels of relaxation, attention (as measured by the WT-attention test), and experiential acceptance in a group of elite Chinese shooters. Ultimately, the goal of this form of training is to teach the athlete to accept that negative thoughts and emotions may arise during performance and help them to redirect their attention to more appropriate or useful cues such as core action components.

Conclusion

This chapter depicted concentration as an ephemeral process that is subject to a host of internal and external distractions. A range of evidence shows that a performer's attentional resources can often be misdirected, resulting in undesirable outcomes such as choking. Reassuringly, however, clutch states reveal that performers can flexibly allocate attention in a manner that allows them to respond to situational demands. Coaches have an important role to play through the introduction of high-pressure training, which enables them to replicate the attentional demands their athletes face during competition. Familiarizing athletes with the mental and bodily states they are likely to experience in competition may help inoculate them against the potentially deleterious consequences of performance pressure. In addition, training under pressure provides athletes with an opportunity to apply various strategies such as self-talk and mindful awareness to ensure they continue to concentrate on task-relevant stimuli. Together, these approaches can be used to help athletes exert attentional control and to maintain performance proficiency in the face of a range of internal and external distractions.

10 | Reflection and Balance

Carlos Eduardo Gonçalves
University of Coimbra

Humberto Moreira Carvalho
Federal University of Santa Catarina

Coaches recognize that the capacity to understand their specific sport is an essential characteristic of contemporary athletes. Coaches also know that learning does not occur spontaneously; it is a function of deliberate stimuli that are intended to cause the expected adaptations and improvements. This chapter addresses the conceptual and terminological imprecision surrounding words such as *understanding, intelligence, decision making, tactical literacy*, and *creativity*. Planning is closely linked to reflective practice of both coaches and athletes. The argument presented in this chapter is that athletes must be encouraged and taught to build their own plans for personal development, becoming more and more autonomous about their self-evaluation and about their strategic choices in training and competition.

The chapter presents a short review of literature on planning and three success stories of interventions with athletes. At the end of the chapter, some guidelines are suggested for coaches about the process of planning and reflecting on successes and failures. The chapter concludes by encouraging coaches to make their own research in action through thoughtful planned and monitored experiments.

Relevance

In a television interview, basketball star LeBron James said that if a team wants to be a champion, a collection of talent is not enough; to succeed at the highest level, a team needs a collection of minds that think beyond the single game. All coaches recognize that the capacity to understand the specific sport is an essential characteristic of contemporary athletes, especially when they need to perform to their fullest potential. Skills such as reasoning, strategic thinking, and intelligent performance from a tactical point of view are considered as indicators of success in competition. Furthermore, elite players are expected to be problem solvers in dynamic situations and proactive when interacting with teammates and opponents. According to this premise, coaches should provide opportunities for their athletes to analyze, interpret, and decide about the content of their training process (Butler, 2016). Simply put, the idea is that having greater understanding of what coaches are trying to achieve and some options for achieving those goals enable athletes to engage in creative ways to improve performance.

LeBron James' observation can also be misleading. Besides being an intelligent performer, he is a superathlete and a technical virtuoso. Interventions with beginners highlight the players' technical fragilities as a limit to the full exploitation of the pedagogical value of reasoning skills (Santos & Morgan, 2019). Coaches know that what is tactically desirable must be both physically and technically possible for the athletes concerned; in other words, the path to expertise is holistic and demands commitment and time. To monitor and then drive progress, it must be measured mechanically but also evolved through training sessions and repetitions. Coaches also know that learning

Brad Smith/ISI Photos/Getty Images

Professional goalkeepers and other elite athletes are expected to be problem solvers in dynamic situations.

does not occur spontaneously; it is a function of deliberate stimuli that are intended to cause the expected adaptations and improvements—even if these stimuli may sometimes be generated by the players, with the generation skillfully manipulated through clever coaching.

Therefore, coaches need to move toward creating strategies that are rooted in coordinated planning approaches and oriented to facilitating long-term athlete development. Beyond the general theories of sport planning, what are the roles of the coach and athlete in this long-term process? The conceptual and terminological imprecision of words such as *understanding, intelligence, decision making, tactical literacy*, and *creativity* are abstractions that people use to reduce the complexity of the living world. Later in the chapter, the meaning and contents attributed to those terms are defined. First, some proposals are offered to define the challenges that coaches and athletes face in the quest for a better understanding of sport participation.

Defining the Coach's Role

Representation of the coaching process evolved from traditional prescriptive models to the emphasis on complexity and uncertainty of sports coaching that is seen as part of a dynamic, ecological system (Seifert et al., 2017). If prescriptive models seem to omit the complexity and nonlinearity of the sport environment, they have the advantage of well-defined guidelines that result in the process, expected outcomes, and eventual performance. Between these two contrasting conceptual positions, the role of the coach as a facilitator, manager, and mentor of the athlete and team development can often be forgotten. In the real world, coaches have limited control over the athletes' and team's behaviors, especially when dealing with conflicting values or expectations; individual, social, and cultural idiosyncrasies demand different context-based approaches.

Based on these premises, the first argument is that coaches matter in all stages of the process, and the effective use of teaching tools depends on good ideas, proper planning, attentive instructions, and corrections. Plans are mental constructions that need to be confronted with reality and evaluated accordingly. Therefore, the full process of coaching connects—in dynamic and dialectic interactions—practice, reflection, and planning for change. Max-Neef (2005) argues that the normative discipline in research and practice is planning, which defines the purpose of knowledge about what exists through the language of reasoning and logic. If disciplines such as pedagogy, psychology, and coaching tell coaches what they are capable of doing, planning organizes separate types of knowledge and allows for the orchestration of thoughtful interventions.

This chapter focuses on the use of strategies on and off the field as a way to foster the athletes' ability to understand the dynamics of a specific sport. The concept of *intelligent learning* refers to the athletes' capacity to build a coherent mental representation of the time, space, and power relationships in their sport. However, the real content of teaching tactics is complex phenomenon, and no single definition or process fits all contexts.

The second argument is that playing games does not teach athletes how to make decisions; it simply provides the context for the players to see what is happening and learn how to deal appropriately with fast-paced, ever-changing situations. The current belief that small-sided games teach tactical awareness is devoid of content if not integrated in the coach plan.

One additional problem is the contemporary quest for creativity, which is pervasive of all human agency. Athletes must be creative, and the best are the most creative ones. Therefore, youth coaches must work to develop creativity among talented athletes (Memmert, 2015). However, the work of Gopnik (2016) demonstrated that human development seems to be a trade-off between plasticity and efficiency. As you become more efficient at making decisions, you gradually lose your capacity to be creative and absorb the things that don't fit with what you know. In fact, as athletes improve their skills and accumulate hours of training, they start to see the sport better and are more able to make the right decision and execute the game plan, but this experience-based knowledge does not mean that the athletes become more creative.

The third argument is that it is time to stop mixing beginner, advanced, and elite athletes. Every developmental stage presents different challenges, so practice sessions must be designed, taught, and assessed accordingly. The tactical meaning of a small-sided game or the analysis of opponents is best perceived by expert athletes, who can figure out the activity's ultimate purpose (Hodge et al., 2014; Hansen & Andersen, 2017). In addition, professional athletes move frequently to new clubs, cities, or countries, and they are expected to perform at a high level regardless of the coach, style of play, teammates, or time to prepare. The ability to adapt to ever-changing conditions is learned and embodied during a long period of apprenticeship. The following sections focus on this process of apprenticeship; they present and discuss differentiated pedagogical approaches for different levels of expertise.

Pedagogical Aspects

It is important to address some pedagogical issues as they relate to coaching. First, reflective practice and planning are not exclusive to coaches. Athletes must be encouraged and taught to build their own plans for personal development, becoming increasingly autonomous in their self-evaluation and in their strategic choices during training and competition. Coaches must be aware that the athletes' ability to think about their sport and increment their knowledge about it is teachable, and it is the coaches' responsibility to teach it.

Another issue is that to think and to plan is not a matter of talent development; all athletes need to have the same opportunities to learn to enhance their cognitive skills and knowledge. This concept is especially important in team sports where all the players need to share the same mental models and the same tactical approach. The real matter is good coaching, individualized teaching, fun, and the education of intelligent participants.

Two corollaries can be deducted from the previous argument. First, not all athletes react to this transfer of autonomy in the same way. Some of them embrace the concept and develop their own strategies to plan their preparation and competitive approaches; others prefer to remain dependent on their coach's planning choices. The second is that the process is nonlinear, and some athletes will develop a good level of reasoning and understanding of their sport but are not capable of translating it into superior performance, their knowledge remaining primarily procedural.

What We Know

Although a body of literature exists about reflective practice and planning, it is of little help for practitioners because of its eclectic intellectual foundations and the limitations of the empirical applications. Consequently, this chapter limits its presentation to the theoretical approaches that are relevant to practitioners and useful for future research.

Three main theoretical concerns are related to teaching and learning how to plan for change:

1. A clear definition of understanding in every sport (e.g., *tactics* and *applied reasoning* have different meanings in track and field, combat, or team sports)
2. The field's incomplete knowledge about the mental mechanisms and processes that underpin tactical and strategic learning
3. The imperfect assessment of the efficacy of teaching and learning to plan

Regarding these concerns, constructivism appears to be the obvious theoretical framework in contemporary sport because it assumes that individuals build their own understanding of the world based on collecting and structuring information that suits their needs and expectations. According to constructivist principles, coaches do not prescribe solutions for tactical problems, limiting themselves to a role of facilitators through observation and questioning. However, as Stolz and Pill (2014) put it, existing research on coaching based on constructivist principles has failed to demonstrate that it is able to take athletes beyond their current performance and knowledge in a consistent way. At the same time—and despite the claims by the various constructivist avatars that their main target is youth sport—consistent empirical findings *are* to be found with world-class performers. In their study with the New Zealand rugby team, which later became world champions, Hodge and colleagues (2014) exposed the ability and autonomy of the players to plan and make decisions about their preparation with little interference of the coaches. Hansen and Andersen (2017) report the same level of planning skills among Norwegian Olympic cross-country skiers.

In a more pragmatic tone, Price and colleagues (2020) suggest that the capacity to reflect on performance is an indicator of understanding; it is viewed as the first step for planning. The same authors argue that the ultimate goal for athletes is to attain a capacity for metacognition about their sport; in other words, the aim is to express the ability to reflect on their own reflections and construct their game plans.

For Den Hartigh and colleagues (2018), the aim of reflective practice is to go from representations to sensorimotor skills. Observation of the athletes' actions in practices and competitions enables the coach and the trained athletes to evaluate the relationships between the actions and their outcomes. The athletes map and integrate relevant information regarding themselves, their teammates, and their opponents.

Indeed, the capacity to structure information in real time (during competitions) is a characteristic of expert performance. To attain higher levels of expertise, athletes must improve their skills to gather and analyze information at ever-increasing levels of complexity in order to build their own strategies and plans for improvement. However, in their study of young soccer players who were recruited by a professional club and asked to watch video clips of soccer matches and verbalize the actions taking place on the field, Den Hartigh and colleagues (2018) cast doubts; they were not convinced that the transfer of cognitive expertise to match situations would result in expert decision making.

One important feature is the tendency toward empirical testing of new ideas; in simple terms, the athlete uses themselves as the focus for experimentation. In their study with Olympic skiers, Hansen and Andersen (2017) report that some athletes do seem able to actively use their knowledge of their sport, acquired through years of intensive practice, when evaluating new equipment and technologies. Facing innovation, these athletes were prone to test new ideas in practice and compare the results with the previous ones. If they found that changes occurred in performance, the skiers made adjustments to their practice through self-reflection. The authors noted that the ability to use the learning-based knowledge and make experiments in the field was not apparent in other skiers, who relied less on reflection and observation of their own training parameters. Even in this case of top world athletes with a high level of autonomy in sport-related decisions, it is important to acknowledge the role of the coach as a facilitator and gatekeeper.

Partially as a consequence of the theoretical and empirical inconsistencies about what is effective reflective practice and planning, more recently researchers began to take interest in the work of Vygotski, namely in the importance of discourse as a learning tool. Vinson and Parker (2019) argue that oral speech and dialogue play a crucial role in the development of all of the higher psychological functions. According to Vygotski (1986), intelligent action is closely linked to speech, especially when integrated with practical reasoning. As an organizing function, speech precedes action and represents a central factor in planning. Other studies corroborate this claim (Richards et al., 2012, 2009); they present slow learning as a step in the athlete's procedural knowledge that facilitates the path to the implementation of knowledge in action. Notably, this approach of thinking slow to think fast is especially important for players of team sports who will watch, review, and talk through game films as an important precursor to then practicing the moves indicated at speed (Bjørndal & Ronglan, 2019).

One unsolved problem is clarifying the mechanisms that underpin the transfer of individual improvement in knowledge and performance to the collective performance on a pitch or court. If an athlete elevates themselves to a superior level of reasoning and decision making, how can it affect the team's performance? Sport science professionals observe a scarcity of experimental research designed to approach the present topic. Time con-straints and the presence of opponents make difficult the evaluation and tuning of strategies, but they don't make it impossible. A consistent body of literature in economic and political sciences (Bonner & Bolinger, 2013; Huang & Hutchinson, 2013; Mesagno et al., 2015; Milch et al., 2009) uses experimental designs to approach planning and strategic choices at individual and team levels. For instance, in studies of performance management, Huang and Hutchinson (2013) found that the lack of knowledge about the team's mental model and the lack of proper planning is more detrimental to performance than the lack of motivation is.

Although cross-sectional and without the presence of adversaries, contri-butions from other sciences, such as economics, can help sport scientists and coaches in designing their own plans. Bonner and Bollinger (2013) sug-gest that teams outperform individuals regarding decision making because of their superior confidence in searching relevant information and better shared understanding of the problems. However, the authors also point out that the accuracy of a group's decision making does not outperform the decision of the best individual. This consideration is especially important for coaches who may deal with exceptionally talented athletes who demand a custom-ized approach when discussing strategies, tactics, or competition plans.

In line with the previous argument, the reflective cycle presented next (Husebø et al., 2015) is picked from medical sciences and used in nurse education programs to foster their readiness to make decisions under pres-sure. Also, anecdotal evidence suggests that elite coaches make the most of their off-season time to study other sciences and talk with scientists and practitioners from different areas of knowledge. They say that going out from the narrow field of coaching makes them more reflective about their own practice and more open to innovation.

Success Story 1: Boys Basketball

Every week, L., a basketball coach of an under-14 boys team, organizes a video session of 15 minutes based on the previous game. While the other players practice with an assistant coach, a group of three players watch two or three video clips edited by the coach and are invited to comment on them. If he thinks it necessary, L. intervenes to orient the athletes' attention to particular topics.

Once a month, usually after the weekend game, L. asks the players to write down at home the description and evaluation of a lived situation. He also has them design an action plan for improvement that follows the steps of the reflective cycle presented earlier. Players return their written sheet to the coach in the first practice of the week.

Here is an example of the responses of one player from the first month of the season:

Description: "I drove to the basket to score, but it was a difficult shot, and I missed."

Evaluation: "It was a bad decision because I did not see that one of my teammates was free for an easy basket."

Action plan: "Listen to the coach's advice to keep my head up and facing the basket."

In the third month of the season, these were the responses of the player:

Description: "I wanted to pass to my teammate in the wing, but I noticed he had the passing lane closed, so I moved the ball to the other side."

Evaluation: "I felt good because I avoided a turnover in a close game."

Action plan: "When we play give-and-go, I must be aware of the position of the close defenders."

In the fifth month of the season, these were the responses of the player:

Description: "In one of our moves, when my teammate A gets the ball in the elbow, I must cut to the basket. But I saw that a defender on the other side was in the help position and waiting for me to cut, so I went to the corner to give A enough space to play one on one."

Evaluation: "We did not score, but I think it was a good play."

Action plan: "I need to watch what our team is doing and what the other team is doing, and how they defend us—with and without the ball."

It is possible to observe the evolution in the complexity of the young player's reasoning as he is confronted with more capable opponents. In the process, he goes from the awareness of his position with the ball to a more comprehensive view of the two teams.

In this case, players learn first what to see and how to make sense of what they see. The reasoning starts through their eyes (Memmert, 2015).

Assessment

This section presents some practical suggestions for coaches on how to teach reflective and planning skills to their athletes. All of them were used and tested across diverse age groups and competitive levels, and in different sports and contexts.

Some premises need to be addressed. The intervention of the coaches to foster knowledge, reasoning, and understanding among the athletes must be deliberate, daily, and planned. Experience (seen as the accumulation of hours of participation) is a necessary requisite, but it is not enough. Cognitive and strategic skills, as well as development of physical qualities or assimilation of tactical movements, must be planned and taught.

The cognitive and strategic skills in mind are thinking structures tied to a specific sport, developed and designed to be applied in real time and in real situations. They evolve in complexity as the levels of competition grow higher and are expected to mirror the development of strategic reasoning. Following Husebø and colleagues (2015), a reflective cycle of six stages is suggested as a starting point for the coach's plan for change elaboration. It is not mandatory to go through all the steps, and coaches may adopt a simplified version to match their particular contexts. The process is designed to help athletes think about their lived experiences in training and especially in competition.

The reflexive cycle combines a description of a chosen situation (*What happened?*) with emotions (*How did you feel when you were on the pitch?*), analysis (*What sense can you make of the situation? Were the experiences of others, teammates and adversaries, different?*), evaluation (*What was good or bad about the situation? Do you think it was positive or negative?*), and conclusion (*What else could you have done?*).

Finally, the coach asks the athlete to draw an action plan (*What can you do if you face similar situations in the future?*).

Assessment using this staged approach will help the coach to promote an effective endpoint to the process while also offering an early warning of flawed thinking that can be corrected before it goes too far.

Depending on the competitive level, age group, or level of experience and knowledge, coaches may let the athletes choose freely the situations, or they can direct their attention for specific topics. Topics include principles of play and tactics, the pace of the game, spacing, cooperation with partners, opposition to known or unknown adversaries, and the logic of the competition when in advantage or disadvantage. They all address the developmental periods in the specialization path, where athletes engage in and embody their chosen sport.

Success Story 2: Girls Field Hockey

Every month, J., a field hockey coach for an elite under-16 female team, organizes a video session with the team. Each player is shown a video clip of another team and has 30 seconds to choose the best decision to score a goal. After players decide individually, they are placed in groups of three with starters and nonstarters mixed together, and they are shown other clips. During the group sessions, the players are allowed to debate the possible solutions.

J. found that the best decision makers when reviewing the video clips were not necessarily the best players on the field, showing that procedural knowledge did not translate to knowledge in action. This time, the strategy resulted in an action plan for the coach. She started to customize the video clips according to the complexity of reasoning exhibited by the players, and she changed the content of her instructions and corrections to meet the needs of the athletes. In the final tournament, J.'s team was the leader in assists for the first time.

Optimization

The three success stories in this chapter suggest that planning is closely linked to reflection and that coaches and athletes should plan their future. However, some qualifications are necessary. Even if a coach can foresee what needs to be taught and learned in the next weeks or months, young athletes live in the present. To succeed in gaining their commitment to engage in thinking and talking about their experiences, coaches must start from real-life situations that have meaning for the youngsters and allow them to express themselves freely, even in a naive manner.

The proper sequence recommended for teaching reflection is to start from the individual, have a good knowledge about the context, and have a clear vision of the pursued goal. The task, important as it is, represents a drill that, if repeated without reflection, risks being transformed into an end in itself. A good example of lack of attention to the individual, the context, and the goal can be seen in the extensive but often unconsidered use of small-sided games for tactical learning purposes. This application needs to be critically evaluated. With repetition, players learn to play the games with efficacy. However, it does not mean that they reach a state of metacognition as described by Price and colleagues (2020). The stimuli represented by small-sided games must grow in complexity and adapt to the quality of the players' responses.

Another recommendation is the use of design thinking as an intellectual and methodological tool to value and leverage what exists and to go beyond an inventory of problems. Coaches and athletes know that they are going to commit mistakes, and they are able to recognize them. Design thinking helps them to start with what they are able to do and figure out what is needed to reach the next level. In fact, strategic thought is a positive idea.

Keep in mind that planning is not equivalent to periodization. In the 2010s, tactical periodization became a popular instrument in professional team sports faced with frequent competitions during 10-month seasons (Delgado-Bordonau & Mendez-Villanueva, 2012; see also chapter 15). The purpose of periodization is to adjust all the preparation to the next competition, through the execution of a game plan, expected to be assumed and followed by every single member of the team with a rigorous tactical discipline. Although the elaboration of the game plan presupposes a deep knowledge about the specific sport and includes cognitive elements, the process is centered on the coaching staff and leaves little room for the autonomous intervention of athletes. Notably, athlete intervention depends on extensive player knowledge that is assimilated during years of specialized training.

Guidelines for Coaches

The following guidelines must be seen as practical suggestions to help coaches and athletes build their own strategies and interventions. Coaches should keep in mind that not all athletes like to talk about strategies or to feel responsible for their preparation. Athlete comfort may also vary between age groups or levels of expertise. Many elite performers expect coaches to plan their training and to make the decisions in competition.

1. Coaching culture and practice should be heavily oriented toward solving typical competitive situations characterized by uncertainty and physical and psychological stress. As presented earlier in this chapter, competition plays a crucial role as a pedagogical environment. There is no learning without opponents, and there is no better occasion and place to engage in a reflective cycle than the competitive field; competitions are vivid, meaningful situations for athletes. As shown in the three success stories, coaches must expose their athletes to an adequate environment. If the adversaries are too strong or too weak, coaching has little effect and learning does not occur.

Coaches must avoid remaining locked in their coaching philosophy. Personal values are important as principles, but pedagogical interventions must be based on facts. Coaches tend to rely on past experiences and on what worked on previous occasions. In contrast, reflection and effective plans look at the athlete's or team's future; they cannot function as justifications for the coach's actions. The solutions that open-minded coaches must consider are those that answer the question *What does the athlete or the team need in order to think and perform better?*

Most coaches have a clear picture of how the specialization path looks and what is necessary for an athlete to reach expertise. However, the young athlete does not share the same long-term vision as the coach. It is better to take small steps while aiming at goals and outcomes that athletes

Ross Land/Getty Images

Competitions are vivid and meaningful experiences for athletes. Lots of learning can arise from competitive challenge.

can see and that are meaningful for them. The competitive season—with its training cycles, team goals, or individual expectations—represents a good opportunity to channel the athletes' attention and reflections in desirable directions. Smaller steps also have the advantage of making it easier to change course when a contradiction or misunderstanding arises. In success story 1, the coach followed the athletes' pace and lines of thought as a scaffold to plan his next teaching intervention. Sometimes the progress seems of small or moderate importance, but its relevance grows over time and paves the way for more significant improvements.

Coaching is based on nonlinear pedagogy; a stimulus oriented to a specific outcome can lead to unexpected responses from the athletes, and the expected outcome seldom correlates perfectly with the magnitude of the stimuli.

2. As a corollary to the previous guideline, coaches know that a sport problem can have multiple solutions. When confronted with a tactical issue, expert athletes weigh multiple alternatives before making a decision. The speed of the competition excludes thinking during execution, but these athletes accumulate an enormous number of off- and on-field situations that allow for a quick, accurate response. Thinking before play restarts can also act to prime the athlete toward a more suitable subset of options.

As seen in success story 2, the best young players have the capacity to find the right solution to a tactical problem, especially in competitive settings. However, there are no normative prescriptions for the right answer for every problem. Therefore, coaches must avoid their natural temptation to have full control of the process; they should abstain from narrowing the possibilities that do not follow a predetermined, linear path.

Coaches' observation skills are crucial because it is their job to connect all the parts in a holistic way. For instance, a technical improvement may offer a new avenue for tactical refinement, or an individual athlete's step further in tactical understanding may force the teammates to adapt, which will affect the team's performance.

3. As in all human social processes, mistakes can happen. However, failures can also contribute to intelligent learning. Coaches should discern which factors contributed to the failure, and they should make clear distinctions between what was a result of a planned action and what happened randomly, answering these questions: *Was it a consequence of carefully planned action or not? What went wrong? Did the plan not match the capacities of the athlete, was it too complex, or was the competitive reality too uncertain?* Effective learning is only viable when the athlete is familiar with the subject, is able to recognize the failure, and wants to correct it.

4. Coaches must have clear expectations about the outcomes and performances they plan for the athletes. Reasonable expectations inform coherent strategies that facilitate development and autonomy. If strategic thinking foresees the future, only a retrospective view can tell if the plan for change was thoughtfully elaborated and applied.

5. Contrary to the tenets of tactical periodization, there is nothing wrong with coaches having a general long-term plan. It draws a steady line of development and it offers benchmarks, but it must also be constantly evaluated and adapted. The potential problem is that, besides unique individual characteristics, athletes' and teams' needs are also constantly changing, demanding continuous observation and assessment. Sometimes the situation forces coaches to improvise and refine their intervention through trial and error.

6. Although no linear pattern exists, coaches must make an effort to unveil what is really effective coaching, such as understanding which plans and actions led to the actual outcomes and performances. Young athletes do not share the same mental models with coaches, nor do they have the same values and expectations. After identifying a problem and developing a plan for change, coaches need to observe carefully eventual discrepancies between suggested actions and actual responses in order to adjust to new situations. All details—whether biological (for instance, growth spurt during adolescence can alter the tactical role of the athlete) or emotional (a bad relation with a teammate affects tactical reasoning)—are important.

7. Effective coaching does not mean to copy effective elite coaches. Coaching at the highest levels is similar to a performative art. Coaches do stage behaviors, events, and even relationships, sometimes using the media space. Their deliberate purpose is to manipulate the athletes' attention to specific aspects or increase or release emotional stressors. However, the ultimate goal for professional and elite athletes is to win competitions, which is not necessarily the case with athletes at the youth sport level.

Professional teams also use a resource known as walkthrough. When a team has no time or necessity to have a formal workout, athletes and coaches can gather before the competition and walk in a park or sit in a quiet place. In this setting, athletes can verbalize and discuss the tasks they are expected to perform a few hours later. When possible, coaches of young athletes could use this model to stimulate procedural knowledge and awareness of the complexity of sport competition, which is in line with Vygotski's (1986) concept about the role of oral speech as a learning tool to develop higher levels of reasoning.

Guidelines for Athletes

Traditionally, athletes are expected to follow the coaches' instructions and corrections. Especially in the learning and specialization years, coaches mediate and translate the knowledge about sport in a way that fits the athletes' capacities and needs. However, it is always a bilateral process that must evolve with time. Nurturing and developing an environment that encourages dialogue, verbal interaction, and mutual understanding is a crucial task for every educator and therefore for every coach too.

Success Story 3: Adult Volleyball

S., a volleyball coach of an adult team, designed a four-on-four game with a constraint that resulted in a momentaneous numeric superiority for one of the teams. Without any instruction from the coach, the groups of four played the game for four weeks, twice a week.

The coach recorded video of all the games, and the players had free access to the recordings. S. observed and registered the solutions implemented by the players to exploit the advantages or to hide the weaknesses when they were outnumbered. In the last week of the experiment, S. asked the players to verbalize the rationale of their tactical choices and the effect they thought they had on their performance.

Based on the gathered information, for the rest of the season S. started to debate with the team the game plans for the next matches, asking for suggestions on how to approach the match and how to adjust to the opponent.

Contrary to the preceding case, in which the coach reacted to unexpected information, S. was proactive, provoking the players to think and talk about their reasoning. For the coach, it represented a priceless opportunity to develop a plan for change in close cooperation with the players.

Conclusion

Coaches can appeal to available tools to develop athlete capacity to think and plan. Technological resources offer new fields for experimentation and practical intervention. For example, Price and colleagues (2017) proposed the use of a video games approach to develop understanding of the game and the planning skills. However, it is not a matter of instruments or technological sophistication; all stems from a deliberate purpose of the coach, who has a clear idea and a plan. This idea is consistent with Cushion (2018), who alerts against the risk of conformism in reflective practice. Coaches need to plan for change, but they should not treat it as a bureaucratic task arising from a coach education program or from an inventory of coaches' need-to-do-tasks. The necessity of planning is born in real practice and not in a coaching textbook. The act of translation and implementation at times results in simplifications and reductive formulations, which can be not only unavoidable but in fact desirable if it makes the concepts comprehensible to the athletes for which it is intended.

A crucial problem is yet to be solved: the assessment of the planned interventions, and the individual and team progress toward superior levels of reasoning. The centrality of time represents an additional factor of uncertainty. Furthermore, development is nonlinear and follows an individual pace, making predictions almost impossible. For example, for the player mentioned in success story 1, it took six months for him to figure out how complex the game is. Notably, however, in the same six months, his teammates were not able to reach that stage of reasoning.

The path to expertise in sport takes several years of learning. The vast majority of criteria for the athletes' evaluation are external and related to competitive outcomes. Coaches must observe, collect, and register all the oral, written, or video information they can. It is the only way to assess how the planned intervention is perceived, processed, and eventually adopted by its recipients. The athletes' perspective and beliefs about their participation in sport are key factors in their development.

Coach education programs emphasize the need for coaches to build a strong personal coaching philosophy that is based on values and a deep knowledge of the specific sport. Usually planning is framed by a successful model. However, models are abstractions; although abstractions are useful, they do not mirror the changing dynamics of the real world.

What really matters is the outcome of the process of planning and learning, not the beginning of the process itself. In this regard, more experimentation is necessary. Because the period of planning is a long-term one, cross-sectional studies are almost always useless. As researchers in action, coaches are the only ones who can do it during the season. Coaches and athletes are pragmatic people who are deeply interested in ideas that work. As this chapter has shown, you can seek inspiration in other scientific areas and take a step further to help athletes think and help them enjoy intelligent participation.

PART III | ENHANCING TEAM PERFORMANCE POTENTIAL

11 | Leadership

Andrew Cruickshank
Grey Matters UK

Throughout the world of high-level sport, leadership is credited as one of the main reasons—and sometimes the sole reason—for the success or failure of individual athletes, teams, programs, or entire organizations. Indeed, leadership provides a common point of conversation for those in most domains of sport as well as for those observing and commenting from the outside (e.g., parents, media, fans, broader public, politicians). The effect of this common conversation can quickly become apparent in organizational decisions. For example, the rate that many professional sport teams fire head coaches or general managers is testament to how quickly leadership issues can escalate, especially given that firing people at the top level (e.g., an NBA head coach or NFL general manager) can cost clubs tens of millions of dollars. Interestingly, *losing the dressing room* (when a manager's leadership style has lost impact with the players) is cited as a much more common reason for these decisions than lack of technical or tactical know-how.

The firing of head coaches or managers in professional sport is just one example. Certainly, the importance of leadership is evident across most (if not all) corners of organized, high-level sport. Whether it be a CEO, a board member, a performance director, a head coach, an academy manager, a captain, or an informal leader or cultural architect, the day-to-day experience of almost everyone is affected by leadership.

In this respect, one reason leadership is so important in high-level sport is that leaders are presumed to have a major impact on their followers. Another reason is that many societies are innately interested in leadership; being a leader or being led are two of the most common experiences humans face.

Relevance

Why exactly is leadership such an important factor when it comes to enhancing training, development, and performance in high-level sport? To address this question, it's useful to begin with this key point: leadership is about influence. In other words, leadership is how one person (or group of people) affects another person (or group of people). Indeed, in any scenario where at least two individuals work toward a shared goal, interpersonal influences play a major role in how a group functions and what it achieves. Success, stagnation, or failure in the largest elite sport organizations, all the way down to a single coach–athlete pairing, can be traced to the way in which people were influenced along the way. In this respect, all groups can clearly benefit from influences that support optimal development and performance. On the flip side, all groups can also clearly suffer from influences that don't support (or actively inhibit) optimal development and performance.

When viewing leadership through the lens of influence, the importance of leadership should therefore come into sharp focus: in group settings, people are all influenced to some degree by others. In sport, as with most environments, this influence is often established and delivered through formal

Andres Alonso/NCAA Photos via Getty Images

Leadership is about influence: how one person (or a group of people) influences others.

leadership roles—positions of influence—which almost everybody involved in high-level sport encounters on some scale. For example, high-level athletes can be influenced by a host of formal leaders, such as the beliefs of the team's captain, the philosophy of the coach, the knowledge of the sport science and medicine coordinator, the funding and selection criteria determined by the sport's performance director or leadership team, and the rules decided by the sport's national or international governing body. In a coach's position, influences on an athlete's work might arrive from the perspective of other specialist coaches on the coaching team, the coach development manager in the organization, or the leader of the national coach accreditation system. In summary, formal leaders can have a big say on how a group functions and what it achieves, in part because they occupy positions in which a level of power is provided to them. Indeed, the ability to influence others is intertwined with the power the person has to do so. Put simply, this power can be provided (as a product of being placed in a formal role) or acquired (as a product of the ongoing work done and the relationships formed with others). In this sense, considering leadership in the environment is also relevant because those who have been provided power by a group's top-level leaders (e.g., a head coach, performance director) can say a lot about the likely direction and way of working that is to follow.

Significantly, however, it is also important to recognize that formal leadership is just one side of the coin and much leadership (influence) in groups, teams, or organizations is also established and delivered through informal channels. For example, many senior athletes may not fulfill formal leadership roles, but their influence on a group can be sizable. From a head coach's view, other coaches or sport science staff further down the organizational chart might play a key role in shaping group dynamics. In short, influence can arrive from many people in many places; it may come through formal or informal channels; and it may enable or inhibit the achievement of goals.

In this sense, the effect of leadership on development and performance in high level-sport, in the majority of cases, is inescapable. Other people regularly influence the actions of athletes. This influence often is delivered through the direct views or actions of leaders, such as the influence of a coach's decisions on what to focus on in a particular block of training or the influence of a captain's feedback to teammates during breaks in a game. However, leadership can also be impactful by its absence, especially when it appears to be missing from those in formal leadership roles. For example, consider the influence of a coach who *hasn't* decided what to focus on in a particular block of training or a captain who *doesn't* provide feedback to teammates at halftime in a game. In this way, the members of any group can be strongly influenced by what others *do* and also by what they *don't*. Keep in mind that not doing something as a leader is not inherently negative or wrong. It might be wrong in a case where the best solution requires the leader to do something. However, sometimes a proactively hands-off approach or intentionally laissez-faire style might be useful if the goal is to provide opportunities for others to take greater ownership of the group's actions (e.g., athletes contributing to the training block design, other players on the team taking responsibility for planning the second half approach). In short, the intention and context matter. Therefore, the significance of a leader's skills in professional judgment and decision making (PJDM) comes strongly to the fore (Cruickshank, 2019; Cruickshank & Collins, 2016).

Three points are useful to keep in mind through the rest of the chapter. First, leadership is about the way people are influenced in pursuit of a collective goal. Second, this influence can come from many different people in many different places. Third, what constitutes effective leadership depends on the context. The following section focuses on what is known about leadership in relation to improving performance in the context of these three features.

What We Know

As suggested in the previous section, leadership can be a complicated process; it has many moving parts, and the job is never done. Nevertheless, some sound, evidence-based principles can guide the work of those in leadership roles. They include the following:

1. Optimizing clarity of the group's goals (what we are trying to achieve)
2. Harnessing influence from across a group (not just leaving leadership to the leaders)
3. Addressing and enhancing both the cognitive side and the behavioral side of leadership (recognizing that leading requires a specialized set of thinking skills in addition to a specialized set of behavioral skills)

A host of other factors plays an important role in leadership, such as the group's identity (Slater et al., 2014) and effective followership (Chaleff, 2003). In other words, the three points listed earlier are part of a much bigger picture. However, the information that follows will help you later evaluate and enhance your roles or experiences against these important selected parts, or it will offer you a starting point to explore these and other areas.

Goal Clarity: What Are We Actually Leading Toward?

As with any performance endeavor, those operating in high-level sport as athletes, coaches, managers, or support practitioners are guided and motivated by goals. Indeed, much research has highlighted the importance of goals for directing attention and effort to the most relevant factors during development, preparation, and ultimate performance. In this respect, the promotion of *goal*-directed or *task*-relevant behavior is inherent across many of the tools recommended by psychology specialists to aid peak performance (as demonstrated throughout this book). For example, the essence of most approaches to performance enhancement, such as competition planning, preperformance routines, reset processes, or communication and coordination strategies, is to encourage athletes or teams to focus on things that are most enabling of a good performance and limit the potential to focus on things that are less relevant, entirely irrelevant, or directly damaging. In this way, leadership is no different. Central to successful leading (or following) is clarity of the goal and the task (cf. Steinmann et al., 2018).

Indeed, if the role of a leader is to influence others in pursuit of a collective goal, then being clear on that goal is essential. It should be the focal point of the entire leadership process whether the formal leaders are in place for a short or long time. In this vein, work on shared mental models (SMMs) has emphasized the value of a shared understanding of the goal and the task across a group or team (Cannon-Bowers et al., 1993; see also chapter 13). Alongside SMMs of who team members are and how they can interact to best effect, SMMs of the goal and task offer a frame for all the work a group undertakes; in other words, it is essential to know who the other team members are and how all members need to interact *relative to the goal and task*. Without this shared understanding, teams are much more likely to experience challenges to their collective cohesion (e.g., through social loafing, personal agendas) and individual role clarity.

Along these lines, much research on leadership in sport has identified the role played by the leader or team's vision (Vallée & Bloom, 2005). This role refers to the future-focused, aspirational, big-picture goal that the team and individuals within it are guided to work toward. In fact, a long-term vision is a foundation of many theories and models of leadership, including one of the most popular in recent times within sport-based research, called the transformational style of leading (Bass, 1990). Considered against the previously mentioned framework of SMMs, transformational leadership uses this logical emphasis: *An effective leader is someone who can help their group to see and buy into a shared goal and task.* However, it is important to note that this long-term vision alone is usually not enough for optimal or sustained success. More specifically, although a long-term vision sets the big-picture destination, it does not necessarily offer the roadmap by which the team will get there. In this respect, high-level athletes, coaches, and support personnel tend to quickly work out leaders (many of whom could be described as transformational) who have ridden the vision wave but carry little else to back it up. In short, it has lots of style, little substance.

At this point, it is useful to reflect on periodized or nested planning. (For more detailed discussions, see chapters 1, 15, and 18.) A core principle of designing a long-term program of work (which leadership also requires) is that every point of action is nested in a three-tier structure that reflects a macro, meso, and micro level of work. Therefore, a leader's or group's vision can be viewed as the macro-level goal; in other words, it's the big picture. However, when this big picture isn't supported by clear meso- and micro-level goals (the finer and the finest levels of detail that make up the big picture), individuals can easily lose sight of or belief in where the group is headed. In this way, clarity on how the group is to achieve the overall goal becomes fuzzy if not entirely opaque. Of course, the opposite also occurs; some leaders are excellent at devising micro- and meso-level goals and plans (e.g., the plan for this season and its subphases), but they are less skilled at seeing and selling a long-term vision. Some leaders are excellent at macro and micro levels, but they struggle to identify and stitch together the meso-level steps. If a group is to be optimally led (or influenced), clarity of macro-level goals is essential, but clarity on meso- and micro-level goals is also key. Simply put, you need to know where you're aspiring to go *and* the series of steps that will take you there. Clarity on these steps can also play a big part in helping leaders to share and promote the group's philosophy (see chapter 1).

Harnessing Influence From Across a Group

One of the most common errors in reviewing and enhancing group performance in sport is the degree to which emphasis is placed on the contribution of formal leaders and the role of leadership itself. Leadership is crucial to the function and performance of a group, team, or organization, and so are formal leaders. However, the balance of input that goes into these areas is often linked to challenges in a group's dynamic. As noted earlier, much research on leadership in sport has focused on formal leaders such as coaches and head coaches and those in management, directorial, or other top leadership positions. If leadership is fundamentally about influence, the net needs to be spread much wider (Fransen et al., 2020).

Indeed, if leadership is about influencing a group in the pursuit of its goals, then it is crucial to recognize that influence can come from many places (see figure 12.1). Also, if leadership occurs at multiple levels (macro, meso, micro), it is logical that different individuals will be better suited to leading on different parts of the overall agenda or even at different times within the same agenda. In this way, the importance of distributed leadership (delegation) comes to the fore. Put simply, *delegation* means getting the best people to do the job that's needed at each particular time instead of asking the same people to do everything all the time. Delegation is important because some leadership jobs will not match up with the skills people have. For example, consider the needs of a team heading into a competitive match. The team needs leadership of the game plan, leadership of building confidence in that plan, leadership of building confidence to execute that plan, and leadership of the team's energy and enthusiasm on the day. During the game, the team needs leadership of their execution of the plan, leadership of their response to problems that the game presents, and leadership of many other areas (e.g., communications with the referee, coaches on the sidelines, etc.). In most cases, one person cannot perform all those leadership duties on their own—certainly not at an optimal level.

Other related research on leadership in sport has explored the role played by informal leaders—those who have significant influence on a group without an official leader title or explicit responsibility. Sometimes regardless of their alignment with those in formal positions, informal leaders can do much to tip the scale in one direction or another. Indeed, if team culture reflects what is usual or expected for a given group, these informal influences are a significant part of the equation (see chapter 12, Optimizing Informal Leadership and Cultural Architects; Railo, 1986).

Covering Both Sides of Leadership: The Role of Thinking Skills

As suggested earlier, effective leadership in groups, teams, programs, or organizations is much more than the role played by formal leaders. It is also much more than how leaders (formal or informal) behave. Indeed, hopefully one of the key messages from this chapter so far is that effective leadership is also determined by the way that leaders think.

More specifically, the ability to act coherently on micro, meso, and macro levels, plus the ability to recognize who are the best people to lead different actions at different times, clearly requires a degree of skilled thinking. To date, however, much research in sport (and in other fields) has tended to focus on the behavioral side of leadership often studied through the lens of certain behavioral styles (e.g., transformational leadership, authentic leadership). Of course, behavior-focused research is relevant and useful. However, as a field, the cognitive skills of leaders in high-level sport have been somewhat underconsidered (Cruickshank & Collins, 2016). Fortunately, research elsewhere can give us a positive steer when it comes to identifying the thinking skills that leaders benefit from (see parallel messages in Cruickshank et al., 2018).

More specifically, research across a range of professions has consistently indicated that expertise is reflected by an individual's ability to do the following:

- Understand *why* a situation has arisen and *how* each part of the puzzle fits together (rather than just *what* the situation is or *what* the parts of the puzzle are).
- Explore and weigh options before deciding on a course of action, including the use of pros and cons trade-offs.
- Develop hypotheses on how certain courses of action will pan out and anticipate what might happen or what will be needed next (i.e., mental simulation).
- Use long-term memory, mental models, perceptual skills, and thinking routines to continually gather, translate, and integrate the most relevant information as situations play out (and get rid of what is less relevant or irrelevant).

- Monitor the impact of their actions (including a comparison with similar prior situations), and revise their strategies or create new strategies when needed.
- Detect early signs that a course of action needs to be adapted or replaced.

While this list points to the complexities of leadership, the bottom line is that expertise in people-dependent roles requires skills in thinking effectively and not just behaving effectively. Indeed, a hallmark of effective leaders is not just the positive outcomes that they deliver but also the relatively few big mistakes that they make; this number can rely on luck, but mostly it depends on the ability to think multiple moves ahead. Consider leadership as another type of performance. Leaders must be skilled as top performers in thinking-heavy activities that are characterized by their ability to work ahead of the curve (e.g., the expert chess player, politician, surgeon, or stockbroker). As such, a focus on your thinking skills should also be at the forefront when it comes to assessing and optimizing your work as a leader or the work of those who lead you.

Assessment

Whether an athlete, coach, manager, director, sport psychology consultant, or any other practitioner in high-level sport, everyone can lead in at least some way and for at least some of the time. Indeed, this leadership may not just be engaged internally (with others involved in the sport) but also externally (e.g., the leadership of a parental or family input into your sport). In this vein, this section considers how to assess the way you or others in your environment are leading in terms of the specific messages presented so far. First, the following text highlights some general approaches to evaluation.

As conveyed throughout this book, the accuracy of any assessment on matters relating to psychology is boosted by using a combination of methods. Broadly speaking, these methods fall under the categories of observation, conversation, or psychometrics. From a psychometric perspective, if you seek extra information on how you are perceived to lead, you may find value in deploying questionnaires. These questionnaires, such as the Differentiated Transformational Leadership Inventory, offer a measure of how a person's general leadership behavior is perceived by others (Callow et al., 2009). For balance, consider how the bright side of leadership behavior balances with the dark side, with each being evaluated by different instruments (Hogan & Hogan, 2009). While it hasn't been a primary feature of this chapter, if you are interested in exploring how the dark side relates to the bright side of leadership, look at some of the authors' previous work in high-level sport (Cruickshank & Collins, 2015) as well as work in other fields that has criticized the excessive and unrealistic positivity of some leadership theories (e.g., Alvesson & Einola, 2019). In short, effective leadership is certainly not as clear-cut as it might seem. Concluding on the theme of psychometrics, some readers might like to use tools that offer a more indirect evaluation of leadership through assessing linked outcomes, such as the Group Environment Questionnaire (Eys et al., 2007) or the Fletcher-Lyons Collective Resilience Scale (FLCRS) (Lyons et al., 2016). In conclusion, a few measures are available to do the job you're after. Keep in mind that asking those you lead to fill in a questionnaire on how you lead them is prone to more than a few biases.

Assessing Goal Clarity

When assessing a group's goal clarity, a number of factors need consideration. One of the easiest ways to check for levels of sharedness is to simply ask individuals what they think the group's goals are and assess whether the answers are consistent with each other. Remember to consider the three levels of leading; in other words, how clear are individuals on a macro level (e.g., what the team is trying to achieve this season), on a meso level (e.g., what the team is trying to achieve in this block of the season), and on a micro level (e.g., what the team is trying to achieve this week)?

Not all individuals need to be clear on goals for all three levels, especially given that better performances often occur when things are kept simple. Therefore, for some levels (usually the meso), some individuals don't need to know the goals; they might even be better off not knowing. However, if a group is to grow and perform optimally, being clear on what you do know (or need to know) is crucial. Lack of clarity is a common pitfall for newly appointed formal athlete leaders (e.g., team captains). More specifically, through the enthusiasm to lead on the team's long-term vision and different phases of the season, they risk spending too much time at macro and meso levels, losing sight of where they can contribute most, namely, the micro level (e.g., the next game). Similarly, many coaches, managers, and directors can succumb to the opposite: they focus too much on the next game and lose sight of the next phase and the whole season. In this respect, it's worth reflecting on the time spent in each of the three levels of leadership in terms of (a) the role that you've been tasked to fulfill; (b) where your greatest contribution to the group lies; and (c) the time of the competitive cycle. In short, are you working in the right area(s), at the right time, for the right duration?

Assessing Influence From Across the Group

As stressed in the Relevance and What We Know sections, many different people in many different places can influence how a group, team, or organization works and performs. As such, considering how leadership or influence is currently spread across your group, team, or organization is also important for maximizing development and performance in the future. To support this knowledge, try a version of a process known as social network analysis (Wasserman & Faust, 1994).

More specifically, this approach involves creating a visual map of where individuals sit within a group and its subgroups. Many use this process to assess relationships (e.g., *Who are the key individuals in my social network? How strong are my relationships with them? And which ones do I need to address or prioritize most?*). From a leadership angle, emphasis can instead (or also) be placed on influence. For example, figure 11.1 shows a spread of all individuals in a leader's group including those who are typically positive influencers (those in circles), those who are typically negative influencers (those in squares), and those who are typically neutral followers (those in triangles); alternatively, the same shape may be used for all individuals (e.g., a circle) but with different-colored outlines or shading used to denote more positive, negative, or neutral influence. Individuals are also all placed in one of three surrounding circles that reflect their closeness to the leader either structurally (the proximity of their position to the leader in the organizational chart) or based on their regularity of contact (how often they interact with

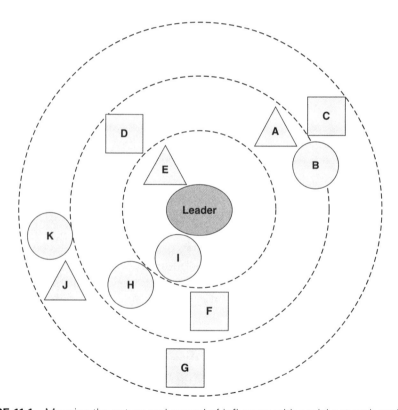

FIGURE 11.1 Mapping the nature and spread of influence with social network analysis.

the leader). In short, this closeness depicts the opportunities to push coherence from the center out and, in the case of positive influencers farther away from the center, opportunities to push coherence from the outside in. Taken against the full picture, the leader can then reflect on the spread of influence across the group, chances being missed to spread (or push) influence further, and threats of negative influencers (or, if positive influencers or neutral followers aren't given enough or the best chance to contribute, then leading to demotivation). Ultimately, assessing in simple ways such as this one can shine a light on key influences in groups regardless of whether these individuals hold formal positions of influence or not.

Assessing the Thinking Skills of Leadership

When assessing the cognitive side of leadership, it's worth returning to the list of cognitive skills in the What We Know section. More specifically, consider these questions from either your own leadership or in relation to the leaders in your environment:

- How much time is spent trying to understand *why* the situation faced is this particular one? And how much time is spent trying to understand why alternative situations have *not* occurred?
- How much time is spent exploring and weighing the pros and cons of different options before deciding on a course of action?
- How often are hypotheses formed, or waymarks identified, that allow for judgments to be made on how effective a decision has been?
- How much time is committed to anticipating how different courses of action might play out, including an identification of their likely roadblocks or derailers?
- How often are solutions to challenges singular solutions (We need to do *this one thing*) versus combination solutions (We need to do *x, y,* and *z*)?
- How clear are the sources of relevant feedback and less relevant or irrelevant feedback before a course of action is rolled out (e.g., *These* things will give us the best indication if we've made a good decision, and *those* things less so)?
- How often is the course of action tweaked or adapted based on incoming feedback and comparisons to previous similar actions?
- How often are early warning signs recognized and responded to (that tell us a course of action might not be working in the intended way)?

In short, using this list for evaluation can help shed some light on the general volume, nature, and balance of thinking done as a leader and where future progress might come from.

Optimization

Now that you have evaluated the way leadership stacks up in some key areas, what is next for enhancing approaches or experiences? This section looks at each of the main themes of the chapter through the lens of optimization.

Optimizing Goal Clarity

As described earlier, in terms of making progress, two desirable outcomes for the overall direction of a group are that it be *clear* and *shared*. Other chapters in this book (1, 13, and 14, and elements of others) describe some of the key processes required to promote enhancing the levels of shared-ness. As such, clarity is the main focus of this section.

Leadership often works best when sufficient clarity exists on the goals that a group, team, program, or organization is being led to achieve. In this respect, issues usually arise when the direction given is either too broad or too detailed; generally, aiming for a just-right balance is key. Asking people to work to too much detail means that they often lose sight of the big picture as well as get frustrated by being micromanaged. On the other hand, asking people to work to too little detail means that they approach the big picture in a way that each individual person believes is best, which usually leads to a mix of inconsistent approaches and much confusion for those on the receiving end (often athletes). Issues with this approach generally worsen when

Cameron Spencer/Getty Images

Leadership works best when sufficient clarity exists on the goals that a team is working to achieve.

performance drops. A losing streak is a great way to expose the cracks in relationships that are often covered—or at least less obvious—when winning and positivity dominate. Therefore, for a group to work as a coherent team while not stifling the autonomy of individuals (see chapter 5), it makes sense for leaders to put particular effort into promoting meso-level clarity. To illustrate this idea, the following success story describes an approach that was taken to establish this balance with one sport's coaching team.

Success Story: Enhancing Meso-Level Clarity in a National Sport's Performance System and Pathway

When it comes to long-term psychobehavioral development, a lot of research indicates that athletes are best served by systems that provide an appropriately coherent experience as they progress (see chapter 14 for more detail). Against this backdrop, colleagues and I have helped a national sport organization to optimize the coherence of coaching throughout their pathway on a psychobehavioral level from early junior all the way to top senior international in both male and female competition. This project aimed to best connect the pathway's micro-level goals (to improve specific psychobehavioral skills in the next year) to its macro-level goals (to develop senior athletes with a certain psychobehavioral profile) through building more clarity on its meso-level goals (the major psychobehavioral challenges that athletes need to overcome in the early junior phase, then late junior phase, then senior phase). In other words, the aim was to help coaches be clear on the critical challenges that their athletes need to overcome so that they could equip them with the best skills for the job (rather than provide skills for a different or less critical job).

To achieve this clarity, the project first focused on establishing the psychobehavioral profile desired of senior athletes (the macro-level goal) or their levels of adaptability, independence, and resilience (Webb et al., 2016). From here, emphasis was placed on identifying the common and critical challenges that most athletes experience and need to negotiate at each stage of the pathway to build toward these ultimate levels of adaptability, independence, and resilience (or, more generally, to fulfill their potential, whatever level it ends up being). More specifically, this process involved each coaching group across the pathway identifying the challenges that had ended, stalled, or hastened the progression of athletes at that stage in the past plus an audit of the challenges currently presented at that stage. Subsequently, a map of the sport's common and critical challenges up and down the full pathway's stages was developed; it was a tool to support meso-level clarity (we know what we're trying to achieve in our part of the big picture). Subsequently, this map was then used as a base in the sport's efforts to optimally align its coaching systems, processes, and practices throughout the pathway (e.g., athlete profiling; see chapter 1) and to inform and integrate the inputs of other stakeholders (e.g., funding agencies, club coaches, parents).

Optimizing Influence From Across the Group

As stressed throughout this chapter, everyone in a group has the potential to influence the way that group functions, develops, and performs at least to some degree. Of course, in most groups, this influence tends to come from certain individuals or subgroups more than others. In terms of direction, this influence can be broadly classed as more group-oriented, more self-oriented, or somewhere in between. For a group to be as successful, the weight of influence clearly needs to lean toward the more group-oriented end of the continuum. In this respect, most groups contain individuals who are naturally more group-oriented than others. However, this fact shouldn't be taken for granted, and it's important that these individuals know the precise contribution that they make and are recognized and rewarded for it (see chapter 14, Operational Principles and Practice). It is also important that efforts be made to secure the best group-oriented contribution of those in the in-between camp and the more self-oriented camp. In short, the more people who influence other people to put the group's goals first, the more likely the group's goals will be met.

Figure 11.2 offers a simple model that can be used to grow the overall leadership of a group. As shown, this model is based on the idea that positively influencing a group depends on individuals being clear on what exactly to influence (or the opportunity to influence), plus the motivation, skills, and confidence to do so. Of course, a number of other factors play a role as well, particularly in relation to how the leader is perceived by others. In this regard, the model is intended to offer a simple and practical starting point rather than the basis for any comprehensive assessment.

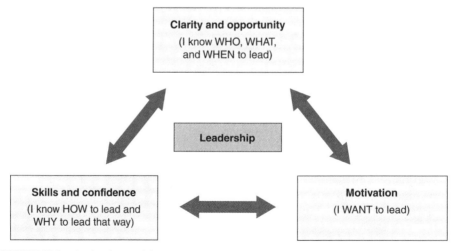

FIGURE 11.2   A simple model to assess and grow leadership.

Usefully, this model can be applied in a number of different ways. In particular, consider the following three:

1. The model can be used to identify and harness individuals who might be best placed to influence the group in the here and now. In short, these individuals are those who check the motivation, skills, and confidence boxes, but they just need a bit more clarity on what exactly they should lead on or they need more opportunities to do so.

2. The model also can be used to solve problems, such as when individuals who know what they should influence and have the opportunities to do so do not deliver. In this respect, the model encourages you to consider whether it might be due to motivation, skills, or confidence issues (or a combination), allowing for subsequent actions to be identified and progressed.

3. Finally, the model can be used for leadership development, whereby individuals can be evaluated according to the three conditions and then supported to close the gaps that might be limiting their leadership potential.

Optimizing the Thinking Skills of Leadership

In the third theme of this chapter, the same list of cognitive skills from earlier should provide you with a basis for moving forward. If you feel like you don't use many of these features or could use them better, then one of the first steps might be to simply create more time and space in which to do so. Indeed, all the features relate to the time that is *proactively* created, then committed, to planning and reflecting on your decisions. (Note that all of these features can also help with making good decisions in any area of your training, development, or performance.)

Time is a precious commodity, especially in high-level sport. For some, it might not be about creating more time and space but being more efficient with the time and space that you have. For example, are you missing any chances to use travel time more productively? Also, how much time is set aside throughout your week or day for slowed-down planning and reflection? Many leaders end up in meeting after meeting after meeting or, put in the frame of this chapter, stuck in the micro level of leadership. It is striking how many leaders made significant progress on meso- and macro-level agendas during the COVID-19 pandemic—a situation that, for many in high-level sport, presented a lot of time and space for slowed-down thinking. Of course, the volumes of time and space that most experienced are clearly not afforded in normal circumstances; however, the pandemic taught many that these resources can—and should—be prioritized over lots of less essential (or even unnecessary) activities so that groups, teams, and organizations can work more effectively, efficiently, and ambitiously.

Shifting from preevent planning to postevent reflection, consider trying the Big 5 structure that Collins and Collins (2021) successfully trialed with coaches. In this approach, individuals are encouraged to develop their declarative knowledge base and future PJDM skills by considering the following five questions:

1. What happened, and what did you do?
2. What other options were available?
3. What made you choose the option you did?
4. What would have made you choose one of the other options?
5. What would you have done if the situation had started to play out differently? What would you do next time?

As Collins and Collins found in their study, this structure offers a useful structure for reflection and developing PJDM skills on an individual level, but significant impact also arrives when it's used on a group level. So, just as leadership works best when it's delivered collectively, this structure can also be used to help groups to reflect collectively and develop their PJDM skills collectively.

Conclusion

As noted at the start of this chapter, leadership plays a central role in the development and performance of most, if not all, involved in high-level sport. To help leaders consider, assess, and optimize their approaches or the approaches of those followed, focus was placed on three main areas: goal clarity, influence across a group, and the thinking skills that positively drive all leadership-related judgments, decisions, and actions. The consequent messages have offered a starting point to make improvements in your own environment, something extra to reflect against, or something to reinforce and refine all the good work currently being done. Whatever the scenario (and in line with the overall purpose of this book), now it is up to you.

12 | High-Performing Cultures

Geir Jordet
Norwegian School of Sport Sciences

Rune Giske
University of Stavanger

For the All Blacks, the highly successful national rugby union team of New Zealand, doing the famous haka dance is a consistent pregame tradition. This ritual has become a powerful carrier of history, tradition, and roots; it unites and energizes the team, and it intimidates their opponents (Kerr, 2013). Another foundation for the All Blacks culture is the so-called "No Dickheads" philosophy (Kerr, 2013). According to All Blacks mental coach Gilbert Enoka, dickheads are "putting themselves ahead of the team, people who think they're entitled to things or expect the rules to be different for them, people operating deceitfully in the dark, or being unnecessarily loud about their work." The culture of the team is for players to directly address and remove any such behaviors in teammates without necessarily bringing it up through management (Austin, 2017, para. 3). Similarly, on the other side of the globe, one of the mottos of the men's alpine ski team of Norway is "No Jerks Allowed." As one of the skiers, Kjetil Jansrud, explains, "We believe there is no good explanation for why you have to be a jerk to be a good athlete. We just won't have that kind of thing on our team" (Ingle, 2018, para. 9). Such rituals and internal team rules are good expressions of high-performing cultures in sport.

Hannah Peters/Getty Images

As mentioned in chapter 6, the New Zealand rugby squad's pregame haka is a ritual that unites and energizes the team.

Relevance

The importance of culture is perhaps best described by this metaphor: If members of a team are fish, their culture is the water surrounding them (Hammerich & Lewis, 2013). Culture is a construct of social cognition that can be defined as "the shared values, beliefs, expectations, and practices across the members and generations of a defined group" (Cruickshank & Collins, 2012, p. 340). This chapter refers to the term *culture* as both about the environment (including infrastructure, buildings, and artifacts) and about what is socially agreed on, held in common, and shared among the participants in a group.

High-performing cultures occur when these environments, values, and practices lead to and support performance. Specifically, high-performing cultures lead to short-term performance, persist over time, are independent of team results (which can fluctuate even though performance is high), and lead to consistent long-term performance relative to the resources they operate with (Cruickshank, 2019; Cruickshank & Collins, 2012).

This chapter reviews what is known about high-performing culture in sport. It addresses ways that coaches, leaders, managers, athletes, and sport psychology consultants can assess, change, and optimize the culture in groups, teams, or organizations regardless of how big they are. Even two people working together create and live in their own culture.

What We Know

Compared with organizational psychology, few studies have been done on high-performing cultures in sport (Cruickshank & Collins, 2012), and most of them were published relatively recently (since the 2010s). Nevertheless, some research has accumulated, and two review studies summarize this knowledge well (Maitland et al., 2015; Wagstaff & Burton-Wylie, 2018).

Schein (1999) features three levels of organizational culture: artifacts, espoused values, and underlying assumptions. *Artifacts* are observable by people outside an organization; they include buildings, facilities, logos, photos on the wall, stories, anecdotes, rituals, ways of communicating, and language. Even though everyone can see or hear these artifacts, the meaning that the members of a team attach to them will vary. *Espoused values* are values and beliefs that are articulated by leaders, but it is also important to consider values that are expressed and shared between members of an organization. *Underlying assumptions* indicate the core or essence of the organization's culture. These assumptions are often assumed without thinking, and individuals typically are unable to explicitly articulate them.

With respect to form, culture can be manifested in different ways, such as through jargon, myths, stories, legends, folklore, jokes, slogans, rituals, ceremonies, celebrations, traditions, heroes, rules, taboos, dress, and physical arrangements (Martin & Frost, 1996), which can be categorized in symbols, language, narratives, and practices (Wagstaff & Burton-Wylie, 2018). The following sections review a selection of studies from high-level sport. These studies have identified factors of high-performing cultures and ways to change culture.

Elite Sport Cultures

Johnson and colleagues (2013) conducted 20 in-depth interviews with past and present All Blacks team captains and coaches to study the core values of the All Blacks in the period of sustained team success between 1950 and 2010. The general results showed a culture characterized by pride in winning, pride in legacy, and embracing change (emphasizing innovation and change in the way the game is being played). The strong emphasis on history and tradition—the All Blacks legacy—combined with a willingness to innovate, adapt, and learn, is deeply embedded in the values and core assumptions of the All Blacks. Further, Cole and Martin (2018) examined the culture in a champion New Zealand rugby team. Among their findings were the recognition of culture as important for team success, including establishing and reinforcing core values, simple and relevant themes that incorporate these core values, informal rituals that are reinforced, a strong informal influence by the players themselves, and a flat organizational structure based on transformational leadership.

Based on an ecological approach, Larsen and colleagues (2013) studied environmental factors contributing to the success of a Danish boys' under-17 soccer team. Many features, such as a strong, open, informal, and cohesive culture, were described; additional features included clear physical manifestations of the desired direction, such as displayed pictures of old club legends and great historical wins as well as trophies visible in the halls, cafeteria, and tactical room. Desired behaviors and values were publicly posted in documents and in the locker rooms. A holistic approach was valued; focus was on player and character development, professionalism, a strong family-like atmosphere, and strong work ethic. Larsen and colleagues (2020) conducted a comparable study at Ajax's youth academy in Amsterdam, which has been successful in developing future male professional players. Visible artifacts, as well as tightly corresponding values and basic assumptions that characterize the entire environment, consistently focused on developing young, talented players for the senior team.

Studies of high-performing cultures have also been conducted with groups of Scandinavian athletes competing in individual sports. Henriksen and colleagues studied environmental factors that influence success in Danish sailing (2010a), a Swedish track and field team (2010b), and a kayak environment in Norway that was known for developing elite senior athletes from its juniors (2011). A common cultural characteristic is that excellence can be achieved by cooperation and open sharing of knowledge. Moreover, they highlighted a strong team orientation with an emphasis on inclusiveness and more passionate focus on performance improvement than on results.

Further, Junggren and colleagues (2018) examined the culture in a swimming club in Denmark that had a record of delivering swimmers to the Danish national team. In addition to the findings from the previously mentioned Scandinavian cultures, the results highlight central values such as long-term development, individualized training, and autonomy as the basis for progress; however, studies, social life, and family are also important.

Henriksen and colleagues (2013) turned the standard research recipe around; they examined a Danish golf club that consistently had limited athletic success in order to see if it would be characterized by features often seen in successful environments. The study revealed that the golf environment had a lack of supportive training groups and role models and an incoherent organizational culture. Among the observed artifacts and behaviors were that often athletes and coaches were late for training, coaches would leave warm-up and strength and conditioning up to the athletes, the structure of the training was loose, and no sanctions were applied if quality or adherence were lacking.

Cultural Change

Some studies have focused more on the culture change process itself. Frontiera (2010) interviewed six primary decision makers on teams that had substantially increased their winning percentage over a certain period of time, about their organizational cultures and the change that took place. They discovered several key findings. First, all participants were aware of symptoms of a dysfunctional culture in place, such as poor facilities, nega- tive values (e.g., selfishness and too much focus on money), and having become accustomed to mediocrity (not winning and substandard processes) when they started. Second, the leaders clearly communicated a philosophy of "My Way" through vision, values, personnel change, growing people, and explicit communication. Third, the leaders "Walked the Talk," which entailed day-to-day attention to details and making physical improvements to the environment to generate artifact impact. Fourth, the new culture was embedded through new successes and significant turning points. Finally, the cultural shift gave birth to a philosophy of "Our Way," characterized by valuing people in the organization, making better organizational decisions, and independently thinking outside the box.

Cruickshank and colleagues (2013) did an in-depth analysis of a cultural change for an English professional rugby union team. The cultural change program was delivered as a holistic, highly integrated, dynamic process. It also changed the physical environment, such as creating an open office environment, using off-site activities, and putting performance data on public display. Among structural changes were helping players choose not to drink alcohol and relying more on objective performance data. Player ownership was regulated and adapted. Change was socially driven, and the team relied on leaders, role models, and cultural architects. Media and the CEO were managed deliberately.

Further, Cruickshank and colleagues (2014) examined cultural change in Olympic sports from interviews with seven performance directors in the United Kingdom. They concluded that cultural change is not effectively conducted in a top–down, linear, and decontextualized way. Rather, cultural leaders need to carefully manage relative to the sport's cultural, political, and performance landscape as well as proactively manage all aspects of the highly fluid and complex social setting that includes external partners and media. Success further depends on arriving at and maintaining shared values, standards, and practices in a two-way interaction with all involved stakeholders.

Finally, Henriksen (2015) conducted and examined an intervention set up to create a high-performing culture in orienteering. Based on the work of Schein (1999), the intervention involved three stages: unfreezing (creating motivation to change the culture), learning (designing new values and testing strategies), and refreezing (implementing the values into daily practice). All three levels of culture were addressed by formulating values, displaying the values in posters on the wall, and incorporating the values and strategies into the team's basic assumptions. Team members identified their top five values, which were facilitated through the positive story of the day, mounting symbols on the walls, deliberately reading and responding to nonverbal communication, and setting individual goals.

Summary

The studies by Henriksen and colleagues (e.g., Henriksen et al., 2010a; 2010b) have collectively identified organizational culture as an important component of talent development environments, showing that a hierarchical system that puts emphasis on open communication, advocating athlete autonomy, and supporting athletes in both education and continuous development are more likely to experience success in sport (Wagstaff & Burton-Wylie, 2018). Much of this research on high-performing culture in sport has been done in countries with small populations (where they have an acute need to nurture the few talents who are available) and flat leadership structure (logically fostering autonomy, emergent leadership, and cultural architects). In addition, Cruickshank and colleagues have done substantial work on culture and culture change in a larger British context (e.g., Cruickshank et al., 2013), showing some of the complexity of these processes and that cultural change is not effectively conducted in a top–down, linear, and decontextualized way.

Assessment

Culture is dynamic, fluid, and interactive; therefore, assessing culture is a complicated feat (Cruickshank & Collins, 2012). It is also difficult because each culture is special and needs to be understood based on its own premises; no one type of culture will lead to success for all groups under all conditions (Cruickshank, 2019). Certain psychological inventories measure subaspects of culture, such as sport-specific team norms (Colman & Carron, 2001), team trust (Costa & Anderson, 2011), and collective orientation (Driskell et al., 2010). However, if you are present, embedded, and actively observing, you will be able to grasp completely different layers of a culture than what you will achieve through structured quantitative measurements (Gilmore, 2013). Thus, this section focuses on the former.

Coaches, leaders and managers, athletes, and sport psychology consultants attempting to assess the various aspects of a culture need to equip themselves with some basic knowledge about high-performing cultures (see What We Know). Based on Schein's (1999) distinction of levels in a culture as artifacts, values, and basic assumptions, this section begins with this question: *How can you assess cultural artifacts?* Because cultural artifacts are the most concrete, tangible form, assessing different types of training facilities is easy; you can see posters, photos on the wall, and the shape of physical facilities. To assess these aspects of culture when you visit a facility, you need to be open, aware, and curious about all these physical manifestations. Assess based on these questions: *What meets you when you first arrive? What do you see on the walls? What are people doing when they meet you? How does the facility make you feel? Do the surroundings inspire you for action?*

Further, *When you observe a team practice or play, can you see (literally with your eyes) if the team has a high-performing culture or not?* Some important behavioral norms, such as punctuality and attendance, are simple to assess as long as you know them. Others, such as mutual performance monitoring of effort, concentration, and quality skill execution, both in practice and in competition, are far more complex. The demarcation line for acceptable and nonacceptable team behavior in such contexts is difficult for outsiders to see and most likely difficult for team participants to verbalize. Further, evidence shows that the majority of information exchanged between people consists of no words; it is nonverbal (Matsumoto et al., 2013). A few studies have examined sport performers' body language during competitive events. Generally they show that participants on successful teams are more positive, appear more dominant, celebrate their successes more intensely, seek out their teammates more, and stay in physical contact more than participants on less-successful teams do (e.g., Jordet & Hartman, 2008; Kraus et al., 2010; Moll et al., 2010). Further, Coyle (2018) lists a series of what he calls *connection cues*, which he would observe in the interactions between people in high-performing cultures. These cues include close physical proximity, a lot of eye contact, physical touch, short and energetic exchanges (no long speeches), everyone talking to everyone, few interruptions, a lot of questions, intensive and active listening, humor and laughter, and small and attentive courtesies (e.g., saying thank you, opening doors for each other). The more accustomed you are to observing different types of teams and athletes in given sports, the better you become at assessing these nuances in people's behaviors and interactions.

You can also assess values by talking to people. Find out the views of a wide range of people across different roles and levels, such as athletes, support staff, previous management personnel, and board members (Cruick-shank & Collins, 2012). One systematic approach to accomplishing this task is to conduct a culture audit (Cole & Martin, 2018; Solomon, 2004; Prosek, 2011). For example, you might interview people using the following process:

1. You ask senior management personnel to list what they see as the current values of the organization.
2. They list what they see as the desired values.
3. You ask the other participants in the organization to list what they see as current values.

4. You compare the lists from senior management and those from the other participants.

5. You work with the organization to alter the most dominant values to match the desired values.

6. Once you have a decent grasp of the values, you ask the question *To what extent are they aligned with the artifacts, symbols, and other physical manifestations of the culture?*

Given that both the real values and basic assumptions in a culture are difficult to accurately assess, you need to explore ways to get under the surface to fully grasp them. If you are a part of a culture over time, it is possible to experience these deeper sets of values. One thing you can do is systematically listen to the words, phrases, or stories that people on a team express to each other and to others outside their group. Another potentially fruitful approach to assessing culture is to observe a culture when it faces problems, is challenged, or is under some type of stress (Gilmore, 2013; Schein, 2010). For example, consider these questions: *What is the communication like when a team has accumulated a string of bad results? Who speaks with whom? What do they say? Do they say and do the same things as when they perform well?*

Be sure that your assessments capture all aspects of a culture and not only what is expressed by the most prominent and opinionated people. McDougall et al. (2020a) argue that one fruitful way to understand culture is the three-perspective approach; it involves using the complementary views of integration (what is shared and consistent in a culture), differentiation (what is contested and disputed), and fragmentation (what is vague and ambiguous). While the majority of this section has focused on the former (the openly shared aspects of a culture), you also need to know, acknowledge, and consider the less obvious aspects, such as the cultural experience of marginalized team members with lower status and authority. Thus, coaches, leaders and managers, athletes, and sport psychology consultants need to be mindful of these different layers and not draw conclusions about a culture merely from listening to the loudest voices in the room.

Finally, assessing culture is a skill; to do it well, you need to constantly educate yourself. McDougall et al. (2020b) argue that practitioners need first to learn about the concept of culture and how cultural meaning is manifested in stories, rituals, and language. It means becoming proficient at reading the cultural landscape, which presupposes some knowledge about cultures and about ways to observe and interpret them. Further, to accurately analyze and decode complex cultural symbols, you need to engage in a process to improve these interpretation skills. Education and training in the methods used by anthropologists or organizational psychologists will be helpful, and the deeper insights you will have into such types of knowledge, the deeper, more sophisticated, and more accurate your insights will be.

Optimization

This section addresses what coaches, performance staff, and athletes can do to build, nurture, change, and optimize a high-performing culture. It is divided into four subsections: artifacts, values, leadership, and cultural architects.

Optimizing Artifacts

Artifacts can be powerful cultural symbols. Leaders and coaches need to make sure that all the different artifacts in their culture consistently and coherently communicate and repeat their team's most important goals, aspirations, directions, paths forward, and values (Coyle, 2018). Structuring culture this way is less about big and bold inspiring statements and speeches, and more about many clear and visible signals that are always present, shown, or shared. It concerns these questions: *How can the physical environment be arranged so it communicates positive messages by use of objects, symbols, or writing on the wall? Can coaches consistently put focus on and communicate the specific effortful bar-setting behaviors that are important to reach the team's goals? What role models can become powerful symbols who call the others to do the right things every day?*

However, cultural artifacts and rituals are not necessarily stable and enduring. Teams need to adapt them to new times and new situations. Constantly revisit old routines to make sure they reflect what they need to reflect. See success story 1 for an example of successfully changing an old ritual.

Optimizing Values

This section elaborates on the ways that values come across in high-performing cultures and addresses how to optimize values in a team. It is important that those on your team who have the most influence embrace the values of your organization. The values explored in this section are performance standards and team orientation.

Performance Standards and Professionalism

Many high-performing athletes have been not only excellent performers but allegedly also their teams' hardest workers (e.g., Cristiano Ronaldo, Kobe Bryant, Michael Jordan, and Mia Hamm). When they consistently exhibit their hard-working behavior, these outstanding players naturally become the benchmark that everyone else on the team strives toward. Consequently, one player's work ethic effectively becomes the work ethic of the group. When performance-facilitating values emerge organically from within the group rather than as a result of a top–down initiative from management, it is conducive to a high-performing culture (Potrac & Jones, 2009; Cruickshank & Collins, 2012).

Success Story 1: Stopping an Old Ritual to Create a New Cultural Artifact

Liverpool Football Club in the English Premier League was the most successful soccer team in England in the 1980s; it earned seven league titles that decade. However, following their win in the 1989 to 1990 season, it took them 30 years to win again (2019-2020 season). In 2015, Jürgen Klopp was hired as the Liverpool manager (head coach). Upon his arrival in Liverpool, among the many things he did to change the culture was to tell his players that they were not allowed to take part in a long-standing tradition at the club: when players walk through the tunnel to get out on the pitch at Anfield, their home ground, all Liverpool players touch the sign above their heads that reads "This Is Anfield." Klopp is reported to have said, "I've told my players not to touch the 'This Is Anfield' sign until they win something" (O'Neill, 2019).

When Liverpool won the 2019 Champions League final and ahead of the 2019 to 2020 season, Klopp's ban was lifted. This temporary break from tradition may have become a cultural artifact in itself; when the team does not touch the sign, they are actively showing an intent to become champions rather than passively adhering to tradition. For practitioners, this case illustrates that culture optimization is a dynamic and ongoing exchange that you constantly need to adapt to the environment and the group itself.

Catherine Ivill/Getty Images

Head coach Jürgen Klopp (left) broke from tradition at Liverpool.

For coaches, this idea reinforces the importance of letting values emerge naturally from within the group. A way to affect it is primarily related to recruitment, which considers who is invited to be a part of the group and what their values are. Once the group is set, the coach needs to make sure that those who express the values the coach wants to promote are given an influential position in the group.

It is important for athletes to be aware of the role they play in setting the team culture, and they should work to be positive role models with respect to performance standards and professionalism. It is particularly important for senior members of a team. Their behaviors are indeed seen and registered by others, and they need to make sure that those behaviors are aligned with the behaviors the whole team needs to have. One of the authors of this chapter was once brought in by team management to work with one specific team member whose body language was so negative that it drained the energy of both other players and staff. The player's response to the question of how to have a positive effect on teammates through his body language was "I don't think my body language matters much as nobody notices me anyway. I'm really invisible in this group!" He was oblivious to the effect he had on others, and we proceeded to change both his perception and the way he appeared to the others.

Attendance and punctuality are foundational to any team activity. Coaches need to be punctual and establish norms for punctuality for the team. Some teams have created a culture where its members are intrinsically drawn to each other and their mutual activity, which is likely a positive force for both individual and collective performance development. Pep Guardiola, the coach of the highly successful FC Barcelona soccer team from 2008 to 2012, said this about what it meant to be in this team: "There are some things that show us what a team is. Today, we had planned to meet at 5. At 4:30, everyone was here. The players know that when we stop doing this, everyone can beat us" (Balague, 2012). For another example, see success story 2.

Team Orientation

The term *team orientation* concerns the extent to which the members of the team are helping each other, being open to each other, and sharing their knowledge with each other. The value of team orientation is about members' belief in the importance of the team goals over the individual goals and the propensity to take others' behaviors into account during group interaction (Salas et al., 2005).

Do you have rituals that connect team members together? In one of the most successful teams in the National Basketball Association (NBA), the San Antonio Spurs, Coach Gregg Popovich constantly hosts elaborate dinners for staff and players (Coyle, 2018). He apparently goes through painstaking effort in selecting restaurants, menus, wine pairings, light, ambience, and seating arrangements. He personally arrives at the restaurants before anyone else to make sure everything is set up correctly, then he affectionately greets everyone on arrival. This ritual accentuates the importance of togetherness and teamwork. As one of the players testifies, "[The dinners] help us have a better understanding of each individual person, which brings us closer to each other and, on the court, understand each other better" (Holmes, 2019, para. 44). Coaches, athletes, and leaders should establish their own social rituals, both in the form of such events (e.g., regular team excursions away from the practice facilities, bringing families to the club a certain number of times each year, seeing nonsport-related landmarks on every away game trip) and with respect to daily interaction (e.g., the way they greet each other every day).

Coaches and leaders can also reinforce the team orientation in a group by increasing members' participation in goal setting, strategizing, and problem solving. Once a month, the San Antonio Spurs organization leaves a time-out in a game for the players to conduct themselves with no involvement from the coaches (Coyle, 2018). Doing so presupposes maturity in the team and that the coach's status is undisputable. Given these premises, it can strengthen player ownership and stimulate the collective orientation on the team. Success story 2 links to these points also.

Optimizing Leadership

An infinite number of leadership aspects are related to optimizing culture. This section touches on a few of the most important, which complement and reinforce some of the messages in chapter 11.

First, group leaders are in charge of making members feel that they belong in the group. The term *psychological safety* describes this sense of security found in human relationships, and it has been consistently shown to facilitate learning and performance in different types of groups (Edmondson & Lei, 2014). People are biologically dependent on receiving confirming signals about group belonging (e.g., *We are close*, *We are safe*, *We share a future*), and high-performing cultures constantly feed these signals to the members of their group so that everyone feels that they belong (Coyle, 2018).

For coaches and athlete leaders, creating a psychologically safe environment is strongly connected to their relationships with others. The quality of these relationships is likely the result of the ability of coaches and athlete leaders to (1) treat athletes or peers as unique and valued individuals, learn about them, show that they are seen for who they are; (2) invest time and energy in athletes or peers, being totally present in every exchange with them; and (3) be future oriented with them, signaling that the relationship will continue (Coyle, 2018). Start with this simple question: *Are you interested in your athletes or peers as people?* The degree of curiosity and care that you have and show for them says a lot. Great coaches and athlete leaders link these relationships to performance.

As highlighted earlier, coaches and other team leaders have a major effect on the culture of their teams through their direct actions. However, leaders also need to create and shape the contexts in which the team operates to encourage and nudge members to make their own decisions with respect to behaviors that might support a culture or not (Cruickshank, 2019). This way leadership will take place in the background as well, to subtly but effectively shape behaviors in the foreground. Further, to successfully change and optimize culture, coaches need to regulate and navigate the power dynamic of a group to keep athletes and staff satisfied, motivated, and united (Cruickshank & Collins, 2012). In most elite team environments, coaches can effectively accomplish this task only if they continually monitor and optimize the program-shaping perceptions of board members, fans, and the media (particularly if faced with initially poor results) (Cruickshank & Collins, 2012). Awareness of stakeholders' proximity, power, and different rationality should permeate all decision-making processes (Cruickshank et al., 2014; Cruickshank et al., 2015). For an illustration of some of the involved stakeholders and dynamics of managing them, see figure 12.1.

Generally, coaches who are experts at navigating these complex cultures are also extremely interested in these aspects of culture. For example, Guus Hiddink, coach of professional soccer teams for more than 30 years in 10 different countries and on three different continents, seemingly has specialized in coaching in different countries. The foundation of his ability may come from his cultural openness, curiosity, respect, flexibility, tolerance, and ability to learn new languages—all while keeping focus on his performance targets (Hiddink & Jordet, 2019).

Optimizing Informal Leadership and Cultural Architects

Sometimes, it is important that coaches let go of control to let leadership grow from within the group of athletes or teammates. One way to do so is to activate, allow for, and reinforce the cultural architects in the team. The term *cultural architect* originally comes from the Norwegian sport psychology consultant Willi Railo (1983). Danielsen and colleagues (2019) defined *cultural architect* as a team member who significantly contributes to cocreating, interpreting, translating, developing, implementing, executing, and enhancing the group's visions and strategies through their attitude and actions (both verbally and behaviorally) and who thereby contributes to development of optimal team coordination and culture. Such athletes are particularly important for coaches because the greater the number of sources of social impact they can have in a social situation, the greater their impact will be (Latané, 1981). Furthermore, the coach's impact increases when his cultural architects have higher status. Cultural architects understand that the coach cannot be the only source of discipline on the team, and they can communicate disapproval toward team members who have different or lower performance

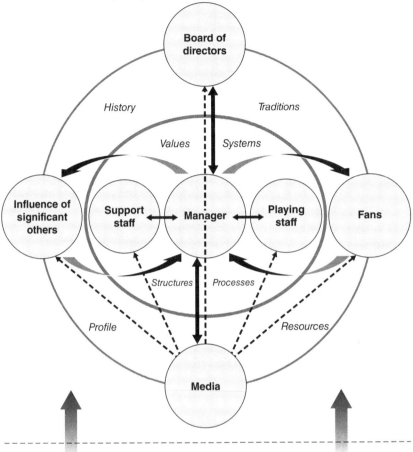

Management of a holistic, integrated, and dynamic social system
- Managing multi-stakeholder perceptions and expectations
- Action-guiding multi-stakeholder perceptions and actions

Initial evaluation, planning, and impact
- Evaluating fitness with the club and board
- Evaluating the performance department
- Setting and aligning multi-stakeholder perceptions and expectations
- Identifying, recruiting, and harnessing social allies and cultural architects
- Withholding initial action in suboptimal conditions
- Delivering instant results

FIGURE 12.1   Manager-led culture change best practice within the performance department of British professional sport organizations. Solid line arrows refer to manager-based interactions; broken-line arrows refer to secondary interactions from the manager through the media.

Reprinted by permission from A. Cruickshank, D. Collins, and S. Minten, "Driving and Sustaining Culture Change in Professional Sport Performance Teams: A Grounded Theory," *Psychology of Sport and Exercise* 20 (2015): 40-50.

standards. Furthermore, they can improve the coach's profiling of productive or unproductive underlying values and norms and contribute to extrapolating the behavior leading up to optimal exploitation of team resources. Success story 2 shows how cultural architects across generations were essential for the Norway men's alpine ski team.

Success Story 2: Culture Change in the Norway Men's Alpine Ski Team

Prior to the 1992 Olympics, the Norwegian men's alpine ski team took a total of three Olympic medals, all in 1952. It took 40 years until they earned the next medal in 1992, and after that one, the team has taken a total of 29 Olympic medals (11 gold). What happened? Aksel Lund Svindal (4 Olympic medals between 2010 and 2018) focused on some of the team's history in his recent autobiography. He attributed parts of the team culture to the outstanding cultural architects that led the others in their respective generations: first Ole Kristian Furuseth; then Kjetil André Aamodt and Lasse Kjus; and finally himself, Kjetil Jansrud, and others (Lund Svindal & Ekelund, 2019). Kjetil André Aamodt, who joined the team around 1990, describes how it started with one specific individual: "The culture [in the national team] was not very professional . . . With one exception: Ole Kristian Furuseth. . . . Fortunately, Furuseth became the first Norwegian to win a World Cup race . . . He had the right mindset. That produced results, and when he won, people stopped laughing at how eager he was, and started training instead. The way I see it, this signaled the start of the good winning culture that the national team has had until now" (p. 107). Many of the cultural artifacts that existed in the beginning still exist now. For example, the team meets every day at 6:45 p.m., and dinner is at 7 p.m. Everyone is punctual (when they say to meet at a certain time, everyone knows that they really need to be there 5 minutes early), and the athletes still share rooms when they are on the road (often, seniors share rooms with juniors, to keep the older one sharp and transfer experience from the older one to the younger one). In addition, the culture is characterized by collective team-orientated values, expressed by what Lund Svindal was told by the team members in the generation ahead of him: "They told me, 'This isn't an NBA team or something like that. You can't be traded or sold to another team. We're all here for life.' Those two guys (Kjus and Aamodt) created a culture of unity, and all we had to do was preserve it" (Pennington, 2018, para. 29).

Conclusion

This chapter addressed high-performing cultures, what is known about them, and how to assess and optimize them. Most importantly, although culture is highly fluid, multifaceted, and complex, coaches and athletes have many concrete and specific ways to influence it in a positive direction. It begins with the individual with curiosity and interest in other people and how the rituals, values, and assumptions that are shared in a team can provide a fertile ground for its members to develop, thrive, and perform.

13 | Shared Mental Models

Pam Richards
University of Central Lancashire

Dave Collins
Grey Matters UK and University of Edinburgh

Whenever a group of people get together, they usually have some discussions relating to differences of opinions. Indeed, many researchers and some leaders and managers see this situation as a *desirable difficulty*—a positive force that generates a creative tension and drive for innovation and keeps organizations fresh. Of course, the conflict must be appropriate for the situation and the group. Quality disagreement—the ability to check and challenge but not fall out over it—is a feature of quality performance environments. This balance marks what we (the authors of this chapter) call the difference between high-perform*ance* (the status of the athletes and team… what most people already work in) and high-perform*ing* (a very effective and efficient system…what many aspire to for optimal success) environments.

The ability to live life in the zone of uncomfortable debate (ZOUD) (Burke, 2011) is an important characteristic of those who aspire to work in high-performing environments (HPE). This chapter outlines evidence and guiding principles for designing HP environments with the objective of facilitating an empowerment culture—a culture in which team members can contribute to performance strategies in an environment that is psychologically safe. Such an environment enables desirable difficulties to be effectively discussed, resulting in enhanced collective performance. The design and development of shared mental models (SMMs; see also chapters 1, 8, and 11) relating to the performance vision are instrumental in facilitating a shared perception of the performance context; they influence a shared understanding of what factors are vital for a successful performance (Richards et al., 2012) and enable team discussions to be positive and collaborative because all members are driven by sharing the same performance objectives. Cannon-Bowers and colleagues (1993) defined SMMs as

> knowledge structure(s) held by each member of a team that enables them to form accurate explanations and expectations . . . and in turn, to coordinate their actions and adapt their behavior to demands of the task and other team members." (p. 222)

How might this desirable state work, and why might it be of interest to those in athletics? Furthermore, is this characteristic important only for team athletes and coaches, or can all high-performance teams or squads (HPTs) see benefit? This chapter aims to answer these practical questions. The chapter offers examples from both team and individual sports, and it outlines some guiding principles that will enable the design, development, and operation of SMMs within your performance context. To get the most out of the chapter for your own practical use, first focus on the principles and mechanisms rather than the exact examples, then apply them to your situation.

Relevance

Although the introduction recognized desirable difficulties as a factor within HP environments, the best way to make team differences more positive is to work toward more "Ah yes, I see" than "That's nonsense" responses during difficult conversations. The way it works is based on the idea of SMMs. Before defining them and exploring their benefits, it might be best to say what they definitely are not. The dark side of SMMs is evident in an idea called groupthink (see McCauley, 1989, for a description of how groupthink might develop and operate). *Groupthink* occurs when members of a group or team all start thinking in the same way. They all pressure each other to conform to the group ideas, with some leading members acting as mind guards to police anyone who metaphorically (or actually) steps out of line. From the inside, everything looks rosy; everyone is furiously agreeing and telling each other how "great we are!" From the outside, however, it looks rather odd, especially when the group's opinions seem impervious to logical argument. Emerging concerns about ethically doubtful (or just downright wrong) behaviors in sport are just one example of groupthink. For example, take drug use in sport. Some people justify their drug use because everyone does it, and after all, "*We* [athletes as a group] think it's OK." From a performance perspective, the group will stagnate, becoming ever more conformist to the central ideas. In almost all cases, groupthink emerges as a problem when, usually without warning (at least to the groupthink team themselves), problems emerge to which the group simply cannot adjust.

In contrast, SMMs operate in a much more positive fashion. Team members exhibit a common understanding of higher-level ideas (e.g., team strategy, the underlying basis of training models), facilitating critical debate between them about the details. In simple terms, members (whether team players or individual-sport athletes interacting with their coach and support staff) are willing to question and offer suggestions, but they do so with all parties seeing fairly quickly where they are coming from (i.e., the suggestions fit into the shared model) even if they disagree. ZOUD-style conversations can take place without the mind-guard pressure to conform and, when led with consideration, the team's buy-in to the eventual plan is enhanced, largely because it is clearly a cooperative group ("we") idea rather than an imposed individual ("I") system. Shared understanding at all levels (the plan, the process, and the goals) will be a positive feature of this approach, which the leader (coach or sport psychology consultants) can access simply by talking and listening to team members as they debate any feature of the team's or group's operation.

Many components presented in the Cannon-Bowers and colleagues (1993) definition will be of relevance later in the chapter as they are explored in the context of HP delivery of SMMs. SMMs contain shared knowledge, allowing teams to work under the same assumptions and have similar expectations regarding roles and responsibilities, leading individuals to similar decision-making (DM) strategies (Salas et al., 1997). SMMs also facilitate

David E. Klutho /Sports Illustrated via Getty Images

Shared mental models contain shared knowledge, leading individuals to complementary decision-making strategies.

communication, coordination, and team performance (Cannon-Bowers et al., 1993). SMMs therefore consist of two components: (1) technical aspects (information, techniques, cues, data points, and positional skill sets relating to the domain) and (2) nontechnical aspects (e.g., communication, inter- and intrapersonal skills, culture, team philosophy, common language). They are addressed later in the chapter.

SMMs are useful across performance domains. Certainly, member buy-in and commitment to the ideas and processes with the employment of SMMs will be much greater. Furthermore, constructive (and even creative) ideas will be much more likely to emerge and be shared across the group. Since more heads usually are better than one, the group will be more likely to pursue and achieve the states of constant but focused innovation that are common features of HP environments. Other advantages also exist. For example, SMMs equip members to anticipate and cater to others' needs, whether it be in making sympathetic passes within a team game plan or offering constructive support when needed. Greater role clarity (*I know what I need to do*), acceptance (*I am happy doing that*), and recognition (*Others reinforce me for doing that*) will keep everyone feeling valued and supported. Finally, the common and commonly understood criteria will generally mean less impassioned debate and questioning of various decisions, such as who gets selected or how training plans are adjusted.

What We Know

The concept of mental models is an old one; it stems from 1940s research into how groups may best operate in industrial settings. Since then, the idea has gained credibility and is effectively employed in a wide variety of performance settings. It is particularly applicable to more pressured environments in which speedy and appropriate group DM is needed; these environments include firefighting, stockbroking, combat, and team sport settings (cf. Eccles & Tenenbaum, 2004). These time-pressured, high-stakes environments necessitate a fast DM style that has been termed *naturalistic decision making* (NDM) (Klein et al., 1993). SMMs are useful in this style because they negate the need for a lot of communication, either in the scenario (e.g., *You do this*) or beforehand (e.g., standard operating procedure or *If they do this, we do that*). Rather, as described earlier, team and group members can anticipate each other's needs and pressure points, taking proactive action almost automatically. In simple terms, knowing and understanding preferences of other team or group members enables this proactive anticipation. Once again, recognize the advantages for individual sports as well. In these situations, SMMs will make athletes more amenable to changes in systems, plans, members of the training group, and so on. People are often wary of change, but the common understanding and shared perception of performance reduces the emotional challenge of such refinements. Indeed, team or group members will be more likely to suggest these changes themselves.

You can now see the development and servicing of SMMs as a big proactive feature of developing expertise within the group or team. Good leaders, whether coaches, sport psychology consultants, captains, or cultural architects (those who lead and encourage others in a nonconfrontational manner; cf. Railo, 1983), will encourage SMM development and deployment, making for more of a united (*us*) environment as opposed to a combative (*you v. me*) one, which can be the result of an overly or inappropriately authoritarian structure. The following section examines some practical and more research-related ways you can develop the levels and operation of SMMs.

The NDM paradigm, which explores DM in high-pressure, naturalistic settings, provides the ideal framework to enhance your understanding of DM in HPE through the use of SMMs. The following section provides an overview of key NDM theories relevant to operating SMMs within a HP context.

Research to date has thoroughly investigated perception in invasion sports (Williams, 2009), but it has failed to adequately examine the link to perception, SMMs, and DM in the dynamic, applied environments in which invasion sports occur. Decisions in sport are performed in complex and often unpredictable conditions, under high pressure, and with extreme time constraints (Klein, 2008). NDM researchers seek to investigate how experts perform tasks in dynamic environments that have ill-structured problems, have shifting and changing objectives, have time constraints, include multiple players, and are influenced by organizational goals. All these characteristics are representative of HPEs, including sport. Given that the emphasis of this chapter is to understand the application of SMMs within HPE, the chapter outlines key NDM approaches relevant to SMMs in sport.

As outlined earlier, SMMs consist of both a technical and nontechnical component (Richards et al., 2009). These components are presented in an interconnected manner with the DM framework (Richards et al., 2016) that has been specifically designed for sport and for the formulation of SMMs in the context of high-pressured DM. This framework is presented in the next section. It is relevant to first understand both the technical (psychomotor) and the nontechnical (psychosocial) parts of SMMs, in order to understand how cues in the environment, information, and data points are personalized and integrated into SMMs tailored to each team or performance setting. Developing a SMM collectively as a team requires understanding what information is important to the individuals *and* the team collectively, as well as in the context of the specific team philosophy, skill sets of its members, and the overarching strategic objectives of the program or competitive focus. To understand the complexity of this process, with the application of SMMs in the naturalistic environment of sport, it is helpful to explore several theoretical concepts.

Klein (1998) proposed the model of recognition-primed decision making (RPD), a dual system that integrates intuition and subjective analysis of the situation. Using RPD for team sports enables an understanding of what cues are attended to, and how they are prioritized and used to inform and influence decisions (Klein, 1993). For example, at a basic level, the cues from where a basketball player is holding or carrying the ball, the angle of their body, and the position of the ball in relation to body angle will inform the defense response in relation to the perceived potential moves the attacking player might make. However, the situation is even more complex than this example because such visual information needs to be seen in the context of game tactics and location (where the situation is occurring on the court). For example, the closer the attacker gets to the opposition's basket, the greater the level of compact play (volume of people within a small area) and the higher the level of threat. Without this contextualization, reliance on a cue-driven approach (what you see) will often result in team DM errors. Therefore, to understand the situational context, in which performance information and cues are embedded, it is useful to introduce a second NDM theory: situational awareness (SA).

SA has been a key factor for developing DM skills (Endsley, 1997; Richards et al., 2016). It presents a hierarchical model consisting of three levels. Level 1 requires the perception of important cues. Level 2 focuses on the comprehension of these cues, and level 3 enables individuals (and members of the team collectively) to predict future situations by integrating past experience to the situation. Caserta and Singer (2007) proposed that level 3 SA distinguishes elite from nonelite performers in any domain. This distinction requires individuals and members of the team to make sense of the information and frame it in context of the relevant factors such as stage of the game, team philosophy, and strategic performance objectives (Richards et al., 2016), tailoring the SMMs to the environment for which they are designed. Therefore, the concept of sensemaking makes a valuable contribution to contextualizing how both cues (RPD) and situation (SA) can be combined to illustrate how performers—and the team collectively—can make sense of key information within a given situation and comprehend it to inform an effective course of action.

Sensemaking as a concept (Klein et al., 2007) goes beyond the comprehension of environmental cues and requires both individual and team to engage in a process of noticing and framing (Hansen & Andersen, 2014) so that important information can be interpreted and made sense of (framed) in context of the HPE. One could argue that sensemaking proposes an approach in which the information and the experience of the individual (and also the team) can be used to frame or comprehend what is happening. As the players and team collectively frame the situation through the process of individual or team reflection, the team places the current situation in context of previous experiences, data points (information and performance cues), and team philosophy, resulting in the team interpreting the context in the same way. Sensemaking enables the performer and team to establish connections and relationships between environmental cues and the team's strategic objectives. Such visual perceptions are contextualized within previous playing experiences. The construction of slow, deliberate learning situations (e.g., through team meetings), whereby individuals (and, in turn, the team) are empowered to reflect and contribute to providing a solution, results in the content of these situations being internalized and stored by individual players and the team as a whole, thereby supporting the development of SMMs. In turn, this internalization produces an increasingly robust SMM where, in future situations, information perceived in the environment is matched, enabling rapid execution of technical and tactical skills (Bate & Richards, 2011; Richards et al., 2012; Richards et al., 2009).

Assessment

You can evaluate SMMs simply by asking individuals about their perceptions of a given situation in terms of what they think is important, what should be done, and why. However, from this simple starting point, you can apply a more complex development process that also offers ongoing evaluation opportunities.

Recognizing the importance of NDM as a theoretical paradigm that can be used to inform your understanding of how SMMs can be developed to improve DM in HPE, a DM framework (Richards et al., 2016) has been designed that integrates RPD, SA, and sensemaking. Refer to Richards and colleagues (2016) for a detailed account of the DM framework. An example of its application is presented in two elite HPEs: field hockey (Richards et al., 2009) and netball (Richards et al., 2012). However, for the purpose of exploring later applications, an overview is provided to inform the success story presented later in this chapter.

The DM framework (Richards et al., 2016) consists of two interconnected models. Model 1 illustrates the psychomotor aspects of the SMM (the technical components outlined earlier in the chapter); model 2 represents the psychosocial (nontechnical) aspects of the SMM.

Model 1 outlines the concepts that facilitate the development of the five layers of information required to develop team SMMs (what to coach). Each layer (as described in the stages discussed in the next section) involves feedback and feedforward mechanisms, facilitating a cyclical process for continual learning and development of playing constructs (the nontechnical components of the model). Although the models are illustrated separately to provide clarity, the five layers interact with and define each other. Through the process of player empowerment, each of the layers addresses the development of cognitive structures (RPD), mental models (MMs) and shared mental models (SMMs), and the contextualization of these structures in the specific HP environmental and performance situations (SA).

Model 2 illustrates the pedagogical process involved in coordinating individual perceptual representations of playing and performance situations so that a collective team cognitive thought process can be obtained (nontechnical). Model 2 (how to coach) presents a framework that illustrates the interaction between the slow, deliberate, reflective off-field environment and the rapid on-field competitive environment with the focus on developing team DM. Model 2 focuses on the concept of empowerment, and it requires coaches to develop an inquisitive approach to performance development rather than a prescriptive style of delivery (Kidman & Hadfield, 2001). Their ability to ask questions and enable individual athletes to develop an inquisitive approach to performance will ultimately result in performers taking ownership of their own learning and performance (Kidman, 2001) and the development of SMMs (Westbrook, 2006; Richards et al., 2012).

The models are delivered and engaged with in environments that are both on and off the field or court. The slow, deliberate, reflective off-field training context (team meetings and debriefings, more akin to classical decision making [CDM]), in which MMs and SMMs are constructed, is transferred and operationalized in high-pressure, in-action (i.e., on-field, on-court, or in-performance) environments. The DM framework proposes that SMMs require the complex interaction of psychomotor processes (e.g., technical execution, cue identification, interpretation of situational information and physical movement) and psychosocial processes (e.g., creating a shared vision and common language among coaches and players within the context of shared team philosophy). The creation of pedagogical processes that address psychomotor and psychosocial mechanisms are outlined in examples in the following sections.

Optimization

The rest of the chapter explores the principles that underpin the design, development, and operation of SMMs. Specifically, it outlines how the two interconnected models presented earlier can be used through a five-stage framework to design, develop, and operate SMMs. The sections outline key processes and factors for practitioners to consider while working in the performance context.

The integration of the two visions requires engaging with multiple processes. For an overview of how the process works from a theoretical perspective, see Richards et al., 2016.

Designing and Developing a Performance Vision (Stages 1 and 2)

The initial two stages involve the construction of a performance vision by the coaching team and support staff (stage 1) and with the performers (stage 2). This vision is tailored to each team and the individuals within it, and it often takes time to build. This early phase is initially shaped by the coach's vision of what the ideal performance ultimately looks like for this particular set of players (an alpha version of the performance vision; see Richards et al., 2009, 2012). The vision is never constructed in isolation; it involves the integration of feedback from other coaching staff and support staff. It is informed by sport intelligence (understanding of the sport, how the best in the environment perform; part of the benchmarking process), performance analysis data, and the identification of the key factors that influence performance in successful teams. This preparation phase is often overlooked or minimized, but the time and energy invested in this stage will reap rewards when the SMMs are transferred to the performance setting.

Once established, the alpha vision of performance is divided into small key aspects of play. Some examples of key aspects might include key tactical phases of the sport (e.g., in soccer, transition play in midfield, attacking the backline, entry into the 18-yard box) or key moments in the game (e.g. restarts, critical incidents) and also set plays (e.g. sidelines, corners, overtaking a rider). Identification of these key aspects is the result of conversations with specialist staff in the performance environment and the sport intelligence gathered as outlined earlier. It is relevant to expand on this initial stage in more detail so that you can contextualize it in your own performance setting.

In its simplest form, an alpha vision of performance (a preparation period; for example, a competitive season usually consisting of a calendar year) may have three to five key aspects of performance identified as essential for ensuring success. In figure 13.1, one alpha vision is represented as involving four key aspects of performance—SMMs that are all progressively connected to the alpha vision of performance. For example, SMM1a, SMM2a, SMM3a, and SMM4a are illustrative of the four key aspects of performance identified within this alpha vision. Each separate SMM (see the inset) contains the detail

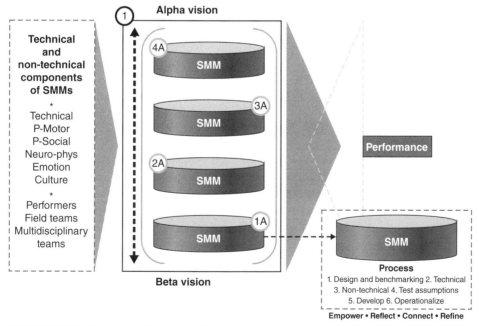

FIGURE 13.1   Sample alpha vision of performance.

Reprinted by permission from P. Richards, *Understanding Decision-Making and Operationalising Shared Mental Models in Olympic Sports* (EIS Performance Team, English Institute of Sport, Virtual/online owing to COVID, 2020).

required for that aspect of performance (SMM) to be successfully designed and built by the coaching team or performance staff and be executed by the performer or team. Each SMM (1a, 2a, 3a, and 4a) is built in a connective manner—sometimes progressively and sometimes simultaneously, depending on the maturity and experience of the team. It is also important to highlight that a process of harmonization exists, where connectivity of SMMs occurs across multiple levels. In an elite sport context, a performance vision may span multiple years, such as an Olympic or Paralympic cycle preparation or a World Cup campaign. In such instances, each phase of preparation will address key aspects of performance over multiple years, so the alpha vision contains multiple levels (multiple phases, multiple years), with each level containing SMMs that are inter- and intraconnected. Figure 13.2 illustrates the concept for a sample two-year program of preparation.

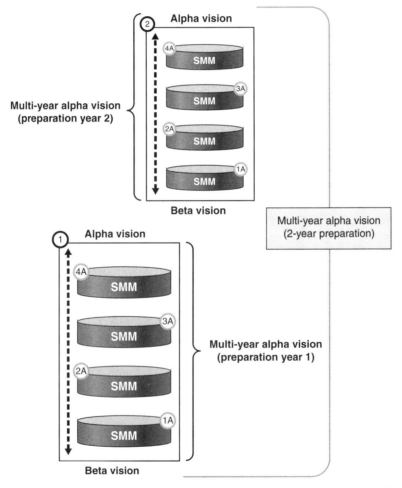

FIGURE 13.2   Sample alpha vision of performance over multiple years of performance preparation.

Reprinted by permission from P. Richards, *Understanding Decision-Making and Operationalising Shared Mental Models in Olympic Sports* (EIS Performance Team, English Institute of Sport, Virtual/online owing to COVID, 2020).

Establishment of the team's concepts (SMMs) is crucial because they provide the framework that will direct attentional focus and determine how knowledge is clustered (Merola & Richards, 2010). During performance preparation, the coach's vision of performance is reshaped as performers are actively encouraged and empowered to add to the performance vision (Bate & Richards, 2011; Merola & Richards, 2010). Incorporation of the performer's perspective (bottom–up approach; Richards et al., 2009; Richards et al., 2012) reshapes the initial vision (alpha version; coaching team and support staff) and results in the construction of the new final beta version of performance. This refinement process is essential and is ongoing throughout the program. Gaining the buy-in from players will facilitate a more meaningful engagement with the SMMs and, therefore, also its ability to be operationalized. Empowering performers to contribute to the development of the beta vision will establish a shared team perception, shared language, and collective thinking relating to key aspects of performance. In reality, a dual process is occurring. The alpha vision (top–down) is guiding discussion and attentional focus, but the beta vision (bottom–up) is continually informing this process from a micro level, because players' thoughts and new sport intelligence is always informing, refining, and shaping how the vision is operationalized.

At the end of the first two stages (integration of thoughts from both management team and performers), the coaching team and performers have developed a collective understanding of the objectives and the content of the alpha vision and the SMMs within it. In other words, they have agreed on what the strategic objectives are, what the key aspects of performance are in relation to those objectives, and how the aspects of performance will be operationalized to achieve a successful outcome. To ensure success, they will each understand their own role and that of all other team members (coaching team and performers) within the strategic context.

Operationalizing SMMs (Stages 3 to 5)

Stages 3 to 5 are therefore focused on operationalizing the alpha vision established in stages 1 and 2. The objective of these later stages is to transfer learning facilitated through team debriefings, team meetings, and discussions (off-field contexts) into on-field (on-court or during event) rapid actions in training games and events, and in competitive match or event settings. Given the creativity of coaches working in the world of sport across the performance spectrum, the intention of this text is not to outline exactly *how* coaches should coach within the performance setting; rather, this section highlights the three key factors that are instrumental in the development and operationalization of SMMs. The first relates to the coaching process and the creativity of the coach to consider the construction of the training environment. In this setting, a cyclic link exists between (1) the physical performance environment, where consideration is given to in-action physical training (on-court, on-field, or in-performance) and (2) the out-of-action nonphysical performance environment (team meetings, debriefing situations, etc.). If SMMs are to be developed, integrating two key processes into the pedagogical delivery is essential. These processes are reflection (at the individual and team level) and empowerment. Therefore, the following section outlines how the coach can create a cyclic learning environment, which can facilitate the design, development, and operationalization of SMMs by integrating the key concepts of reflection and empowerment.

Integrating In-Action and Out-of-Action Training

The cyclic relationship between in-action (on-field, on-court, or in-performance) training and competitive situations and out-of-action (off-field, off-court, nonperformance) debriefs or team meeting environments facilitates the development of a team-focused, direct stimulus system (out of action) and an intuitive, experience-based system (in action). These two systems result in the development of SMMs and more effective collective DM in competitive situations. The out-of-action environment facilitates the development of robust SMMs that players personalize to their playing position and therefore construct internalized plans (understanding of their own role in that specific situation; Richards et al., 2009). Established SMMs and internalized plans are used in future playing situations, allowing the deployment of enhanced rapid DM skills at an individual and team level.

Facilitating Individual and Team Reflection

During these slow, deliberate, reflective encounters, coaches create training environments that simultaneously provide two functions. The first is to integrate core components of physical, technical, and tactical elements into a player's internalized plans (their own mental model relating to their specific role on the team or within the performance). The second function is to facilitate team SMMs (integrating all aspects of performance) capable of being adapted to a variety of contexts.

Hansen and Anderson (2014) note that the reflective process allows individuals to make sense of situations through engaging with the interpretation process; *interpretation* is the evaluation of what is noticed and how individuals make sense of this information. The reflective process enables the individual and team collectively to engage with the processing of key information, which they attend to collectively owing to the establishment of the SMM (the original alpha vision) now being adapted by the performers, resulting in the beta vision. The process of reflection (sensemaking) results in the members and team collectively noticing and framing key elements during team meetings and debriefings. The individuals and team collectively use the process of interpretation to make sense of what is noticed and how it is framed. Sensemaking offers an approach in which the experience of the individual and that of the team can be used to comprehend (frame) a playing situation. As the players and team individually and collectively frame the situation through the process of reflection (i.e., place it in context of previous experiences), data points (performance cues) in competition can be identified, interpreted, and collectively responded to. Sensemaking enables the performer and the team to establish connections and relationships between environmental cues. Such visual perceptions are contextualized in previous playing experiences. The construction of slow, deliberate learning situations, whereby individuals (and, in turn, the team) are empowered to reflect and contribute to providing a solution, results in them internalizing and storing the content of these situations; thus, they establish robust SMMs.

Creating such cognitive structures (SMMs) provides performers and teams with a framework to structure, order, and prioritize relevant information, thus facilitating optimal DM. Formulation of these SMMs also enables individuals to learn and comprehend the nature of the situation more quickly (Ross et al., 2003) while perceiving the environment in the same way as teammates. The establishment of the shared performance vision enables information to be simultaneously transferred and integrated from a top–down knowledge process (alpha performance vision) and a bottom–up knowledge process (MMs and SMMs developed by both players and coaches; Richards et al., 2009). Such MMs and SMMs incorporate players' skill sets, individual roles, team principles of play, and recognition of unique situational factors relating to a specific SMM (as outlined in figure 13.1). This process enables players to cluster information and construct SMMs that facilitate improved DM at an individual, unit, and team level. Richards (2005) highlighted that performers need to develop their own internalized plans through which tactical team plans can be personalized to the players' own roles performed during match play. These plans in turn are situated within the context of team SMMs (Richards et al., 2009, 2012). Such a process results in the development of a collective thought process, a shared common language, and the development of SMMs as all members come to perceive tactical situations in the same way. These two interactive processes are instrumental in operationalizing SMMs in the competitive context.

Empowerment

In regard to developing SMMs, ensuring the engagement and buy-in of players is essential if individuals and teams are to deploy such concepts in the split-second environment that typifies elite sport. Integrating in-action and out-of-action training environments enables the cyclic link to occur when SMMs can be designed, developed, and operationalized in highly competitive situations. For this integration to occur, such learning environments must facilitate individual reflection, team reflection, and empowerment of the team as individuals and as a collective. Furthermore, although many of the applications offered so far seem more appropriate for team rather than individual sports, empowerment is equally important across all settings.

Harry How/Getty Images

Empowering athletes enables them to process information in the context of the task being performed.

The term *empowerment* has been defined as "a process by which individuals gain mastery and control" (Sorensen & Roberts, 2005, p. 1) and more specifically as "the process by which individuals develop skills and abilities to gain control . . . and take action to improve their life situations" (Gutierrez, 1999, p. 149). The thread that runs through most definitions relates to the process by which people gain more control over their decisions. Empowering athletes to engage with the learning process enables them to prioritize and attend to knowledge that they perceive to be important. This attention in turn enables individuals to process information in the context of the task being performed, hence maximizing learning.

Arai (1997) argues that performers move through four stages to become empowered. First, the coach interacts with the performer by asking meaningful questions; this process helps the performer improve their self-awareness. Second, the performer identifies their role in the learning process with support from the coach. In the third stage, the empowerment of the performer becomes evident; through continued support, the performer becomes a decision maker as they ask questions relating to their learning. During this stage, the performer becomes more aware of their own performance and starts to engage in the learning process. In the final stage, the performer contributes to their own learning and development; this reflective process provides a framework for the performer to become empowered and take responsibility for their own learning (Richards, 2005; Richards et al., 2009). Empowering the performer to reflect not only develops a greater level of knowledge and deeper understanding of issues, it also facilitates performers transferring learning from the training context to the competitive environment.

The concept of empowerment is therefore essential in the formulation of sustainable SMMs of individuals, whether team members or athletes in individual sports. More specifically, empowerment enables athletes to integrate their own positional or personal specific skill sets into performance settings (Richards et al., 2009) in the context of SMMs (Richards et al., 2012) to enable the team to collectively operationalize strategic objectives. The following success story provides an example of how the DM framework was embedded into a performance context to result in the design, development, and operationalization of a SMM.

Success Story: Netball

This success story provides an applied example using the DM framework in preparation of an under-21 (U21) international competition in the sport of netball. Richards and colleagues (2016) provide more detail through the five stages of the framework outlined earlier in this chapter, and they describe how it was employed for this case study.

This case study relates to the preparation for the World Youth Netball Championships (which became the Netball World Youth Cup in 2017). The focus was to develop three SMMs that were identified as significant aspects of play. One SMM related to attacking center passes; the attacking center pass (ACP) is a key player in netball. Center passes alternate between the two teams, so converting your own center pass is an essential component of a game-winning strategy.

As outlined in the chapter, members of the coaching team formulated an alpha vision of performance (stage 1) and progressed by sharing it with the players (stage 2) to ensure that players bought in to the vision and to empower them to shape the vision from their individual and team perspectives. This process resulted in the establishment of the beta vision of performance, a vision that coaching staff and players agreed to.

Over 31 days, which included a preparation camp and international tournament, coaching staff creatively designed a performance environment in which players engaged in both on-court training and off-court learning. This cyclic link between practical on-court sessions and reflective off-court sessions enabled the team to design, develop, refine, and operationalize SMMs.

In off-court sessions, players were empowered to reflect (individually and collectively) on SMMs relating to ACP players. Players watched six video clips (each 14 seconds long), and they reflected on key aspects. Players collectively discussed key aspects of the videos (noticing) and contextualized these observations in the context of agreed SMMs (framing). The session empowered the performers and team to reflect on the videos in a structured approach that required the content of SMMs to be built. SMMs created in the team meetings were operationalized on court during competitive matches.

> continued

> *continued*

SMMs were evaluated and monitored through the following:

1. Analysis of data relating to performance
2. The capture of increased similarity of SMMs relating to the ACP, indicating similar perceptions of the same tactical situations, and the comparison of individual player SMMs with the head coach's (expert) SMM
3. Individual players and the collective team recording more detail relating to ACPs as the complexity of SMMs developed over the time period

Statistical evidence also supported these three points; inferential statistics confirmed an improvement in match performance and results.

The key findings from the work identified the following: Creating a cyclic link between on-court and off-court training accelerated the development of SMMs relating to performance. Such SMMs improved on-court performance of individuals and, more importantly, the team collectively. Empowering athletes by involving them in reshaping the alpha vision of performance and establishing a collective beta vision of performance, enabled coaches and performers to agree to strategic objectives and understand the contribution each member would make to achieve success. It is essential that players be empowered to contribute to the alpha version of performance (development of beta vision) if they are to be autonomous decision makers and work effectively as a team. The research illustrated that the DM framework enabled complex information to be layered to construct complex SMMs that could be used in natural settings, resulting in a team cultural intelligence that led to more effective team DM.

Conclusion

This chapter considered the concept of SMMs and their application to enhancing the HPE. Use of specific theories from naturalistic decision making (NDM; namely, recognition-primed decision making [RPD], situational awareness [SA], and sensemaking) has been demonstrated though processes to be used in a team sport setting (Richards & Collins, 2020). One of many innovative but crucial elements is the parallel consideration of psychomotor and psychosocial elements, a combination that strengthens both buy-in by and effect on players.

However, the ideas in this chapter also have important applications for individual sports. Indeed, any situation that involves a group working together can benefit from the use of SMMs. Getting everyone on the same page facilitates the work of a support system, a coaching team, or even the family network around a particular athlete. The SMM construct is apparent in several chapters in this book. The ideas underpin the approach and the methods used—most notably empowerment—as vital tools for any coach who works with people.

14 | Macrostructures and Microsystems

Dave Collins

Grey Matters UK and University of Edinburgh

The old adage *Fail to prepare means prepare to fail* is an unavoidable idea that is important for all concerned in the field of sport and other performance. Nevertheless, many people resist learning the lesson it teaches. In fact, preparation and the structures that go with it have received bad press. Critics have even suggested that overly tight structures can stifle creativity in both coach and performer. Some have said that the coaching environment is so inherently variable that structure is impossible. Others have claimed that coaches should learn to adapt and react to how the performers are behaving rather than try to anticipate it in structures that serve as negative constraints.

Most of these concerns are understandable. However, these problems are a feature of bad structures and poor coaching rather than of structures per se. In short, good planning and well-designed structures will prepare you for the essential adaptation but also help you to think through your objectives ahead of time, making the planning session(s) more goal directed. Accordingly, this chapter covers some ideas on structure, which will help you in the effective planning process and also to optimize the impact of that process.

Relevance

Humans are undoubtedly social animals. One of several consequences of this truth is that coaches need to consider the interpersonal interactions that will inevitably occur. Indeed, they are so prevalent in the sport environment that even the greatest technical and tactical coach would be severely limited if they failed to consider various levels of interpersonal politics. These considerations extend from the smaller, or micro level (e.g., coach and athlete interactions) through the slightly more complicated, or meso level (e.g., the structure of the training or learning environment) through the multi-actor, or macro level (e.g., the way a training group, club, or even national sport governing body may operate).

Reflecting these considerations, this chapter offers an overview of ways to optimize these various contexts for interaction in order to achieve sport goals. (Of course, the goals must be clear in the first place; review part II of this book.) Although the chapter covers most implications for managers and coaches, athletes will also benefit from considering ways to use the proposed ideas to modify the environment around their own experience. The chapter begins with macrostructures and how they apply to and cascade down to the meso- and microsystems that coaches might use.

The considerations in this chapter are not only for team sport situations but for individual sports as well. Even track and field athletics involve a complex hierarchy of interactions, such as coach–athlete, coach–athlete with wider training group, training group with support staff, training group with other training groups, and training groups with the sport hierarchy.

The following section considers examples from the literature to inform interactions with the macro–meso–micro hierarchy.

What We Know

In simplest terms, this entire chapter is about communication. High-quality communication is essential for any effective performance environment. A broad range of literature supports this point; as one example, consider work done in talent development. Many of the examples in this chapter come from talent development, and they apply equally to all other aspects of the sport milieu.

Research has consistently demonstrated that quality communication underpins successful talent development environments and talent development coaching (Henriksen & Stambulova, 2017; Martindale et al., 2005). Importantly, this communication takes place both inside and outside of this system. Indeed, the quality of communication and associated relationships are often the major deciding influence on the outcomes (cf. Storm et al., 2014).

Macro Structures: Vertical and Horizontal Coherence

As a macro level, work by Webb and colleagues (2016) has offered insights into the organizational structure of a sport environment and how it may influence communication at all levels. The model is presented diagrammatically

High-quality communication is essential for any effective performance environment.

in figure 14.1. First, consider the athlete's progression upward along the pathway and how it is structured to be genuinely progressive—what Taylor and Collins (2020) refer to as *vertical integration*.

Figure 14.1*a* provides a model in which vertical integration is extremely tight and commonly understood. In other words, all the developing athletes experience a tightly constrained set of activities, all focused toward a clearly defined and narrow goal. Consequently, the developing athlete receives a coherent provision at each stage, in that every activity is clearly building toward a specific target outcome. This process is clearly positive in creating exactly what the system wants to create. However, a downside always exists; in this case, the cloning process results in performers with lower levels of adaptability. In short, such an athlete would find it hard to swap from the environment for which they were trained to another one. Considering that athletes may move several times in their careers, this lack of adaptability can be extremely limiting. As an additional challenge, either the rules or regulations may change (e.g., modern pentathlon becoming a one-day event) or the style of the game may result in different demands (e.g., changes in scrum laws in rugby union leading to need for a balance of various skills in props). The point is that things change, so it is best that coaches equip athletes to deal with those changes.

Figure 14.1*b* provides a much wider-ranging pathway that shows a clear lack of integration. Coaches engaged at the different stages of athlete progression tend to stick to their own views on what is important and what is

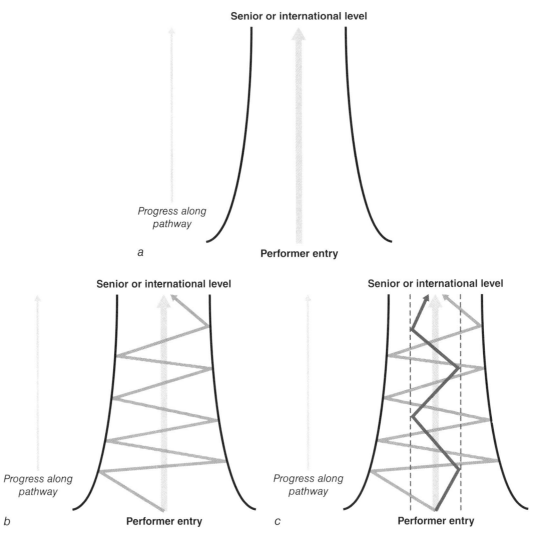

FIGURE 14.1 Schematics of typical progress in pathways that provide *(a)* low variability, *(b)* extreme variability, and *(c)* managed variability.

not. Consequently, the resulting athlete has a wide range of experiences and, assuming the athlete hasn't been burnt out by the variations in challenge, a very adaptable performer will result. Unfortunately, however, the toggling from level to level can be disconcerting for the athlete, who may end up burnt out through trying to cope with the multiplicity of demands or even lose motivation and drop out.

As shown in figure 14.1*c*, a happy medium exists. Integration is apparent in the core of activities that the athlete experiences, but coaches have some freedom to add their own emphasis. In this way, the athlete receives a variety of stimuli and experiences that build their capacity for adaptability while also providing a coherent and clear set of goals. Note that the more gifted and talented the athlete, the potentially wider this balanced zone can be. For the moment, though, consider that placing some constraints—more positively, clearer guidelines—on a core of content will help to ensure an adaptable and motivated adult. Having a system where progressive experiences clearly build toward a commonly understood goal can be considered vertically integrated, leading to a more coherent experience for the athlete.

Of course, it is also important that messaging and goals are consistent *within* the different levels through which the athlete will progress; in other words, they are horizontally integrated. The messages they are receiving should be complementary and consistent rather than contradictory. To ensure this relationship, the sensible coach makes sure that all stakeholders involved in working with the athlete (e.g., the sport's national governing bodies [NGBs], managers, parents) have an agreed-upon and well-understood set of targets that are mutually supported. When this mutual support is ensured, the athlete works with clear messaging on what is needed. This lack of horizontal turbulence ensures that the athlete knows exactly where they are, and they are consistently encouraged toward common goals. The next section covers this horizontal integration in more detail. At this stage, coaches and athletes should consider whether they clearly understand what part each element of their training is—down to play, where they are going, and why; they need to know that all elements are consistent with what they are trying to achieve.

Operational Principles and Practice

Several chapters in this book will attest to the importance of a common understanding, a feature the literature refers to as shared mental models (SMMs; see chapter 13). SMMs are useful in a number of ways, most particularly in the present context because they will aid both vertical and horizontal coherence. Asking for and understanding the reasons why certain decisions are made is important for optimizing organizational systems. Often, people avoid this questioning for fear that it would be seen as confrontational. In fact, high-performing environments are built on quality disagreement, in which people are respectful of each other's opinions while also being able to question and debate to ensure optimal outcomes for the athletes concerned.

One place where these issues tend to arise is around role clarity. It is an essential precursor in performance settings, and it provides the important bridge between role efficacy (how good someone thinks they are at the role) and their eventual performance (Bray & Brawley, 2002). The author's own work (Collins & Taylor, 2019) has suggested three factors related to roles that, when fully addressed, will help to optimize performance. First is role clarity (knowing what everyone is expecting you to do). In addition, you need to check role expectation (what they are actually expecting) and role recognition (the extent to which they will acknowledge and reinforce it if you do it). Applying these three Rs will ensure that SMMs exist and are effective. (This idea and its assessment are addressed later in the chapter; see 3Rs System: What Aspects of Role are Recognized and Rewarded).

Role clarity doesn't apply only to individuals working within groups, it also applies to groups interacting with each other. For example, Pankhurst and colleagues (2013) looked at role clarity in terms of underlying principles for a talent development pathway. Using a set of literature-derived principles, they asked participants to report their own sense of agreement and disagreement with each using a Likert scale. Comparisons between the NGB, coaches, and parents of players in tennis showed significant differences in scores, illustrating a lack of clarity. However, the study went further by asking the three parties to score what they thought the other two would think. This question yielded yet more significant differences, showing that participants were not just different in their perceptions but also in what they thought the other groups expected. In short, it was indicative of a lack of sharing in the SMMs. These findings hold importance for all elements of the macro–meso–micro model, once again stressing the importance of communication.

Of course, disagreement is not completely bad. Drawing on a deep knowledge of organizational psychology, Burke (2011) suggests that people working in target focused groups should live life in the zone of uncomfortable debate (ZOUD; see also chapter 13). This perception of conflict as a positive influence on group operation has been around for a long time. Indeed, Tuckman (1965) talked about the different stages of group formation, acknowledging the importance of a storming stage, although his focus was more on the development of a within-group hierarchy. The author's own research (Alfano & Collins, 2021) is unequivocal in stressing that this internal questioning approach is an essential component, especially in groups aiming for high levels of performance. Of relevance, higher-ability (and perhaps more self-confident) groups are more susceptible to cooperating on change through persuasive argument, while lower-ability groups tend toward splits emerging through a process of social comparison (cf. Sieber & Ziegler, 2019). As a result, you might be selective regarding circumstances under which you do (or don't) debate with colleagues about how to make improvements. For the present purpose, the point is that you should not only insist on knowing *why* things go on but also feel confident in contributing to the ongoing refinement of the organizational systems within which you work.

Consider the role of the coach, especially if it is as part of a developmental pathway. For example, a high school coach clearly wants the team to be successful. It is also at the very least a positive bonus if athletes from the program get drafted to college with scholarships. Indeed, even grassroots athletes want to get better, and the good coach will cater to these desires by setting out a longer-term plan on how their athletes can be developed.

Mesosystems: Ensuring Horizontal Coherence

As a medium (meso) level, coherence relates to the extent to which the athlete is receiving consistent messages on what they need to do. In simple terms, it could be seen as ensuring everyone involved is on the same page.

It certainly applies across any environment, and several other chapters in this book emphasize it (e.g., see chapter 3 on integrating different aspects of athlete life).

Original work by Martindale and colleagues (2005), later supplemented and extended by Henriksen and colleagues (e.g., Henriksen et al., 2010), points to the important role that horizontal (as well as vertical) coherence plays in the design of optimal talent development environments (TDEs); Henriksen and colleagues (2010) refer to athlete talent development environments (ATDEs). As shown in figure 14.2, the vertical coherence of what people are trying to achieve is underpinned by horizontal coherence through a focus on holistic development.

Consider the items down the left-hand column as being the essentials that need to be addressed through vertical integration—that is, the aspects of the pathway that need to be ensured as progressive as athletes move from stage to stage. In the middle column of figure 14.2, the items describe factors that need to be considered within levels, such as the extent to which all stakeholders are aiming for the same things, the extent to which autonomy is being encouraged and, most importantly in a talent development setting,

Key features	Key methods	Nature of model
Long-term aims and methods	Develop a long-term vision, purpose, and identity.	
	Develop systematic planning and implementation.	
	Provide coherent reinforcement at a variety of levels.	
Wide-ranging coherent messages and support	Provide coherent philosophies, aims, and methods at a variety of levels (e.g., parents, coach content, practice and reward systems, selection, funding, competition structure, NGBs).	
	Educate and involve parents, schools, peers, coaches, and important others.	
	Use role models at a variety of levels.	
	Set up a variety of support networks (e.g., peer, coach, sport staff, family) over the long term.	
	Provide forums for open and honest communication patterns at a variety of levels.	Integrated, holistic, and systematic
Emphasis on appropriate development, NOT early success	De-emphasize winning as success at development stages.	
	Provide clear expectations, roles, and meaning within the big picture at every level.	
	Provide stage-specific integrated experiences and teaching, including fundamental physical and perceptual skills, fundamental mental skills (learning and development, life, performance-related), sport-specific skills (technical, tactical, mental, physical, perceptual), and balance.	
	Encourage increasing responsibility and autonomy in learning and development.	
	Develop intrinsic motivation and personal commitment to the process.	
	Promote personal relevance, athlete understanding, and knowledge.	
Individualized and ongoing development	Provide opportunities and fundamentals to as many youngsters as possible.	
	Provide flexible systems to allow variation in performance and physical development.	
	Identify, prepare for, and support individuals through key transitions.	
	Provide regular individual goal setting and review processes.	
	Provide systematic reinforcement contingencies.	

FIGURE 14.2 Key features of effective talent development environments.

Reprinted from R.J. Martindale, D. Collins, and J. Daubney, "Talent Development: A Guide for Practice and Research Within Sport" *Quest* 57, no. 4 (2005), 353-375.

the levels of coherence between parents, coaches and the young athletes themselves.

Microelements: One-to-One or -Two Interpersonal Relationships

Whether this element comes at the top or the bottom of your imaginary hierarchy (a top–down or bottom–up approach), there is no doubt that strong relationships between athletes (or between coach and athlete) are key to performance. The world leader in this field is Sophia Jowett, who has been investigating coach–athlete relationships in her work for a number of years. Importantly, such relationships will have affective, cognitive, and behavioral elements, which interact to produce an overall picture. Notably, however, relationships between the coach and athlete can be very effective but still unsuccessful. Therefore, the key issue is for the coach and athlete to identify an appropriate balance unless they think that performance success and an effective and productive relationship can both be achieved.

A key model in this work is the 3C+1 model (e.g., Jowett & Chaundy, 2004), which describes the four components of the coach–athlete relationship as follows:

*C*loseness: How the coach and athlete perceive their relationship in an emotional sense

*C*ommitment: How both parties commit to the relationship to achieve their agreed targets

*C*omplementarity: The closeness of fit between the two; whether actions by one party create a consistent and expected response in the other

*C*o-orientation: In achieving this complementarity, how well the two parties fit together, matching each other's states and targets

The model has been applied widely, including to executive coaching (e.g., Jowett et al., 2012), and it offers a robust structure through which to examine the coach–athlete relationship. The only concern with this element is the extent to which a close relationship has unequivocally been shown between the relationship and performance. For the moment, return to the aspects of role clarity; in short, both sides of the relationship need to know what they want from it. That concept returns the focus to the macro end of the structure. You know that relationships are as key to organizations (cf. Peters & Waterman, 1982) as they are to individuals (Baumeister, 1998). As stated earlier, it all comes down to communication, both in establishing goals and methods and also then negotiating how they may best be achieved.

Again, putting these ideas together offers a hierarchy and flow that can work in either direction: macro–meso–micro or vice versa. The main issue is one of coherence, specifically, how well all these relationship elements fit together and work toward an agreed-upon set of goals. It is important to keep this interactive nature in mind when assessing or developing any one or all of the elements. To that extent, examining the links top to bottom *and* bottom to top is usually a useful auditing process.

Assessment

Scientists in general and psychologists in particular are notorious for overintellectualizing things. Therefore, the authors of this book have intentionally avoided adding too many questionnaire measures. Although they are great as research tools, accessibility and interpretation problems sometimes make them difficult for practitioners to get their hands on and use effectively.

At the most basic level, assessment of coherence from macro- to microsystems can be a matter of simply talking things through The idea is that if the people concerned develop the SMMs that feature so heavily in this chapter and indeed in the whole book, at least all will be better integrated and the athlete experience will be coherent. Such conversations should focus as much on the *why* as the *what* and *how* so that you know not only the goals that you and your colleagues and collaborators hold but also the reasons underpinning them.

These conversations need not occur too often. All coaches know of the risks inherent in paralysis by analysis, and too much navel gazing is never good for any system (or any player in it). Importantly, however, good practice should include regular reviews so that all are certain and feel confident that they are proceeding in the optimal fashion.

The Big 5: A Structured Approach

Regular reviews should be a part of any planning process. However, as a more frequent and ad hoc method, an approach called the Big 5 can deliver a lot of benefits. The idea is that through regular (but not *too* regular) structured conversations, coaches are encouraged to consider wider alternatives to the methods they have employed. When used as a coach development tool, the Big 5 is focuses on the *how*, with decisions driven by consideration as to *why* a particular method was used. Turning it around slightly can change the focus on the *why* which, as stated earlier, is the main concern in a drive for coherence.

The idea is that after a coaching episode the coach, with one or more colleagues or internally to themselves, explores options through consideration of the following five questions:

1. What did you do?
2. Why? (In simple terms, what were you trying to achieve?)
3. What alternatives did you consider? (Usually it's best to limit them to three options.)

4. What would have changed in the circumstances or context to make you choose one of these other options?

5. When and how would you be able to see whether your decision was the best one or not?

This approach has already been shown to be effective with several groups of coaches, most recently with a group of adventure sports coaches who used the technique for a year (Collins & Collins, 2020). For the present purpose, it exposes the reasoning underpinning certain actions, with this reasoning then overt as a focus for clarification and debate. In short, once colleagues ensure a common set of *whys*, they are much more likely to be on a common track and coherent in their actions.

3Rs System: What Aspects of Role are Recognized and Rewarded

The 3Rs system includes clarity, expectation, and recognition. As mentioned earlier, role clarity ensures that everyone knows what they should be working on. Importantly, however, high-performance environments are as social as any other environment where humans interact. Therefore, it is not only important for any individual to know where they fit into the system and what they should be doing. In addition to role clarity, the individual must also accept what it is they are being required to do. Finally, others in the group must recognize, acknowledge, and support those behaviors. Research shows the power of positive feedback (Mouratides et al., 2008), which can add to feelings of competence to create a positive feedback loop for all concerned.

Having conversations between team members is an essential part of checking for this important characteristic. However, a slightly more structured approach is often useful. When called in to work with group dynamics, it is useful to follow this four-stage process:

1. Ask a line manager or leader what particular people in the system are expected to do.

2. Next, ask those people in person what they think they are expected to do.

3. Then ask each person's peers what they think that person is required to do (in particular, what they do when they are doing their job really well).

4. Finally, observe how people behave, looking at the extent to which each person is recognized, acknowledged, and praised when they do certain things.

In an effective 3Rs system, the answers from all these four elements will be almost identical. In other words, someone knows what they're expected to do, how it fits with what their leader expects, what their peers recognize and, crucially, that the behavioral consequence of behaving this way is positive and consistent. In short, members of the group will consistently recognize and reward (reinforce) important aspects of each other's roles, keeping the whole group moving along the same agreed-upon optimal track.

This idea sounds simple; however, it isn't common. Interpersonal issues, lack of clarity, too many assumptions, and too little communication all combine to generate a system where people are often pulling in different directions. Add the understandable human traits of the need to protect your own position while seeking positive affirmation, and the potential challenges to a coherent system are all clear. Note that the 3Rs idea applies equally well across macro-, meso-, and microelements.

Clarity on Targets and Values: What Are We Trying to Achieve?

After all the ideas presented, it is clear that you need to become coherent in the most macro idea of all—what everyone is trying to achieve. However, it is surprisingly common that, through a combination of lack of role clarity and different ideals, people end up with a lack of coherence across systems and organizations at all levels. The underpinning reasons relate to public recognition and praise.

For example, consider the case of a coach working in an academy system. The academy will understandably stress the importance of the long-term outcome—that the aim of the whole academy is to get players through to first team level or onto a professional contract. However, this goal represents a very long sales loop. It is a rare person who can set goals and await their reward over the five- or six-year period that this one may take. Furthermore, go back to their peers and see how much more likely they are to relate to and reinforce the team's performance last Saturday or how well the athlete has achieved this season, rather than remember (and publicly praise) five or six years later what contribution the athlete made to this eventual senior success.

This case clearly exploits the motivational powers of positive feedback mentioned earlier (cf. Mouratides et al., 2008). Things don't all need to be positive, however. Shame can drive people toward a desire for change (Lickel et al., 2014), while negative feedback is much more effective at getting them to engage in thinking through ways to improve their performance (Taylor & Collins, 2020). Therefore, the skilled coach, manager, or administrator (or parent!) will use a combination of both stick and carrot in developing their systems.

Reflecting this idea, and as detailed in the previous sections, good management and in-team interaction will work for a sound base of coherence between stated aims and values and observed behavior in praising players or coaches. This idea of coherence in word *and* deed is an important one, and it is discussed in the final section of this chapter.

Every coach, manager, or leader needs to keep a careful eye on both the outcomes and drivers of coherence within their systems, teams, and organizations. The common difference between what is said and what people interpret and then do should show you the important task of making sure that all are aligned in the same direction. The next section explores some ways in which this task can be done.

Optimization

Optimization or promotion of your system or organization comes down to clarity of communication. Consequently, the whole of this section is about providing various methods whereby communication can be enhanced and coherence can be monitored, promoted, and improved. As the U.S. poet Emily Dickenson said in 1862, "The heart wants what it wants, or else it does not care." Similarly, an organization NGB, team, or coach can publish as many mission statements or make as many speeches as it likes; however, unless all involved buy into the same targets, even a heavy-duty and draconian system of monitoring and regulation will not ensure that the objectives—however valid or desirable—will be achieved. For example, many cases of athlete abuse may stem from a combination of either willful or ignorant dismissal of what were espoused as the underpinning philosophies of the program. It is important to recognize the power of social pressures against goals and reward structures of individuals. In short, changing behavior is best achieved through the use of social pressures and personal buy-in as well as central leadership. Stoszkowski and Collins (2012) emphasize how coach development is a very social enterprise. As with many other human interactions, people will be encouraged or discouraged from certain actions under significant influence from the social milieu in which they work.

Therefore, it is worth any coach, manager, or leader ensuring that all stakeholders understand and buy into the objective set for any program intervention or initiative. It is wise to check that everybody is on board before setting sail.

Moving away from this talent development setting, consider the example of a different environment, such as a grassroots coach who works with adults aiming at improving but also who enjoys the process of their involvement in sport. Once again, getting everybody on the same page is an important consideration. For example, are coach and athletes consistent in what they are trying to achieve? If the athletes are looking for a good social setting but the coach is driven by achievement of league championships or cups, their goals are clearly inconsistent. In a different setting, such as for a National Collegiate Athletic Association (NCAA) coach, cohesiveness is important; however, adding sufficient variation helps to meet individually stated (or covert) needs. Some athletes may be focused on exploiting their scholarship to achieve the best academic results. Others may be focused on achieving

Success Story 1: Long Road to an Olympics

The road of progress toward an Olympics is clearly a long one. Indeed, Eastern European systems used to look at a 12- or 16-year cycle toward achievement of high levels (a gold medal) at an Olympics. In simple terms, athletes would go to their first Olympic Games to check out the environment, a second to perform, then a third (plus preferably a fourth) to medal. The point is that achieving in this very special, indeed peculiar environment, means that many different factors are catered to. All the athletes I have worked with report that (1) Olympics are special, (2) they are different from every other competition experienced, and (3) each one is different from the others. In short, they are worth careful and specific preparation. Although not all athletes will achieve this level, all will experience a major competition that is a similarly unique challenge.

Preparation with teams for an Olympics has always been of a longer duration than for other events. From a uniqueness perspective (and for most sports where viewing figures are somewhat lower than the average Premiership soccer or Diamond League athletics numbers), the step up is particularly different and especially effective. Of course, these effects are not solely on the athlete; they also have an effect on the social dynamic the athlete experiences within their own training group or team or (of equal importance but less attended to) their families as well.

Therefore, this success story describes my experience working with curling teams developing toward a Winter Olympics. Attention was paid at a macro,

DANIEL LEAL-OLIVAS/AFP via Getty Images

No matter the sport or event, preparing for the Olympics presents a unique challenge.

> continued

> continued

meso, and micro level. As a macro concern, we were particularly focused on ensuring that messages on procedures and expectations were well managed across the NGB but also NSO financing bodies.

From a meso level, we ensured that all members of the team had contributed, understood, and were fully committed to the plan of campaign. For example, we considered how much emphasis was placed on the various qualifying and practice events, who from the five- or six-person squad would play in each event, how selection criteria would be applied or varied, and the detail of the immediate plan into the Olympics itself.

From a micro perspective, we were particularly careful to engage family members and interested parties from the curling community. For the first group, we made sure that everybody knew where the points of pressure would take place. It was important for us that the athletes' immediate families knew when selection pinch points would occur, and what they would mean to the athletes and their chances of selection and performance.

From the second perspective, we wanted to ensure that the curling community in our target country were both aware of and informed about the rationale and intent underpinning the decisions made. In short, if we were to maintain and benefit from the community so important in this tight-knit and socially based sport, we needed to make sure that gossip and assumptions where minimized while informed and carefully evaluated decisions were shared.

As a result, both men's and women's teams performed well and maintained these performances through subsequent events. In conclusion, coaches and managers need to take the trouble to ensure that the intent and rationale underpinning decisions taken are clearly understood and, where possible, endorsed.

levels of performance that attract professional scouts. A few athletes may be looking to enjoy their time at college and make the most of their social status as collegiate athletes. The good coach will take steps to learn of all these experiences and then develop a plan to satisfy the majority view while also offering something to the perhaps significant minority with diverse aims.

Coaches, managers, and leaders will take a variety of steps to make sure that the message on *what we are trying to achieve* is both clearly and consistently transmitted, thus it is consistent in communication and behavior. One common example of such a dissonant mismatch is a coach who says they are committed to long-term development but then picks the best team all the time in order to win every game. Indeed, ensuring consistency forms a great deal of the author's work with parents in academy settings. It is also equally important when dealing with families. As the first success story 1 shows, getting everybody on board with the master plan in the run-up to a major championship is an excellent idea; it avoids conflict down the line while also imbuing team members and significant others with the confidence in what has been designed.

Therefore, it is always worth looking at what has been developed, published, and circulated around any organizational scheme whether at the macro, meso, or micro level.

Psychological Safety: Ensuring Positive Conflict and Constructive Criticism for Growth

With all this emphasis on clarity of communication, it's easy to assume that high-performance environments (or even high perform*ing* environments) are easy places to exist. As the points made earlier emphasize, ZOUD living is an important feature to encourage and commit to. Literature has started to emphasize the role of psychological safety in such environments. *Psychological safety* is defined as "being able to show and employ one's self without fear of negative consequences for self-image, status or career" (Kahn, 1990, p. 708). In simple terms, it is the need for all to feel comfortable to express concern and constructively criticize what is happening. A simple Likert scale questionnaire is available at https://psychsafety.co.uk/measure-psychological-safety. Be aware that this tool isn't a psychometric instrument but rather a set of questions you can use to stimulate discussion.

Although psychological safety is an important factor, timing is crucial, as is who you communicate with. Therefore, standard operating procedures that tell people how, when, and to whom criticisms can be passed are an important feature of ensuring psychological safety. Proper procedures maintain the environment for constructive criticism while also ensuring that the whole plan doesn't fall apart because of internal strife. For the moment, it is probably best presented as a case of disagreeing in private and promoting a common front in public—a simple but often-neglected factor in many interpersonal settings.

RIB Approach: When Is Behavior Out of Order?

Sport has been part of society for many generations, and social standards have changed considerably over the years. Certain coach, athlete, and leader behaviors that used to be socially acceptable may now be considered inappropriate, abusive, and even criminal. It is beyond the scope of this chapter to fully describe or debate these changes, but the point is that the social landscape is ever evolving. Therefore, judging whether behavior is appropriate is more of a skill than a set of specific rules. This section covers an approach that has proved useful in high-performing settings (both in and outside the sport realm). In the rationale–intention–behavior (RIB) approach, three elements must be considered in parallel when judging whether behavior is appropriate: the rationale for the behavior, the intent behind the behavior, and the behavior itself. It is crucial that the cultural leader clearly communicate what the group should expect and why. At the very least, the RIB approach offers a good basis for debate. It can also serve to highlight points of contention to be addressed proactively, preventing much strife down the line. Success story 2 presents an example of how the RIB approach might be applied.

Success Story 2:
RIB—Making Expectations Mutual and Overt

This success story emphasizes the role of the RIB principles described in the chapter, namely, making sure that people understand what is to be done and, more importantly, with what intent and why.

It examines the need for communication between athletes and coaches in the challenging sports of free skiing and snowboarding, specifically the disciplines of park and pipe, where athletes must execute a series of inherently hazardous tricks toward a score awarded on aesthetic rather than purely technical grounds.

Training must inevitably involve risky practice. The challenge for coaches is in deciding when such risks are or are not appropriate. In this case, coaches came up with a set of criteria for the day's goals including identifying days when push, drill, or play was the order of the day. On push days, athletes were warned and would expect to be trying their hardest tricks, accompanied by the use of airbags and other safety precautions. Most importantly, the mindset was established that on this day, they were going for it. By contrast, on drill days, athletes accepted the fact that practice would be targeted at establishing sound execution of tricks that were 7 out of 10 in degree of difficulty. Finally (and in stark contrast), play days enabled the athletes to remind themselves of why they started the sport in the first place. The goal was to rediscover the joy that skiing or snowboarding had offered them, often exploiting recent falls of powder snow to hammer the point home.

The effect of this approach has been documented elsewhere (e.g., Collins et al., 2018; see also chapter 15). The idea of presenting the rationale and intent underpinning behavior, then sharing it with the athletes, has made a positive contribution to the SMMs that are essential between athletes and coaches.

Ensuring a Cohesive and Comprehensive Model

Finally, reflecting the ideas of cohesiveness throughout this chapter, this section presents a model for those involved in athlete development that can ensure all aspects are addressed. A few of these models are available around the world. A popular model that has enjoyed a long life in English soccer is the four corners model, which sees player development as built on tactical, physical, mental, and social components. This approach is a little bit lacking because it fails to reflect the dynamic nature of how these different factors may wax and wane in importance as the player develops, but it led to the development of the five rings model (figure 14.3).

This model considers several factors. Most importantly, the coach, manager, or leader ensures a comprehensive treatment for athletes through their development pathway and even when they hit the senior level. Even for full-time and well-seasoned senior internationals, effective systems will cater to variety of support—not focusing solely on pitch, track, or court

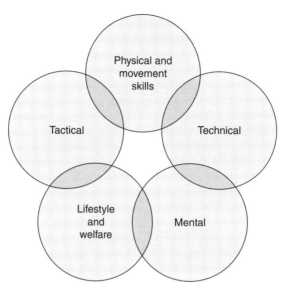

FIGURE 14.3 Five rings model.

performance. The second feature is that the most important factors (and the interrelatedness of these factors) will change with age. As one example, departure from a home environment to college, university, or work places an extra emphasis on mental and lifestyle issues (cf. MacNamara & Collins, 2010). This transition, which is common at around age 18 in most societies, means that an effective system will address and prepare for these factors well in advance (see chapter 17).

Conclusion

This chapter highlighted a number of organizational and structural considerations which, if attended to proactively, will avoid clashes and concerns while also raising the efficacy and impact of coaching inputs. Note that these considerations operate at a series of usually overlapping but distinct levels: the macro, meso, and micro levels. Coaches can address these levels separately; indeed some individuals will see one as their business while ignoring the rest. However, in the shared mental model (SMM), you are usually best thinking about and tweaking the system as a whole, albeit it is a big job. Take the time to add your own particular considerations to the generic ideas presented. Remember to be careful; it's a (sociopolitical) jungle out there.

PART IV | PREPARING INDIVIDUALS AND TEAMS FOR OPTIMAL PERFORMANCE

15 | Program Integration

Tom Willmott

Head Coach, Park and Pipe, Snow Sports New Zealand

I (the author of this chapter) have had extensive personal experience with program integration (PI). Therefore, in this chapter I use my own situation to exemplify its importance. As head coach of the Snow Sports New Zealand (SSNZ) park and pipe program, my role has evolved over more than 14 years. I started as the only full-time coach in the snowboard program, where I was responsible for three athletes and worked with intermittent part-time service providers. As a budding young coach in a fledgling organization, I was highly motivated, but I lacked experience; through both successes and failures, it was a steep learning curve. In my current role, I am responsible for leading a team of six other coaches, collaborating with an athlete performance support team of at least 12 specialist providers, and working closely with a senior leadership team that includes our high-performance director, performance services manager, and high-performance athlete development manager. We currently have 12 carded athletes and 12 national development athletes in the park and pipe program; they range in age from 10 to 25. Our athletes have achieved a host of results spanning the competition landscape, including multiple major event podiums; World Cup, X-Games, and World Championship wins; and two Olympic medals at the 2018 Winter Olympic Games.

As our program has evolved over time, we have needed to repeatedly focus on PI. With program growth in size and complexity, integration has been crucial. It ensures that performance, progression, and well-being have remained at the heart of what we do; that our systems, structures, and cultures have continued to develop; and that all of our people have continued to improve. Simply put, without good integration, any program will fail to work as effectively as it could. We certainly still have work to do in order to optimize PI throughout our program.

The following section explores the relevance of PI, once again referring to my own situation as a practical example. As a result, I propose several principles for effective PI that are then explored from a theoretical perspective in the What We Know section. The Assessment section offers some practical ways in which you can check your own settings before the final part of the chapter explores ways to optimize it.

Relevance

For around six months of the year (from May to November), our program is centralized in Wanaka (South Island, New Zealand), with our offices, gym, trampoline, and off-snow compound at one location and our main on-snow training area a 35-minute drive away; we call it our *domestic* season. Over this period, most of our staff are in the same location and cross paths regularly (both informally and formally). A few staff members live elsewhere in New Zealand and overseas, so efforts must be made to ensure they are incorporated appropriately. For the other six months of the year (usually from late November to May), the majority of our athletes, coaches, and support staff are in the northern hemisphere training and competing. In the park and pipe program, we have numerous groups of athletes. Three main clusters compete in different disciplines and on different schedules along with our national development crews; at times they are spread around the globe, and at other times they come together. We call this period our *international* season. One might assume that PI is easier in the domestic season and harder in the international season. In fact, different and significant challenges exist for PI in both.

Domestically, we have the advantage for PI of a centralized system. It makes communication easier, utilization of staff across different groups of athletes more efficient, and alignment among staff clearer. We use either side of the domestic season for all-staff workshops, debriefings, and planning and professional development opportunities; these meetings allow integration both vertically (from leadership and management down to coaches and athletes) and horizontally (across different disciplines). One disadvantage for PI of the domestic season is that both staff and athletes have a lot going on in their lives, such as family, friends, study, other sports, hobbies and interests, distractions, and time commitments. Ultimately, it means less time in the day is available for focusing on snow sports, which can make PI a challenge. Careful planning, prioritization, and periodization are paramount. Another disadvantage is that with so much interaction going on, potential exists for more fatigue, frustrations, and social discord to ensue. Encouraging quality downtime for athletes and a suitable leave policy for staff aims to avoid the pitfalls of fatigue, while putting energy into formal and informal team-building activities is a proactive form of relationship management.

Internationally, we have the advantage of a focus on snow sports, which is the primary reason that everyone is overseas; as a program, we have a captive audience. On the downside, PI is a challenge because people are spread far and wide in multiple time zones with differing levels of support based on SSNZ's priorities. Our international season is made up of competition blocks and training camps that either stand alone or function as preparation for competition. With some periods of successive events on different continents, finding time for program-wide communication and ongoing program integration can certainly be a challenge. We combat this challenge with monthly performance team meetings, which function as a safety net; they supplement the expected ongoing communication from the lead coach to members of an athlete's tight team (people in their trusted inner support circle). Some coaches are better than others at this key task; likewise, some tight team members are more proactive than others on the communication front.

Program Philosophy and Shared Mental Models

For full PI, everyone must be aligned. What does *alignment* really mean, and how is it achieved? The program's strategic plan—identifying a clear vision, mission, goals, and values—is a good place to start. Without a clear overarching vision that everyone can buy into and a clear roadmap of how the vision will be achieved, the organization lacks shared purpose; individuals are more likely to operate in a self-serving way, which risks failure to achieve the collective goals of the program. For example, our program has a goal of achieving multiple medals in multiple winter Olympic cycles. Accomplishing this goal innately requires PI because it is virtually impossible for any one person in the program to achieve this goal alone. Specific, measurable, achievable, realistic, and time-phased (SMART) goals within the strategic plan are encouraged, while clarity regarding an organization's values will help foster desired behaviors. The strategic plan sets the roadmap for an organization and will include the program's philosophies.

The strategic plan will help build shared mental models (SMMs) at the macro level in terms of setting the focus, philosophy, and objectives with external stakeholders, including funding organizations and partners. For example, *Athlete Focused, Coach Led, Performance Driven* is a philosophy of the way that we operate at SSNZ. Everyone understands that this philosophy underpins how decisions are made, therefore they have the opportunity to critique a decision if it goes against these criteria.

Finding the balance that ensures the criteria are complementing each other rather than competing against one another is part of the art of PI. It is important that all members of the organization understand the shared meaning and nuances associated with these criteria; they can achieve this understanding through staff workshops; in communications; and by referring to them in the meeting room, on documents, and in regular program reviews. At the meso level, the efficacy of the strategic plan to encourage SMMs across the program will be influenced by how the plan is communicated. When it comes to alignment, focus on the details of communication; words matter, as do their meaning and interpretation. It is important to achieve PI for the program to regularly visit, review, and keep this plan live and to check that shared meaning is held among staff, athletes, and stakeholders. Any program can write a beautiful strategic plan that is tucked away on the CEO's hard drive, but fewer can live and breathe it across the whole organization day in, day out.

At the micro level, when newcomers are introduced to the program, a thorough introduction of the vision, mission, goals, and values of the program is required. This detailed initiation ensures that the newcomer understands the philosophy underpinning decision making in the program and the associated support and behavior they should expect to experience along with the behavior expected of them. Proactive leadership is required. Regular communication to ensure that staff and athletes maintain behavioral expectations should be accompanied by swift feedback and consequences when behavior does not meet expectations.

SMMs at the meso level include a shared understanding of performance among an athlete's tight team; it is crucial in order for different members of a support team to be able to integrate effectively. When members of the support team are comfortable with where each other's strengths lie and can contribute in a complementary manner, the benefits of PI will mean support staff are affecting performance in a multiplicative rather than an additive manner, thereby increasing the power of that support. Principles including the overall approach to the periodization of training and competition need to be understood and shared by all members of the athlete's team including the athlete themselves, so the right balance of overload (from the various types of stimuli such as technical, physical, emotional), along with the resulting opportunity for recovery (and learning), can be achieved. SMMs held by a coaching team with regard to technical performance are paramount in a team-coaching situation, where athletes are exposed to multiple coaches (see Team-Coaching Approach later in this chapter). To achieve these SMMs, coaches need to work together; they should be constantly discussing and debating performance, sharing the same performance language, and even designing and sharing models of performance that everyone can agree with.

At the micro level, it is important that individual relationships (most importantly, the athlete–coach dyad) include SMMs; people need to be speaking the same language, picking up what others are putting down. At the developmental level, the athlete is learning the language of performance. Layers of complexity are added appropriately as the athlete matures. Then, at the elite level, the language is sometimes simplified again to the critical few performance components.

Support and Challenge

During the time I have been in my role, I have experienced moments of too little of the right type of support and also moments of too much of the wrong type of challenge. To become or operate as a high-performance organization, the organization needs to have the right and complementary level of support and challenge along with systems and structures to foster that balance.

Early Days: Finding Our Feet and Establishing Performance

In our early years as a high-performance organization, just after the turn of the 21st century when multidisciplinary support teams were in vogue, expertise from existing high-performance sports was applied to ours. We applied an approach to snow sports that was successful in other sports (e.g., cycling, triathlon, rowing) focusing on the physiological requirements of the sport and making gains through physiological advancement and adaptation. While coaches and athletes certainly had room to grow in advancing athletes' physiological capacities at the time, the approach lacked collective buy-in from the participants. The culture of the sport prioritized creativity and art over science, so coaches and athletes prioritized on-snow progression over off-snow development. Athletes who had been drawn to the sport by its autonomous, supportive climate were not adequately supported through the challenge of grueling workout sessions and struggled to see the long-term payoff for their effort. We were still learning about the sport and what it took to win, we were building our support team, and the approach could certainly be described as *multi*disciplinary rather than *inter*disciplinary.

Aspirational Days: Understanding Performance and Achieving It

It took time for the cultures both within the program and in the wider sport to evolve to a point where, for example, strength training in the gym is seen at worst as a necessary evil and at best as a crucial component of performance. These days, most of the athletes understand the link to their performance and protection from injury, while coaches understand and prioritize the importance of physicality and robustness. This acceptance and understanding have been achieved through careful PI of the key components of performance where each is valued appropriately and periodized effectively. When a shift was made from executing to educating, funnily enough, buy-in increased! An integral part of this shift was the development of a profiling

Andy Cross/The Denver Post via Getty Images

For many athletes, emotional periodization can be just as important as physiological periodization.

tool that identifies *all* the key components of performance in our sport (see the Profiling section and figure 15.1).

By getting a clearer understanding of performance in our sport, and ensuring the right balance and focus of the requisite specialties, we have achieved better PI. Having the right people in the room, and resourcing roles with the right amount of capability and capacity has been a crucial structural element that has allowed PI to occur. We now have a full-time physical therapist working proactively on reducing the biggest risk to performance: injury. We have also shifted our focus to learning about and enhancing skill acquisition in a skill-based sport. Optimizing and periodizing performance has seen a model where not only is physical adaptation periodized but emotional periodization is prioritized too (Collins et al., 2018). Where a physiologically based sport such as rowing will rightly focus on physiological periodization, for our athletes (who need to constantly progress their level of performance and learn new tricks), emotional periodization is just as (if not more) important. We structure training at the macro, meso, and micro levels in terms of the emotional demands our athletes face in being required to constantly progress their level of technical difficulty in competition. In our program, the *who we are* (people) and the *what we are doing* (performance) have certainly evolved.

Into the Future: Shifting From Multidisciplinary to Interdisciplinary

We have been working hard on ways to enhance PI across our program. We had to ask ourselves if we were a *multi*disciplinary organization or an *inter*disciplinary organization. A multidisciplinary approach can be effective in some environments. However, at SSNZ we believe the whole is greater than the sum of the parts, that when people get **T**ogether to solve the performance puzzle, **E**veryone can **A**chieve **M**ore; in other words, we believe in a TEAM approach. To see a group of talented people collaborating with a shared purpose, to bounce ideas off each other, and to brainstorm, model, test, build, critique, develop, and redevelop—in an interdisciplinary manner—is the essence of optimal PI. With the coach usually operating as the central agent, at least an elementary understanding of each of the specialist disciplines is useful, and an in-depth understanding is even better. However, no coach is going to be an expert in all elements of performance, and the responsibility also lies with the discipline specialist to sell their area of expertise and also to consider how they can combine with other disciplines in a complementary manner. A key skill that the expert coach requires is the ability to get the most out of the people around them. At times it includes getting the most out of people in the support team, who were not necessarily selected by the coach.

Some of the barriers to an interdisciplinary approach include the following:

- A lack of knowledge from coaches on the application of sport science
- A lack of knowledge from performance support on complementary disciplines
- Egos overshadowing reason, such as when individuals are unwilling to park their own issues, take feedback personally, or assume other staff have a fixed mindset
- Communication challenges, especially with part-time staff who do not have as much bandwidth or availability
- Performance support staff waiting to be led by the coach as opposed to being proactive when they are aware of an opportunity for performance enhancement
- Patterns of alliance (or perceived alliance) among certain members of the support team
- Different interpretations of the problem and the appropriate solution
- Differing opinions on and approaches to client or athlete confidentiality
- Social loafing, especially where support team group size is too large

Solutions to enhance interdisciplinary functioning include the following:

- Regular, efficient team meetings to identify performance puzzles and work together on solutions

- A team culture that encourages feedback, challenge, and continuous improvement
- A supportive and collaborative environment where all ideas are heard and actions are followed up on, and where people are accountable for following through
- Openness to exploring multipronged approaches to solve the performance puzzle

Systems and Structures

Over the years we have refined our systems and structures. This section takes a more detailed look at some specific examples, including an athlete profiling tool that we have developed, our approach to planning and communication, our team coaching approach, and the way we periodize PI itself.

Profiling

We use a profiling tool based on the Dreyfus model of skill acquisition (Dreyfus & Dreyfus, 1980). It includes a breakdown of the various performance components we believe are necessary to achieve a gold medal, such as technical skills, tactical skills, mental skills, and physical skills. Each subset of skills is broken into the most important components; five indicative levels of performance exist within each skill component from the regional development level of performance through to the elite podium level of performance. Each subset was devised by the respective specialists in that field; for example, our strength and conditioning coach and physical therapist have the most input into our physical skills, and our sport psychology practitioners have the most input into our mental skills. Given that the sport is still a relative newcomer and objective performance levels are improving continually subsets are regularly reviewed and updated. The tool we call the SSNZ rocket ship skills profile (figure 15.1) provides SMMs of the performance puzzle and helps clearly identify opportunities for each athlete to make performance gains following a biannual self- and coach review of their performance profile. A healthy debate on the prioritization of these rocket ship tasks is conducted during performance planning sessions with the athlete, coach, and other members of the athlete's tight team; the athlete is ultimately responsible for confirming and committing to these priorities.

Planning

High-quality planning is critical for PI occurring at various levels in the organization. The strategic plan at the highest level may look at least eight years into the future, while quad plans at the team and individual level (based on the four-year Olympic quadrennial) will guide annual plans, season plans, and specific competition and training camp plans.

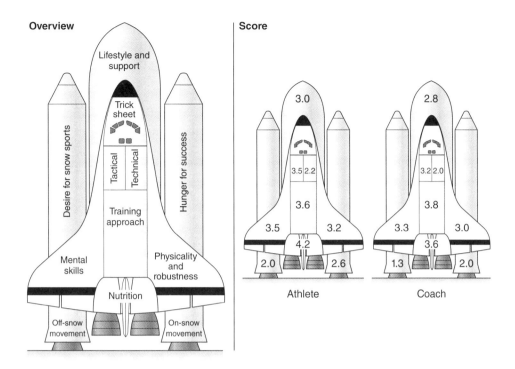

FIGURE 15.1 The SSNZ rocket ship skills profile.

One of the key communication structures enabling PI is the athlete's performance plan. It is a live document that the athlete reviews with their tight team at the end of each training phase (every four to six weeks). Specific goals are set for various facets of performance along with strategies to achieve those goals for the upcoming phase; the athlete is aided with guidance from the coach and input from specialist members of the athlete's support team. Accountability for goal achievement is then a shared agreement between the athlete, the coach, and relevant members of the support team. Regular reviews provide the opportunity for everyone involved to evaluate goal achievement and to establish what to focus on next (or what needs to change) for the goal to be achieved next time. Healthy debate over the prioritization of goals is encouraged along with a system for settling disputes. Usually the coach or the experienced athlete has the final say on the plan.

An athlete's performance plan guides their development. For staff, performance and development plans identify the support they need around them in order to perform and also include professional development activities and opportunities in order for them to get better at what they do. A focus on the well-being of all people within the organization is a fundamental bedrock of PI, while a systemic approach to looking out for people when they are struggling and supporting them through tough times is a cornerstone of sustainability. Members of the coaching and support team are often highly focused on their athlete's performance needs. Reminders to focus on self-care in order to be of better service to the team are a crucial and a valuable message from members of the leadership group to also model and champion. Physical, mental/emotional, and family/social well-being components are often easily visible. A less-understood component of well-being is the spiritual component—an individual's belief structure and their desire for purpose, meaning, and interconnectedness with others. All staff are encouraged to include a well-being component in their performance and development plan that identifies what *well* and *un-well* look like for them as individuals, how to maintain and promote *well* and how to avoid or treat *unwell*. A buddy system among staff to look out for each other's well-being, check in with each other, and reach out for help is a structure aimed at increasing well-being and proactively avoiding illness and burnout. Regular well-being measures inclusive of all the people in the organization through objective (e.g., number of training days lost to injury, illness, sick days) and subjective (e.g., informal check-ins, self-report surveys) indices are important ways for understanding the magnitude and types of well-being issues to be addressed.

The next step is having the capacity and resources (potentially internal or external to the program) to provide support and find solutions. The athlete well-being advisory is a live document that coaching and performance support staff update with regular structured check-ins at performance team meetings. It is a useful tool to alert staff to potential well-being issues with athletes so that they can work together on solutions and ideally address issues before they have a negative effect on performance.

Communication

I have already introduced some of our formal communication structures, including the athlete's performance plan, the SSNZ rocket ship skills profile, and the performance team meetings, among others. As far as direct communication with the athlete goes, in our context, an athlete's lead coach takes the main responsibility for it. Other members of the tight team, including additional team (assistant) coaches and performance support, communicate either directly with the athlete either with the lead coach's endorsement or through the lead coach to ensure a clear and useful message that is conducive to performance enhancement. Mixed messaging and misalignment can undermine both performance and trust, so it should be avoided. On one hand, it is important for differences of opinion to be discussed openly at the right time so that anyone involved can respectfully challenge something. On the other hand, it is important for all members of the support team to be cognizant of specific rules of engagement to avoid the risk of differences of opinion driving performance in counterproductive directions. The *disagree and commit* approach is a useful one for all members of an athlete's support team to understand and be able to apply appropriately. For example, advice on the tactical approach at a competition may be provided by a team coach positioned at the bottom of the course to the lead coach at the top of the course through a closed-circuit radio system (with an earpiece to avoid feedback and comments being shared directly with an athlete). The lead coach is responsible for taking the tactical advice and considering it along with closer insight into the athlete's capabilities and how the athlete is feeling, coping, and performing at that point in time. The lead coach may choose to take the advice onboard or may choose to opt for a different approach. Whether they agree or disagree, the team coach should unequivocally support whatever approach the lead coach deems most appropriate during any direct communication they have with the athlete at the bottom of the course. This show of support ensures a united front that promotes clarity and confidence for the athlete, which is crucial especially in a high-pressure competition situation. Skillfully debriefing any differences of opinion after the event can enhance the learning effect for all members of the coaching team and is an additional tool to maximize the quality of communication.

Team-Coaching Approach

At the national team level at SSNZ, we pride ourselves on a low coach-to-athlete ratio of around one to three. This level of coaching capacity helps PI to directly affect athlete performance. Each lead coach in the park and pipe program reports to me as the head coach, allowing my role to roam across the three discipline groups to facilitate ongoing PI. A construct central to PI is our team-coaching approach, strategically adopted and refined since 2014. While each athlete can define who their lead (primary) coach is from the selection of skilled and experienced coaches employed, a second layer of support and cover is in existence, in both an overt and a covert fashion with respect to the athlete. Athletes spend time at different training camps and competitions. They are exposed to coaching input from multiple coaches within the coaching team; coaches combine in pairs or threes to provide competition cover in lead and team (assistant) coach capacities at major events. Behind the scenes, coaches have input into the performance planning of other athletes within the program; they are encouraged to be involved in brainstorming solutions to various performance questions both formally and informally as a team. A coaching team charter was devised to ensure role clarity and that rules of engagement are understood and followed. Regular reviews of the charter allow for check-ins, debriefings, and updates following blocks of coaching.

The approach has had many benefits. Coaches working more collaboratively (in contrast to a previous more siloed approach) have seen an increase in the richness of feedback provided to athletes; collaboration promotes a more reflective and curious coach who has a community of practice to engage with to solve problems and address concerns. From a long-term perspective, sustainability is promoted with multiskilled coaches in long-term roles who continue to hone their skills and experience. This approach is preferred over the previous scenario in which new coaches arrived at the high-performance environment with "their" athletes; the coaching role was at risk following athlete injury or loss of form. In the thick of a training session or at a competition, the coach can turn to their colleagues to provide a second opinion. This external input from a different perspective offers an additional level of support and feedback that can complement the internal audit of the decision-making process in real time. We call this process *coach triangulation*.

One of the most effective elements of the team-coaching approach has been the positive ability of supporting (not lead) coaches to cover coaching responsibilities at major events. The current coaching team is poised with the nimbleness and agility to adapt to changing situations and circumstances (e.g., injury to athletes, arrival of new athletes, unavailability of coaches, loss of form, or de-carding of athletes) with complementary skill sets that can provide an essential challenge to the status quo.

Periodizing PI

PI needs its own planning and periodization. Our generic approach to building peak athletic performance in a four-year Olympic quadrennial, the four Ps model (prepare, progress, perform, peak, cf. forming, storming, norming, performing; see Tuckman, 1965) can also be applied to PI. For the whole program, year 1 is all about preparation. It is a great time for trying out new approaches, experimenting, integrating new people, and moving people on. Other preparations include embedding any changes to strategy. Year 2 can progress elements from year 1, testing people's relationships, capabilities, and capacities further by increasing the load, expectations, and stressors. Examples include giving new staff more leadership responsibility and increasing the pressure of time on the road incrementally. Year 3 is about performance, and it coincides with the start of the Olympic qualifying period. An example of the PI focus at the micro level in year 3 is the successful performance of an athlete's tight team in competition. At the macro level, the work will have been done with funding bodies for the current Olympic cycle and the focus will shift to securing support for following cycles. Year 4 is about preparing to peak when it counts. It is not the time to be trying too many new things (especially for older or more established athletes), and the same philosophy applies at the program level. Relationships within the athlete's tight team and the general ecosystem of the wider program should be as stable as possible to allow a focus on the crucial few things that matter for achieving peak performance. Of course, this model is simplistic and theoretical; external constraints and influences will always arise (e.g., COVID-19 in 2020); they highlight the need for a nimble program that can be agile and adapt to curveballs. It is important to strike the right balance between stability and agility in order to take advantage of new opportunities and innovations as they arise at any stage in the quadrennial; the goal is to achieve continuous improvement while peaking at the right time.

Culture: How We Behave Here

A famous Maori proverb states, *He aha te mea nui o te ao? He tangata, he tangata, he tangata.* It means "What is the most important thing in the world? It is the people, it is the people, it is the people."

For any program to be successful and achieve its goals, the culture—how the people within the program behave—will have a huge impact. The people are the most important thing, so we need to nurture them. We must look after them, encourage them, guide them, empower them, harness their maximum potential, help them to achieve their goals and dreams, and have fun along the way. With respect to how support teams work together, Reid and colleagues (2004) hit the nail on the head when they said, "a climate of cooperation and collaboration needs to be *actively* fostered in what is potentially an environment that fosters competition and conflict" (p. 205). Program leaders have the biggest responsibility for influencing the culture within the organization. This influence can be achieved in many ways, including paying special attention to the language that is used, recognizing achievement and celebrating success appropriately, ensuring that everyone is learning from both success and failure, ensuring that expectations are met, and ensuring that everyone adheres to ethics and discipline. The standard that we walk past is the standard that we accept; while program leaders set the tone, everyone in an organization has a role to play in influencing the culture. While a deeper delve into culture is beyond the scope of this chapter (and some further reading is identified later in the What We Know section), it is important to highlight its significance and relevance to PI.

Leadership and Trust

As previously discussed, any good system that involves people is built on a common understanding—a SMM. We need to integrate the athletes and their parents. We also need to manage a host of external stakeholders, including agents, sponsors, team managers, and others. The agent at the center of this integration is the coach, and the medium is effective communication. If a coach is at the early stage of their career or is lacking in leadership capability, this role needs to be supported. In our context, the lead coach's primary focus is on the coach–athlete–performance relationship, while the head coach can take on responsibility for leadership of an athlete's tight team and wider support group (if this focus is more appropriate). A transition toward a more lead-coach-led (rather than *head*-coach-led) approach can be achieved as the lead coach grows in experience and capability.

Internally, we need the generalists (the coaches) to lead the overall campaign plan; we need the specialists (the performance support) to lead their discipline; we need an organization full of leaders; and with all those leaders running around, we certainly need good followership. We also need a lot of trust between our people if we are going to have a suitable platform from which to challenge each other to achieve excellence. Trust does not happen by accident; it is earned when given and takes time to develop through shared experiences and the actions that people take when challenged. Trust needs to be nurtured through a combination of authenticity, empathy, and logical reasoning. When inevitable trust hiccups occur, they need to be nipped in the bud; usually viewing a situation through the lens of authenticity, empathy, or logical reasoning helps you find the best approach to restoring trust.

What We Know

The need for SMMs is a consistent message throughout this book. A large and growing body of literature supports the importance of this construct for almost any interpersonal setting (cf. Jonker et al., 2011). SMMs are fundamental to our program philosophy. Given that the literature shows an ongoing interest in innovative ways of building SMMs (e.g., Fletcher & Sottilare, 2018), this construct is likely to be a ubiquitous feature of programs with good PI.

Support and Challenge: From Multidisciplinary Teams to Interdisciplinary Teams

The use, advantages, and disadvantages of interdisciplinary teams has been explored in depth in the health care sphere (e.g., O'Connor et al., 2013; Grace et al., 2016). However, the effectiveness of interdisciplinary teams in sport settings is yet to receive much attention. Carson and colleagues (2014) outline an interdisciplinary approach to injury recovery in a case study, and Youngson (2018) provides an insightful master's thesis exploring the evolution from multidisciplinary to interdisciplinary teams from a strength and conditioning perspective. Reid and colleagues (2004) provide commentary on the construct of the multidisciplinary support team including evaluating inherent issues. Research is beginning to examine the interdisciplinary structure and how it might work to best effect. Much has already been written from an anecdotal level, whereby practitioners report on their own experiences in the field (e.g., Ingham, 2016). In an early attempt to develop some empirical underpinnings, Alfano and Collins (2020) conducted interviews with a cross-section of providers (e.g., sport psychology practitioners, strength and conditioning coaches) and consumers (e.g., performance directors). This study showed the importance of interpersonal skills as much as technical prowess as an enabler of well-integrated practice. A follow-up study by the same authors (Alfano & Collins, 2021) completed a longitudinal tracking of young practitioners in an attempt to see how they thought the interdisciplinary environment was developed. Reflecting earlier comments about how we developed our own PI environment, their participants stressed elements such as leadership and coherence in objectives as key.

Leadership and Trust

Trust is a critical aspect of any high-performance relationship. The coach–athlete relationship has received attention in the literature (e.g., Jowett & Cockerill, 2003; Jowett, 2017), while the conditions under which trust thrives in an organization have also been addressed (Kramer, 2010). As stated previously, it is also a key issue for support staff (cf. Alfano & Collins, 2021) in that trusted leadership from seniors, whether on the performance side (e.g., head coach or performance director) or from more experienced support practitioners, is highly valued.

The other explicit output from leadership is the clarity and coherence of direction. Building from the literature on SMMs, a growing body of work supports the importance of commonality in support teams, including an emphasis on role clarity (e.g., Eys et al., 2006) and on the development of SMMs in young practitioners (cf. Alfano & Collins, 2021; Floren et al., 2018).

Culture

Cole and Martin (2018) explored developing an effective team culture, while Cruickshank and Collins (2012) presented the bigger challenge of changing team culture and the role of the sport psychology practitioner. In both studies the authors stress the importance of multifactorial messages; they are cohesive in sending the same content through several routes but varied in that all concerned—athletes, coaches, and support staff—are receiving guidance from different sources. This combination of cohesiveness and variation helps to ensure that messages are clear, and they are also more likely to be received and internalized.

Assessment

A people × performance matrix is a useful approach for establishing whether the system is working. It is important to know what success looks like. Conversely, you also need to know how to identify when things are not working in order to be able to effect change. Tables 15.1 and 15.2 identify some examples of people- and performance-related questions that can help evaluate some of the important components of PI, along with what success and failure might look like in each instance.

It is unlikely that any organization will achieve a perfect success score on each of these dimensions all the time. Regular profiling, setting goals for improvement, and continually tinkering with the system is a key role of the senior leadership team. Thus, they can continue to get better, make the most of each staff member's abilities, and increase the collective capability and capacity of the system to achieve the overarching goals, whereby they can focus on optimization.

TABLE 15.1   People-Related Questions

ARE THE RIGHT PEOPLE ON BOARD?	
Success	**Failure**
You have a passionate, committed, hardwork-ing, and reflective group of individuals who are experts in their fields and can also work as a team, and they respect the expertise of others to get the best out of each other.	Motivation to improve is lacking, egos get in the way of what is best for the program, people are unwilling to rock the boat.

ARE THEY IN THE RIGHT ROLES?	
Success	**Failure**
Each member of the interdisciplinary support team has role clarity; they know which seat is theirs, and they stay in it while trusting others but also challenging the status quo.	A lack of trust and respect exists between staff members.

DOES AN APPROPRIATE LEADERSHIP AND FOLLOWERSHIP DYNAMIC EXIST?	
Success	**Failure**
Each member of the team has some form of leadership responsibility. They step up when required and can pull in behind other leaders (e.g., picture a track cycling team) to help make the team go faster.	Different people are leading the team in dif-ferent directions and sometimes at the same time.

TABLE 15.2   Performance-Related Questions

DOES EVERYONE HAVE A CLEARLY DEFINED AND COMMONLY SHARED PURPOSE?	
Success	**Failure**
Everyone understands and buys into the over-arching goals of the organization.	People show up, but they do not really know why they are there, what they are trying to achieve, and where they are trying to go.

ARE LEARNING, DEVELOPMENT, AND CONTINUOUS IMPROVEMENT PRIORITIZED?	
Success	**Failure**
Everyone subscribes to an action learning cycle (plan, act, review, learn). Each staff member buys into their own personal and professional development plan.	Mistakes are covered up. Excuses are made, and others are blamed. Things are done a cer-tain way because that's the way they've always been done.

IS A SYSTEMATIC REFLECTION AND DEBRIEFING PROCESS IN PLACE TO MAXIMIZE LEARNING AND IMPROVING NO MATTER WHAT THE OUTCOME HAS BEEN?	
Success	**Failure**
The process and performance are more of a focus than the outcome. Regular formal and informal reflection and debriefing occurs at all levels of the organization, affecting decision making and action.	Occasional reviews occur, usually only when things go wrong.

DOES TENSION EXIST ON THE LINE?	
Success	**Failure**
People can have skillful, courageous perfor-mance conversations in order to get the best out of each other. They passionately fight for what they think is best and are also able to disagree and commit if required.	Conflict is avoided in favor of artificial harmony.

Optimization

Getting all the different parts of a program to effectively work together and getting all the coaches and athletes on board at the same time is more of an art than a science. In fact, it relies heavily on emotional intelligence (EQ), which is required for interacting well with other people. High-quality leadership is at the heart of program optimization from the coach at the athlete and campaign level, from the head coach and management at the discipline and major event level, and from the performance director at the system level. The performance of all leaders in the organization relies on building trusting relationships, managing those relationships, and developing strong networks of support. The equilibrium of an organization is tested sporadically, PI is challenged, and dynamic adaptation to changing constraints is required. The optimal approach is one that is constantly looking to the future and anticipating these challenges, keeping an ear to the ground for changes of direction and opportunities that arise. It is important that leaders in the organization have enough bandwidth available to be future focused as opposed to staying caught up in fighting fires and managing day-to-day events.

Maja Hitij/Getty Images

Getting all the parts of a program to effectively work together is as much art as science.

As an example of a recent challenge to the optimization of PI, massive upheaval has occurred in life around the globe, not least in sport, because of the COVID-19 pandemic. As with other industries or businesses, sports that have been able to pivot effectively have flourished, while others have struggled. Sport programs that have thrived in the chaos and used flexible and agile approaches to PI have achieved a competitive advantage for their athletes. Rather than allow new performance barriers to block them, these programs have focused on the opportunities to create solutions and move beyond the barriers, and they have focused on solving problems rather than being weighed down by the magnitude of those problems. Rather than become paralyzed, they make progress; they keep moving—one mindful step at a time.

Conclusion

In this chapter, I used my role as head coach of the Snow Sports New Zealand (SSNZ) park and pipe program as an example of why program integration (PI) is important. I explained how the program that I work in has evolved over multiple Olympic cycles toward a functioning model of PI. I introduced some of the systems, structures, and other facets that are important in order for PI to occur, and introduced some of the barriers and solutions to effective PI. The chapter identified a nonexhaustive list of theory and research for wider reading and understanding of the topic, and it provided some ideas about optimization. Clearly, given that one of the central agents in PI is the coach, it is important that coach education address leadership, relationship management, and wider system knowledge for effective PI to occur; it will not happen by accident. My take on program integration is intended to provide some practical insight and ideas for nurturing and optimizing PI in your own context.

16 | Motoric Considerations

Maurizio Bertollo
G. d'Annunzio University of Chieti-Pescara

Antonio De Fano
G. d'Annunzio University of Chieti-Pescara

Performance optimization is the ultimate stage that finalizes the process of performance enhancement (Siekanska et al., 2021). Athletes aim to constantly improve sport performance, prevent underperformance, and achieve and maintain maximum performance, leading to an optimal or outstanding result (Kimiecik & Jackson, 2002). Optimizing performance is an essential feature of a successful performance, and it is usually based on adapting what has been learned during training to the needs of the competition (Gröpel & Mesagno, 2019). Sport performance optimization can involve not only the athletic, technical, and tactical aspects but also the psychological aspects, which are necessary to control and manage the competitive situations that inevitably (and often unpredictably) affect athletic performance.

Within the field of sport psychology, performance optimization has been traditionally achieved through the application of cognitive behavioral approaches that are mainly focused on affective and cognitive functions (Winter & Collins, 2015). More recently, however, researchers and sport psychology consultants have shifted attention to the action to be performed and the motoric factors of performance (Carson et al., 2021). Since the turn of the 21st century, researchers have developed, scientifically tested, and applied several action-centered approaches.

The general idea underlying these relatively new psychological approaches to sport performance optimization is that focusing on athlete movements and enhancing their action-related awareness is an effective and efficient strategy; ideally it is used as an addition to the more usual cognitive and emotional focus that has characterized sport psychology to date. This chapter presents the most recent and most used action-centered approaches that include a specific focus on the motoric aspects of sport performance.

Relevance

Optimal performance in sport is achieved through consistent practice that is invested in both training and competition. During training, athletes improve their abilities, learn new skills and competencies, and refine those already learned for performance enhancement (Carson & Collins, 2016a). However, technical training alone is not sufficient to optimally perform during competition, which is a well-known stressful and demanding situation that usually affects athletes' performance (e.g., see Davids et al., 2015) and can lead athletes to choke under pressure (Gröpel & Mesagno, 2019). In simple terms, being trained for an optimal performance is not enough; athletes' training needs to develop both the performance and the optimal emotional state in tandem, with control of both seen as parallel demands. Anxiety and fatigue are just two examples of the many factors that may moderate performance during competition (Carson et al., 2021). For this reason, the experience associated with optimal performance can vary across athletes; *optimal performance* is an umbrella term for the subjective states of peak experience, peak performance, and flow (Harmison & Casto, 2012). In short, recent research suggests that athletes can get *in the zone* by just letting it happen or through making it happen, experiencing this unique state in a very idiosyncratic manner (Swann et al., 2016).

A pragmatic example of this situation was reported by Ana Maria Popescu, one of the fencers who led Romania to win the gold medal in the women's team épée fencing competition at the 2016 Olympics in Rio de Janeiro. In describing her experience during the quarterfinals against Courtey Hurley, Popescu used the following words:

> I can't find my rhythm . . . Trying to get that touch, I get other four . . . After her [the opponent's] last point, I turned my gaze to the end of the fencing strip, where my team seemed to be standing still, paralyzed . . . Less than a minute and three touches to recover. After the third consecutive touch of the opponent, I realized that I was in a state of [unproductive] trance. (personal communication, February 28, 2019)

Although the International Fencing Federation (FIE) ranked Popescu number 1 in épée, she was not immune to the effects of anxiety and fatigue. In fact, one can observe traces of difficulty in executing the desired optimal performance (e.g., "I can't find my rhythm"). Moreover, it seems that the more she tried to act, the worse the situation became ("Trying to get that

FABRICE COFFRINI/AFP via Getty Images

At the 2016 Olympics, Romanian fencer Ana Maria Popescu (right) felt the effects of anxiety and fatigue.

touch, I get other four"). The social pressure deriving from responsibility toward the team ("I turned my gaze to the end of the fencing strip, where my team seemed to be standing still, paralyzed") and the rush of having to find a solution in the shortest possible time ("Less than a minute and three touches to recover") only made the situation worse. At a certain point, however, Popescu realized that she was in an inappropriate psychological state ("I realized that I was in a state of unproductive trance"). It is a clear example of how competitive situations unpredictably affect athletes' performance regardless of their level and experience. Although people like to think this scenario wouldn't occur in their own sport, it likely happens in all of them. For instance, tennis athletes with the ability to put the ball in specific parts of the court sometimes report a worsening of accuracy during competition. Similarly, in sports that require a choreographed performance, such as dance sport, ice skating, and artistic swimming, the pressing situation of competition may lead athletes to underperform (e.g., lose the crucial amplitude of movements) or even to forget steps and lose synchronization with teammates.

Popescu's words highlight that psychological strategies could determine an athlete's ability to control these influential factors, with consideration leading to adapting what has been learned during training to competition demands. Sometimes athletes are able to manage these factors, executing an optimal performance that leads to success. However, on other occasions, these influential factors are not effectively managed, and the risk of failure increases considerably. Notably, achieving and maintaining high-level performance under the demanding and ever-changing situation of competition is an essential characteristic of successful performance (Gröpel & Mesagno, 2019).

Based on Popescu's example, it is clear that the meaning of the term *performance* goes beyond the mere athletic, technical, and tactical aspects; it includes psychological abilities, such as efficiency and vulnerability of mental functioning and social interaction in performance settings (Nitsch & Hackfort, 2016). In this vein, mental skills training becomes fundamental in supporting athletes and coaches in the process of performance optimization (di Fronso et al., 2017; Harmison & Casto, 2012).

Within the field of sport psychology, the cognitive behavioral model is the dominant approach (Winter & Collins, 2015). Based on this model, emotions and cognition receive the major attention at the expense of movement control. However, Carson & Collins (2016b) highlighted the tendency to under- and misrepresent the motoric factors of performance in the broad field of sport psychology. They suggested a greater inclusion of motoric aspects (skill establishment) be made in empirical research as well as in practice. Focusing on motoric aspects of performance with the aim to optimize it means to move toward a more complex conceptualization of athletes' needs (Carson et al., 2021). Consequently, an increase in the chances of achieving the desired result (performance optimization) could be expected because motoric consideration affords several key alternatives and advantages to existing applied practice (Collins et al., 2015).

Success Story 1: Focusing on Motoric Aspects to Change the Game

Think back to the experience of Popescu during the 2016 Olympics. Regardless of the result, the goal is to understand how Popescu turned the game around by focusing on the motoric aspects of performance. In a personal communication, she stated the following:

> The only way was to change something, firstly to activate me and second to get her out of the rhythm, to break her tactics . . . I began to move chaotic, I must somehow destabilize her, impose a rhythm . . . and the touch did not delay appearing . . . A few seconds later, the score was equal, and the decisive touch follows . . . I was getting to feel the determination, the pace, the distance, the decision, the time [of the action] . . . I have trained a whole life for it! It was my moment, my touch, our team's day! (personal communication, February 28, 2019)

Focusing on her action and its characteristics in relation to the opponent's movements (e.g., pace, distance, time), Popescu was able to regain control of her own psychological state in a situation characterized by anxiety, fatigue, and pressure. This turnaround was the result of Popescu's hard work (both physical and mental) done in the years before the competition. In fact, Popescu and her staff applied an action-centered model, called the multi-action plan (MAP) (Bortoli et al., 2012), among other applied interventions.

The following section provides an overview of the main sport psychology–related models focused on motoric aspects. Then, the text delves into the MAP model with the aim of providing practical indications for athletes, sport psychology consultants, and other staff members who want to assess and optimize performance by focusing on motoric aspects.

What We Know

Failing to perform up to individual or team potential, or achieving desired results in training but not in competition, are traditionally linked to difficulties in managing emotions, therefore they have been usually managed through emotion-based coping strategies (Hanin & Hanina, 2009a). Aimed to provide an alternative or complementary perspective to this approach, however, different models have been designed. These models rely on the general idea that focusing on athletes' movements and enhancing their action-related awareness is also an effective and efficient strategy for optimizing performance.

Since the early 2000s, several action-centered approaches have been developed. Some of them are exclusively focused on the motoric aspects, while others also include the affective dimension of performance, adopting a more integrated approach (see table 16.1).

Structural Dimensional Analysis-Motoric Method

The structural dimensional analysis-motoric (SDA-M) method (Schack, 2012) has been specifically designed for measuring movement-related mental representations, called basic action concepts (BACs), and improving athletes' technical preparation (see Schack & Frank, 2020 for a more recent review). Athletes are required to hierarchically cluster and serially order a series of sub-actions (i.e., BACs) presented as textual descriptions, pictures, or video clips. For instance, serve-related BACs in tennis include ball throwing, racket acceleration, and racket follow-through movements. Once clustered and ordered, the BACs are displayed as dendrograms and compared with the actual biomechanical demands of the action. Depending on the potential differences between how sport actions are mentally represented and how they are executed (a feature that coach observation can easily evaluate), specific motoric aspects are selected to enhance motor control during practice (Schack & Frank, 2020). Previous studies showed that the higher the athletes' expertise, the better the match between mental representation structures and biomechanical demands of the task (e.g., see Land et al., 2013). Moreover, the SDA-M method can also accelerate and optimize the learning process, bringing novices' mental representation structures closer to those of experts (e.g., see Frank et al., 2016).

Similar results were found when the SDA-M method was applied to team sports with the aim of assessing and improving mental representations

TABLE 16.1 Applied Sport Psychology Models Focused on Action-Centered and Action- or Emotional-Centered Approaches

ACTION-CENTERED APPROACHES			
Reference	**Model**	**Primary aim**	**Applications**
Schack, 2012	Structural dimensional analysis-motoric (SDA-M) model	Measure movement-related mental representations to improve athletes' technical preparation.	Tennis Windsurfing Volleyball Golf Futsal Soccer Classic dance
Hanin & Hanina, 2009a	Identification-control-correction (ICC) program	Measure subjective experiences of performances to improve athletes' optimal movement pattern awareness and control of performance in competitions.	Javelin throwing Hammer throwing Shooting Diving Pole vault Swimming Soccer Ice hockey Volleyball Car racing Sailing
Carson & Collins, 2011	Five-A model	Refine or regain processes of already learned techniques to achieve, maintain, and improve athletes' optimal performance and its control in competition.	Golf Javelin throwing Swimming Weightlifting
Bortoli et al., 2012	Multi-action plan (MAP) model	Measure subjective experiences of performances to improve awareness and control of the athletes' core components of action and their capability to shift from a suboptimal to optimal performance in competition.	Shooting Dart throwing Cycling Car racing Running Golf Tennis
ACTION- OR EMOTION-CENTERED APPROACHES			
Robazza et al., 2016	Multi-action plan (MAP) model, advanced version	Extends the MAP model by including the measurement of subjective perceived control and hedonic tone associated with sport performance. In this way, athletes could improve the capability to shift from suboptimal to optimal performance in competition relying not only on action but also on emotion.	Shooting Cycling Running Golf Tennis Ice-hockey
Hanin et al., 2016	Task execution design (TED) approach	Manipulate individual action-shaping constraints to control emergent performance patterns with the purpose of achieving the competitive expected results.	Shooting Shot put Rhythmic gymnastics Pole vault
Ruiz, Bortoli, & Robazza, 2020	Multi-states (MuSt) theory	Describe and understand idiosyncratic performance experiences, predicting performance, and identifying the most effective self-regulation strategies.	Archery

related to team actions. For example, experienced soccer players mentally represented team-level tactics in a higher functionally organized manner compared to less experienced participants, and their representations matched well with the task demands (Lex et al., 2015). Furthermore, futsal players' mental representations of team-level tactics (see figure 16.1*a*) improved after a four-week intervention focused on team actions, bringing the experimental group's mental representations closer to those of experienced futsal players (figure 16.1*b*; Frank et al., 2018). Therefore, the SDA-M method is a useful tool for assessing and improving athletes' mental representations not only at an intrapersonal level but also at an interpersonal one.

Identification-Control-Correction Program and Task Execution Design Approach

Hanin and Hanina (2009a) also shared the aim to optimize performance by focusing solely on motoric aspects and relying on the concept that actions can be mentally represented as a movement sequence characterized by specific core components. Thus, they created the identification-control-correction (ICC) program. The first step of this program requires athletes to retrospectively recall both successful and unsuccessful performances. Then, athletes generate a subjective image of the motor task and create a chain of subjectively relevant core components. Once conceptual awareness is gained, the next step is to become physically aware of their optimal and nonoptimal movement patterns through practice. Altogether, these two steps form the identification stage of the ICC program. Then, in the control stage, athletes learn how to deliberately control the entire movement execution by paying attention to the interactions between the individual core components with the aim to standardize them within optimal ranges (with a functional variability). Finally, during the correction stage of their usual errors, athletes replace models of wrong movement with a new learned model that they stabilize through practice (see success story 2).

One of the main differences between the SDA-M method and the ICC program is the identification stage of the core components. In the SDA-M method, mental representations are identified choosing the BACs from a set of action components predefined by sport-specific experts (e.g., coaches; sport psychology consultants). In the ICC program, this task is carried out by the athlete independently through orthodox technical execution. Consequently, the core components identified by the ICC program can be different among athletes even in the same sport, a feature that determines the idiosyncratic nature of the method. This difference represents an advantage for athletes because the work will be tailored to their personal needs and individual characteristics.

Notably, like the SDA-M method, the ICC program could be applied to individual as well as team sport situations. In relation to team sports (e.g.,

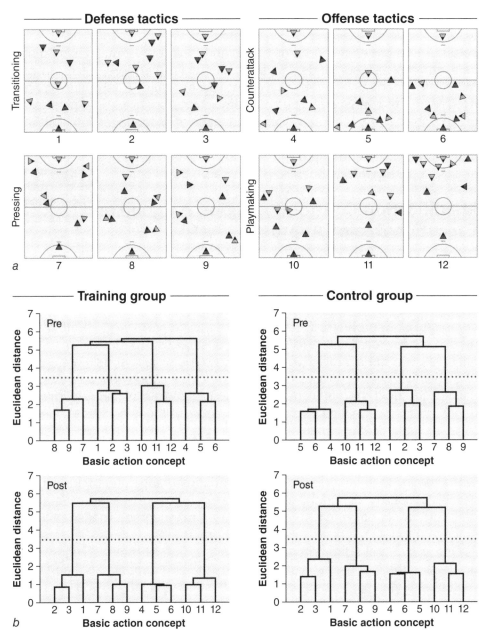

FIGURE 16.1 *(a)* BACs of team-specific futsal tactics. Each of the 12 BACs can be function-ally assigned to one of four team-specific futsal tactics: transitioning and pressing (defense), and counterattack and playmaking (offense). The following numbers below each of the stimuli refer to the different BACs, and they do not reflect a particular order. *(b)* Mean group tree diagrams of the training and control groups for pretest and posttest. The numbers on the *x*-axis relate to the BAC number, and the numbers on the *y*-axis display Euclidean distance. The lower the link between related BACs, the lower the Euclidean distance. Links between BACs above the horizontal dotted marks are considered not related.

Reprinted by permission from C. Frank et al., "Team Action Imagery and Team Cognition: Imagery of Game Situations and Required Team Actions Promotes a Functional Structure in Players' Representations of Team-Level Tactics," *Journal of Sport and Exercise Psychology* 40, no. 1 (2018): 20-30.

Success Story 2:
ICC Implementation With an Olympic Diver

Hanin and Hanina (2009b) worked with an Olympic diver who wanted to deal with fear that did not disappear after an emotion-focused intervention. Through the identification stage, they identified a dive elements chain, and they described the individual ideal performance of each component based on the diver's past experiences as follows:

> I can do this dive quite well, but I focused on wrong things. . . . I focused on rotation, but forgot to focus on the pre-jump which is the most important element for the good take off. . . . I did all that was possible to do in the air. But an error happened in the pre-jump and this disrupted the rhythm of my dive and water entry was spoiled. . . . (p. 85)

The analysis of the diver's past experiences revealed that "feeling in the rush" was due to insufficient time in prejump and especially a poor takeoff. In particular, the diver realized that the takeoff was the core component of the dive, which affected the entire performance process and therefore the final results. In the subsequent stages, the diver and sport psychology consultant could optimize performance by focusing attention on the new identified core component of the dive as a strategy to reduce the negative effect of fear on performance.

soccer, ice hockey) or complex and long-duration sport activities (e.g., car racing and sailing), the ICC program suggests splitting the game into manageable parts. For instance, car racing could be split into six main parts: preparation, starting procedure, early laps, mid race, conclusive laps, and finish. Then, each of these parts should be further divided into smaller sequences, which consider other important elements that the athlete could identify as core components (e.g., turns in racing; Hanin & Hanina, 2009b).

Potentially considered a further extension and development of the ICC program, the task execution design (TED) approach is aimed at helping athletes to adapt their performance based on unexpected events that may occur during competition (Hanin et al., 2016). Indeed, the TED approach suggests manipulating personal constraints to effectively control performance patterns. More specifically, the action-centered strategy of the TED approach involves identifying three action-shaping constraints through the identification stage of the ICC program (Hanin & Hanina, 2009a). These constraints are (1) an initial position, which needs to be controlled because a mistake in this position usually compromises the entire action; (2) core components; and (3) effort intensity (e.g., force or energy level), which, if controlled, allows athletes to maintain the action within the range of functional variability.

Five-A Model

A further model focused on the motoric aspects of performance is the five-A model (Carson & Collins, 2011), which shares the idiosyncrasy with the ICC program. The five-A model (the five A's are analysis, awareness, adjustment, reautomation, and assurance) was designed to refine and regain sport techniques (for a more recent implementation, see Carson & Collins, 2016a). Refining a technique means modifying it so that optimal performance can be maintained as sport equipment changes or the opponent's technique evolves; thus, it is different from skill acquisition (Carson & Collins, 2014). Regaining a technique means returning from current sub-optimum technique to an earlier stage when execution was more effective (Carson and Collins, 2016a). Therefore, the ultimate purpose of the five-A model is to achieve, maintain, and constantly improve athletes' optimal performance also under pressing competitive situations (see success story 3).

Understanding whether it is a case of refining or regaining a technique is an objective of the first A of the model, the analysis stage. Once provided with a diagnosis of and prescription for the identified problem (which always actively involves both athlete and coach or sport psychology consultant), contrasting drills are used to increase the athlete's awareness of the correct versus incorrect actions (the second A, the awareness stage). Then, during the third stage (adjustment), the technical flaw is modified and corrected. In the fourth stage (reautomation), athletes internalize the new key movement characteristics until further changes in the technique are no longer needed (the fifth A, the assurance stage). Studies based on the five-A model highlight the relevant contribution of motoric aspects in implementing technical developments in this dynamic process toward optimal performance (Carson & Collins, 2016a).

Success Story 3: Implementation of the Five-A Model With an Olympic Weightlifter

Carson and Collins (2014) reported a case study of an Olympic weightlifter who needed to refine the snatch technique because of an injury from incorrect execution of the technical requirements repeated over time. Through the analysis stage, the athlete re-created the position that had caused the injury and manipulated it toward a new, more effective, and less injury-prone technique. Then, during the awareness stage, the athlete identified cues for the different feelings and positions, and he performed correct lifts followed by incorrect ones; this sequence emphasized the differences between the two lifts in terms of kinesthetic sensations. Gradually the incorrect trials were faded out. Based on this work, the athlete first adjusted his technique by means of visual and kinesthetic training sessions, then reautomatized it by gradually increasing the weight of the bar. Once maximal weight was achieved, competitive simulations were carried out to ensure the correct execution of the refined technique occurred also under high-pressure situations.

Multi-Action Plan Model and Multi-States Theory

Currently, the most recent action-centered approach to be developed is the multi-action plan (MAP) model (Bortoli et al., 2012). Relying on the assumption that combining different approaches provides more chances of success in performance optimization, these authors extended the model by including the emotion-centered perspective (Robazza et al., 2016). Therefore, the MAP model can be considered an integrated psychological approach to sport performance. The main idea underlying the MAP model is to take advantage of self-regulatory strategies focused on both affective and motoric components of sport actions by using an idiosyncratic approach to performance optimization (di Fronso et al., 2017). However, the current section will deal with only the motoric contribution, which is at the core of the current discussion.

The MAP model's authors describe four types of performance defined by the interaction between performance level (optimal and suboptimal) and attentional-control level (controlled and automatized) during action execution (figure 16.2). In type 1 performance, athletes are self-confident, in full control of the situation, and their well-learned movements are executed in an automatic, effortless, and consistent manner. Every athlete would like to be in such a state when performance level is high (optimal level) and attentional control level is low (automatic level). Unfortunately, competition-related contextual factors (e.g., distress, fatigue, anxiety) may disrupt this state, leading to an increased need for attentional control (i.e., controlled level) and suboptimal level of performance (type 3 performance). However, suboptimal performance may also occur when athletes execute actions

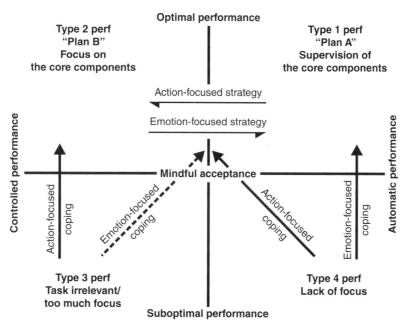

FIGURE 16.2   Conceptualization of the multi-action plan (MAP) model.

Reprinted by permission from L. Bortoli et al., "Striving for Excellence: A Multi-Action Plan Intervention Model for Shooters," *Psychology of Sport and Exercise* 13, no. 5 (2012): 693-701.

investing a low level of attentional control (automatic level) but are not fully involved or interested in the task, such as in the type 4 performance. Whenever the plan A of performing in an optimal-automatic manner (type 1) is not an option, athletes may switch to a plan B (type 2) to avoid having a suboptimal performance. This plan involves focusing attention on core components of the individual's action identified during practice that could exert functional effects on performance also in endurance tasks, such as cycling (Bertollo et al., 2015).

The assessment and optimization intervention of performance based on the MAP model will be explained in detail in the following paragraphs. Meanwhile, drawing on the MAP model, Ruiz and colleagues (2020) developed the multi-states (MuSt) theory. This further-applied model is aimed to predict and optimize performance by proposing to regularly revise and refine the core components with a direct and longitudinal assessment of their accuracy before or after actual competitions. When athletes perform within a functional and optimal range of variability (in-the-zone condition), successful performance can be predicted. In contrast, poor performance is expected when accuracy levels are out of this zone (out-of-zone condition). These predictions are subsequently verified and eventually confirmed based on subjective experience and performance. Finally, to achieve and remain in the in-the-zone condition, athletes can apply action-centered self-regulation strategy by directing attention to their core components of action.

Assessment

The first phase of the MAP model requires identifying the core components of a given action. To this aim, athletes are required to describe their usual optimal sequence (the action chain) in an accurate and extensive fashion, providing a step-by-step description of the entire movement sequence. In selecting core components, athletes are helped by coaches or sport psychology consultants in reflecting and increasing awareness and movement-related critical thinking. An example of such an open question is, "What are the actions that when executed in a less accurate manner cause your scores to drop from optimal to suboptimal level?" (Bortoli et al., 2012). In the case of Popescu presented earlier, one of the intervention purposes was to optimize her flèche action, an aggressive offensive fencing technique mainly used with épée. Following the indications of her sport psychology practitioner, Popescu reported a flèche-related action sequence characterized by six parts: starting moment, back arm extension, front arm clean extension, lateral burst, timing, and finishing moment.

Once the action chain is defined, the second phase consists of selecting relevant components of the chain associated with an optimal performance (Bortoli et al., 2012). Notably, the core components are not necessarily the most salient parts of a sport action as one might suppose. Furthermore, they are not even related to biomechanical components of action. Instead, with the term *core components*, the MAP model's authors refer to elements of the movement chain not completely automatized or that show nonfunctional accuracy fluctuations under stressful conditions (e.g., in competition). This thinking is also in line with one of the most accredited theories of motor control and coordination, namely the uncontrolled manifold hypothesis (Scholz & Schöner, 1999). According to this theory, working on the core components could mean driving the central nervous system to create a subspace of independent elemental variables (e.g., joint angles) and organize their covariation to restrict much of their variability, thus increasing movement stability, also under different constraints or conditions (Latash et al., 2010). Among the six components of the flèche action sequence defined by Popescu, the two core ones were the first and last part of the chain (the starting and finishing moments, respectively). Following the reflection and awareness work done on the flèche action, the athlete dwelled on two specific motoric factors: the optimal distance from the opponent at the beginning of the action (*misura*, a fencing term meaning "measure") and the rate or pace at which the action is performed (tempo).

Next, the sport psychology consultant and coach analyzed many of Popescu's actions, correlating attention on the core components with performance results, using the procedure described by Bortoli and colleagues (2012). They applied a specific statistical analysis (hierarchical linear regression) to control the effectiveness of the two core components (misura and tempo) athletes could use in the definition of the individual zone of optimal performance (Kamata et al., 2002). Misura was noted to be more consistent than tempo, so it was selected as the motoric element of the action on which the athlete should focus attention to manage difficult circumstances and optimize performance.

In the assessing stage, Popescu and her staff used psychophysiological tools, such as electrocardiography (ECG) and psychometrics, according to the model suggested by Bertollo and colleagues (2020) for performance monitoring (see figure 16.3). In fact, previous studies showed an association between specific psychophysiological states and the four types of performance defined by the MAP model (di Fronso et al., 2017). For example, types 2 and 3 performance of shooters and dart throwers were characterized by higher levels of skin conductance compared to types 1 and 4; It could be related to the higher action control requirements in types 2 and 3 (Bertollo et al., 2013). Another example comes from a study conducted with professional drivers. In relation to optimal performances, the controlled one (type 2) showed higher heart and respiratory rates compared to the automatized type 1 (Filho et al., 2015). Finally, the same research group found that the four types of performance also presented different neural cortical activities (Bertollo et al., 2016; di Fronso et al., 2018). Briefly, the automatized types of performance (types 1 and 4) were characterized by higher levels of neural synchronization in frequency bands commonly associated with attention requests (theta [4-8 Hz] and alpha [8-12 Hz] bands). However, the

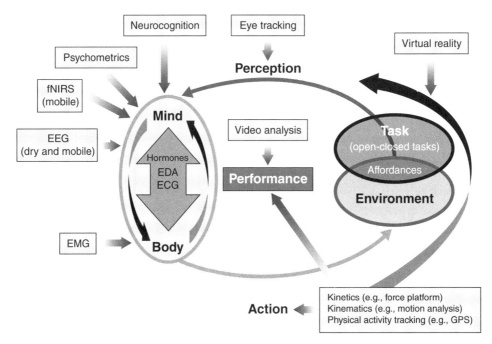

FIGURE 16.3 Integrated use of technology in the multidimensional and multimodal psycho-physiological monitoring of the processes involved in performance proficiency during practice.

Reprinted by permission from M. Bertollo, M. Doppelmayr, and C. Robazza. "Using Brain Technology in Practice," in *Handbook of Sport Psychology*, 4th ed., edited by G. Tenenbaum and R. Eklund (Hoboken, NJ: Wiley & Blackwell, 2020), 666-693.

type 4 performance showed a more distributed synchronization than type 1. Conversely, the controlled types of performance (types 2 and 3) were both characterized by a higher desynchronization in the alpha band, although the type 2 had a higher theta synchronization; this difference is probably because of the higher attention required by the task under high-pressure situations. Findings in line with these results were also reported in expert golfers (Wang et al., 2019) and cyclists (di Fronso et al., 2018).

As shown in figure 16.3, the main technologies for monitoring athletes' mental processes are neurocognitive and psychometric tools as well as neuroimaging tools, namely the mobile functional near-infrared spectroscopy (fNIRS) and the dry and mobile electroencephalography (EEG). Athletes' body processes can be monitored by using electromyography (EMG). The interrelation between mind and body can be detected by measuring hormone concentration as well as electrodermal (EDA) and electrocardiac (ECG) activities. Virtual reality can be useful to monitor the task and the opportunity for movement in a specific environment (affordances). Kinetics (e.g., force platform), kinematics (motion analysis), and physical activity tracking (e.g., using a global positioning system [GPS]) can be used to monitor action as well as perception and the whole sport performance. Finally, two other tools—eye tracking and video analysis—can be used specifically to monitor perception and sport performance, respectively.

The earlier-mentioned studies highlight the usefulness of combining various technologies, such as EEG, EMG, eye tracking, and motion capture to assess sport performance from a multimodal and multidimensional perspective (Bertollo et al., 2020; see figure 16.3). Such technologies help make it possible to obtain otherwise inaccessible information that allows for a better understanding of the relationships between athletes' perception, emotions, actions, and cognition related to the specific action to be optimized. This understanding, in turn, allows for the development of more effective and efficient MAP model–based interventions that take into account the person (athlete), the task, and the environment.

Optimization

The optimization stage begins with the practice of the action while focusing attention on the core components. It is also used to confirm selection of core components. More specifically, athletes are required to perform the selected action a number of times; the exact number varies among sports and athletes. The minimum number of repetitions is established according to the specific sport, the athlete's level of expertise, and an individual preparation program established by the technical staff as well as by statistical constraints. In previous studies, shooter athletes performed 60 (Bortoli et al., 2012; Robazza et al., 2016) to 121 shoots (Bertollo et al., 2013; 2016), while 122 was the number chosen for dart-thrower flights (Bertollo et al., 2013). In the case of Popescu, the number of flèche actions was set at 50 repetitions. In fencing, the evaluation of performance is already categorized as binary (success or failure).

During this practice phase, athletes assess themselves by rating the hedonic tone level (i.e., the degree of pleasantness or unpleasantness aroused by their experience) before and after each action repetition as well as the perceived result and control level of each core component after each action repetition and before seeing the actual outcome (Bortoli et al., 2012; Robazza et al., 2016). However, some situations exist in which the information related to the actual result is automatically available to athletes, therefore evaluation can be biased by this information (Bertollo et al., 2013). For example, it is the case of dart throwers who have direct and immediate access to the performance outcome on the dartboard, but it could be the same for soccer and basketball players during a penalty kick and free throw, respectively. In these circumstances, Bertollo and colleagues (2013) suggested asking athletes to report only the levels of control and accuracy of the core component of the action. The rating scale used to self-evaluate control and accuracy levels is a modified 11-point Borg category ratio (CR-10) scale (see Bortoli et al., 2012).

At this point, different subjective data are available, such as the level of control of core components and perceived action result. These data could be compared to the objective ones, such as the actual action result. Different analytical methods could be used to evaluate this aim (e.g., logistical ordinal regression; see Kamata et al., 2002). After having explained to athletes that the main aim of the analyses is to determine whether the core components can discriminate performance levels, individual probability curves are estimated. Whether core component scores discriminate performance outcomes, the optimization process goes further with the last phase. Otherwise, new core components must be identified and subsequently tested (Bortoli et al., 2012). If statistical competencies are not available, coaches, sport psychology consultants, and athletes can use qualitative approaches comparing the athlete's perception of the core component with previous videorecorded competition and check whether the core component was associated with action instability in skill execution.

The last phase of the MAP model consists of several practice sessions during which the most influential core components are further tested under conditions of distress and fatigue. Such conditions could be induced by mental or physical exertions in tasks performed before the practice session (cf. combination training; MacPherson et al., 2008). These exertions are designed to elicit unfavorable mental and bodily states similar to those during competition. In fact, as already asserted, competition can negatively affect performance, where performing in an optimal and automatic fashion (type 1 performance, plan A) is not possible. The main aim of this phase is enhancing athletes' awareness related to their new meta-experiences, leading them in the process of mindful acceptance of mental and bodily distress, and teaching them to focus attention on the core components of action in order to switch to a plan B (type 2 performance) whenever plan A is not feasible because of the stressful competition conditions (see figure 16.4). During this phase, athletes learn the strategies to shift from one type

Success Story 4: Applying the MAP Model With an Olympic Gymnast

Drăgulescu was supported by the same sport psychology consultant as Popescu, who used a MAP model–based intervention to train the gymnast to either perform in a flow state of mind (plan A) or, when in a high-pressure situation, to focus more on the motoric elements that were under his control (plan B). Regarding his performance at the Olympic Games qualification competition in Rio de Janeiro, Drăgulescu reported that he entered the competition feeling very determined. Then, following early mistakes, the distress related to the significance of competition and the eustress related to the fact that the favorite gymnast had already failed, negatively interfered with his plan A. So, he decided to switch to the well-trained plan B. Although the latter plan was highly mentally consuming, it proved efficient in a time of crisis and allowed him to qualify for the vault final.

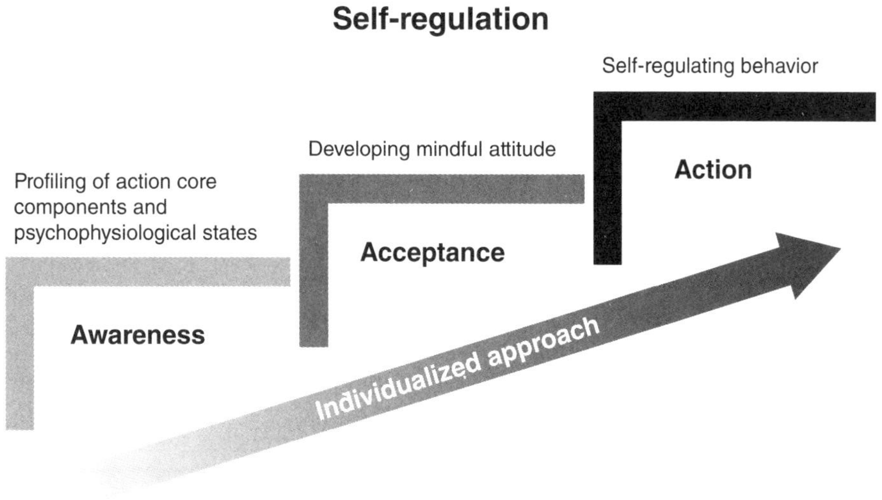

Self-regulation

FIGURE 16.4 The self-regulation process starts with profiling of action core components and psychophysiological states to enhance athletes' awareness related to their new meta-experiences, leading them in the process of mindful acceptance of mental and bodily distress, and teaching them to self-regulate their own behavior in order to optimize performance.

of performance state to another, using both action and emotion coping strategies (see figure 16.2). It is exactly what Marian Drăgulescu did during the floor exercise at the qualification competition for the 2016 Olympics (see success story 4). Drăgulescu is a Romanian Olympic artistic gymnast who introduced the famous and difficult Drăgulescu vault.

As introduced in the Assessment section, the optimization stage of the MAP model can be further implemented with psychophysiological monitoring. Popescu and Drăgulescu's sport psychology practitioner did so with her athletes; she used ECG to measure heart rate variability (HRV). The use of such instruments could be crucial for intervention effectiveness considering the association between MAP model–related types of performance and specific psychophysiological states already discussed at the end of the previous section (Christie et al., 2020). Moreover, because of the similarity with real game situations, this kind of information is more useful when psychophysiological technologies are used in an ecological scenario. However, the use of these technologies needs a high level of expertise to enable interpretation of results, make inferences, and draw conclusions for performance optimization (Bertollo et al., 2020, 2021). It is worth noting that biological signals could also be used as feedback to help athletes develop higher awareness and control of their psychophysiological states during competition (di Fronso et al., 2017). In fact, brain–body computer interfaces, biofeedback, and neurofeedback systems have been developed to allow people to visualize their own biological signals and use them to evaluate and self-regulate their psychophysiological processes in real time. This technology will ultimately lead to self-regulation in performance optimization (Bertollo et al., 2021; di Fronso et al., 2020). Modern technological development in sport has made all these tools available to the general practitioner; very inexpensive HRV monitors (e.g., Elite or Polar), EEG headsets (e.g., Muse, Neurosky, or Epoc), eye tracking devices, and virtual reality systems can assess and improve performance and implement effective perceptual-cognitive training (see Bertollo et al., 2021).

Conclusion

The effectiveness and efficiency of the action-centered approaches in the process of performance optimization have been widely tested. Some of these approaches are exclusively focused on the motoric aspects of sport performance, such as the SDA-M method (Schack, 2012), the ICC program (Hanin & Hanina, 2009a), the Five-A model (Carson & Collins, 2011), and the MAP model (Bortoli et al., 2012). Other action-centered approaches also integrated the affective dimension of performance, such as in the advanced version of the MAP model (Robazza et al., 2016), the TED approach (Hanin et al., 2016), and the MuSt theory (Ruiz et al., 2021).

These approaches have been applied in a variety of sports, also implementing different approaches in the same sport. However, no one has performed a comparison among the approaches in the same sport. Therefore, currently no specific prescription exists for the best action-centered approach to implement for each sport. An evidence-based practice is currently a pragmatic solution that a sport psychology consultant might implement; thus, they can understand what would be the best action-centered approach(es) to optimize athletes' sport performance, and they can gain insights and useful information.

Thank you to Alina Gerghisan (sport psychology practitioner), Ana Maria Popescu, and Marian Drăgulescu (athletes of the Romanian Olympic Committee) for sharing their experiences for this chapter.

17 | Talent Development

Áine MacNamara
Dublin City University

In the competitive landscape of sport, a continuous pressure exists to identify and select the best young performers, then develop them to an elite standard. Therefore, talent identification and development (TID) has become a key focus for national governing bodies (NGBs), professional clubs, coaches, and athletes across all sports. In turn, an increasing evidence base informs TID and drives coaches' and athletes' decision making and practice. Unfortunately, the efficacy and scientific foundations of some TID practices are strongly questionable. For example, early talent identification (TI) measures, where young children are selected into training programs based on their physical, anthropometric, or performance profile, have been criticized based on the low predictive value and lack of validity attributed to these programs. Simply, many TI programs have not been very effective at detecting and identifying young people with the potential to develop into successful senior performers.

When people decide to employ early TI schemes, many factors are at play. In this regard, the starting point of the talent development pathway in different sports is typically influenced by physiological demands, sport structures, and even tradition. For example, serious gymnastics training typically starts in the prepubescent years based on the physiological and performance demands of that sport. Soccer follows a similar chronological trajectory; professional academies recruit players starting as young as 5 years of age. However, recruitment in soccer appears to be a result of market forces (recruit the child before someone else does), tradition, and competition as opposed to physiological or performance demands (Williams, Ford, & Drust, 2020). In short, approaches to TI are often shaped by sport- and culture-specific pressures and assumptions (and sometimes myths) about how to best develop young performers.

Significant evidence shows that early TI, especially when completed before physical maturation, is neither appropriate nor effective in a lot of (if not most) cases (e.g., Miller et al., 2015). Certainly, the nonlinearity of development, combined with other influences, such as the relative age effect (RAE) (Cobley, 2009), athlete's birthplace (e.g., Turnnidge et al., 2014), or pure luck (Bailey, 2007), can make TI a lottery, especially when conducted through snapshot trials that take place on a single occasion. The majority of high-performing young athletes do not go on to elite or even sub-elite careers (Kearney & Hayes, 2018); conversely, many adult elite performers were not identified through the standard talent pathways, nor were they precociously gifted as young children. Despite this lack of evidence and the considerable data that illustrate the inefficiencies of early TI (e.g., over 90% of those recruited to Premiership U.K. soccer academies will never play for the first team), sports continue to invest considerable resources, time, and funding into talent spotting.

Despite considerable investment in talent identification, many high-performing young athletes do not go on to elite or even sub-elite careers.

Given the relative inefficiency of TI, and to offer you something far more concrete on which to base your journey to senior success, this chapter emphasizes the determinants of talent *development* (TD) and the range of factors that underpin the capacity of a young athlete to realize their potential. This discussion should provide coaches, athletes, sport psychology consultants, and others in high-level sport with evidence-informed guidelines that support their practice in TD. Moreover, although development potential might slow down over time, it does not disappear; therefore, the discussion allows senior-end athletes and coaches to consider their developmental journey. It also allows them to reflect on how they acquired their skill set as well as potential missed development opportunities that could be compensated for even at a more mature stage of development.

Relevance

Regardless of sport, a range of factors influence the journey to excellence, and the process is driven by opportunities offered both within and outside of the arena of sport. For example, the process of TD is mediated by exposure to and practice with specific knowledge, psychological and social skills, and the broader environment that the individual inhabits (Coutinho et al., 2016). As such, the development of talent is modifiable by coaching, training, and exposure to appropriately timed opportunities such as competition, selection to teams, and higher standards of competition. In short, athletes, coaches, sport psychology consultants, and others can have a major impact on eventual senior success through the actions that they take (or don't take) in the developmental pathway.

This understanding of TD as a process is juxtaposed with a traditional conceptualization of sport ability as unitary, genetically inherited, and measurable (Abbott & Collins, 2004). Current performance, especially in prepubescent athletes, can be a poor indicator of ability because it is mediated through a host of other influences such as training, support, parental investment, and societal values. Instead, it is important to think of TD as multifactorial, requiring the performer to develop a range of skills and abilities (such as physiological, biomechanical, psychological, and physical) within a favorable development environment (Simonton, 2001). Each of these components interact in a multiplicative (rather than additive) manner, and multiple components contribute to the development of talent. TD is therefore the result of an interaction between abilities, social learning, and cultural learning; this interaction of processes undermines simplistic correlations of ability and performance.

Many approaches to talent development fail to recognize—or sufficiently cater for—this complexity. In this respect, aspects of this chapter will be relevant for leaders of talent pathways as well as athletes, coaches, and sport psychology consultants. For example, development in sport has typically been explained and organized in terms of a pyramid-based model, a broad base of participation followed by increasingly higher levels of performance engaged in by fewer and fewer people. However, despite its popularity and prevalence, numerous criticisms have been leveled at the pyramid approach (Bailey & Collins, 2013). The narrowing of the pathway that is built into the pyramid's design means that some athletes are systematically excluded as they progress; no matter how good they are in absolute terms, fewer and fewer players progress to the next level. Pyramid models also presume that successful progression is indicative of later or emergent ability; in most cases, this presumption is not accurate. As noted earlier, progression is typically based on the evaluation of a limited range of discrete variables (typically a single performance or physical measurements), with a failure to recognize the dynamic nature of development. As such, pyramid approaches to TD may well be excluding athletes with potential who might not be performing at that point in time. Indeed, traditional models such as the pyramid approach or Côté's developmental model of sport participation (DMSP) (Côté & Hay, 2002) present talent development as a relatively linear progression along a continuum from childhood to retirement. However, even a cursory look at the biographies of successful performers will highlight the nonlinear, dynamic, and idiosyncratic nature of development (Coutinho et al., 2016).

Indeed, and as this chapter explores in more detail, the dynamic, nonlinear, and idiosyncratic nature of development seems to be a common feature of successful senior athletes' journeys; therefore, understanding and supporting the developmental experiences of young athletes, including those of a psychological nature, should be an essential element of a coach's, athlete's, or sport psychology consultant's toolkit. Indeed, coaches, athletes, sport psychology consultants, and others should focus on equipping young athletes with all the psychological tools they will need to realize their potential. In this respect, TD is a process that propels individuals on trajectories from potential to competence to expertise (Subotnik et al., 2019). The rest of this chapter focuses on some key principles of progression from a psychological perspective, how athletes and those who support them can assess this progress, and finally, how progression might be optimized. As you read the rest of this chapter, consider your own context and seek to understand how the principles presented can be implemented to guide practice in your domain.

What We Know

Considerable evidence focuses on different approaches to supporting the TD journey in sport. Notably, much of this research has examined the developmental histories of elite athletes to identify the factors that affect an athlete's journey in sport. As you investigate this evidence base, it is important to consider the multiplicity of influences and their interactive effect on the athlete rather than uncritically extrapolating these findings to influence your own context.

Rocky Road to Success

The idea that young athletes benefit from a variety of challenges to facilitate eventual superior adult performance has attracted significant attention. Interestingly, youth sport often seeks to minimize the number—and impact—of developmental challenges for best-performing young athletes. In this vein, a feature of some talent development systems is to provide a greatly supportive environment to minimize challenge and allow young athletes to focus on their sport commitments. However, the low transfer of youth to senior success (Kearney & Hayes, 2018) would attest to how smoothness often precedes a fall in terms of TD. It may be that a young athlete needs to experience a degree of challenge and adversity in order to build and acquire the confidence, resilience, and other psychological characteristics needed to achieve at the highest level.

People are increasingly recognizing that for aspiring elite athletes, overcoming a degree of challenge is desirable. This approach might include sport-specific challenges such as playing up an age group, playing out of position, deselecting or selecting for particular competitions, or increasing training load. Indeed, in the 2016 paper "Super Champions, Champions, and Almosts," Collins and colleagues defined *super champions* as those who had won five or more world or Olympic medals or at least 60 international caps. In their study, super champions were differentiated from their less successful counterparts by their use of positive, proactive coping and their *learn from it* approach to challenge. In sum, the mechanism for the benefits of this approach appears to relate more to what athletes bring to the challenges than what they experience. For example, when asked to reflect on their developmental journey, super champions described a range of high-quality and challenging experiences that were overcome through a number of skills that they brought to each situation, such as personal organization, focus, goal setting, planning, and other psychobehavioral skills that form part of the mental skill set required for success. In contrast, *almosts* (defined as a successful junior who failed to reach the highest level of senior competition) described a smooth, nonlinear journey to a certain level where they then either reached a plateau or dropped out of the sport because of a lack of the psychobehavioral skills and motivation required at the elite level. The following section considers what is known about these psychobehavioral skills in more detail.

Negotiating the Rocky Road: Psychobehavioral Determinants of Talent Development

A significant body of literature suggests that equipping performers with the right attitude to succeed is an essential part of the development process and negotiating the rocky road described previously. Related to this idea, Carol Dweck's (2006) work on growth mindset and Duckworth and colleagues' (2007) work on grit have both gained a lot of traction in TD. *Growth mindset* is attitudinal and espouses the advantages of a growth over a fixed mindset; it sees talent as something one can develop through appropriate effort rather than as something one is merely born with (or without). Dweck and colleagues have completed an impressive series of studies that show how possession of a growth mindset changes one's attitude to practice (Haimovitz & Dweck, 2016), coping with disappointment and failure (e.g., Yeager & Dweck, 2012), and working with others (Dweck, 2017). In similar fashion, *grit* describes the perseverance required for the attainment of long-term goals. Grit can be assessed behaviorally (e.g., through direct observation) or by short questionnaires (e.g., Duckworth & Quinn, 2009). A further impressive array of empirical studies attest to the associations between grit and performance in a range of settings, including passing out of the U.S. Military Academy at West Point (Maddi et al., 2012); success in the National Spelling Bee; and performance in sport, academics, and music (Duckworth et al., 2007). In sum, from a TD perspective, incremental theories such as growth mindset and grit, which see ability as something that can be developed, have strong face validity and strong supporting evidence.

Of course, for athletes and their supporting practitioners, it is also important to consider how constructs such as growth mindset and grit actually operate and influence development. In short, how do people actually *develop* them? Growth mindset may relate to (or even be a product of) self-regulatory learning (e.g., Burnette et al., 2013). Examining grit in a mechanistic manner also points to the positive effects of grit as attributable to perseverance, which is related to motivation and self-drive (Credé et al., 2017). It is also important to consider the context-specific nature of these constructs; young athletes may manifest a growth mindset in one dimension of their lives but a fixed mindset in others (e.g., a young soccer player has a growth mindset and an incremental belief that their soccer ability will improve as a result of effortful practice but has a fixed mindset toward their academic work because they believe they are not smart; Burnette et al., 2013).

All in all, it is clear that growth mindset and grit are important features in the development of talent. However, it is also clear that both—and other similar psychological outcomes (e.g., resilience)—are driven by a set of underpinning skills; in other words, these skills help an athlete to achieve or exhibit a growth mindset, to be gritty, or to be resilient. Indeed, young athletes clearly need to have a range of psychobehavioral skills (obtained through experience or attitudinal) that enable them to cope with the various challenges and opportunities they will face as they progress on the talent pathway. In fact, the literature in this field shows significant evidence of the causative influence of psychological skills, particularly in the area of self-regulation (Toering et al., 2011). As such, if psychobehavioral skills are important mechanisms of successful development, they should be purposefully developed on the pathway. To this end, the next section focuses on psychobehavioral skills as one particular key process of development and a logical way to prepare young athletes for the ups and downs of development. In short, by focusing on the process and teaching of psychobehavioral skills and by optimizing both planned and naturally occurring developmental experiences, athletes can generate the outcome deliverables (e.g., growth mindset, grit, and resilience) that support achievement.

Psychological Characteristics of Developing Excellence

In terms of TD, a range of psychobehavioral factors have been shown to play a key role in the realization of potential. MacNamara and colleagues (2010a, 2010b) term these factors *psychological characteristics of developing excellence* (PCDEs); they are listed in table 17.1. PCDEs are not just mental skills, such as imagery or goal setting; they also include psychobehavioral characteristics, such as commitment. Accordingly, possession and systematic development of PCDEs seems a logical step, allowing young athletes to interact effectively with the developmental opportunities they are afforded (Côté & Hay, 2002; Simonton, 2001; Van Yperen, 2009). Of course, equipping young athletes with these developmental skills will not necessarily guarantee high-level performance, because a wide range of other variables influence the likelihood of reaching the top. However, it will provide aspiring elites with the capacity and competencies (including growth mindset, grit, and resilience) to strive to reach their potential. In this respect, a key strength of the PCDE approach is that it is both comprehensive (it caters to the full

TABLE 17.1   Psychological Characteristics of Developing Excellence (PCDEs)

PCDE	Definition
Commitment	How well a performer can commit to the focus and levels needed for success
Focus and distraction control	Knowing what is important, knowing how to stay concentrated on it, and knowing what to do to both avoid and counter distractions
Realistic performance evaluation	The ability to accurately know what was good and what was not so good in a performance, plus the willingness to do something about it
Role clarity	Knowing what is needed and expected to be optimally effective at a role or job
Self-regulation	Knowing how—and being able—to control the effects of pressure
Planning and self-organization	Being optimally organized in any given situation and accounting for all the factors that need to be addressed for optimal performance
Goal setting and self-reward	Planning the steps needed to achieve a given target and rewarding the steps needed to take to achieve a long-term goal
Quality practice	Knowing what to do—and having the motivation—to achieve high-quality practice
Effective and controllable imagery	The ability to develop effective images that can be used to structure mental practice of a particular skill or goal
Seeking and using social support	Building on, and making use of, a network of friends, family, and stakeholders to support progress

range of challenges and contexts that athletes are likely to encounter) and proactively developable as the athlete proceeds along an inherently nonlinear and dynamic pathway.

PCDEs as Facilitators of Transfer

Of course, it would be naive to ignore context-specific differences that undeniably exist across performance domains when it comes to the relevance of the PCDEs; these potential differences are acknowledged in the Optimization section (see table 17.2). However, in spite of those differences, some key features of the talent development process from a psychological perspective do seem to be generic. For example, significant evidence suggests that the same PCDEs are important regardless of performance domain (Kamin et al., 2007). As such, TD processes that promote PCDEs not only encourage and facilitate athletes to achieve their potential in their current performance domain, they also allow for the cross-fertilization of talent into other domains at later stages of development (e.g., talent transfer approaches; Collins et al., 2014). Or, even if an athlete does not change domain, PCDEs will help them adapt their performance to the different situations and contexts inherent in their activity (Abbott & Collins, 2004) and the broad range of other challenges (e.g., adolescent lifestyle, education, and personal life), which can be equally powerful derailers (Taylor & Collins, 2019).

The long-term health benefits of promoting and developing PCDEs in young people are equally significant. The PCDEs that underpin development in achievement domains also seem to be the same psychological characteristics that promote uptake of and adherence to a physically active lifestyle (MacNamara et al., 2011). In this vein, the three worlds continuum (Collins et al., 2011) is an interesting way to consider how the TD pathway nurtures the potential of young people; it prepares them to be the best they can be by reconceptualizing how they define excellence. More specifically, the three worlds continuum (as depicted in figure 17.1) refers to three different types of excellence: elite-referenced excellence, personal-referenced excellence, and participation for personal well-being. These three types of excellence are defined as follows:

> *Elite-referenced excellence (ERE)*: Excellence in the form of high-level sporting performance, where achievement is measured against others with the ultimate goal of winning at the highest level possible.
>
> *Personal-referenced excellence (PRE)*: Excellence in the form of participation and personal performance, where achievement is more personally referenced by completing a marathon or improving one's personal best.
>
> *Participation for personal well-being (PPW)*: Taking part in physical activity and sport to satisfy needs other than personal progression, such as making and keeping friends or staying in shape.

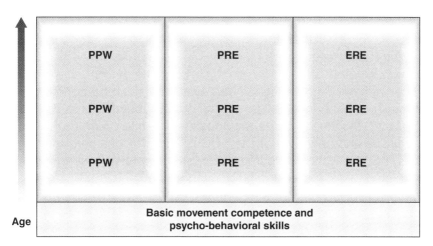

FIGURE 17.1   Three worlds continuum.

In TD terms, the important point is that the three worlds are interrelated. Built on a common fundamental skills base that encompasses both basic movement and psychobehavioral skills in particular, young athletes should be empowered to progress back and forth among the three types of activity contexts as they progress. For example, elite performers can subsequently stay involved at a participation level, while late developers or returners can attempt to move into the ERE and PRE worlds at any age. In fact, young athletes might even inhabit multiple worlds concurrently.

Much research indicates that psychobehavioral skills are one of the key mechanisms that facilitate progression along and between the three worlds (MacNamara et al., 2011); they do so through influencing an individual's capacity to be physically active and their competence and determination to make appropriate health and exercise choices. Again, the operational mechanism of these factors may well be evidenced by examining constructs such as self-determination or self-regulation. Given that a TD pathway should prepare young athletes for a range of destinations, the systematic development of PCDEs offers significant broader benefit. In short, from both performance and educational perspectives, it appears that substantial benefit is gained from the systematic development and facilitated deployment of these generic skills.

Assessment

As emphasized earlier, it is important to view the principles presented in this chapter in your particular context. These principles support the aim to guide young athletes as they develop a comprehensive skill set on their path to the next level. For example, young athletes should have experienced input and application for all of the PCDEs by the time they reach the tail end of the pathway. This developmental curriculum prepares them for the sharp end of the development pathway when pressures rise significantly. As they progress, athletes will therefore ideally be working on an intentional and systematically supported subset of the full PCDE curriculum at particular stages.

To check whether athletes are on track, completing formative evaluations at regular intervals is essential. These evaluations can be conducted using a self-report questionnaire such as the PCDE Questionnaire 2 (PCDEQ2) (Hill et al., 2019). The PCDEQ2 provides a self-rating on different elements (both positive and negative) of the PCDEs and provides an opportunity for coaches, sport psychology consultants, and others to assess athletes on seven related factors: active coping, imagery and active preparation, seeking and using social support, self-directed control and management, clinical indicators, adverse response to failure, and perfectionistic tendencies; these factors have been shown to discriminate between more or less successful performers. Figure 17.2 shows a PCDEQ2 output of a 16-year-old soccer player; the dotted line shows the player's PCDE profile, and the solid line illustrates an ideal PCDE profile. The output provides a detailed breakdown of an athlete's PCDE skill set, which a practitioner (with specialist training) can subsequently use as a basis for training and development.

The important feature is the formative use of the PCDEQ2. It is not a selection tool; rather, it is one way to gain a picture of what is happening. The results of the questionnaire should therefore be triangulated with coach evaluations, performance data, and independent reports, providing a comprehensive picture of each athlete's development and a useful resource for reviewing and refining the athlete's development plan in conjunction with key stakeholders. Of course, these strategies can be employed effectively

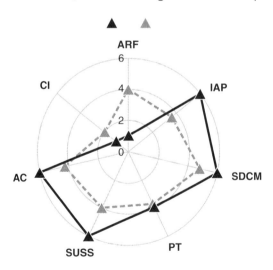

Adverse Response to Failure (ARF); Imagery and Active Preparation (IAP); Self-Directed Control and Management (SDCM); Perfectionistic Tendencies (PT); Seeking and Using Social Support (SUSS); Active Coping (AC); Clinical Indicators (CI)

FIGURE 17.2   Sample PCDEQ2 output. The darker, solid-line shape depicts the target skills profile. The lighter, dotted-line shape depicts an example athlete's current skills profile.

and independent of the questionnaire, supported by established methods and processes in the performance environment such as video, diaries, reflection, and performance analysis by the athlete, coach, and sport psychology consultant. In these cases, the PCDEs can still be applied as a framework to guide evaluations, offering a basis for discussion (e.g., *What are my strengths and weaknesses in seeking and using social support?*) and deciding on future actions (e.g., *I need to talk more to senior players to understand what they do for focus and distraction control purposes*).

It is also worth considering how your sport assesses potential in young athletes more broadly. A range of different approaches are now common in sport and are grounded in skills and expertise (e.g., Faber et al., 2015), psychometrics (e.g., Höner et al., 2015), genetic testing (e.g., Breitbach et al., 2014), web-based approaches (e.g., Louzada et al., 2016) or current performance (e.g., Allen et al., 2014). Most of these measures are employed—and justified—because they are reflective of high performers in that sport; for example, people look for tall basketball players and powerful sprinters. Critically, you should consider the extent in which these measures actually enable prediction (McCall et al., 2017), the representative of the selection task to the eventual sport performance (Pinder et al., 2011), and the extent to which unidimensional tests can evaluate multidimensional potential (cf. Mann et al., 2017).

Optimization

Reflecting the importance of developing psychobehavioral characteristics and skills as part of the talent development process, this section considers how to teach, develop, and refine PCDEs in the coaching process and as a key part of the developmental diet of young athletes.

Promoting PCDEs in Talent Development Environments

Although psychological skills training is often included in support programs aimed at senior elite performers, a more effective approach is to systematically incorporate these skills into TD processes specifically oriented toward imminent events. As such, it is important to consider how PCDEs can be included in the TD agenda. Again, athletes should have experienced input and application of all the PCDEs by the time they reach the tail end of the pathway; for those reaching or already at senior level, the aim is to have a clear idea about which skills might need to be honed most or compensated for. Against the much preferred proactive approach, a developmental curriculum ensures that athletes who are making the transition to elite sport are prepared for the pressures and challenges they will face. As mentioned earlier, teaching PCDEs as part of the developmental diet will have multiple benefits. PCDEs will support the transition of athletes cut from elite sport pathways, facilitating talent transfer (Vaeyens et al., 2009) or life after sport (Williams & MacNamara, 2020). As such, PCDEs are useful from both a specific (focus on this sport) and generic (transfer to other activities) performance perspective together with a much broader educational agenda encompassing achievement after sport and lifelong physical activity participation (cf. the three worlds mentioned in Collins et al., 2011).

Although coaches typically value psychological and mental skills and attempt to teach these skills to their athletes, this training is not always conducted in a systematic or intentional manner. Furthermore, the skill level of the coach mediates the ease with which these psychological skills are taught. Skilled coaches typically use a variety of well-thought-out and articulated strategies (e.g., team meetings, modeling behavior, feedback) to teach psychological skills. Conversely, less-skilled coaches teach psychological skills in an ad hoc manner. Aspiring elites benefit from coaches who carefully consider and prioritize PCDEs as part of their educational focus.

PCDEs in Practice

As a first step of a proactive, systematic approach, PCDEs must be defined as clear and observable behaviors that are meaningful to the athlete and the context in which they perform. This process allows coaches, sport psychology consultants, and the athletes themselves to assess, monitor, measure,

Coaches need to consider their own behaviors and how they provide feedback and reinforcement to help athletes develop PCDEs.

and reinforce progress and behavior. Simply put, each PCDE should be operationalized based on aspects that will strengthen the athlete's performance, development, and mental skills profile. Table 17.2 illustrates some sample PCDE behaviors. It highlights how multiple definitions might exist, thus conveying how the PCDEs can be tailored to different sports, goals, and development phases. The behavior should be visual (something that can be seen and measured), behavioral (something that can be promoted), and positive (not a lack of something).

In order to promote and reinforce PCDE behaviors, a series of coach behaviors and systems are required that encourage, prime, and reinforce the desired actions, as shown in table 17.3. This systematic approach is important as coaches, sport psychology consultants, and other stakeholders must consider how their own behaviors and the system in which they operate promote desired (and sometimes dysfunctional) behaviors in athletes. As a first step, it is important to limit the focus to a couple of PCDEs to prevent the athlete from becoming overwhelmed and confused with too much change. Second, coaches, sport psychology consultants, and others need to consider their own behaviors and how they provide feedback and reinforcement (within a supportive environment) to the athlete that indicates their progress toward achieving the desired behaviors. Third, coaches need to put in place systems that set conditions to encourage, teach, and promote the desired behaviors; these systems clarify what behaviors are expected and the consequences of

TABLE 17.2 Sample PCDE Behaviors

Psychological characteristic	Sample behavior
Commitment	Arrives early to train Works hard at own level
Focus and distraction control	Remains focused under distraction Displays a consistent preperformance routine
Realistic performance evaluation	Is able to analyze what they do well and what they don't Is able to attribute success and failure appropriately
Role clarity	Understands how their role varies in different game contexts Understands how their role fits with others in different contexts Understands the standard expected of them at the training ground
Self-regulation	Is aware of adaptive and maladaptive influences on performance
Planning and self-organization	Is able to balance lifestyle commitments Is able to prioritize different activities
Goal setting and self-reward	Is able to set short-, medium-, and long-term goals Is able to set appropriate goals
Quality practice	Is able to maximize understanding in training Understands why the coach is doing what they are doing
Effective and controllable imagery	Uses imagery to rehearse new skills Uses imagery to simulate new environments
Seeking and using social support	Knows when and how to seek out support from others

TABLE 17.3   PCDE Coach Systems and Behaviors

Player behavior	Coach behavior	System
Show confident behavior under pressure	• Identify confident behaviors and body language • Reinforce appropriate behaviors through feedback • Model the behavior: Having fear is all right, but teach how to overcome it	• Simulated pressure situations in training • Keeping a record of behaviors in competition and training • Senior players talking about coping with pressure
Motivated and confident to do their best on competition day	• Emphasize links between training and competition (what they need to do, show they can do it) • Emphasize roles and process goals of competition (with player involvement)	• Simulated specific pressure training • Review of roles and goals in competition, leading to goal setting
Can overcome mistakes	• Teach solution and emotional coping • Stress long-term successes from short-term failures	• Encourage 3 goods and 3 work-ons postgame or postpractice • Use goal ladders to encourage climbing back

engaging (or not engaging) in those behaviors. In fact, teaching, deploying, and culturally encouraging PCDE behaviors as a feature of everyday practice is a particularly important element of this approach. More specifically, the procedural element of the coaching system is important because it keeps the skills central to the athlete's experience and embeds them within the culture of the environment. As such, coaches will design their practice for explicit outcomes such as improving technique, tactics, or fitness, but also for implicit outcomes such as increasing self-regulation or commitment—in other words, PCDEs. The PCDEs are seen as an essential part of the sport rather than a peripheral aspect that might be useful.

Ultimately, it is through the interaction of coach systems and coach behaviors that the athlete is encouraged to engage in the PCDE behavior. A consistent and coherent approach will then lead to the athlete accepting and internalizing these behaviors so that they occur independently to the benefit of their performance.

Teach, Test, Tweak, Repeat

In order to ensure young athletes are provided with opportunities to develop PCDEs, a teaching, challenging, evaluating, and refining (or more simply, *teach, test, tweak, repeat*) cycle also needs to be used (see figure 17.3). This model ensures that the coach behaviors and systems are systematically designed to provide the athlete with the opportunity to learn skills before having to implement them against meaningful challenge. In the teach phase,

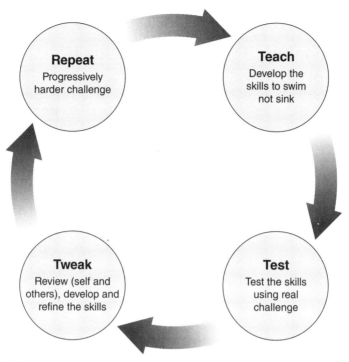

FIGURE 17.3   Teach, test, tweak, repeat cycle.

athletes experience a gradual development of psychological skills as part and parcel of their training. The skillful use of coach behaviors and systems (table 17.3) ensures that the athlete learns the skills before they are tested under pressure in the test phase of the model. In the test phase, the PCDEs are tested against realistic challenges from within their environment. For example, an academy player might train with the senior team or be asked to practice advanced skills. Again, skillful use of reinforcement, modeling, and evaluation by the coach through their own behavior and the environment created will ensure an optimal outcome from this formative evaluation of the skills. After the challenge, coaches and others (involving parents is also a useful practice depending on the age of the athlete) engage the athlete in review—the tweak phase. This process allows the athlete to develop their capacity to self-evaluate and self-manage with support and feedback from teachers and others. As the athlete progresses, the complexity of the challenge increases, which requires them to develop and deploy a more sophisticated skill set. In tandem, the balance of challenge to support also increases. Critically, though, and reflecting the developmental agenda, athletes must be given time to reflect on the process and refine the required skills. Integral to this is the requirement for the athlete to learn from, develop, refine, and crucially secure confidence in their capacity to use the PCDEs. As such, it is important that athletes get periods of adaptation where they return to familiar and comfortable surroundings to maximize opportunities for growth.

Success Story:
Managing the Junior to Senior Transition

In my experience, the most effective means of developing PCDEs is to integrate them into the coaching and playing structures of a specific environment. First, effective PCDE curriculum approaches take care to ensure that the application has a customized feel (in terms of language, procedures, and emphasis) that makes it relevant to the players, sport, and context. Second, the planned use of challenge to support the development of PCDEs has been a very effective method. For example, in one rugby academy, players are systematically placed in senior level competitions or training for short periods of time, or they are sent on loan to lower-level leagues to gain exposure to different environments. On occasion, academy players warm up at a senior session as an effective coach system of developing and refining PCDEs. As another coach system, academy players complete a skills session at halftime of a premiership game to gain experience performing in front of a real crowd and as a test of their ability to cope with the pressure of the occasion.

Third, the teach, test, tweak, repeat cycle ensures that players have the skills to swim and not sink. For example, in my work on a national hockey pathway, considerable time was spent teaching PCDEs before incremental exposure to challenge over the course of a 24-month development program. An important feature was that coach behaviors such as engaging players in regular reviews and encouraging them to self-evaluate, self-reflect, and use feedback ensured PCDEs were bullet-proofed before they came under fire at an important tournament. Finally, the success of the PCDE curriculum across all these contexts was that it was seen as part and parcel of the overall development approach, was embedded into the procedural and coaching decisions at all levels, and was reflective of day-to-day interactions.

Conclusion

Psychological characteristics of developing excellence (PCDEs) offer an evidence-based route by which young athletes can increase their chances of overcoming the roadblocks and derailers inherent in their talent development (TD) journey and realize their potential. Significantly, the approach to TD outlined in this chapter should facilitate the pursuit of excellence at the athlete's chosen level of achievement but also their potential to achieve in other domains. Indeed, the transferability and generality of PCDEs is a positive feature of this approach; the same PCDEs appear important regardless of domain or stage of development, and they equip athletes to cope with developmental challenges from both in and out of sport across the life span. Overall, this chapter has emphasized the following:

1. The PCDE approach is skills based; it uses a careful periodization of challenge and support to teach, test, and tweak skills, then repeat them, creating a positive cycle.

2. The skills are taught through a combination of formal, informal, and procedural methods, then they are tested against realistic challenges.

3. Teachable moments should be used to engage the athlete in review to consider what happened and why. This approach helps the athlete secure confidence in the use of the PCDEs.

4. The formal teaching of PCDEs usually involves a sport psychology consultant (if available) and the coach presenting the skill. It is an individualized and gradual approach backed up by a variety of informational interactions. The use of peers to model effective application of the PCDEs in realistic challenges is a useful strategy.

5. The PCDEs should be taught, deployed, and encouraged as part of everyday practice and interactions so that athletes see the PCDEs as an integral part of their development.

6. Starting early offers a greater chance to develop and embed PCDEs, provides skills to counter roadblocks or life events before they occur, and offers plenty of opportunity for gradual, incremental progression.

7. PCDEs can be thought of as equipping the athlete with a hand of cards that are then deployed to achieve or counter challenges in their current or future environments.

This chapter presents a case for the role of psychology as an important and influential mechanism in the TD process. Because this development process is nonlinear, complex, and dynamic, it is vital that aspiring elites are supported to develop, test, and refine a comprehensive set of skills so that they can negotiate their own highly individual pathways to excellence.

18 Practice and Transfer to Competition, Peaking, and Performing

Boris Blumenstein
College of Management Academic Studies (Rishon LeZion)

Iris Orbach
College of Management Academic Studies (Rishon LeZion) and Wingate Institute

Psychological skills are central components of athletic performance. The aim of this chapter is to review the benefits of practicing psychological skills training (PST) and transferring psychological skills associated with peak performance from laboratory to field. Integrating PST with other athletic preparations (i.e., physical, technical, tactical) according to the periodization principle helps to achieve the transfer of psychological skills from laboratory to field quickly and precisely.

This chapter introduces the five-stage PST model, which integrates biofeedback training with other psychological strategies as one intervention package. The five-stage PST model includes some objective measurements for evaluating psychological readiness associated with peak performance. In addition, the chapter addresses relevant questions that coaches and staff might ask. Based on the scientific and practical knowledge included in this chapter, a success story of applying the five-stage PST model while working with a professional athlete is presented.

Relevance

An increasing number of athletes and coaches have come to understand that the winner is the mentally strongest athlete or team on any given day. Therefore, most elite athletes and teams pay special attention to psychological preparation. Psychological preparation is posited as effective for attaining optimal athletic performance and is widely researched and practiced (Krane & Williams, 2015; Vealey, 2007; Weinberg & Gould, 2015). For example, a positive performance effect was found in more than 85 percent of the studies across different sports, such as golf (e.g., Ramsey et al., 2008), basketball (e.g., Burke, 2006; Lidor et al., 2007a, 2007b), combat sports (e.g., Blumenstein et al., 2005), soccer (e.g., Dosil, 2006), and high-intensity sports (e.g., Birrer & Morgan, 2010). At the same time, most of the athletes who took part in another study indicated the importance of psychological preparation. However, only 44 percent made frequent use of psychological strategies and techniques in competitions compared to practice settings, which does not allow for optimal psychological preparation (Frey et al., 2003). It is an absurd situation that in competition, athletes use mental techniques they do not learn and practice in their daily regimen. However, according to Weinberg and Gould (2015), PST can be applied to athletes at all levels. In addition, PST has been applied in business, to artists, to police officers, to army officers, to firefighters, to drivers, and to soccer and basketball referees

Harry How/Getty Images

Psychological skills training can be applied to athletes at all levels, from youth participants to Olympic competitors.

to improve their performance (e.g., Bar-Eli, 2017; Blumenstein & Orbach, 2014b; McCrory et al., 2013).

Psychological skills are not innate. In addition, only after the systematic and consistent practice can those psychological skills be applied in training and competition for the purpose of peak athletic performance. Unfortunately, most coaches do not understand these facts, and they may be intimidated by the involvement of a third person such as a sport psychology consultant. They may believe that psychological skills cannot be improved, and they may not have enough knowledge about the possibility of measuring and evaluating progress in the use of psychological skills. At the same time, sport psychology consultants may not understand the theory and methodology of sport training in the specific sport discipline, so they too can benefit from learning something new. As the famous soccer coach Fabio Capello states, "It is crucial that a sport psychologist working in elite soccer completely understands soccer. . . . and is prepared to understand the problems related to this type of activity" (Freitas et al., 2013, p. 89). Sport psychology consultants should understand that they are part of the team that helps athletes achieve excellence. The next section discusses knowledge about PST and peak performance.

What We Know

Overall, a successful psychological program is based on the following fundamental principles:

- Systematic PST
- Planned psychological programs
- Integration in training processes
- Collaboration with the coach and medical staff
- An established link between scientific research and training practice
- Ethics and morals in PST application (e.g., Bompa et al., 2019)

When a sport psychology consultant is not involved, athletes and coaches should still consider these principles as much as possible.

Each sport has unique demands for the psychological skills that may guarantee peak performance. Common psychological skills and strategies that are typically used in different sports to achieve peak performance include relaxation and self-regulation of arousal, concentration and attentional focus, self-confidence, self-talk, imagery, goal setting, and biofeedback training (see Acharya & Morris, 2014; Blumenstein & Orbach, 2014a, 2018; Henschen, 2005; Lidor, 2007; Moran, 2010; Vealey, 2007; and Vealey & Forlenza, 2015). In team sport, techniques focused on group cohesion, communication, and leadership play an important role in the team's success (e.g., Weinberg & Gould, 2015) as highlighted in earlier chapters of this book.

Most of these techniques are widely used by sport psychology consultants, and they have shown significant positive effects on athletic performance. Each of these techniques can be used alone or as part of a psychological intervention package (Blumenstein & Orbach, 2012a, 2012b, 2018; Vealey, 2007). Moreover, these psychological strategies are characterized by individual content and context, determined by the different sport demands and sport situations. All techniques should also be linked and coordinated with the training phases. For example, the concentration style in shooting is different than the concentration style in basketball; relaxation in the preparation phase and relaxation in the competition phase have different goals and therefore should be practiced accordingly. Overall, one of the most important psychological strategies or techniques to help transfer learned skills from laboratory settings to the field is biofeedback training (Beauchamp et al., 2012; Blumenstein & Orbach, 2018; Zaichkowsky 2009).

Biofeedback Training

Biofeedback training is a technique used for gaining control of self-regulation; it is based on information (feedback) received from an athlete's body and mind. Substantial reasons exist for successfully using biofeedback training as part of an athlete's psychological preparation. First, similar to physical training, biofeedback training is based on the educational approach, which includes the following: clear training goals, a varied collection of psychological strategies and exercises as a means of training, a plan and structure for training sessions in which improvement can be observed, and transference of learned skills to the field. Second, psychophysiological monitoring of an athlete's emotional state represents an objective source of information. Finally, using psychophysiological measurement can promote an understanding of the athlete's brain and the complexity of sport performance (Blumenstein & Orbach, 2014a; Collins & McPherson, 2006; Zaichkowsky 2009).

Today, biofeedback training is used in research and practical programs as an integral component of PST in a variety of sport disciplines, such as archery, soccer, swimming, and wind surfing. One example of a newly developed approach is the three-dimensional learning–modification–application (LMA) approach (Blumenstein & Orbach, 2014a, 2018). This approach is a multifaceted psychological program that integrates biofeedback training with other psychological strategies into one intervention package based on the periodization principle; it mainly focuses on applied work with elite athletes. *Periodization* is a basic principle in sport training that enables the coach to plan and manage the training process. For the complete transfer of psychological skills from laboratory to field, the authors of this chapter have developed another periodized approach; it is called the simulation training exercise program (STEP) (Blumenstein et al., 2007; Blumenstein & Orbach 2012a, 2012b, 2015, 2018), and it is discussed in the next section.

Simulation Training Exercise Program

Based on numerous applied studies and the scientific and practical work of the authors of this chapter, the simulation training exercise program (STEP), including the main objective of each phase and its psychological correlates, is presented in table 18.1. As indicated, this program is composed of special exercises and simulated competition situations alleged to improve the athlete's psychological skills and performance. The motor tasks are practiced during mental training sessions, and the psychological techniques are used to improve performance and positive transfer to competition. STEP is usually provided as an independent program or as part of an intervention package that is applied in specific preparation and competition phases based on the periodization principle before to important events. A typical training program consists of three main phases: preparatory (general and specific), competitive, and transition. The practice during these phases includes these four different preparations: physical, technical, tactical, and psychological. In the ideal training program, each of the four preparations should be coordinated with the other preparations in each training phase (Bompa et al., 2019; Mujika et al., 2018). STEP includes three further stages (initial, advanced, and realization). It also includes different motor exercises (e.g., stop reaction exercise, time reproduction exercise, and reaction training program). In the $STEP_{initial}$ stage, athletes learn and practice two of the three motor exercises—time reproduction exercise and stop reaction exercise—which are provided in the general preparatory phase of the training periodization. The goal in this stage is to learn a movement and to connect it to the relevant psychological strategies (e.g., muscle relaxation, concentration, self-talk, or imagery). In

TABLE 18.1 Periodization of Psychological Preparation

	PREPARATORY PHASE			
	General preparation	**Specific preparation**	**Competition phase**	**Transition phase***
Main aims	Learn basic psychological strategies for developing self-regulation abilities.	Modify psychological skills and strategies based on sport-specific demands.	Transfer and apply psychological skills to the field and competition.	Use psychological techniques for recovery and rest between seasons.
Special attention	Have a positive attitude toward the daily training load and sport regimen, weekly recovery, and sport motivation.	Combine dominant psychological skills relevant to sport discipline.	Keep optimal sport form and self-confidence, stress management, coping skills, and preperformance routine.	Evaluation and recovery between competition events and seasons

*During the transition phase, athletes are directed to use psychological techniques for recovery and rest in both laboratory and home settings.

the STEP$_{advanced}$ stage, which takes place in the specific preparatory phase, the athletes continue to perfect the movement with relevant psychological strategies while being exposed to different demands, which allows for better results in task performance. Finally, in the STEP$_{realization}$ stage, which is provided in the competitive phase, athletes practice the exercises under situations and conditions that are designed to be similar to real-life, sport-specific competition demands.

Overall, the combination of the LMA and the STEP programs continually contributes to the application of psychological skills in training and competition. The full potential of PST in competition can be seen when it is part of the athlete's overall preparation and is based on the periodization principle (Blumenstein et al., 2007; Blumenstein & Orbach, 2018; Bompa et al., 2019). The special exercises, simulated situations, and psychological techniques used as part of the LMA and STEP programs are adjusted based on the demands of the sport (e.g., individual or team), the periodization of the specific sport, and the needs of the athletes and the coaches (Blumenstein et al., 2007; Blumenstein & Orbach, 2012a, 2012b, 2015).

In summary, coaches and athletes should be aware that psychological skills can be learned and practiced; psychological skills can be monitored through objective and introspective measures; and psychological preparation can be linked to an athlete's training goals and become part of their regular practice (Blumenstein et al., 2007; Blumenstein & Orbach 2012b, 2018; Bompa et al., 2019; Holliday et al., 2008; Mujika et al., 2018). Furthermore, sport psychology consultants should have enough information regarding the theory and methodology of sport training to provide psychological preparation in the training process (Blumenstein & Orbach 2012b, 2018; Bompa et al. 2019).

Assessment

To help coaches, athletes, and sport psychology consultants assess their approach to transferring psychological skills to competition and peak performance, consider some topics regarding PST processes. This section provides tools for realistic assessment and commitment to PST.

Integration and Transfer of PST to Competition

As outlined earlier, periodization is a basic principle in sport training that enables the coach to plan and manage the training process. The full potential of any psychological program can be achieved when PST is part of the athlete's overall preparation and is based on the periodization principle, sport-specific discipline, and athlete or team abilities (Balague, 2000; Blumenstein et al., 2007; Blumenstein & Orbach, 2018; Bompa et al., 2019; Mujika et al., 2018).

For example, the best time to initially implement PST is during the off-season or preseason when the stress level is low. It allows enough time for the athletes to integrate their new knowledge and psychological skills into actual competitions. The following section discusses recommendations to coaches and sport psychology consultants regarding the incorporation of PST into the training process.

Preparatory Phase: General Preparation

The main objective of general preparation in the preparatory phase is to help athletes improve their physical and motor abilities as required by the specific sport (e.g., Bompa & Buzzichelli, 2019). Athletes can achieve this goal with hard, voluminous, monotonous work with numerous exercise repetitions. Therefore, PST should be oriented toward physical and psychological rest, recovery, relaxation, daily and weekly motivation, concentration under fatigue, positive attitude, and clear goal setting. Athletes can learn basic psychological techniques and strategies, such as progressive muscle relaxation (Jacobson, 1938), imagery (e.g., Morris, 2010), concentration (e.g., Moran, 2010), biofeedback training (e.g., Blumenstein & Orbach, 2014a;), and goal setting (e.g., Gould, 2015).

Preparatory Phase: Specific Preparation

The main objective of specific preparation in the preparatory phase is to further develop the athlete's physical abilities according to the unique physiological characteristics of a specific sport, including the athlete's sport form and readiness for competition (Blumenstein et al., 2007; Blumenstein & Orbach, 2012a, 2012b; Bompa & Buzzichelli, 2019). Accordingly, as the intensity of practice increases, the number of repeated exercises substantially decreases. The main objective of PST in specific preparation is to practice psychological skills and strategies to enhance the physical, technical, and tactical skills required for a specific sport type. In this phase, it is especially important to consider the technical preparation, in which mental and motor control play a vital role.

In the specific preparation phase, the athlete is exposed to a variety of actual environmental factors related to a competition situation. Therefore, psychological techniques need to be performed under special stress distractions and are modified toward sport-specific demands. In addition, during this period the athlete participates in some competitions. Therefore, the psychological skills training in the individual sport should focus more on parameters such as self-confidence, self-regulation, and concentration. In team sports, the psychological skills training centers on developing team cohesion, communication, leadership, group dynamics, and the relationships among players. If present, the sport psychology consultant takes part in athlete or team practice, introduces psychological techniques in training, identifies weaknesses in the athlete or team psychological preparation, and finally optimizes the precompetitive routine. In this period, it is important to pay special attention to the interactions among the psychological, tactical, and technical preparations.

In short, in the preparatory phase the athlete develops a framework for the physical, technical, tactical, and psychological preparations for the upcoming competition phase (Lidor et al., 2016). Eventually, during the specific preparation, the psychological techniques are modified toward the sport-specific skills of each chosen sport.

Competitive Phase

The main objective of the competitive phase is to improve the athlete's motor and psychological abilities in as many competitions as possible so that they can achieve peak performance. During this phase, the intensity of the performed technical elements increases and the repetitions decrease while the total time of training decreases. In addition, the athlete intensively participates in a variety of competitions. The ultimate goal of PST in this period is to transfer a large part of the mental training from the laboratory to the field and to apply the psychological strategies in different training and competition situations. Moreover, the psychological strategies are modified to the training and competition demands, such as the duration and specificity of the sport. Therefore, in this period, psychological skills are an integral part of the precompetitive routine, more related to the kind of sport and the actual environment factors of competition (Blumenstein et al., 2007; Blumenstein & Orbach, 2018; Weinberg & Gould, 2015; Weinberg & Williams, 2015). Special attention in this phase is given to preperformance routines (Cotterill, 2010), concentration (Moran, 2010), self-confidence (Feltz & Oncu, 2014), short versions of muscle relaxation (Jacobson, 1938), biofeedback training (Blumenstein & Orbach 2014a), and recovery following training and competitions (Elbe & Kellmann, 2007).

Transition Phase

The objective of the transition phase is to enhance physical and psychological rest and to ensure that an acceptable level of the athlete's general preparation is maintained. Athletes are advised to remain active during this phase so that they will be better conditioned for the next preparation phase in a new training cycle. The main objective of PST during the transition phase is mental recovery, using methods such as relaxing, listening to special individualized music, and breathing exercises, while incorporating biofeedback games (Blumenstein & Orbach, 2012a, 2012b; Elbe & Kellmann, 2007).

Allowing Enough Time for PST

Practice literature indicates that within five to six months (depending on the sport discipline and the athlete's characteristics) of systematic weekly PST practice, athletes can experience the first positive results in training and competitions. Similar to other types of preparation (physical, technical, or tactical), the athlete or team should continually practice PST to achieve stability and performance excellence for the long term.

Personnel to Provide the PST

Ideally, PST programs should be provided by a qualified sport psychology consultant who takes part in athlete or team practice, plans PST programs, introduces psychological techniques in training, identifies weaknesses in the athlete or team psychological preparation, and optimizes the precompetitive routine. To accomplish all these tasks, the sport psychology practitioner should increase their own sport-specific knowledge. However, coaches should acquire and use psychological knowledge (e.g., Phil Jackson and Pat Riley in the NBA), which can be seen in special projects in countries such as Portugal, the United States, Australia, and England (Pain & Harwood, 2004).

Evaluation of a PST Program

Because PST is integrated with other preparations, evaluating a PST program is not easy. However, related remarks on some indicators of success and how to gauge them are presented as follows:

- When the athlete or team achieves their best results in training and competition and overcomes challenging situations, it is a good indication that PST, together with the other preparations, has yielded positive results.
- The athlete or team and coach would like to continue cooperation with the sport psychology consultant involved in psychological preparation. For example, the first author worked with the same athletes during two or three Olympic Games and numerous World and European Championships.
- In terms of the evaluation process, interviews, questionnaires, evaluation forms, behavioral observation, and analyzed practices and competitions should be used for understanding the impact of a PST program.
- Most important is to establish whether a positive linear relationship exists between the use of a PST program and the athlete's and team's achievement.

Optimization

Since 2002, the authors' framework of psychological preparation has been applied with encouraging outcomes in various sports and to numerous elite athletes. The effectiveness of this program and its elements were investigated in numerous research projects and practical work with athletes at varied ages, skill levels, and sport disciplines (e.g., Blumenstein & Orbach, 2012a, 2012b, 2014a, 2015, 2018; Lidor et al., 2007b). To help you think further on what can be done to optimize your own psychological preparation, the PST model is introduced. This model was primarily designed to inform the work of sport psychology consultants, but coaches and athletes can also consider the principles to inform their own practice.

The PST model integrates biofeedback training with other psychological strategies as one intervention package that includes the LMA approach and STEP. Like the LMA and STEP, the innovation of this program is its integration with the athlete's or team's training process and incorporation of the periodization principle. Throughout the training program, psychological skills are learned and practiced, becoming more specific to sport and the athlete's or team's practice.

The PST model is composed of five stages (see table 18.2) that overlap with the LMA and STEP models mentioned earlier.

Stage 1: Introduction

In the first stage, *introduction* (usually at the beginning of the sport season for general preparation), the sport psychology consultant visits the athlete's practices during the first training month to observe the athlete's daily regimen. The main goal is for better understanding of the training process and the qualities of sport discipline. The main instruments are observations and conversations with the coach and athletes and study of specific literature relevant to the sport discipline, including reports of famous athletes of this sport. For example, the first author of this chapter (BB) began his work with a top windsurfer while visiting and observing training in the sea and talking

TABLE 18.2   Main Intervention Programs in the PST Model

	PREPARATORY PHASE				
	General preparation		**Specific preparation**	**Competition phase**	**Transition phase***
PST model	Introduction	Learning	Modification	Application	Analysis and recovery
LMA stages		Learning	Modification	Application	
STEP stages		STEP$_{initial}$	STEP$_{advanced}$	STEP$_{realization}$	
Lab/field ratio %	20/80	70/30	50/50	30/70	60/40
Place of PST	Mainly in field	Lab	Lab and field	Field	Lab and competition results

*During the transition phase, athletes are directed to use psychological techniques for recovery and rest in both laboratory and home settings.

with the coach about the training process and the athlete's performance daily. In addition, while working with team sport, BB traveled with a soccer team for a training camp that lasted one month. These experiences can be titled as *deep immersion* in the training process. This kind of cooperation with the sport psychology consultant can allow the athlete or team and the coach to harmoniously cross to the next stage.

Stage 2: Learning

The second stage, the *learning* stage, is provided as part of the general preparation of the athlete. The main objective of practice in this phase is to strengthen the physical, technical, and psychological foundations of the athlete. A high volume of training, long-duration practice sessions, and moderate intensity are the main characteristics of the general preparation phase in most sports (Bompa et al., 2019). In this stage the athlete practices the main psychological strategies and interventions, such as biofeedback training, muscle relaxation, concentration, imagery, and self-talk. The process is usually accompanied by biofeedback control, such as heart rate (HR), electromyography (EMG), and electrodermal activity (EDA) (also known as galvanic skin response [GSR]). Moreover, basic psychological strategies are learned and practiced according to a stress distraction scale that was developed from the authors' work with biofeedback training in a variety of athlete levels and sport disciplines.

   In the learning stage, the athlete learns and performs basic psychological strategies under light stress distractions in laboratory settings (*light* stress = levels 1-2 on a 7-point scale). The duration of this stage is approximately two months (i.e., 7-8 sessions) during which the sport psychology consultant visits the athlete's practice two or three times a week. For example, regarding relaxation skill, the athlete initially learns the basic version of relaxation and uses it for recovery purposes after intensive practice. At this stage the relaxation should last 10 to 15 minutes. At the end of this stage, the athlete can use the relaxation skill independently during practice according to sport discipline demands.

Stage 3: Modification

The third stage is the *modification* stage, which is applied parallel to the specific preparation phase of the athlete's training. The main objective of the specific preparation phase is to further develop the athlete's physical ability according to the unique physical and physiological characteristics of the sport (e.g., Bompa et al., 2019; Blumenstein & Orbach, 2018). Moreover, at this stage athletes integrate into their practice the technical and tactical components of their preparation. Therefore, the mental sessions and psychological strategies are modified according to the practice. For example, during the mental sessions, athletes focus on concentration and imagery techniques, in which they visualize technical elements of themselves or their opponents (e.g., in combat sports). Moreover, the length of the psychological interventions and their packaging are relevant to the sport discipline. For example, in judo, the biofeedback training includes short relaxation for 1 to 3 minutes (i.e., preparation time before the match) followed by imagery for 4 minutes (i.e., the length of the real-life match). The overall length of the modification stage is approximately two months (i.e., 7-8 sessions). These sessions are provided in a lab or training setting under *moderate* stress distractions (level 3-4 on a 7-point scale). In training settings, the equipment used are portable biofeedback devices.

Stage 4: Application

The fourth stage is the *application* stage, which is linked to the competition phase of the periodization principle. The focus of this stage is to practice the technical and tactical elements of the athlete's performance. The practice includes simulation of previous competition events and generating real-life situations using a variety of stress distractions. Therefore, mental training sessions in this period include the practice of skills such as short relaxation, fast concentration, and performance imagery with biofeedback control under competitive stress. For this purpose, competitive noises and scenes are prepared and practiced (stress distractions level 5-7).

For example, a major feature of the application stage is the simulation and practice of the event itself. This process is accompanied by biofeedback training, while the goal is to perform psychological skills quickly and accu-

Richard Langdon/Getty Images

Practicing PST helps the athlete to bring all their training together in critical moments of competition.

rately under actual competition time. Therefore, during mental sessions, the imagery for rhythmic gymnasts lasts about 1 minute, 30 seconds, which is similar to real competition performance time; relaxation for taekwondo lasts about 1 minute and is applied 3 times, with a pause of 1 minute between periods; relaxation and imagery for swimming lasts 10 to 20 seconds and is accompanied with the command *step up, take your mark, go*.

Ultimately, the practice of the PST model helps the athlete to bring all their training together in critical moments of competition. It allows the athlete to integrate mental skills as part of the precompetitive and preperformance routine as well as for performance enhancement. The practice can entail performing a package of psychological exercises and achieving specific results that are linked to the athlete's psychological readiness in different sports as outlined in table 18.3. The data in this table are based on more than 30 years of experience working with elite athletes from a variety of sport disciplines and countries (Blumenstein & Orbach, 2012a, 2012b).

The reaction training program consists of three reaction training tasks that are practiced on a computer device: (1) simple reaction training (1 stimulus and 1 response); (2) choice reaction training (2 stimuli and 2 responses); (3) discrimination reaction training (2 stimuli and 1 response) (Blumenstein et al., 2005). Regarding the table's details, pay attention to the ratio data. In the simple reaction training, the judo example includes 10 attempts (9 fast

TABLE 18.3 Sample Measurements for Evaluating Psychological Readiness Associated With Peak Performance

	Reaction training program: **10 simple** **20 choice** **20 discrimination**	**STEP:** **Stop reaction exercise** **Time reproduction exercise**	**Δ GSR (kΩ)** **(30 sec, 1 min)**	**Performance time during imagery**
Judo N = 25	115-145 msec; ratio: 9:1 140-168 msec; ratio: 8:2 127-136 msec; ratio: 9:1	0.06-0.07 sec 4.94-5.06 sec (±0.06)	Δ 600-700 (1 min)	N/A
Taekwondo N = 16	127-130 msec; ratio: 8:2 140-164 msec; ratio: 8:2 122-138 msec; ratio: 9:1	0.06-0.08 sec 4.95-5.05 sec (±0.05)	Δ 600-650 (1 min.)	N/A
Rhythmic gymnastics N = 16	N/A	N/A 4.95-5.05 sec (±0.05)	Δ 450-500 (30 sec)	Individual: 1.29-1.30 Group: 2.29-2.30 Δ 500-600 (30 sec)
Swimming N = 5	N/A	0.11-0.13 sec 4.95-5.05 sec. (±0.05)	Δ 500-600 (30 sec)	Approximately the personal best time
Rowing N = 4	N/A	0.13-0.14 sec 4.94-5.06 sec (±0.06)	Δ 500-600 (30 sec)	Approximately the personal best time

and 1 slow). However, in the choice and discrimination reaction training, the attention is only on the dominant side of the athlete; therefore, the ratio is based on only 10 attempts and not 20.

The STEP includes two motor exercises: (1) stop reaction exercise and (2) time reproduction exercise. In the stop reaction exercise, the athlete holds a wide stopwatch with the thumb pressed on the start–stop button. The main goal of this exercise is to start and stop the time as fast as possible. To achieve good results, the athlete must learn how to relax their muscles and concentrate on the act itself while finding the optimal balance between muscle tension and the necessary concentration level. In the time reproduction exercise, the athlete is asked to reproduce a time period of 5 seconds without looking at the time clock. After three or four training attempts, the athlete has five attempts. The goal is to reproduce a time close to 5 seconds based on the sport discipline (see table 18.3).

Another measurement is the galvanic skin response (GSR) (kΩ). In this biofeedback exercise, athletes are asked to relax and concentrate for a specific time period (e.g., 30 sec in combat sport and 60 sec in other sports). The Δ achieved indicates the ability of the athlete to self-regulate.

Finally, the last exercise is performance time during imagery. The goal is to imagine a clean performance within the ideal competitive performance time, such as the personal best time in 100-meter swimming or a rhythmic gymnastics routine performed within the required competition time limit (e.g., 1:30 min). In some cases, both the coach and the athlete should make the necessary corrections in the athlete's preparation to compensate for not achieving the desired measures. For example, measures of the reaction training program and STEP based on table 18.3 inform the athlete about their speed of decision making, concentration, and the ability to create an optimal balance between concentration and relaxation. If the athlete demonstrates an insufficient result in these exercises, they must pay more attention to the technical details of their performance (especially with a ratio of 7:3 or 6:4 in the reaction training program). Similarly, corrections are necessary in the warm-up preparation and tactical preparation for the upcoming fight in combat sports. In addition, throughout the competition process, an athlete may achieve their best results in the reaction training program and STEP exercises. For example, after a first victory in judo and in the preparation process for the second fight, the athlete may achieve 0.06 seconds in the stop reaction exercise, and 4.97 seconds, 5.01 seconds, and 4.96 seconds in the three attempts of the reaction training exercises.

Stage 5: Analysis and Recovery

Returning to table 18.2, the fifth and final stage of the psychological skills training model, *analysis and recovery,* includes analysis, recovery, and correction of possible mistakes. The objective of this stage is to help the athlete to start recovering from the extreme physical and psychological efforts they have made during the competition phase. Included are an analysis of the positive and negative sides of the competition's results together with relaxation techniques while listening to music. During this stage, it is recommended that a few individual and team sessions be conducted regarding future cooperation with the sport psychology consultant and new goals for the next season.

The authors' practice based on the psychological skills training model has helped athletes successfully prepare for four Olympic Games and numerous European and World Championships during more than 30 years. It allows the athlete to integrate mental skills training as part of the precompetitive and preperformance routine, as well as for performance enhancement, as outlined in the following success story.

Success Story: The Road to Medals

The judoka R., one of Israel's best combat athletes, immigrated to Israel at the age of 11. He learned and trained at the Youth Sport Academy at the Wingate Institute. In 2000, he began participating in senior competitions on international levels.

At first, judoka R. said, "I don't need help. I am strong with good will and high motivation. I do not understand what your role is in training and in what way you can control this process. Psychology is only talking. It's science without measurements." This athlete had a strong character, had faced many injuries and comebacks in training, and had experienced problems finding a suitable coach. Until meeting with B.B. (the first author), the athlete had not achieved significant results in international competitions.

Three months before the European Championship, the athlete approached B.B. and asked for his help in getting ready for the competition. The meetings were based on training using the five-stage PST model.

Approximately one week before the competition, the athlete achieved the following results in the reaction training program (15-30-30):

- Simple: 175 msec; ratio = 9 fast: 6 slow
- Choice: 180 msec; ratio = 8:7
- Discrimination: 165 msec; ratio = 9:6

For comparison purposes, the athlete's results from the beginning of the intervention in the reaction training program (15-30-30) were as follows:

- Simple: 195 msec; ratio = 7:8
- Choice: 215 msec; ratio = 5:10
- Discrimination: 190 msec; ratio = 6:9

Reaction training program results indicate that the athlete improved his self-regulation, concentration, and reaction-time skills during the three months, although during the last month before the competition, the results were taken

> *continued*

> continued

while the athlete was being exposed to different levels of stressful factors. Moreover, movement quality improved, as is evident in the ratio between fast and slow reaction time. In the athlete's report, he remarked, "I perform my movements in the training match very fast, similarly to my performance in the psychologist's session (175 msec or 0.06-0.07 sec)." The competition took place during May, three months after the initial meeting between R. and B.B. For the first time the athlete achieved a respectful fifth place in a European Championship.

From October, the athlete and B.B. started joint systematical work based on the periodization principle (see tables 18.1 and 18.2). The two basic subprograms focused on during the psychological training were LMA and the reaction training program. During the preparatory phase (October-December), the first two steps of the LMA were applied. In addition, as part of the reaction training program, the typical workload was 15-30-30 with no stress factor. Intervention strategies such as concentration, exercise, and imagery were modified based on the sport's demands (imagery time changed to 4 min to reflect a real-life match). In addition, the goals were modified from long-term training goals to short-term performance goals.

In the competitive phase (February-May, next year), the athlete worked on steps 2 to 4 of the PST model, which dealt with competitive and training stressors. In the reaction training program, the workload was shorter (10-20-20) and included stress factors. Intervention strategies were modified to reflect more specifically competitive factors. For example, imagery and concentration exercises included stress factors and goal setting focused on technical and tactical goals. The precompetitive routine included strategies, game plans, and self-talk with key words such as *focus*, *fast*, and *relax*.

In the transition phase, two relaxation sessions with music were provided.

Judoka R. and B.B. worked together systematically for the next two years. During this time, the athlete achieved two second places in the European Championships, met the Olympic criterion, and had honorable results (two victories) in Olympic events. B.B. recalls that a day before the European Championship, the athlete asked B.B. to check his reaction training program abilities. B.B. hesitated, but he decided to take the risk. The results of the reaction training program (10-20-20) were as follows: 143 msec (9:1), 168 msec (8: 2), and 135 msec (10:0). The judoka had achieved his best results, but he was suspicious about the reliability of the equipment (computer). After taking a walk, the athlete went to sleep. The next day during his match, he was very focused, aggressive, and confident. That was the first silver medal the athlete had achieved. In addition to the European Championships, the athlete achieved numerous medals in A-level tournaments. Unfortunately, in the next season the athlete decided to train on his own, and in the subsequent years the athlete did not have any significant achievements.

Conclusion

The integration of psychological preparation into an athlete's training process can be realized by using the periodization principle as a guideline for sport psychology interventions. Therefore, psychological skills training (PST) programs should be modified and practiced based on an athlete's training and preparation phases. Biofeedback is a particularly effective tool for prompt realization of the argument. More broadly, the learning–modification–application (LMA) and simulation training exercise program (STEP) models provide athletes and coaches with a framework that allows for the transfer of learned psychological skills from the laboratory to the field as well as for the integration of PST into the athlete's wider preparation. Modern educational programmers of sport psychology should include relevant professional knowledge in sport science with a focus on the theory and methodology of sport training; in the case of coaches, they should also include knowledge in applied sport psychology with an emphasis on PST.

19 | Countering Slumps and Adversity

Andreas Stenling
Umeå University and University of Agder

Andreas Ivarsson
Halmstad University and University of Agder

Athletes often have to deal with slumps and adversity. Common issues that athletes encounter include high levels of stress, external and internal pressure, and injuries. When an athlete is struggling to cope with slumps and adversity, such as precompetitive anxiety and stress, periods of poor performance, or recovery from injury, it can have severe short- and long-term consequences for the athlete's motivation and well-being, and it sometimes leads to career termination. Therefore, working proactively to prevent slumps and adversity as well as help athletes cope with difficult events and periods are crucial for healthy and sustainable sport participation.

This chapter focuses on how athletes can enhance their autonomous motivation and well-being, which can reduce the risk of stress, injury, and psychological ill-being. It also focuses on how coaches, leaders, sport psychology practitioners, or other support practitioners can help to support these areas. The chapter provides examples of potential tools to use in sport environments to assess these factors. Finally, the focus of the chapter moves to behaviors that athletes, coaches, and other social agents in the sport environment can use to create a need-supportive and motivating environment.

Relevance

Participation in organized sport is associated with several positive consequences, such as physical, psychological, and social well-being. However, negative consequences of sport participation (e.g., high injury rates and prevalence of mental health problems) are also frequently reported (Nilsson et al., 2016; Nylandsted Jensen et al., 2018). Approximately 3.7 million sport-related injuries were reported in the United States in 2019 (National Safety Council, 2021). Research has also shown that approximately one out of five elite athletes are at risk for anxiety- or depression-related problems (e.g., Åkesdotter et al., 2020).

Experiences of physical (e.g., injuries) or psychological (e.g., anxiety) ill-being can have negative consequences at the individual, team, and club levels. At

An injury can have short- and long-term effects on an athlete's career.

the individual level, research shows that an injury can have short- and long-term effects on the athlete's career and career development (e.g., Schinke et al., 2018). Several studies have shown that sport injuries in a substantial number of cases have a negative effect on athletes' physical (e.g., Maffulli et al., 2011) and psychological health (e.g., Wiese-Bjornstal et al., 2020). Another negative consequence is that in many cases, severe injuries may lead to career termination (e.g., Park et al., 2013). At the team and club levels, higher injury rates are associated with poorer team performance (lower league ranking at the end of season) in league play and European cups in male professional soccer (Hägglund et al., 2013).

Stress has been highlighted as a particularly potent risk factor for both physical injuries and psychological ill-being. Previous research has shown that high levels of stress are related to increased psychological health complaints (Gerber et al., 2018) and an increased risk of injuries (e.g., Ivarsson et al., 2017a) among athletes. According to researchers, athletes are exposed to multiple stressors, and these can be divided into three broad categories: competitive stressors, organizational stressors, and personal stressors

(Sarkar & Fletcher, 2014). What Fletcher and colleagues (2006) refers to as *organizational stressors* are of particular interest for the current chapter, and examples of organizational stressors are factors intrinsic to the sport (e.g., training and competition load, insufficient recovery), sport relationship and interpersonal demands (e.g., lack of social support), athletic career and performance development issues (e.g., position insecurity, career and performance advancement), and organizational structure and climate of the sport (e.g., coaching style, lack of autonomy, and belonging).

Not being able to adequately cope with stressors is related to an increased risk of physical (e.g., injuries; Ivarsson et al., 2017a) and psychological (e.g., stress symptoms; Kuettel & Larsen, 2020) ill-being. Athletes can use various strategies and intervention programs to enhance their ability to cope with the stressors and consequently decrease their risk of physical injuries and psychological ill-being. Although strategies and interventions are available, barriers exist such as negative attitudes toward help seeking, poor mental health literacy, and motivational factors that can affect athletes' likelihood to adopt strategies and engage in certain behaviors (e.g., injury prevention or rehabilitation; Chan & Hagger, 2012a; Purcell et al., 2019).

Coaches, sport psychology consultants, physical therapists, and other social agents in the sport environment play a key role in helping athletes cope with stressors and supporting them to engage in adaptive behaviors. Research has shown that sociocultural norms can exist where athletes are expected to play through injury and pain, which can aggravate and extend the negative effects of the injury, pain, and psychological ill-being (e.g., Wiese-Bjornstal, 2010). Coaches can help prevent such negative effects if they help normalize and support help-seeking behaviors among athletes to overcome potential stigma to acknowledge physical and psychological problems (Bissett et al., 2020). These types of behaviors from the coach can increase the likelihood of athletes engaging in adaptive behaviors, which decreases the risk of injuries and psychological ill-being. In addition, several programs have been developed to prevent injuries and psychological ill-being (e.g., mindfulness- and acceptance-based approaches). However, the motivation and adherence to such programs are generally low among athletes (Moreland et al., 2018). Social agents in the sport environment, such as coaches, physical therapists, or sport psychology consultants, can therefore play an important role when introducing programs and support athletes' motivation and adherence to follow a protocol.

What We Know

Psychological theories that explain broad motivational phenomena have shown great promise for enhancing people's understanding of behaviors and conditions that facilitate athletes' health, well-being, and optimal functioning (Standage & Ryan, 2020). This section focuses on a particular motivation framework, self-determination theory (SDT) (Ryan & Deci, 2017), which provides athletes, coaches, and other social agents in the sport environment with tools to create and maintain a health-conducive and motivating environment and reduce the adverse effects of stressors. This framework is also discussed more broadly in chapter 5.

Underpinning Principles of SDT

As noted in chapter 5, SDT is a macro-level theory of human motivation, personality, and emotion. It is guided by the assumption that people are active organisms with evolved tendencies toward growth, mastery, and integrating new experiences into a coherent sense of self (Ryan & Deci, 2017). These evolved tendencies toward development require ongoing social support and essential nutrients; they do not operate automatically. The social context can either support or thwart these natural tendencies toward growth, active engagement, and coherence. For example, athletes might notice how features of their own environment, such as support or pressure from the coaches or parents, influence how they train. SDT is underpinned by an organismic dialectical approach, where the dialectic between the active organism and the social context is the basis for predictions about behavior, experience, and development. Put more simply, the interaction between factors in the social environment, such as how the coach of a team interacts with the athletes and how athletes experience these interactions, can influence both athletes and coaches in various ways.

The essential universal nutrients for healthy development, effective functioning, and optimal motivation are specified within SDT using the concept of basic psychological needs. The needs are viewed as innate (rather than acquired), and they are defined at the psychological (rather than physiological) level (Ryan & Deci, 2017). These needs are for autonomy (endorsement of one's actions, flexibility, absence of pressure, and a sense that one is engaging in the action voluntarily), competence (that a person wants to interact effectively with the environment and experience a sense of adequate ability), and relatedness (desire to feel connected to significant others, to be cared for, and to care for others in a safe environment). Therefore, a soccer player's or ice hockey player's needs might be supported by a coach who provides choices during practices and takes the athlete's perspective (support for autonomy), clearly communicates goals and expectations (support for competence), and listens actively to the athlete's responses and feedback during practices (support for relatedness).

Under circumstances that continuously support need satisfaction, people thrive and experience optimal motivation and well-being (e.g., Li et al., 2019; Stenling et al., 2015), whereas conditions in which the needs are frustrated will contribute to nonoptimal motivation, poor functioning, and ill-being (e.g., Bartholomew et al., 2010, 2011; Bhavsar et al., 2020;). Hence, an athlete who feels pressured (frustration of autonomy), isolated (frustration of relatedness), and that their competence is being questioned (frustration of competence) in the sport environment will experience nonoptimal motivation and ill-being.

This correlation highlights the importance of facilitating need-supportive conditions to promote optimal motivation and counteract and reduce the adverse effects of stressors that athletes encounter.

Autonomous Motivation and Controlled Motivation in SDT

SDT outlines various types of motivation that can vary in strength and quality. Within SDT, a broad distinction exists between autonomous and controlled types of motivation (Standage & Ryan, 2020). Besides intrinsic motivation, autonomous motivation includes extrinsic types of motivation (integrated and identified) toward activities that the person has integrated and identified as important and in line with their values. *Autonomous motivation* has been integrated into the person's sense of self, and autonomously motivated people experience volition and self-endorsement. This type of motivation is reflected in an athlete who engages in sport primarily for the inherent enjoyment and because they value the positive consequences of engaging in sport. *Controlled motivation*, on the other hand, consists of external regulation, where one's behavior is driven by external rewards or punishments; or introjected regulation, where the behavior is a function of avoidance behaviors, contingent self-esteem, or ego involvement. Controlled motivation leads people to experience pressure to think, feel, and behave in certain ways. This type of motivation would be reflected in an athlete who tries to prove themselves to others (e.g., the coach or parents) or is striving to achieve some external reward.

In contrast to autonomous and controlled motivation, which energize and direct behavior, *amotivation* refers to a lack of motivation and intention. In the appropriate (need-supportive) social conditions, people take in and accept values and norms that regulate and guide behavior by the process of internalization. Behaviors that previously were considered as external prompts can become increasingly integrated into the person and self-regulated (i.e., motives for tasks become more autonomous; see Ryan, 1995) over time.

Research shows that autonomous motivation is related to more adaptive outcomes among athletes, such as better performance (Gillet et al., 2010), less dropout (Pelletier et al., 2001), better well-being and vitality (Gagné et al., 2003), better adaptive coping (Gaudreau and Antl, 2008), and more injury prevention and rehabilitation intentions (Chan & Hagger, 2012b). Controlled motivation and amotivation, on the other hand, have generally been linked to maladaptive outcomes among athletes, such as burnout (Lonsdale & Hodge, 2011), nonadaptive coping (Gaudreau & Antl, 2008), and negative affect (Gagné et al., 2003).

Role of Coaching and Need Support in SDT

Under the umbrella term of *need support*, SDT outlines three dimensions of social inputs that support the basic psychological needs and autonomous motivation. These dimensions are autonomy support, competence support, and relatedness support (Ntoumanis, 2012; Standage & Ryan, 2020). Although they are presented as supporting a particular need, they often support more than one basic psychological need. *Autonomy support* is provided when the coach takes the athlete's perspective; provides a meaningful rationale; provides relevant choices and information; acknowledges negative feelings; and minimizes coercion, demands, and pressure. *Competence support* (sometimes called structure) involves providing clear and understandable guidelines, expectations, and goals; provision of informational and positive feedback; optimal challenges; and task involvement. *Relatedness support* (sometimes called involvement) is displayed when the coach communicates a genuine interest in the athlete and the athlete's well-being and spends considerable time, energy, and resources on them. It also involves promotion of seeking social support and providing opportunities to help others.

In contrast, a *need-thwarting* (or controlling) style is characterized by pressuring athletes to think, feel, or behave in specific ways, which undermines psychological need satisfaction (Ntoumanis, 2012). Coaches with a need-thwarting interpersonal style place value on control and power-assertive techniques that pressure athletes to comply (Mageau & Vallerand, 2003). In contrast to need support, need-thwarting coaches prioritize their own perspectives and let them overrun the athletes' perspective through intrusion and pressure (Bartholomew et al., 2009, 2010).

Intervention studies support the positive effects of need-supportive conditions on a range of athlete outcomes. In youth Gaelic football coaches, a need-supportive intervention increased coaches' need-supportive behaviors and decreased their controlling behaviors (Langan et al., 2015). While burnout symptoms and amotivation increased among athletes in the control group, no such increase was observed among the athletes in the experimental group. These findings suggest that coaches' autonomy support can prevent increases in athlete burnout over the course of a season, which might have long-term consequences for athletes' performance and well-being. One SDT-based intervention has been performed in a high-stakes competitive sport context with participants in the 2012 London Paralympic Games (Cheon et al., 2015). The intervention showed consistent effects across athletes' and coaches' self-reports, rater-scores, and objective-dependent measures. A longitudinal deterioration was observed for athletes and coaches in the control group on all measures of coaches' interpersonal styles, need frustration and satisfaction, and engagement. Athletes and coaches in the experimental group maintained or increased their levels on all measures of coaches' interpersonal styles, need frustration and satisfaction, and engagement. Athletes in the experimental group also won more medals compared to athletes in the control group. The authors concluded that an autonomy-supportive coaching style can function as an antidote to coaches' otherwise situationally induced controlling style. Reynders and colleagues (2019) showed similar effects in youth sport settings where an SDT-based intervention increased need-supportive behaviors and decreased controlling behaviors among coaches in the intervention group. Athletes in the intervention group also increased in autonomous motivation and engagement compared to athletes in the control group.

SDT and Injury Rehabilitation

In addition to the positive effects of need-supportive conditions on athlete motivation and well-being, several scholars have highlighted the role of need support and need satisfaction for successful injury rehabilitation and

Success Story: A Season-Long Stress Reduction and Prevention Program

This case study is based on applied work on an elite soccer team focused on improving the players' ability to cope with stressors inside and outside the soccer context. The approach involved need-supportive features, such as providing a meaningful rationale (supporting the need for autonomy), inviting the players to dialogue (support for relatedness), and learning new strategies for stress reduction and prevention (support for competence).

The coaches and the team's sport psychology consultant met with the players early in the season to present one of the focus areas for the upcoming season. For this meeting, the coach and sport psychology consultant had prepared a presentation that included both research findings and examples from the elite soccer context showing that lower levels of stress were related to better health, well-being, and performance.

One week after the initial meeting, the sport psychology practitioner introduced the concepts of mindfulness and acceptance to the players to start the process of working with this focus area. In this introductory session, the players engaged in various mindfulness and acceptance exercises and were encouraged to use these exercises on their own to reduce and prevent stress. During the season, the players were provided with opportunities to perform these exercises as a part of a pregame or prepractice routine.

Another part of the stress management program was that players were encouraged to register their perceived levels of stress and well-being every morning in an application. The players, coaches, and medical support staff all had access to a graph of the players' trajectories of stress and well-being. When introducing this application, the coaches informed the players that data would be used only as a basis for discussion during the season between each player and coach as well as between each player and medical support staff. In the postseason evaluation, the players expressed that they perceived lower levels of stress during this season compared to the previous season. In addition, fewer injuries were observed in the team during this season compared to the three previous seasons.

return to sport (Ardern et al., 2013; Podlog et al., 2011; Truong et al., 2020). An injured athlete faces several threats to their sense of autonomy, competence, and relatedness. Feeling a pressure to return to sport and a lack of control of the rehabilitation process can frustrate the need for autonomy. Re-injury anxiety, lack of confidence in performance capabilities, and self-presentational concerns are common issues among injured athletes that can frustrate the need for competence. An injured athlete can also feel isolated and disconnected from their sport and team, which can frustrate the need for relatedness. Thus, creating a need-supportive environment for the injured athlete can help counteract these threats to need satisfaction and foster well-being and autonomous motivation toward injury prevention and rehabilitation (Ardern et al., 2013).

Another positive consequence of a need-supportive environment during injury rehabilitation is that it can increase athletes' adherence to the rehabilitation plan (e.g., Lonsdale et al., 2017). Adherence to the rehabilitation protocol has been identified as a key behavior for a successful rehabilitation process (Ivarsson et al., 2017b), and it affects multiple rehabilitation outcomes, such as functional outcomes and return to sport (Wiese-Bjornstal, 2010).

SDT and the unifying principle of basic psychological needs provide a coherent framework for understanding conditions that reduce adverse effects of stressors in the sport environment and that facilitate athletes' physical and psychological health and well-being. Thus, creating conditions in the sport environment that support athletes' basic psychological needs is worthwhile given the wide range adaptive outcomes (e.g., well-being, rehabilitation adherence, performance) that these three needs explain.

Assessment

This section provides examples of various tools to collect information about health, well-being, motivation, and need support in sport environments. Many of these tools can be used repeatedly to assess how these factors change over time, such as the duration of a competitive season. Such data can be crucial for understanding how these factors vary and provide information about whether a specific type of intervention or prevention program is needed at a specific time point during the season.

Evaluation of Athlete Health and Well-Being

Information about athletes' health and well-being can provide the coach and the athletes themselves with valuable input regarding how to best approach training and performance activities. Completing these types of questionnaires can also facilitate athletes' ability to reflect on their current situation. Self-reflection is an important skill that has been found to reduce

Information about an athlete's health and well-being can provide a coach with valuable input regarding how to best approach training and competition.

stress in athletes (e.g., Cowden & Meyer-Weitz, 2016). Two examples of measures assessing athlete health and well-being that are frequently used in the sport context are the five-item World Health Organization Well-Being Index (WHO-5; Topp et al., 2015) and the Short Recovery and Stress Scale (SRSS; Kölling et al., 2020). The WHO-5 questionnaire is focused on well-being, whereas the SRSS is designed to capture both stress (i.e., muscular stress, lack of activation, negative emotional stress, and overall stress) and recovery (i.e., physiological performance capability, mental performance capability, emotional balance, and overall recovery).

Evaluation of Athlete Motivation and Intention

Information about the athlete's motivation and intention to engage in certain behaviors can be beneficial for athletes and coaches because these factors are known to direct future behavior. Chan and Hagger (2012a, 2012b) used the Treatment Self-Regulation Questionnaire (TRSQ) and questions about behavior intentions to capture athletes' autonomous and controlled motivation and intentions to engage in injury prevention and rehabilitation. Although these measures were developed for injury prevention and rehabilitation, they can easily be adopted to collect information about other behaviors. Collecting this information can be used, to highlight whether efforts might be needed to increase athletes' autonomous motivation and intentions to engage in certain behaviors, which are factors that increase the likelihood that athletes will engage in such behaviors.

For athletes, conducting a motivational diagnosis (Teixeira et al., 2013) can be useful to assess the degree of autonomy and self-determination toward specific activities (e.g., practice and competition, injury rehabilitation). Such diagnosis (see table 19.1) can involve asking yourself three simple questions:

1. For whom am I doing this?
2. Toward what am I striving?
3. How do I feel when engaging in this activity?

With regard to the first question, an answer of *Mostly for myself* reflects a higher degree of autonomy and self-determination, whereas an answer of *Mostly for others* reflects a lower degree of autonomy and self-determination. With regard to the second question, if the answer indicates intrinsic goals, such as *Skill development, mastery, and enjoyment*, it reflects a higher degree of autonomy and self-determination. If the answer primarily indicates extrinsic goals, such as *To outperform others*, *To make money*, or *For social recognition*, it reflects a lower degree of autonomy and self-determination. With regard to the third question, if the answer is *Energetic*, *Challenged*, *Stimulated*, *Positive*, *Relaxed*, or *Volitional*, it reflects a higher degree of autonomy and self-determination, whereas *Pressured*, *tired*, *Forced*, *Tense*, or *Anxious* reflects a lower degree of autonomy and self-determination. Conducting motivational diagnosis regularly will highlight whether the sport environment is need supportive (if athlete responses reflect a higher degree of autonomy and self-determination) or if adding need-supportive features

TABLE 19.1   Motivational Diagnosis

	High degree of autonomy	Low degree of autonomy
For whom am I doing this?	Mostly for myself	Mostly for others
Toward what am I striving?	Intrinsic goals: Skill development Mastery Enjoyment	Extrinsic goals: To outperform others To make money Social recognition
How do I feel when engaging in this activity?	Energetic Challenged Stimulated Positive Relaxed Volitional	Pressured Tired Forced Tense Anxious

in the environment (if responses mostly reflect a low degree of autonomy and self-determination) is necessary.

Evaluation of Need-Supportive Conditions

The Interpersonal Behaviors Questionnaire (IBQ) (Rocchi et al., 2017) can be used to capture athletes' perceptions of coaches' (or other social agents') need-supportive and need-thwarting behaviors, but it can also be used to assess coaches' self-ratings of their interpersonal behaviors. The questionnaire consists of 24 items and six subscales assessing autonomy-supportive, autonomy-thwarting, competence-supportive, competence-thwarting, relatedness-supportive, and relatedness-thwarting interpersonal behaviors. By capturing perceptions of both need-supportive and need-thwarting behaviors, the IBQ provides a detailed picture of interpersonal behaviors in the sport environment. The IBQ can be used by athletes and coaches, which provides opportunities to examine the agreement in perceptions between athletes and coaches with regard to the level of need support and thwarting. The Tripartite Measure of Interpersonal Behaviors of Coaches (TMIB-C) (Bhavsar et al., 2019) is another measure of perceptions of coaches' interpersonal behaviors. In addition to need-supportive and need-thwarting coach behaviors, this 22-item scale also includes need-indifferent behaviors, which are demonstrated when a coach is inattentive to their athletes' basic psychological needs. Need-indifferent behaviors are proposed to be less motivationally damaging in comparison to need-thwarting behaviors, because they do not actively undermine the three psychological needs. However, being indifferent to athletes' basic psychological needs is a missed opportunity to provide need support and can still be motivationally damaging.

Another useful approach to capture need-supportive behaviors and conditions is to use observations of the coaches or other social agents' (e.g., physical therapists') behaviors in the sport environment (see Smith et al., 2016). One useful tool that has been included in multiple intervention studies (e.g., Cheon et al., 2015) is a behavior rating scale that captures six need-supportive behaviors and six need-thwarting behaviors. One or several observers provide a rating on a bipolar scale ranging from 1 (never, not at all) to 7 (frequent, always) to assess the extent to which a coach engages in behaviors that represent a particular type of need support. More detailed observational tools have also been developed in other contexts (e.g., physical education; see Haerens et al., 2013); they can be adopted if a higher level of detail and additional need-supportive behaviors are warranted.

Ntoumanis and Mallett (2014) suggested that if coaches become more aware of how they communicate with their athletes (e.g., videorecording and reviewing their sessions or seeking feedback from athletes and other coaches), it could guide the shift toward a more need-supportive approach to coaching. A part of this process could be to respond to and reflect on questions such as the following:

- What are the most common need-thwarting behaviors you use? What is the frequency of those behaviors?
- What are the most common need-supportive behaviors you employ? What is the frequency of those behaviors?
- What do you think might be the short-, medium-, and long-term consequences of any need-thwarting behaviors?
- Are you interested in changing any need-thwarting behaviors? If so, which ones, and how?
- How is your interpersonal style contributing to your athletes' psychological need satisfaction (autonomy, competence, and relatedness)?

A systematic use of such questions and documentation of the responses over time will provide coaches and other social agents in the sport environment with an easy-to-use monitoring tool to track need-supportive behaviors.

Optimization

With the basic psychological needs as a unifying principle, SDT outlines how conditions and qualities that are supportive of autonomy, competence, and relatedness can be linked to adaptive behaviors and outcomes (e.g., motivation, adherence, well-being, performance) among athletes. Thus, SDT provides clear avenues for intervention to optimize the conditions under which athletes can thrive, perform, and experience physical and psychological well-being. Several empirically supported situational components that have been shown to support athletes' basic psychological need satisfaction are presented in table 19.2. Coaches and other social agents who engage in these need-supportive behaviors will create conditions in the sport environment that facilitate need satisfaction and optimal motivation (Standage & Ryan, 2020).

The available evidence also suggests that need support plays a vital role in injury rehabilitation and return to sport (Truong et al., 2020). Throughout the acute stage (i.e., immediately after injury or surgery), rehabilitation stage, and return to sport stage, involving athletes in the recovery process (e.g., helping them understand their injury and diagnosis, manage emotions, and deal with athletic identity loss) can support their need for autonomy. Working with active coping strategies to manage setbacks and problem-based coping can also support athletes' autonomy. Supporting the need for competence can be done by finding ways to overcome barriers to progress (e.g., by handling fear of reinjury, handling fear of not being able to return to sport, and establishing realistic expectations for rehabilitation and return to sport). Social support is important to satisfy the need for relatedness, but the sources of social support change throughout recovery. In the early stages,

TABLE 19.2 Need-Supportive Behaviors

AUTONOMY SUPPORT

TONE AND SENTIMENT WHEN TRYING TO MOTIVATE ATHLETES.
THE TONE IS HIGHLY RESPECTFUL OF THE ATHLETE'S PERSPECTIVE,
AND IT IS SUPPORTIVE OF THEIR INITIATIVES.

Behavior	Description
Take the athlete's perspective.	Try to understand the athlete's perspective before providing feedback, instructions, and the like. Ask for the athlete's perspective before providing feedback, giving instructions, or making suggestions.
Provide a meaningful rationale.	Explain why you ask athletes to do activities, why in this particular way, and how it can improve the team or individual.
Provide relevant choices.	Offer choices whenever possible: for example, about drills, practice structure, or level of difficulty.
Encourage initiative and curiosity.	Welcome and invite ideas, feedback, and suggestions from the athletes, and let them try their ideas.
Acknowledge negative feelings.	Show and express that you accept emotional expressions (positive and negative) from the athletes. Strong emotional expressions are often valid reactions to (exaggerated) control, demands, and structures.
Minimize coercion, demands, and pressure.	Avoid being overly prescriptive and controlling. For example, avoid words and phrases that can be perceived as controlling and prescriptive, such as *you have to*, *you must*, or *you should*; instead, use words and phrases that support autonomy, such as *you can try* or *you might want to*.

COMPETENCE SUPPORT

CLEARLY COMMUNICATE EXPECTED OUTCOMES, GOALS, PLANS, STANDARDS,
AND THE LIKE, AND HOW YOU CAN HELP ATHLETES ACHIEVE THEM.

Behavior	Description
Provide clear and understandable expectations, guidelines, and goals.	Clearly communicate expectations and guidelines (in an autonomy-supportive way). Communicate short- and long-term goals with the activities athletes do. This clarity of focus helps athletes understand how they can develop necessary skills, meet expectations and demands, and deal with challenges.
Provide informational and positive feedback.	Informative feedback targets a specific action performed by the athletes, such as performance during a drill in practice. Do not only communicate if the athlete performed well (or not), but clearly communicate what was performed well (or not) and how the athlete can improve the next attempt.
Provide optimal challenges.	Find activities that are neither too easy nor too difficult for the athletes. Optimal motivation is facilitated by challenges that are slightly above the athletes' current level.
Promote task involvement.	Encourage athletes to reflect and ask questions about their performances in practice and competitions or games. Ensure that the athletes are highly involved during practices and competition and that they are not just doing as they are told.

> *continued*

Table 19.2 *> continued*

RELATEDNESS SUPPORT	
SHOW THAT YOU CARE ABOUT YOUR ATHLETES BY GIVING THEM YOUR TIME AND RESOURCES. PAY ATTENTION TO YOUR ATHLETES' BEHAVIORS AND EMOTIONAL EXPRESSIONS, AND OFFER THEM A SAFE AND SECURE SOCIAL CONTEXT.	
Behavior	**Description**
Show a genuine interest in the athletes.	Show that you care about the athletes, ask them how they feel, monitor signals from the athletes, and adjust activities and instructions to the situation.
Practice active listening.	Pay attention, and listen to the athletes' point of view. Give them opportunities to express their opinions without judgment or evaluation.
Promote social support seeking.	Provide activities that facilitate social-support seeking among athletes. Ensure that everybody feels included in the team or group, and monitor if anyone appears to be left out.
Provide opportunities to help others.	Provide opportunities for athletes to help each other and share skills, knowledge, and experiences.

support from family, friends, and teammates is more important, whereas support from coaches, physical therapists, and other medical staff is more important in later stages.

Aside from need support from coaches, physical therapists, sport psychology consultants, or other important social agents in the sport environment, athletes can use several strategies to counter slumps and adversity. Mindfulness and acceptance-based approaches have shown promising results in relation to athlete well-being and performance as well as injury prevention (Henriksen et al., 2020; Ivarsson et al., 2015, 2017a). Mindfulness has also been linked to need satisfaction and a higher degree of self-determination (Donald et al., 2020). *Mindfulness* refers to paying attention in a particular way, on purpose, in the present moment, and nonjudgmentally. It involves paying attention to both external events and internal experiences as they occur. For athletes, it might refer to observing their thoughts before or during a practice, rehabilitation session, or competition without labeling them as good or bad thoughts and having no intent to eliminate or change them. *Acceptance* refers to opening up and making room for a wide range of thoughts, feelings, and sensations (negative and positive ones), which are a natural part of life and sport. Adopting an acceptance approach means not struggling with emotions but instead giving them space without being overwhelmed. If you learn to accept, it is easier to let emotions come and go without draining your energy or negatively influencing your performance (Henriksen et al., 2020).

Motivational techniques are also available for athletes to identify and reduce need-frustrating factors and enhance need-supportive factors (Knittle et al., 2020). These techniques involve such things as task crafting—restructuring tasks (e.g., practices) to make them more enjoyable and congruent with the individual's skills and ability—which can enhance need satisfaction for autonomy and competence. Actively seeking practical and emotional social support from people in one's surroundings can enhance relatedness need satisfaction. Finally, identifying sources of pressure and ways of dealing with pressure, and acknowledging one's own ability for choice, can enhance autonomy need satisfaction. In short, multiple techniques are available for facilitating need satisfaction and motivation.

Conclusion

This chapter outlined need-supportive behaviors that coaches can adopt to enhance athletes' well-being, motivation, and performance. It also outlined several techniques and approaches that athletes can use to optimize motivation and well-being, which in the long-run will have a positive effect on performance. Optimizing motivation, health, and well-being requires an understanding of the complex interactions between environmental and individual factors and conditions that contribute to adaptive outcomes. It also requires an understanding of stressors and conditions that can produce adverse effects, such as physical and psychological ill-being. Self-determination theory (SDT) provides a coherent motivational framework for understanding conditions in the sport environment that facilitate adaptive behaviors, health, and well-being in athletes. Sport environments that support basic psychological needs will substantially decrease the likelihood of adverse effects and increase the likelihood of high-quality sport experiences for both athletes and coaches.

Getting Help: What to Look for and What to Expect in a Consultant

Andrew Cruickshank
Grey Matters UK

Dave Collins
Grey Matters UK and University of Edinburgh

As you reach the conclusion of this book, the authors recognize that different readers will have arrived at this point from different levels of engagement based on their own interests and needs. Some might have read the whole book. Some may have read a section, others may have read one chapter, and some may have turned to this section first. For those who have read at least some of the book up to here, the content has probably generated one or more of three broad outcomes: (1) It has reinforced what you already knew; (2) it opened your eyes to ideas that you have not yet recognized, evaluated, or optimized as much as others in the past; or (3) it has challenged your previous understanding or beliefs. In any of these cases, one of your follow-up questions (or perhaps your starter question) has probably been *Who should I look to support me on this?* This epilogue aims to answer that question. For clarity, all of the content that follows is applicable or transferable to athletes and coaches alike—as well as any other individual exploring or evaluating the use of sport psychology services.

Although the central focus of this epilogue is on what you should look for and expect in a consultant, a few key points are worth noting. First, the term *sport psychology consultant* has been used consistently throughout this text. For clarity, mention of this title also represents other titles used in other countries to signify someone who is accredited to provide sport psychology services to clients by a recognized professional body (e.g., Certified Mental Performance Consultant in the United States). Second, the structure of this epilogue is slightly different from that of the chapters. In addition to the Relevance and What We Know sections, it includes a section called What to Look for and What to Expect in a Practitioner. Finally, this epilogue makes connections to all preceding chapters to indicate how the concepts fit together, and it includes some pointers on which chapters you might like to (re)visit in the future.

Relevance

When weighing the potential merits and uses of sport psychology support, three primary factors to consider are who sport psychology can help, what sport psychology can help with, and what sport psychology may not help with. We now describe each of these three factors in more detail.

Who Can Sport Psychology Help?

The ideas and suggestions offered by all contributors to this book target two main groups: athletes and coaches. Indeed, athletes and coaches have been particularly prominent consumers of professional psychology resources or services in sport to date. However, a host of other individuals can engage with professional sport psychology as well; they include leaders, managers, sport science and sports medicine practitioners, and parents. In this way, professional psychology input can be useful for almost everyone in high-level environments whether that support is for personal benefit or for the benefit of those an individual works with, for, or through. Put more simply, sport psychology can deliver direct benefits to the individual as well as indirect benefits to those the individual engages with. Supporting this approach, practitioners and researchers in sport psychology have long argued for the value of supporting all those involved in the athletic development and performance process; indeed, they have shown the benefits of it (as evidenced throughout this book). Similarly, the preceding chapters of this book have emphasized that sport psychology can also help on a group level whether that group represents a pair, unit, team, department, or entire organization. In short, sport psychology has the potential to help any individual or group in which psychological factors play a part in day-to-day functioning, development, and performance.

What Can Sport Psychology Help You With?

The chapters in this book have provided just a taste of the important work that can be done using sport psychology. Indeed, as with any book of this nature, many important topics have received limited coverage or no coverage at all. While some of the content in the book has offered a starting point for exploring some of these other areas in more detail, it has focused on a basic set of topics that are relevant and informative to readers who aspire to high-level performance in a broad range of sports.

More specifically, part II of the book focused on some consistently foundational mental factors in high-level sport: motivation (chapter 5); confidence (chapter 6); imagery (chapter 7); self-regulation (chapter 8); and concentration, focus, and attentional control (chapter 9). The word *consistent* in the previous sentence has two meanings. First, the links between these mental factors and higher levels of performance are consistent across a host of sports. Second, these factors have also been consistent across time. In this respect, be careful not to overlook these psychological basics, although getting them all to fire in the best way can be complicated. Indeed, these factors form part of the mental bedrock that is often undervalued or underplayed in favor of more niche or fashionable approaches. Mental toughness, resilience, and psychological safety are just three examples of such approaches; these perfectly valid if rather ill-defined constructs can offer something valuable to performers and coaches, but they can do so only once the underpinnings are addressed. Put simply, many in high-level sport (and other domains) fall into the trap of focusing on the candles rather than the cake. However, any good sport psychology consultant will be able to offer support that enables you to progress in these essential areas.

Similarly, part III highlighted some factors that sport psychology can help with from a group perspective. Once again, the four chapters in this section clearly don't provide a complete picture of practice in this area. However, they cover some particularly prominent aspects of group performance from an applied view. Indeed, getting on top of leadership (chapter 11), culture (chapter 12), shared mental models (chapter 13), and system alignment (chapter 14) will put any group on a strong footing—factors that make up a big chunk of the proverbial cake.

Finally, part IV has helped to further demonstrate what sport psychology can help with when it comes to some wider areas of preparing to perform. In particular, this section provided a range of examples on how principles and practices from sport psychology can be integrated with those from parallel disciplines in high-level sport. More specifically, chapter 15 and chapter 18 looked at the alignment and integration of psychology work into wider coaching and competition processes, chapter 17 into talent development processes, chapter 19 into physical and mental health processes, and chapter 16 into motor control processes.

What Can Sport Psychology Not Help You With?

Of course, while a sport psychology consultant might be able to help you in many of the areas covered in this book, clearly limits exist to their services based on their training, experience, and judgment. In this respect, practitioners are duty bound to work within their areas of expertise which, as the title suggests, covers sport and psychology. Importantly, it means that a sport psychology consultant can clearly help you with psychology as it relates to your sport (e.g., optimizing your confidence in an area of practice), while many practitioners might also be able to help (to varying degrees) with psychology as it relates to you in a wider sense, including for nonsport matters (e.g., managing stress related to family dynamics). In other words, the challenge or goal doesn't necessarily have to be sport related for a sport psychology consultant to be able to help, as long as that individual is working within their limits of personal and demonstrable expertise. As such, when it comes to what a sport psychology consultant might not be able to help you with, it is important to consider aspects beyond just the locality of the challenge (whether the challenge is occurring in sport or more broadly in life).

When deciding whether a sport psychology consultant can help you (or for a sport psychology consultant to decide if they can help you) work on matters related more to emotion, well-being, and mental health (whether these matters are directly related to the individual's sport or not), consider the following factors (in no particular order):

- The *effect* of the challenge (the scale of the cognitive, emotional, or behavioral effects being experienced by the individual)
- The *frequency* of the challenge (how often it's experienced)
- The *duration* of the challenge (how long the challenge has been present)
- The *robustness* of the challenge (the extent to which past solutions—or attempted solutions—are not effective)
- The *generality* of the challenge (the extent to which the challenge is present across different parts of the individual's life)
- The *ambiguity* of the challenge (the extent to which the roots or triggers of the challenge are unclear)
- The *confidentiality* of the challenge (the level of privacy the individual desires)

Generally, the higher the levels in these aspects and the more of them are at play, the greater the chance that you need another type of specialist to help you, such as a counseling psychologist, clinical (sport) psychologist, or (sport) psychiatrist.

What We Know

Assuming that a sport psychology consultant is the best person to help you achieve your goals or overcome the challenges faced, now consider some important knowns in terms of how this type of support works best.

Importance of Client Motivation

As emphasized in chapters 5 and 19, motivation is a critical factor in any human endeavor; working with a psychologist is no different. Indeed, the lower the motivation to address the challenges that you face or to make strides in the areas that you wish to progress, the lower the chance that you will achieve these outcomes. In other words, change requires some hard work; the bigger the change that you're trying to make, the bigger the effort needed to get there. This point is consistent with many established theories of behavior change, such as the theory of planned behavior (Azjen, 1991) and the transtheoretical model of change (Prochaska et al., 1992). It is also a core feature of professional ethics. In short, psychologists can support only individuals who proactively request and consent to their help apart from in certain extreme situations.* Given the importance of client motivation, it is therefore important to identify a consultant who will work to help *you* and *your* goals which is different to *their* goals for you (or, unfortunately in some cases, *their* goals for *them*). If you're already working with a sport psychology consultant, it's worth checking that your current work is being driven by what you are most motivated to address, unless the consultant has offered a cogent and acceptable reason for doing something else with you.

Importance of Client–Consultant Fit

Linked to these points on client motivation, a big success factor in psychological support is the fit between client and practitioner. This fit operates on many levels, with interpersonal fit clearly one of the essentials. A sign of a good interpersonal fit is that you are comfortable talking to each other. Another essential is expertise fit; in other words, the consultant has the appropriate knowledge and skills to address the client's specific challenge or goal. Generally, sport psychology consultants are able to support clients in developing the skills and confidence to achieve the following:

- *Psychological goals* (to overcome cognitive processing challenges, emotional challenges, motivational challenges)
- *Psychosocial goals* (to overcome relationship challenges, group dynamics, culture challenges, and organizational challenges including system design)
- *Psychomotor goals* (to acquire, refine, and establish movement skills)

Most readers are less familiar with the psychomotor goals (as covered in chapters 9 and 16 in particular) than the *psychosocial* or *psychological* goals. The many reasons for this focus include shifts in the typical education and training of sport psychology consultants together with applied trends (what

---

*In the United Kingdom, this practice is known as *sectioning*, whereby an individual with severe mental problems is detained in care for their own protection. For more information, see www.mind. org.uk/information-support/legal-rights/sectioning/overview. Also check the conditions and regulations that apply to your own country. For example, psychologists usually assure clients of an appropriate age that all conversations will be confidential unless they see evidence that a client is at risk of harm to self or others.

is currently in fashion). However, it most certainly is an area sport psychology consultants can or should be able to help with. Indeed, you probably can't think of a sport that doesn't involve an interaction between what the athlete's brain does and how the athlete's body moves. In this respect, it is important to recognize that a sport psychology consultant can be more than an emotion and relationship expert. In fact, knowledge of psychomotor principles can also significantly inform work that might appear to be more psychological or psychosocial in nature. For example, an athlete's frustration or anger at not being able to execute a skill in competition might have much more to do with the technical training that they have done to establish (or pressure-proof) their skill rather than how they managed their emotions on the day (cf. Carson & Collins, 2015). Ultimately, some sport psychology consultants will be better equipped to help clients with particular areas more than others. For example, some practitioners specialize more in psychosocial areas, others specialize more in psychomotor areas, and others specialize in more psychological areas. Often, the types of sports that the sport psychology consultant has worked in can clue you in to category or categories that their skills might fall into. For example, it would be reasonable to assume that a practitioner with more experience in team sports might be more attuned to psychosocial matters than someone who had worked more heavily with individual clients in individual sports.

You know that sport psychology consultants come in many shapes and sizes of expertise. It might be useful to think of practitioners as being more I-shaped, more T-shaped, or more M-shaped (see figure E.1). As described by Maw (2019), this idea originated from the then head of Elite Rugby Coach Development at the Rugby Football Union (and former Wales national coach), Kevin Bowring. Expressing concerns about the increasingly limited specialisms of skills coaches, Kevin suggested the need for a T-shaped expertise—having a breadth of knowledge across a number of areas in parallel to a depth in one.

As these examples indicate, more I-shaped practitioners are those who know a lot about one of the aforementioned categories. For instance, they might know a lot about psychological parts of development and performance but not much on the psychosocial or psychomotor parts. In contrast, the more T-shaped practitioner may be characterized by a more specialized area, but they may also have a general breadth of knowledge and skills across the other two categories. The more M-shaped practitioner might have a similarly broad knowledge and skill set across all categories, but they may also have areas of greater specialty within each category. The point is that different sport psychology consultants are able to do different things and help clients work toward their psychological goals, psychosocial goals, or psychomotor goals in more separate or more combined ways. Accordingly, don't just look for any sport psychology consultant; look for someone who can do the job that you need, a principle that any sport psychology consultant you approach should also prioritize. In this respect, a sign of a good practitioner

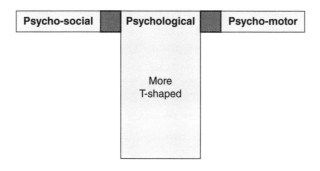

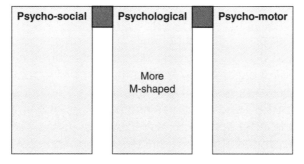

FIGURE E.1   Different shapes of practitioner.

is knowing what they can and can't help you with and knowing who might help you better instead.

Importance of Being a Critical Consumer

Another key factor in effective support is understanding the approaches that the support practitioner will take or has already taken. It might partly involve understanding the values and beliefs that form the practitioner's philosophy; broadly, it means understanding who they are (cf. points made in chapter 4). Another part is understanding more about what they do and why. Indeed, knowing how and why things work (or are intended to work) are key drivers of both motivation and fit for the client, which are themselves key drivers of learning and development (cf. Martindale & Collins, 2005). In this vein, everyone who engages with a sport psychology consultant should frequently ask, "So, how does that work?" "Why do you think that will work for me?" "Why are we not doing this instead?" As well as providing you with the chance to boost your knowledge and control of the change process, asking these questions acts as an important check on the quality of your supporting practitioner. In short, if they can't accurately describe the mechanisms by which something works, it's a strong signal that they don't understand them well enough (Winter & Collins, 2015). In this respect, finding out whether the practitioner has a record of published research may offer some extra pointers as you evaluate your options. More specifically, publications might offer some insight on the practitioner's levels of commitment to generating and engaging with peer-reviewed research, which is a key source of evidence-based practice in sport psychology as it is in other professions. Simply put, ask the practitioner what research is informing their work with you.

In line with these checks on how things work and why, if you are assessing your support options, you are encouraged to consider how a practitioner's approach differs in relation to other approaches. You can then make the most informed call on the approach you would like to engage with. This consideration is particularly important given the actual or apparent overlap in many offerings. For example, approaches grounded in acceptance and commitment therapy are part of the third wave of cognitive behavioral therapy (CBT), but they have been argued to share a number of underpinning mechanisms with second-wave therapies, such as rationale emotive behavior therapy (REBT) (Arch & Craske, 2008). This overlap may be subtle, but it can be confusing in terms of knowing exactly how the practitioner will work with you.

To illustrate this idea, table E.1 shows some of the overlaps in principles and practices of REBT and principles and practices of chimp management (Peters, 2012); the latter approach has received significant media and public attention in the United Kingdom since its inception. To help with your interpretation of the table, the chimp model uses a range of metaphors to represent different parts or processes of the brain, such as the chimp (the emotional team within the brain that thinks and acts for you without your permission), the human (the conscious, thinking, analyzing being who works with facts and truth and then makes deductions using logical thinking), the computer (something that acts as a memory programmed to take over if the chimp or human is asleep or if allowed to run ahead of the chimp or human with preformed decisions and beliefs that guide its action); and gremlins (an unhelpful or destructive belief or behavior that is removable from the brain). For more information, see the chimp management website (https://chimpmanagement.com/the-chimp-model) and book (Peters, 2012).

While some major differences exist between REBT and chimp management, many overlaps exist too. In this case, the chimp model was created after REBT, and its author may not recognize or simply does not acknowledge that the model has built on other work. It can be confusing when

TABLE E.1   Comparison of REBT With Chimp Management

REBT principle or practice (from Neenan & Dryden, 2011)	Parallel chimp management principle or practice (from Peters, 2012)
Rigidity is at the core of psychological disturbance (e.g., presence of *must, should, ought*).	"Gremlins are often statements that contain rigid words such as *must* and *should* . . . they are often inappropriate and can be damaging" (p. 102).
Flexibility is at the core of psychological health.	"How flexible and adaptable you are to different situations will also determine how successful you will be in your ventures" (p. 123).
Rational thinking is a conscious choice.	"Most people don't realize that the Chimp is merely making an offer and not a command. You do not have to follow your emotions; you have a choice" (p. 52).
Help clients to discriminate irrational from rational beliefs.	"It is important to recognize the differences between the Chimp and the Human" (p. 43).
Help clients to dispute their irrational and rational beliefs.	"The Human can search out facts and evidence not only to support the [emotional] idea (which the Chimp will agree with) but also to dispute the idea" (p. 68).
Dispute beliefs with empirical arguments.	"Sit down with a piece of paper and pretend you are going to represent yourself in court and put a light on the situation. Write down all the evidence (no feelings or might be's, only fact) both for and against how you are behaving and why" (p. 291).
Dispute beliefs with logical arguments.	"If the chimp is thinking in black and white terms, stop and ask yourself what the alternatives are or if there is any middle ground" (p. 68). "You can only do your best in everything that you do. You cannot do better than your best; this is illogical" (p. 264).
Dispute beliefs with pragmatic arguments.	"Ask yourself: How important is this situation to the rest of my life?; Is this situation going to last forever or will it pass and things change?; What are the really important things in my life, and is this one of them, or has it changed them?" (p. 203).
Use humor in disputation style.	"Depending on how serious the situation is, try to see the lighter side of it. Laugh at yourself if you have overreacted. Laughing at yourself, or situations, is one of the most powerful ways to remove stress from the Chimp" (p. 204).
Encourage clients to engage in self-observation.	"Gremlins have a nasty habit of returning so watch out for them. You need to be vigilant and try to address them every time you recognize them" (p. 104).
Encourage clients to engage in regular psychological workouts.	"Think about each [recommendation] on a day-by-day basis. Remember that developing happiness is like developing emotional skills. It takes effort and a lot of time, but you will get there" (p. 319).
Help clients design a core rational philosophy.	"The stone of life is your ultimate reference point. It is where your Truths of Life, Values and Life Force are all inscribed. The Chimp and Human gauge everything by the Stone" (p. 86).

two similar approaches use different terminology. Therefore, discriminating between different approaches to psychological support is challenging. As such, you don't need to be an expert in psychology to identify and use psychology support; instead, it makes sense to check that the practitioner can explain why and how things work with their approach as well as how it differs to alternatives. If their account of the why and how isn't convincing, other approaches sound more appealing, or few details are offered on alternative approaches, it could be an early sign to reconsider the options. Given this complexity, you should recruit a friend, family member, coach, colleague, teacher, or other psychologist who can help you run through the information provided.

What to Look for and What to Expect in a Practitioner

Although a range of practitioner shapes and often some fuzziness between different approaches exist, you can use a number of further checks to help sort through them and be as precise as possible with all choices. You should also (re)visit part I of this book to further inform your approach when it comes to understanding how psychologists might work to best support individual goals. Specifically, it may be useful to reflect (or reflect again) on the messages on blending mental training into a performance program (chapter 1), as well as those on the assessment and strategy design process (chapter 2), the integration of athlete- and performance-centered approaches (chapter 3), and the application of a sound philosophy of sport psychology (chapter 4).

Accreditation and Certification

Making sure that a practitioner has the appropriate accreditation to work as a sport psychology consultant is an early priority. It offers a level of assurance that the practitioner has the education and credentials to be able to work with clients in a professional capacity. It also offers assurance that the practitioner is required to follow a code of standards and ethics that have been professionally established and regulated; in other words, they don't just work to their own personal standards and ethics. As one particularly important feature of these codes, accreditation means that your practitioner is required to work within an established set of rules around confidentiality, providing clients with confidence to be as open as necessary. Overall, the key reason for choosing an accredited practitioner is to receive a professional service in which the client is prioritized and protected by the rules of the profession (cf. Winter & Collins, 2016).

Keep in mind that unfortunately, a *professional* service does not equate to an *excellent* service or even a *good* service. Instead, given that many professional training systems currently prioritize the assessment of psychologists against behavioral competencies and minimum standards of practice, many practitioners might operate closer to this minimum standard than you would like (Cruickshank et al., 2020). Accordingly, sourcing some previous customer reviews is a sensible step before committing to working with someone. Similarly, the advice to seek out an accredited practitioner should not overlook the fact that some people who aren't professionally qualified or recognized may offer excellent psychology-focused advice. In this regard, many athletes, coaches, leaders, managers, sport scientists, and sport parents have a strong understanding of psychological principles and practices through their own experiences and learning. In fact, some may demonstrate a deep understanding of the psychology of their sport. However, these cases are rare; it is much more common that people either have a depth of understanding in a narrow set of psychological factors, shallow understanding across a broader set of factors, or not much understanding at all. The bottom line is that you should be careful in your choice.

Just as an accredited physiotherapist can address rehabilitation goals, or an accredited physiologist can address physical capacity goals, an accredited psychologist can help clients address psychological, psychosocial, or psychomotor goals in an accredited way. You might also want to check if the practitioner is accredited in any other related professions or roles. For example, an understanding of sport coaching is valuable for optimal practice in that it helps the sport psychology consultant to understand wider development and performance processes, meaning that interventions can be designed and fitted in the most effective ways. For those reading this section alone, you might want to go back to read chapter 1 to consider this suggestion in more detail. Similarly, but with a focus on the value of understanding principles of periodization, you also might (re)visit ideas presented in chapters 15 and 18.

Process of Support

Assuming a sport psychology consultant can do the job required and fits the bill in accreditation terms, what should clients notice about the way in which the support plays out? Initially, you should expect to go through a case formulation or needs analysis process, a process in which the psychologist gathers information relating to the client's presenting challenge or goal. This process is detailed in chapter 2, and you are encouraged to (re)visit this chapter to get a sense of what this process should look and feel like. Although its breadth and depth will vary based on a host of factors, such as the philosophy of the sport psychology consultant (see chapter 4) and the immediacy of the client's need, this process should be experienced early in the interaction with any sport psychology consultant or when the primary support goal changes in longer-term support relationships. Indeed, without establishing a specific understanding of *you* and *your* goals, the advice you receive can only be generic or even just based on guesswork. Sometimes clients think this generic approach is enough, and they decide that the advice will be effective even before receiving it. Research has shown this tendency to be a genuine inhibitor for the positive impact of work with psychologists (Tinsley et al., Barich, 1993). In most cases, however (unless the practitioner gets really lucky), this generic advice will fall short of the specific impact that the client requires or that would lead to greatest returns.

As another marker to look out for, any support received should be coherently adaptive. *Adaptive* means that support should be responsive to the client's evolving progress and situation. In this respect, it is important to remember that sport psychology input is not administered in a lab where conditions can be carefully controlled and monitored. Instead, in most cases, input is provided in the complex and dynamic environment of real life. In real life, things change, progress is not linear, and a host of interacting factors (e.g., other people) are present. As such, the support received should adjust and respond to these oscillations rather than try to ignore and plow through them.

In this regard, practitioners and their clients are typically well-served by adopting a foxlike rather than hedgehoglike style to their unfolding situation (Tetlock, 2006). However, a key caveat to this point is that it's about balance. More specifically, adapting works best when you have a plan to coherently adapt; in other words, you need substance to make the adaptations all link together. Otherwise, what might seem to be an adaptive approach could well be more of an erratic approach or an incoherently adaptive experience. Some signs that your work with a sport psychology consultant is more erratic than adaptive (or incoherent) would be the sense that you regularly shift focus, or you try one thing for a short time, then something else, then something else. In contrast, coherently adaptive support is indicated by a sense that everything you do still connects and makes sense (which might not be immediately apparent); you regularly return to the same core themes, ideas, tools, and strategies; and you experience regular aha moments.

As well as feeling a level of coherence in your work with a sport psychology consultant, another key marker to look out for—*if* you have consented to share details of your work together—is a level of coherence in the views and actions of those around you. In this regard, all behavior is situated in context; for humans, much of that context is social. As such, patterns of behavior in individuals inevitably have links (some more obvious and significant than others) to the behavior of those around them. Consequently, you should also anticipate efforts from your sport psychology consultant to integrate their support with the work that others do with you (e.g., with your coach if you are an athlete). Alternatively, if this integration is not possible or desired, then you should ask many questions about how you can manage and harness the role that others play in relation to your goals.

Finally, you should pay particularly close attention to the practitioner's rationale—*why* they're saying and doing what they're saying and doing. In this respect, one of the key factors in effective psychology work is the practitioner's ability to establish a clear rationale behind their actions or to form *intentions for impact* (Martindale & Collins, 2005). To reiterate earlier points, you should proactively check your practitioner's rationale throughout your work together. However, you should also note that better practitioners will provide this rationale without you having to ask.

Outcomes of Support

While the process of support is an important feature of a client's experience with a sport psychology practitioner, the bottom line is clearly what is achieved through that process. In other words, clients should also expect their work with a sport psychology consultant to lead to success in achieving agreed-upon goals. It is not uncommon to find clients working with practitioners for substantial periods of time without achieving obvious progression on outcome measures, such as improved performances. Given that the responsibility of a psychologist is to respect and promote the autonomy of their clients, you should therefore expect a psychologist to clearly highlight when progress on outcome goals is not being made. Then, you should engage in discussion around the reasons for it (on both practitioner and client parts), any remedial actions, and (where relevant) the potential transition to alternative support (e.g., a referral to another practitioner) or termination of the support. To provide a level of confidence that you won't reach this type of conversation, you should therefore expect some waymarks to be identified; in other words, have an idea of what mini outcomes will be achieved (on how you're thinking, feeling, or behaving) along the way to reaching your ultimate goal.

Conclusion

This chapter offered clarity and direction in seeking and using (or continuing to use) sport psychology support to address any current challenges or to maximize your potential and performance. If you can find the right practitioner for you and your goals, the impact of working on the mental side can be anything—a handy check that you are on the right path, or game-changing when it comes to your functioning, development, and performance. As emphasized from the beginning of this book, much of this work can be incorporated into the things that you are already doing instead of adding a lot of extra work into an already busy schedule. For most people, it's not a case of finding more time; it's about using your time in a different way or with a different focus. Your personal circumstances will clearly dictate the extent to which the integration of evidence-based, professional sport psychology consulting is possible. This book has aimed to show that your efforts to optimize this integration are well worth it.

REFERENCES

Chapter 1

Abraham, A., & Collins, D. (2011). Taking the next step: Ways forward for coaching science. *Quest, 63*, 366-384.

Bompa, T.O., & Haff, G.G. (2009). *Periodization: Theory and methodology of training.* Human Kinetics.

Brunswik, E. (1955). Representative design and probabilistic theory in a functional psychology. *Psychological Review, 62*, 193-217.

Butler, R.J., & L. Hardy. 1992. The performance profile: Theory and application. *The Sport Psychologist, 6*(3): 253-264.

Collins, D., Abraham, A., & Collins, R. (2012). On vampires and wolves: Exploring and countering reasons for the differential impact of coach education. *International Journal of Sport Psychology, 43*, 255-271.

Collins, D., & Collins, J. (2010). Putting them together: Skills packages to optimise team/group performance. In D. Collins, A. Button & H. Richards (Eds.), *Performance Psychology: A Practitioners' Guide* (pp. 361-380). Elsevier.

Collins, D., & Cruickshank, A. (2015). Take a walk on the wild side: Exploring, identifying, and developing consultancy expertise with elite performance team leaders. *Psychology of Sport & Exercise, 16*, 74-82.

Collins, D., Downes, D.P., & Moody, J. (2021). Role and competency for the S & C coach. In I. Jeffreys & J. Moody (Eds.), *Strength and conditioning for sports performance* (2nd ed., pp. 3-11). Taylor & Francis.

Collins, D., Willmott, T., & Collins, L. (2018). Periodisation and self-regulation in action sports: Coping with the emotional load. *Frontiers in Psychology, 9.* https://doi.org/10.3389/fpsyg.2018.01652

Counsilman, J.E. (1968). *The science of swimming.* Prentice Hall.

Dhami, M.K., Hertwig, R., & Hoffrage, U. (2004). The role of representative design in an ecological approach to cognition. *Psychological Bulletin, 130*(6), 959-988. https://doi.org/10.1037/0033-2909.130.6.959

Fliegel, J. (2015, October 28). Winning philosophies of 7 legendary coaches. *Inc.* www.inc.com/jordan-fliegel/winning-philosophies-of-7-legendary-coaches

Jones, J.G. (1992). The role of performance profiling in cognitive behavioural interventions in sport. *The Sport Psychologist, 7*(2), 160-172. https://doi.org/10.1123/tsp.7.2.160

Jowett, S., Kanakoglou, K., & Passmore, J. (2012). The application of the 3+1Cs relationship model in executive coaching. *Consulting Psychology Journal: Practice and Research, 64*(3), 183-197. https://doi.org/10.1037/a0030316

Karp, J.R. (2010). Strength training for distance running: A scientific perspective. *Strength and Conditioning Journal, 32*(3), 83-86. https://doi.org/10.1519/SSC.0b013e3181df195b

Kiely, J. (2018). Periodization theory: Confronting an inconvenient truth. *Sports Medicine, 48*, 753-764. https://doi.org/10.1007/s40279-017-0823-y

Martindale, A., & Collins, D. (2005). Professional judgment and decision making: The role of intention for impact. *The Sport Psychologist, 19*(3), 303-317.

Martindale, A., & Collins, D. (2012). A professional judgment and decision making case study: Reflection-in-action research. *The Sport Psychologist*, *26*(4), 500-518.

Selye, H. (1956). *The stress of life*. McGraw-Hill.

Simonton, D.J. (2001). Talent development as a multidimensional, multiplicative, and dynamic process. *Current Directions in Psychological Science*, *10*(2), 39-43. https://doi.org/10.1111/1467-8721.00110

Tamarit, X. (2015). *What is tactical periodization?* Bennion Kearney.

Tee, J.C., Ashford, M., and Piggott, D. (2018). A tactical periodization approach for rugby union. *Strength and Conditioning Journal*, *40*(5), 1-13.

Verkhoshansky, Y.V., & Siff, M. (2003). *Supertraining* (6th ed.). Supertraining Institute.

Chapter 2

Abraham, A., & Collins, D. (2011) Taking the next step: Ways forward for coaching science. *Quest*, *63*, 366-384.

Butler, R.J., & Hardy, L. (1992). The performance profile: Theory and application. *The Sport Psychologist, 6*, 253-264.

Cruickshank, A. (2013). Case study 1: A professional judgement and decision making (PJDM) approach to consultancy with an elite junior judo player. *Sport & Exercise Psychology Review*, *9*(1), 15 -23.

Downes, P.W.M., & Collins, D. (2021). Examining the roles and consequent decision-making processes of high-level strength and conditioning coaches. *Societies*, *11*(3), 76. https://doi.org/10.3390/soc11030076

Eells, T.D. (2002). Formulation. In M. Hersen & W. Sledge (Eds.), *The encyclopedia of psychotherapy* (pp. 815-822). Academic Press.

Eells, T.D., Lombart, K.G., Kendjelic, E.M., Turner, L.C., and Lucas, C. (2005). The quality of psychotherapy case formulations: A comparison of expert, experienced, and novice cognitive-behavioural and psychodynamic therapists. *Journal of Consulting and Clinical Psychology, 73 (4)*, 579-589.

Glaser, R., & Chi, M.T.H. (1988). Overview. In M.T.H. Chi, R. Glaser, & M.J. Farr (Eds.), *The nature of expertise* (pp. XV-XXVIII). Lawrence Erlbaum Associates.

Heil, J., & Henschen, K. (1996). Assessment in sport and exercise psychology. In J.L. Van Raalte & B.W. Brewer (Eds.), *Exploring sport and exercise psychology* (pp. 229-256). American Psychological Association.

Kreber, C. (2002). Teaching excellence, teaching expertise and the scholarship of teaching. *Innovative Higher Education*, *27*, 5-23.

Lazarus, A.A. (1997). *Brief but comprehensive psychotherapy: The multimodal way.* Springer.

Lazarus, A.A. (2003). Multimodal behavior therapy. In W. O'Donohue, J.E. Fisher, & Steven V. Hayes (Eds.), *Cognitive behavior therapy*. Wiley.

Lazarus, A.A. (2004) Multimodal therapy. In R.J. Corsini & D. Wedding (Eds.), *Current psychotherapies*. Wadsworth.

MacNamara, Á., & Collins, D. (2011). Development and initial validation of the Psychological Characteristics of Developing Excellence Questionnaire. *Journal of Sports Sciences, 29*(12), 1,273-1,286.

Martens, R., Vealey, R.S., Burton, D., Bump, L., & Smith, D.E. (1990). Development and validation of the Competitive Sports Anxiety Inventory 2. In R. Martens, R.S. Vealey, & D. Burton (Eds.), *Competitive anxiety in sport* (pp. 117-178). Human Kinetics.

Martindale, R.J.J., Collins, D., Wang, J.C.K., McNeill, M., Lee, K.S., Sproule, J., & Westbury, T. (2010). Development of the Talent Development Environment Questionnaire for Sport. *Journal of Sports Sciences*, *28*(11), 1,209-1,221.

Martindale, A., & Collins, D. (2012). A professional judgment and decision making case study: Reflection-in-action research. *The Sport Psychologist, 26*(4), 500-518.

Poczwardowski, A., Sherman, C.P., & Henschen, K.P. (1998). A sport psychology delivery heuristic: Building on theory and practice. *The Sport Psychologist, 12*, 191-207.

Schön, D. (1991). *The reflective practitioner: How professionals think in action.* Arena.

Chapter 3

Appleton, P.R., Ntoumanis, N., Quested, E., Viladrich, C., & Duda, J.L. (2016). Initial validation of the coach-created Empowering and Disempowering Motivational Climate Questionnaire (EDMCQ-C). *Psychology of Sport and Exercise*, 22, 53-65.

Aquilina, D. (2013). A Study of the relationship between elite athletes' educational development and sporting performance. *The International Journal of the History of Sport, 30*(4), 374-392.

Brewer, B.W., & Petitpas, A.J. (2017). Athletic identity foreclosure. *Current Opinion in Psychology, 16*, 118-122.

Bryan, C., O'Shea, D., & MacIntyre, T. (2019). Stressing the relevance of resilience: A systematic review of resilience across the domains of sport and work. *International Review of Sport and Exercise Psychology, 12*(1), 70-111.

Bundgaard, J. (2016). *Sportslige toppræstationer hos danske student-athletes i 2016* [Top sports performances of Danish student-athletes in 2016]. IDAN.

Carless, D., & Douglas, K. (2013). "In the boat" but "Selling myself short": Stories, narratives, and identity development in elite sport. *The Sport Psychologist, 27*(1), 27-39.

Cartigny, E., Fletcher, D., Coupland, C., & Taylor, G. (2021). Mind the gap: A grounded theory of dual career pathways in sport. *Journal of Applied Sport Psychology, 33*(3), 1-22.

Collins, D., MacNamara, Á., & McCarthy, N. (2015). Super champions, champions, and almosts: Important differences and commonalities on the rocky road. *Frontiers in Psychology, 6*.

Collins, D.J., MacNamara, Á., & McCarthy, N. (2016). Putting the bumps in the rocky road: Optimizing the pathway to excellence. *Frontiers in Psychology, 7*, 1-6.

Cosh, S., & Tully, P.J. (2014). "All I have to do is pass": A discursive analysis of student athletes' talk about prioritising sport to the detriment of education to overcome stressors encountered in combining elite sport and tertiary education. *Psychology of Sport and Exercise, 15*(2), 180-189.

Coulter, T.J., Mallett, C.J., & Singer, J.A. (2016). A subculture of mental toughness in an Australian Football League club. *Psychology of Sport and Exercise*, 22, 98-113.

De Brandt, K., Wylleman, P., Torregrossa, M., Defruyt, S., & Van Rossem, N. (2017). Student-athletes' perceptions of four dual career competencies. *Revista de Psicología Del Deporte, 26*(4), 28-33.

Dohsten, J., Barker-Ruchti, N., & Lindgren, E.-C. (2020). Caring as sustainable coaching in elite athletics: Benefits and challenges. *Sports Coaching Review, 9*(1), 48-70.

Gould, D., & Carson, S. (2008). Life skills development through sport: Current status and future directions. *International Review of Sport and Exercise Psychology, 1*(1), 58-78.

Gouttebarge, V., Bindra, A., Blauwet, C., Campriani, N., Currie, A., Engebretsen, L., Hainline, B., Kroshus, E., McDuff, D., Mountjoy, M., Purcell, R., Putukian, M., Reardon, C.L., Rice, S.M., & Budgett, R. (2020). International Olympic Committee (IOC) Sport Mental Health Assessment Tool 1 (SMHAT-1) and Sport Mental Health Recognition Tool 1 (SMHRT-1): Towards better support of athletes' mental health. *British Journal of Sports Medicine*. https://doi.org/10.1136/ bjsports-2020-102411

Haraldsen, H.M., Nordin-Bates, S.M., Abrahamsen, F.E., & Halvari, H. (2020). Thriving, striving, or just surviving? TD learning conditions, motivational processes and well-being among Norwegian elite Performers in music, ballet, and sport. *Roeper Review*, *42*(2), 109-125.

Harrison, C.K., Lawrence, S.M., Bukstein, S., Carr, K., & Osika, L.B. (2016). Dear Basketball (PS I love you): A qualitative investigation of Kobe Bryant's sport career termination and retirement from the NBA. *Kinesiologia Slovenica*, *22*(3), 41-61.

Henriksen, K., Schinke, R., McCann, S., Durand-Bush, N., Moesch, K., Parham, W.D., Larsen, C.H., Cogan, K., Donaldson, A., Poczwardowski, A., Noce, F., & Hunziker, J. (2020). Athlete mental health in the Olympic/Paralympic quadrennium: A multi-societal consensus statement. *International Journal of Sport and Exercise Psychology*, 1-18.

Henriksen, K., Stambulova, N., & Roessler, K.K. (2010). Holistic approach to athletic talent development environments: A successful sailing milieu. *Psychology of Sport and Exercise*, *11*(3), 212-222.

Henriksen, K., Storm, L.K., Kuettel, A., Linnér, L., & Stambulova, N. (2020). A holistic ecological approach to sport and study: The case of an athlete friendly university in Denmark. *Psychology of Sport and Exercise*, *47*, [101637].

Hill, A., MacNamara, Á., & Collins, D. (2019). Development and initial validation of the Psychological Characteristics of Developing Excellence Questionnaire version 2 (PCDEQ2). *European Journal of Sport Science*, *19*(4), 517-528.

Into, S., Perttula, V.-M., Aunola, K., Sorkkila, M., & Ryba, T.V. (2020). Relationship between coaching climates and student-athletes' symptoms of burnout in school and sports. *Sport, Exercise, and Performance Psychology*, *9*(3). 1-16.

Ivarsson, A., Stenling, A., Fallby, J., Johnson, U., Borg, E., & Johansson, G. (2015). The predictive ability of the talent development environment on youth elite football players' well-being: A person-centered approach. *Psychology of Sport and Exercise*, *16*, 15-23.

Jones, M.I., & Lavallee, D. (2009). Exploring the life skills needs of British adolescent athletes. *Psychology of Sport and Exercise*, *10*(1), 159-167.

Jowett, S. (2003). When the "honeymoon" is over: A case study of a coach-athlete dyad in crisis. *The Sport Psychologist*, *17*(4), 444-460.

Jowett, S. (2017). Coaching effectiveness: The coach-athlete relationship at its heart. *Current Opinion in Psychology*, *16*, 154-158.

Jowett, S., & Ntoumanis, N. (2004). The Coach-Athlete Relationship Questionnaire (CART-Q): development and initial validation. *Scandinavian Journal of Medicine & Science in Sports*, *14*(4), 245-57.

Jowett, S., & Poczwardowski, A. (2007). Understanding the coach-athlete relationship. In S. Jowett & D. Lavallee (Eds.), *Social psychology in sport* (pp. 3-15). Human Kinetics.

Kidman, L. (2005). *Athlete-centred coaching: Developing inspired and inspiring people*. Innovative Print Communication.

Knapp, D. (2012). *Performance of student-athletes at Olympic Games*. Australian University Sport.

Knight, C.J., Harwood, C.G., & Sellars, P.A. (2018). Supporting adolescent athletes' dual careers: The role of an athlete's social support network. *Psychology of Sport and Exercise*, *38*, 137-147.

Küttel, A. (2020). From Olympic athlete to sports psychological consultant within the ski jumping context: A self-narrative. *Journal of Career Studies*, *3*, 1-10.

Küttel, A., Boyle, E., & Schmid, J. (2017). Factors contributing to the quality of the transition out of elite sports in Swiss, Danish, and Polish athletes. *Psychology of Sport and Exercise*, *29*, 27-39.

Küttel, A., Christensen, M.K., Zysko, J., & Hansen, J. (2020). A cross-cultural comparison of dual career environments for elite athletes in Switzerland, Denmark, and Poland. *International Journal of Sport and Exercise Psychology*, *18*(4), 454-471.

Küttel, A., & Larsen, C.H. (2019). Risk and protective factors for mental health in elite ath-letes: A scoping review. *International Review of Sport and Exercise Psychology.* https://doi.org/10.1080/1750984X.2019.1689574

Lavallee, D. (2019). Engagement in sport career transition planning enhances performance. *Journal of Loss and Trauma, 24*(1), 1-8.

Lavallee, D., & Robinson, H.K. (2007). In pursuit of an identity: A qualitative exploration of retirement from women's artistic gymnastics. *Psychology of Sport and Exercise, 8*(1), 119-141.

Lebrun, F., MacNamara, A., Rodgers, S., & Collins, D. (2018). Learning from elite athletes' experience of depression. *Frontiers in Psychology, 9*, [2062].

Lorimer, R., & Jowett, S. (2013). Empathic understanding and accuracy in the coach-athlete relationship. In P. Potrac, W. Gilbert & J. Denison (Eds.), *Routledge handbook of sports coaching* (pp. 321-332). Routledge.

MacNamara, A. (2011). Psychological characteristics of developing excellence. In D. Col-lins, A. Abbott, & H. Richards (Eds.), *Performance psychology for physical challenge* (pp. 47-62). Elsevier.

Maitland, A., Hills, L.A., & Rhind, D.J. (2015). Organisational culture in sport: A systematic review. *Sport Management Review, 18*(4), 501-516.

McCann, S. (2008). At the Olympics, everything is a performance issue. *International Journal of Sport and Exercise Psychology, 6*(3), 267-276.

Pink, M., Saunders, J., & Stynes, J. (2015). Reconciling the maintenance of on-field success with off-field player development: A case study of a club culture within the Australian Football League. *Psychology of Sport and Exercise, 21*(11), 98-108.

Rynne, S.B., Crudgington, B., Dickinson, R.K., & Mallet, C.J. (2017). On the (potential) value of coaching. In J. Baker, S. Cobley, J. Schorrer, & N. Wattie (Eds.), *Routledge handbook of talent identification and development in sport* (pp. 285-301). Routledge.

Sandström, E., Linnér, L., & Stambulova, N. (2016). Career profiles of athlete-coach rela-tionships: Descriptions and interpretations. *International Journal of Sports Science & Coaching, 11*(3), 395-409.

Schlossberg, N.K. (1981). A model for analyzing human adaptation to transition. *The Coun-seling Psychologist, 9*(2), 2-15.

Sorkkila, M., Aunola, K., & Ryba, T.V. (2017). A person-oriented approach to sport and school burnout in adolescent student-athletes: The role of individual and parental expectations. *Psychology of Sport and Exercise, 28*, 58-67.

Stambulova, N. (2003). Symptoms of a crisis-transition: A grounded theory study. In N. Hassmén (Ed.), *SIPF Yearbook 2003* (pp. 97-109). Örebro University Press.

Stambulova, N. (2010). Counseling athletes in career transitions: The five-step career plan-ning strategy. *Journal of Sport Psychology in Action, 1*(2), 95-105.

Stambulova, N., Engström, C., Franck, A., Linnér, L., & Lindahl, K. (2015). Searching for an optimal balance: Dual career experiences of Swedish adolescent athletes. *Psychology of Sport and Exercise, 21*(11), 4-14.

Stambulova, N., & Ryba, T.V. (2013). *Athletes' careers across cultures.* Routledge.

Stambulova, N., Ryba, T.V., & Henriksen, K. (2020). Career development and transitions of athletes: The International Society of Sport Psychology Position Stand Revisited. *International Journal of Sport and Exercise Psychology.* https://doi.org/10.1080/16121 97X.2020.1737836

Stambulova, N., & Wylleman, P. (2019). Psychology of athletes' dual careers: A state-of-the-art critical review of the European discourse. *Psychology of Sport and Exercise, 42*, 74-88.

Steele, A., van Rens, F., & Ashley, R. (2020). A systematic literature review on the academic and athletic identities of student-athletes. *Journal of Intercollegiate Sport, 13*(1), 69-92.

Turnnidge, J., & Côté, J. (2016). Applying transformational leadership theory to coaching research in youth sport: A systematic literature review. *International Journal of Sport and Exercise Psychology*, *16*(3), 1-16.

van Rens, F.E., Borkoles, E., Farrow, D., & Polman, R.C. (2018). Domain specific life satisfaction in the dual careers of junior elite football players: The impact of role strain. *Journal of Clinical Sport Psychology*, *12*(3), 302-315.

Wylleman, P., De Knop, P., & Reints, A. (2011). Transitions in competitive sports. In N.L. Holt & M. Talbot (Eds.), *Lifelong engagement in sport and physical activity: Participation and performance across the lifespan* (pp. 63-76). Routledge.

Yopyk, D.J., & Prentice, D.A. (2005). Am I an athlete or a student? Identity salience and stereotype threat in student-athletes. *Basic and Applied Social Psychology*, *27*(4), 329-336.

Yukhymenko-Lescroart, M.A. (2014). Students and athletes? Development of the Academic and Athletic Identity Scale (AAIS). *Sport, Exercise, and Performance Psychology*, *3*(2), 89-101.

Chapter 4

Aoyagi, M.W., & Poczwardowski, A. (2011). Models of sport psychology practice and delivery: A review. In S.D. Mellalieu & S. Hanton (Eds.), *Professional practice issues in sport psychology: Critical reviews* (pp. 5-30). Routledge.

Baltzell, A. (2011). *Living in the sweet spot: Preparing for performance in sport and life*. FiT Publishing.

Collins, L., & Collins, D. (2016). Professional judgement and decision-making in adventure sports coaching: The role of interaction. *Journal of Sports Sciences, 34*(13), 1231-1239. https://doi.org/10.1080/02640414.2015.1105379

Collins, D., Burke, V., Martindale, A., & Cruickshank, A. (2015). The illusion of competency versus the desirability of expertise: Seeking a common standard for support professions in sport. *Sports Medicine, 45*, 1-7. https://doi.org/10.1007/s40279-014-0251-1

Cruickshank, A., Collins, D., & Minten, S. (2015). Driving and sustaining culture change in professional sport performance teams: A grounded theory. *Psychology of Sport and Exercise, 20*, 40-50. https://doi.org/10.1016/j.psychsport.2015.04.007

Dweck, C.S. (2006). *Mindset: The new psychology of success*. Random House.

Eubank, M., Nesti, M., & Cruickshank, A. (2014). Understanding high performance sport environments: Impact for the professional training and supervision of sport psychologists. *Sport and Exercise Psychology Review, 10*(2), 30-37.

Gardner, F.L., & Moore, Z.E. (2007). *The psychology of enhancing human performance: The Mindfulness-Acceptance-Commitment (MAC) approach*. Springer.

Haberl, P. (2012). Dr. Peter Haberl. In M. Aoyagi and A. Poczwardowski (Eds.), *Expert approaches to sport psychology: Applied theories of performance excellence* (pp. 51-70). Fitness Information Technology.

Haberl, P., & McCann, S. (2012). Evaluating USOC sport psychology consultant effectiveness: A philosophical and practical imperative at the Olympic Games. *Journal of Sport Psychology in Action, 3*(2), 67-756.

Hayes, S.C., Strosahl, K., & Wilson, K.G. (1999). *Acceptance and commitment therapy: An experiential approach to behavior change*. Guilford Press.

Henriksen, K., Diment, G., & Hansen, J. (2011). Professional philosophy: Inside the delivery of sport psychology service at team Denmark. *Sport Science Review, 20* (1-2), 5-21.

Hill, K.E. (2001). *Frameworks for sport psychologists: Enhancing sport performance*. Human Kinetics.

Hoigaard, R., & Johansen, B.T. (2004). The solution-focused approach in sport psychology. *The Sport Psychologist, 18*, 218-228.

Nash, C., Martindale, R., Collins, D., & Martindale, A. (2012). Parameterising expertise in coaching: Past, present and future, *Journal of Sports Sciences*, *30*(10), 985-994. https://doi.org/10.1080/02640414.2012.682079

Newburg, D., Kimiecik, J., Durand-Bush, N., & Doell, K. (2002). The role of resonance in performance excellence and life engagement. *Journal of Applied Sport Psychology, 14*, 249-267.

Orlick, T. (1989). Reflections on sport psych consulting with individual and team sport athletes at Summer and Winter Olympic Games. *The Sport Psychologist, 3*, 358-365.

Poczwardowski, A. (2019). Deconstructing sport and performance psychology consultant: Expert, person, performer and self-regulator. *International Journal of Sport and Exercise Psychology, 17*(5), 427-444. https://doi.org/10.1080/1612197X.2017.1390484

Poczwardowski, A., Aoyagi, M., Fritze, T., & Laird, M. (2020). Revisiting "Gaining Entry": Roundtable Discussion 25 Years Later. *The Sport Psychologist, 34*(3), 153-161. https://doi.org/10.1123/tsp.2018-0189

Poczwardowski, A., Sherman, C., & Ravizza, K. (2004). Professional philosophy in the sport psychology service delivery: Building on theory and practice. *The Sport Psychologist, 18*, 415-429.

Prochaska, J., & Norcross, J. (2013). *Systems of Psychotherapy: A transtheoretical approach* (8th ed.). Cengage Learning.

Ravizza, K. (1988). Gaining entry with athletic personnel for season-long consulting. *The Sport Psychologist, 2*, 243-254. https://doi.org/10.1123/tsp.2.3.243

Webb, V., Collins, D., & Cruickshank, A. (2016). Aligning the talent pathway: Exploring the role and mechanisms of coherence in development. *Journal of Sports Sciences*, *34*. https://doi.org/10.1080/02640414.2016.1139162

Chapter 5

Bartholomew, K.J., Ntoumanis, N., & Thøgersen-Ntoumani, C. (2009). A review of controlling motivational strategies from a self-determination theory perspective: Implications for sports coaches. *International Review of Sport and Exercise Psychology, 2*(2), 215-233.

Clancy, R.B., Herring, M.P., & Campbell, M.J. (2017). Motivation measures in sport: A critical review and bibliometric analysis. *Frontiers in Psychology, 8*, 348.

Cresswell, S.L., & Eklund, R.C. (2005). Motivation and burnout among top amateur rugby players. *Medicine & Science in Sports and Exercise, 37*, 469-477.

Deci, E.L., & Ryan, R. M., (2000). The "what" and "why" of goal pursuits: Human needs and the self-determination of behavior. *Psychological Inquiry, 11*(4), 227-268.

Doran, G.T. (1981). There's a S.M.A.R.T. way to write management's goals and objectives. *Management Review, 70*, 35-36.

Elliot A.J., Murayama, K., & Pekrun, R. (2011). A 3 × 2 achievement goal model. *Journal of Educational Psychology, 103*(3), 632-48.

Gillet, N., Vallerand, R.J., Amoura, S., & Baldes, B. (2010). Influence of coaches' autonomy support on athletes' motivation and sport performance: A test of the hierarchical model of intrinsic and extrinsic motivation. *Psychology of Sport and Exercise*, *11*(2), 155-161.

Hare, B. (2017). Survival of the friendliest: *Homo sapiens* evolved via selection for prosociality. *Annual Review of Psychology, 68*, 155-186.

Hogue, C.M., Fry, M.D., & Fry, A.C. (2017). The differential impact of motivational climate on adolescents' psychological and physiological stress responses. *Psychology of Sport and Exercise, 30*, 118-127.

Mallett, C., Kawabata, M., Newcombe, P. Otero-Forero, A., & Jackson, S. (2007). Sport Motivation Scale-6 (SMS-6): A revised six-factor sport motivation scale. *Psychology of Sport Exercise, 8*, 600-614.

Mascret, N., Elliot, A., and Cury, F. (2015). Extending the 3 × 2 achievement goal model to the sport domain: The 3 × 2 Achievement Goal Questionnaire for Sport. *Psychology of Sport and Exercise, 17*, 7-14.

Maslow. A.H. (1943). Preface to motivation theory. *Psychosomatic Medicine, 5*, 85-92.

Newton, M., Duda, J.L., and Yin, Z. (2000). Examination of the psychometric properties of the Perceived Motivational Climate in Sport Questionnaire-2 in a sample of female athletes. *Journal of Sports Sciences 18*(4), 275-290.

Nicholls, J.G. 1984. Achievement motivation: Conceptions of ability, subjective experience, task choice, and performance. *Psychological Review, 91*, 328-346.

Pelletier, L.G., Rocchi, M.A., Vallerand, R.J., Deci, E.L., & Ryan, R.M. (2013). Validation of the revised Sport Motivation Scale (SMS-II). *Psychology of Sport and Exercise, 14*, 329-341.

Pelletier, L.G., K.M. Tuson, M.S. Fortier, R.J. Vallerand, N.M. Briére, and M.R. Blais. (1995). Toward a new measure of intrinsic motivation, extrinsic motivation, and amotivation in sports: The Sport Motivation Scale (SMS). *Journal of Sport and Exercise Psychology, 17*, 35-53.

Roberts, G.C., Treasure, D.C., & Balague, G. (1998). Achievement goals in sport: The development and validation of the Perception of Success Questionnaire. *Journal of Sports Sciences, 16*, 337-347.

Ryan, R.M., & Deci, E.L. (2000). Intrinsic and extrinsic motivations: Classic definitions and new directions. *Contemporary Educational Psychology, 25*, 54-67. https://doi.org/10.1006/ceps.1999.1020.

Ryan, R.M., and Deci, E.L. (2017). Self-determination theory: Basic psychological needs in motivation, development, and wellness. The Guilford Press.

Schaller, M., Kenrick, D.T., Neel, R., & Neuberg, S.L. (2017). Evolution and human motivation: A fundamental motives framework. *Social and Personality Psychology Compass, 11*(6), Article e12319.

Smith, A., Ntoumanis, N., & Duda, J. (2007). Goal striving, goal attainment, and well-being: Adapting and testing the self-concordance model in sport. *Journal of Sport and Exercise Psychology, 29*, 763-782.

Smith, A., Ntoumanis, N., & Duda, J. (2010). An investigation of coach behaviors, goal motives, and implementation intentions as predictors of well-being in sport. *Journal of Applied Sport Psychology, 22*, 17-33.

Weinberg, R. (2010). Making goals effective: A primer for coaches. *Journal of Sport Psychology in Action, 1*(2), 57-65.

Weinberg, R., and Butt, J. (2015). Goal-setting and sport performance: Research findings and practical applications. In A. Papaioannou & D. Hackfort (Eds.), *Routledge Companion to Sport and Exercise Psychology* (pp. 343-355). Routledge.

Weiner, B. (1972). Attribution theory, achievement motivation, and the educational process. *Review of Educational Research 42*(2), 203-215.

Chapter 6

Bandura, A. (1986). Social foundations of thought and action: A social cognitive theory. Prentice-Hall.

Bandura, A. (1997). *Self-efficacy: The exercise of control*. W.H. Freeman.

Bandura, A., & Wood, R. (1989). Effect of perceived controllability and performance standards on self-regulation of complex decision making. *Journal of Personality and Social Psychology, 56*(5), 805814. https://doi.org/10.1037/0022-3514.56.5.805

Brewer, B.W., & Redmond, C.J. (2017). *Psychology of sport injury*. Human Kinetics.

Bruton, A.M., Shearer, D.A., & Mellalieu, S.D. (2019). Who said "there is no 'I' in team"? The effects of observational learning content level on efficacy beliefs in groups. *Psychology of Sport and Exercise*, *45*, 101563. https://doi.org/10.1016/j.psychsport.2019.101563

Carver, C.S., & Scheier, M. (1998). *On the self-regulation of behavior*. Cambridge University Press.

Chmielewski, T.L., Zeppieri, G., Lentz, T.A., Tillman, S.M., Moser, M.W., Indelicato, P.A., & George, S.Z. (2011). Longitudinal changes in psychosocial factors and their association with knee pain and function after anterior cruciate ligament reconstruction. *Physical Therapy*, *91*(9), 13551366. doi: 10.2522/ptj.20100277

Collins, R. (2005). *Interaction ritual chains*. Princeton University Press.

DeRue, D.S., Hollenbeck, J., Ilgen, D., & Feltz, D. (2010). Efficacy dispersion in teams: Moving beyond agreement and aggregation. Personnel Psychology, *63*(1), 140. https://doi.org/ 10.1111/j.1744-6570.2009.01161.x

Dowrick, P.W. (1999). A review of self modeling and related interventions. *Applied and Preventive Psychology*, *8*(1), 2339. https://doi.org/10.1016/S0962-1849(99)80009-2

Feltz, D.L., Chase, M.A., Moritz, S.E., & Sullivan, P. J. (1999). A conceptual model of coaching efficacy: Preliminary investigation and instrument development. *Journal of Educational Psychology*, *91*(4), 765776. https://doi.org/10.1037/0022-0663.91.4.765

Fletcher, D., & Sarkar, M. (2012). A grounded theory of psychological resilience in Olympic champions. *Psychology of Sport and Exercise*, *13*(5), 669678. https://doi.org/10.1016/j.psychsport.2012.04.007

Fransen, K., Kleinert, J., Dithurbide, L., Vanbeselaere, N., & Boen, F. (2014). Collective efficacy or team outcome confidence? Development and validation of the Observational Collective Efficacy Scale for Sports (OCESS). *International Journal of Sport Psychology*, *45*(2), 121-137. https://doi.org/10.7352/IJSP.2014.45.121

Fransen, K., Mertens, N., Feltz, D., & Boen, F. (2017). "Yes, we can!" review on team confidence in sports. *Current Opinion in Psychology*, *16*, 98103. https://doi.org/10.1016/j.copsyc.2017.04.024

Galli, N., & Vealey, R.S. (2008). Bouncing back from adversity: Athletes' experiences of resilience. *The Sport Psychologist*, *22*, 316335.

Gardner, F.L., & Moore, Z.E. (2006). *Clinical sport psychology*. Human Kinetics.

Hauw, D., Gesbert, V., Crettaz von Roten, F., & Rolland, J-P. (2021). A multilayer approach for assessing the psychological needs of aspiring soccer players. Implications for overseeing talent development [manuscript submitted for publication]. *Professional Psychology: Research and Practice*.

Hays, K., Thomas, O., Maynard, I., & Bawden, M. (2009). The role of confidence in world-class sport performance. *Journal of Sports Sciences*, *27*(11), 11851199. https://doi.org/10.1080/02640410903089798

Heuzé, J.-P., Raimbault, N., & Fontayne, P. (2006). Relationships between cohesion, collective efficacy and performance in professional basketball teams: An examination of mediating effects. *Journal of Sports Sciences*, *24*(1), 5968. https://doi.org/10.1080/02640410500127736

Larson, H.K., McHugh, T.-L.F., Young, B.W., & Rodgers, W.M. (2019). Pathways from youth to masters swimming: Exploring long-term influences of youth swimming experiences. *Psychology of Sport and Exercise*, *41*, 1220. https://doi.org/10.1016/j.psychsport.2018.11.007

Michel, D. (2019, March 30). Entretien Gabriel Medina (Interview of Gabriel Medina), L'Equipe Mag, 9-25. https://www.lequipe.fr/abonnement/kiosque/le-magazine/f6c94e2c-11dd-4607-8701-452eeca9e1d5

Martens, R., Burton, D., Vealey, R.S, Bump, L., & Smith, D.E. (1990). Competitive State Anxiety Inventory-2. In R. Martens, R.S. Vealey, & D. Burton, Competitive anxiety in sport (pp. 117-213). Human Kinetics.

Mellalieu, S.D., Hanton, S., & Thomas, O. (2009). The effects of a motivational general-arousal imagery intervention upon preperformance symptoms in male rugby union players. *Psychology of Sport and Exercise*, *10*(1), 175185. https://doi.org/10.1016/j.psychsport.2008.07.003

Short, S.E., Sullivan, P., & Feltz, D.L. (2005). Development and preliminary validation of the Collective Efficacy Questionnaire for Sports. *Measurement in Physical Education and Exercise Science*, *9*(3), 181202. https://doi.org/10.1207/s15327841mpee0903_3

Tasa, K., & Whyte, G. (2005). Collective efficacy and vigilant problem solving in group decision making: A non-linear model. *Organizational Behavior and Human Decision Processes*, *96*(2), 119129. https://doi.org/10.1016/j.obhdp.2005.01.002

Vealey, R.S. (1986). Conceptualization of sport-confidence and competitive orientation: Preliminary investigation and instrument development. *Journal of Sport and Exercise Psychology*, *8*(3), 221246. https://doi.org/10.1123/jsp.8.3.221

Vealey, R.S., Hayashi, S.W., Garner-Holman, M., & Giacobbi, P. (1998). Sources of sport confidence: Conceptualization and instrument development. *Journal of Sport and Exercise Psychology*, *21*, 54-80.

Warnick, J., Wilt, J., & McAdams, D.P. (2016). Dancers' stories: A narrative study of professional dancers. *Performance Enhancement and Health*, *4*, 35-41. https://doi.org/10.1016/j.peh.2015.12.002

Zaccaro, S.J., Blair, V., Peterson, C., & Zazanis, M. (1995). Collective efficacy. In J.E. Maddux (Ed.), *The Plenum series in social/clinical psychology. Self-efficacy, adaptation, and adjustment: Theory, research, and application* (pp. 305-328). Plenum Press. http://doi.org/10.1007/978-1-4419-6868-5_11

Chapter 7

Arvinen-Barrow, M., Clement, D., & Hemmings, B. (2013). Imagery in sport injury rehabilitation. In M. Arvinen-Barrow & N. Walker (Eds.), *The psychology of sport injury and rehabilitation* (pp. 71-85). Routledge.

Bandura, A. (1982). Self-efficacy mechanism in human agency. *American Psychologist, 37*, 122-147. https://doi.org/10.1037/0003-066X.37.2.122

Bierton, J., Gorman, A., Lloyd, M., Gorman, A., Parker, J.K., & Lovell, G.P. (2019). Investigating the predictors of intrusive visual imagery in elite athletes. *Journal of Imagery Research in Sport and Physical Activity*, *14*. https://doi.org/10.1515/jirspa-2018-0011

Brewer, B.W., & Redmond, C.J. (2017). *Psychology of sport injury*. Human Kinetics.

Brewin, C.R., Gregory, J.D., Lipton, M., & Burgess, N. (2010). Intrusive images in psychological disorders: Characteristics, neural mechanisms, and treatment implications. *Psychological Review*, *117*, 210-232. https://doi.org/10.1037/a0018113

Cumming, J., & Williams, S.E. (2013). Introducing the revised applied model of deliberate imagery use for sport, dance, exercise, and rehabilitation. *Movement & Sport Sciences*, *82*, 69-81. https://doi.org/10.1051/sm/2013098

Cumming, J., Cooley, S.J., Anuar, N., Kosteli, M.C., Quinton, M.L., Weibull, F., & Williams, S.E. (2016). Developing imagery ability effectively: a guide to layered stimulus response training. *Journal of Sport Psychology in Action*, *8*, 23-33. https://doi.org/10.1080/21520704.2016.1205698

Deci, E.L., & Ryan, R.M. (2012). Self-determination theory. In P.A.M. Van Lange, A.W. Kruglanski, & E.T. Higgins (Eds.), *Handbook of theories of social psychology* (p. 416-436). Sage. https://doi.org/10.4135/9781446249215.n21

Hall, C.R., & Martin, K.A. (1997). Measuring movement imagery abilities: A revision of the Movement Imagery Questionnaire. *Journal of Mental Imagery*, *21*, 143-154.

Hall, C.R., Mack, D.E., Paivio, A., & Hausenblas, H.A. (1998). Imagery use by athletes: Development of the Sport Imagery Questionnaire. *International Journal of Sport Psychology*, *29*, 73-89.

Holmes, P.S., & Collins, D.J. (2001). PETTLEP approach to motor imagery: A functional equivalence model for sport psychologists. *Journal of Applied Sport Psychology, 13*, 60-83. https://doi.org/10.1080/10413200109339004

Lang, P. (1979). A bio-informational theory of emotional imagery. *Psychophysiology*, *16*, 495-512. https://doi.org/10.1111/j.1469-8986.1979.tb01511.x

Marshall, B., & Wright, D.J. (2016). Layered stimulus response training versus combined action observation and imagery: Effects on golf putting performance and imagery ability characteristics. *Journal of Imagery Research in Sport and Physical Activity*, *11*, 35-46. https://doi.org/10.1515/jirspa-2016-0007

Martin, K., & Hall, C. (1995). Using mental imagery to enhance intrinsic motivation. *Journal of Sport and Exercise Psychology, 17,* 54-69. https://doi.org/10.1123/jsep.17.1.54

Martin, K.A., Moritz, S.E., & Hall, C.R. (1999). Imagery use in sport: A literature review and applied model. *The Sport Psychologist*, 13, 245-268. https://doi.org/10.1123/tsp.13.3.245

McCarthy-Jones, S., Knowles, R., & Rowse, G. (2012). More than words? Hypomanic personality traits, visual imagery and verbal thoughts in young adults. *Consciousness and Cognition, 21*, 1375-1381. https://doi.org/10.1016/j.concog.2012.07.004

Miller, M., & Munroe-Chandler, K. (2019). Imagery use for injured adolescent athletes: Applied recommendations. *Journal of Sport Psychology in Action, 10*, 38-46. https://doi.org/10.1080/21520704.2018.1505677

Morris, T. (1997). *Psychological skills training in sport: an overview* (2nd ed.). National Coaching Foundation.

Morris, T., Spittle, M., & Watt, A.P. (2005). *Imagery in sport*. Human Kinetics.

Murphy S., Nordin, S., & Cumming, J. (2008). Imagery in sport, exercise, and dance. In T.H. Horn, Advances in sport psychology (3rd ed., pp.297-323). Human Kinetics.

Munroe-Chandler, K., & Gammage, K. (2005). Now see this: A new vision of exercise imagery. Exercise and Sport Sciences Reviews, 33, 201-205. https://doi.org/10.1097/00003677-200510000-00009

Norman, E., Pfuhl, G., Sæle, R.G., Svartdal, F., Låg, T., & Dahl, T.I. (2019). Metacognition in psychology. *Review of General Psychology*, *23*, 403-424. https://doi.org/10.1177/1089268019883821

Paivio, A. (1985). Cognitive and motivational functions of imagery in human performance. *Canadian Journal of Applied Sport Sciences*, *10*, 22S-28S.

Parker, J.K., & Lovell, G.P. (2009). Characteristics affecting the use of imagery: A youth sports academy study. *Journal of Imagery Research in Sport and Physical Activity, 4*, Article 8. https://doi.org/10.2202/1932-0191.1034

Parker, J.K., & Lovell, G.P. (2012). Age differences in the vividness of youth sport performers' imagery ability. *Journal of Imagery Research in Sport and Physical Activity, 7*, Article 7. https://doi.org/10.1515/1932-0191.1069

Parker, J.K., Jones, M.I., & Lovell, G.P. (2015). An investigation into athletes' intrusive visual imagery. *Sport and Exercise Psychology Review*, *11*, 34-42.

Parker, J.K., Jones, M.I., & Lovell, G.P. (2017). Involuntary imagery predicts athletes' affective states. *Sport and Exercise Psychology Review*, *13*, 22-31.

Parker, J.K., Lovell, G.P., & Jones, M.I. (2021). An examination of imagery ability and imagery use in skilled golfers. *Journal of Imagery Research in Sport and Physical Activity, 16,* 20210006. https://doi.org/10.1515/jirspa-2021-0006

Schmidt, R.A., & Lee D.L. (2021). Motor learning and performance: From principles to application (6th ed.) Human Kinetics.

Schuster, C., Hilfiker, R., Amft, O., Scheidhauer, A., Andrews, B., Butler, J., Kischka, U., & Ettlin, T. (2011). Best practice for motor imagery: A systematic literature review on motor imagery training elements in five different disciplines. BMC Medicine, 9, 75. https://doi.org/10.1186/1741-7015-9-75

Sheard, M., & Golby, J. (2006). Effect of a psychological skills training programme on swimming performance and positive psychological development. International Journal of Sport and Exercise Psychology, 4, 149-169. https://doi.org/10.1080/1612197X.2006.9671790

Slimani, M., Chamari, K., Boudhiba, D., & Chéour, F. (2016). Mediator and moderator variables of imagery use: Motor learning and sport relationships: A narrative review. *Sport Sciences for Health*, *12*, 1-9. https://doi.org/10.1007/s11332-016-0265-1

Tod, D., Edwards, C., McGuigan, M., & Lovell, G.P. (2015). A systematic review of self-directed cognitive strategies' effects on strength performance. *Sports Medicine, 45*, 1589-1602. https://doi.org/10.1007/s40279-015-0356-1

Vadocz, E.A., Hall, C.R., & Moritz, S.E. (1997). The relationship between competitive anxiety and imagery use. *Journal of Applied Sport Psychology*, *9*, 241-253. https://doi.org/10.1080/10413209708406485

Wakefield, C., & Smith, D. (2012). Perfecting practice: Applying the PETTLEP model of motor imagery. *Journal of Sport Psychology in Action, 3*, 1-11. https://doi.org/10.1080/21520704.2011.639853

Weinberg, R. (2008). Does imagery work? Effects on performance and mental skills. *Journal of Imagery Research in Sport and Physical Activity*, *3,* 1-21. https://doi.org/10.2202/1932-0191.1025

Wells, A., & Cartwright-Hatton, S. (2004). A short form of the metacognitions questionnaire: properties of the MCQ-30. *Behaviour Research and Therapy*, *42*, 385-396. https://doi.org/10.1016/S0005-7967(03)00147-5

Williams, S., Cooley, S., & Cumming, J. (2013). Layered stimulus response training improves motor imagery ability and movement execution. *Journal of Sport and Exercise Psychology*, *35*, 60-71. https://doi.org/10.1123/jsep.35.1.60

Williams, S.E., & Cumming, J. (2011). Measuring athlete imagery ability: The Sport Imagery Ability Questionnaire. *Journal of Sport and Exercise Psychology*, *33*, 416-440. https://doi.org/10.1123/jsep.33.3.416

Chapter 8

Adie, J.W., Duda, J.L., & Ntoumanis, N. (2012). Perceived coach-autonomy support, basic need satisfaction and the well-and ill-being of elite youth soccer players: A longitudinal investigation. *Psychology of Sport and Exercise*, *13*(1), 51-59.

Baker, J., & Young, B. (2014). 20 years later: Deliberate practice and the development of expertise in sport. *International Review of Sport and Exercise Psychology*, *7*(1), 135-157.

Bartulovic, D., Young, B.W., & Baker, J. (2017). Self-regulated learning predicts skill group differences in developing athletes. *Psychology of sport and Exercise*, *31*, 61-69.

Bartulovic, D., Young, B.W., McCardle, L., & Baker, J. (2018). Can athletes' reports of self-regulated learning distinguish deliberate practice from physical preparation activity? *Journal of Sports Sciences*, *36*(20), 2340-2348.

Baumeister, R.F., & Tierney, J.M. (2012). *Willpower: Rediscovering the greatest human strength*. Penguin.

Collins, D., Willmott, T., & Collins, L. (2018). Periodization and self-regulation in action sports: Coping with the emotional load. *Frontiers in Psychology*, *9*, 1652.

De Ridder, D.T., Lensvelt-Mulders, G., Finkenauer, C., Stok, F.M., & Baumeister, R.F. (2012). Taking stock of self-control: A meta-analysis of how trait self-control relates to a wide range of behaviors. *Personality and Social Psychology Review*, *16*(1), 76-99.

Dorris, D.C., Power, D.A., & Kenefick, E. (2012). Investigating the effects of ego depletion on physical exercise routines of athletes. *Psychology of Sport and Exercise*, *13*(2), 118-125.

Elferink-Gemser, M.T., De Roos, I., Torenbeek, M., Fokkema, T., Jonker, L., & Visscher, C. (2015). The importance of psychological constructs for training volume and performance improvement: A structural equation model for youth speed skaters. *International Journal of Sport Psychology*, *46* (6), 726-744.

Englert, C., & Bertrams, A. (2012). Anxiety, ego depletion, and sports performance. *Journal of Sport and Exercise Psychology*, *34*(5), 580-599.

Englert, C., & Bertrams, A. (2014). The effect of ego depletion on sprint start reaction time. *Journal of Sport and Exercise Psychology*, *36*(5), 506-515.

Englert, C., & Wolff, W. (2015). Ego depletion and persistent performance in a cycling task. *International Journal of Sport Psychology*, *46*(2), 137-151.

Englert, C., Bertrams, A., Furley, P., & Oudejans, R. R. (2015). Is ego depletion associated with increased distractibility? Results from a basketball free throw task. *Psychology of Sport and Exercise*, 18, 26-31.

Englert, C., Zwemmer, K., Bertrams, A., & Oudejans, R.R. (2015). Ego depletion and attention regulation under pressure: Is a temporary loss of self-control strength indeed related to impaired attention regulation? *Journal of Sport and Exercise Psychology*, *37*(2), 127-137.

Erikstad, M.K., Høigaard, R., Johansen, B.T., Kandala, N.B., & Haugen, T. (2018). Childhood football play and practice in relation to self-regulation and national team selection: A study of Norwegian elite youth players. *Journal of Sports Sciences*, *36*(20), 2304-2310.

Ertmer, P.A., & Newby, T.J. (1996). The expert learner: Strategic, self-regulated, and reflective. *Instructional Science*, *24*(1), 1-24.

Furley, P., Bertrams, A., Englert, C., & Delphia, A. (2013). Ego depletion, attentional control, and decision making in sport. *Psychology of Sport and Exercise*, *14*(6), 900-904.

Giske, R., Rodahl, S.E., & Høigaard, R. (2015). Shared mental task models in elite ice hockey and handball teams: Does it exist and how does the coach intervene to make an impact? *Journal of Applied Sport Psychology*, 27:1, 20-34. https://doi.org/10.1080/10413200.2014.940431

Gould, D., Dieffenbach, K., & Moffett, A. (2002). Psychological characteristics and their development in Olympic champions. *Journal of Applied Sport Psychology*, *14*(3), 172-204.

Hadwin, A.F., Järvelä, S., & Miller, M. (2011). Self-regulated, co-regulated, and socially shared regulation of learning. *Handbook of self-regulation of learning and performance*, *30*, 65-84.

Hagger, M.S., Wood, C., Stiff, C., & Chatzisarantis, N.L. (2010). Ego depletion and the strength model of self-control: A meta-analysis. *Psychological Bulletin*, *136*(4), 495.

Hardy, L., Roberts, R., Thomas, P.R., & Murphy, S.M. (2010). Test of Performance Strategies (TOPS): Instrument refinement using confirmatory factor analysis. *Psychology of Sport and Exercise*, *11*(1), 27-35.

Harkin, B., Webb, T.L., Chang, B.P., Prestwich, A., Conner, M., Kellar, I., Benn, Y., & Sheeran, P. (2016). Does monitoring goal progress promote goal attainment? A meta-analysis of the experimental evidence. Psychological Bulletin, *142*(2), 198.

Hofmann, W., Baumeister, R.F., Förster, G., & Vohs, K.D. (2012). Everyday temptations: An experience sampling study of desire, conflict, and self-control. Journal of Personality and Social Psychology, *102*(6), 1318.

Jordalen, G., Lemyre, P.N., & Durand-Bush, N. (2016). Exhaustion experiences in junior athletes: The importance of motivation and self-control competencies. *Frontiers in psychology, 7*, 1867.

Jordalen, G., Lemyre, P.N., Durand-Bush, N., & Ivarsson, A. (2020). The temporal ordering of motivation and self-control: A cross-lagged effects model. *Journal of Sport and Exercise Psychology, 42*(2), 102-113.

Jordet, G. (2009). When superstars flop: Public status and choking under pressure in international soccer penalty shootouts. *Journal of Applied Sport Psychology, 21*(2), 125-130.

Jordet, G. (2016). Psychology and elite soccer performance. *Soccer Science*, 365-388.

Jordet, G., Hartman, E., & Sigmundstad, E. (2009). Temporal links to performing under pressure in international soccer penalty shootouts. *Psychology of Sport and Exercise, 10*(6), 621-627.

Jowett, S., & Arthur, C. (2019). Effective coaching: The links between coach leadership and coach-athlete relationship—From theory to research to practice. In M. H. Anshel, T. A. Petrie, & J. A. Steinfeldt (Eds.), *APA handbook of sport and exercise psychology*, Vol. 1. Sport psychology (pp. 419–449). American Psychological Association. https://doi.org/10.1037/0000123-022.

Karabenick, S.A., & Newman, R.S. (2009). Seeking help: Generalizable self-regulatory process and social-cultural barometer. In M. Wosnitza, S. A. Karabenick, A. Efklides, & P. Nenniger (Eds.), *Contemporary motivation research: From global to local perspectives* (pp. 25–48). Hogrefe & Huber Publishers.

Kitsantas, A., & Zimmerman, B. J. (2002). Comparing self-regulatory processes among novice, non-expert, and expert volleyball players: A microanalytic study. *Journal of Applied Sport Psychology, 14*(2), 91-105.

Landers, D.M., & Arent, S.M. (2010). Arousal-performance relationships. In J. Williams (Ed.), *Applied sport psychology: Personal growth to peak performance* (6th ed.), pp. 221-246. McGraw-Hill.

Massey, W.V., Meyer, B.B., & Naylor, A.I. (2015). Self-regulation strategies in mixed martial arts. *Journal of Sport Behavior, 38*(2).

McCardle, L., Young, B.W., & Baker, J. (2019). Self-regulated learning and expertise development in sport: Current status, challenges, and future opportunities. *International Review of Sport and Exercise Psychology, 12*, 112-138. https://doi.org/10.1080/1750984X.2017.1381141

Mischel, W., Ayduk, O., Berman, M.G., Casey, B.J., Gotlib, I.H., Jonides, J., Kross, E., Teslovich, T., Wilson, N.L., Zayas, V., & Shoda, Y. (2011). 'Willpower' over the life span: Decomposing self-regulation. *Social Cognitive and Affective Neuroscience, 6*(2), 252-256.

Orlick, T., & Partington, J. (1988). Mental links to excellence. The Sport Psychologist, *2*(2), 105-130.

Phillips, E., Davids, K., Renshaw, I., & Portus, M. (2010). Expert performance in sport and the dynamics of talent development. *Sports Medicine, 40*(4), 271-283.

Roberts, G.C., Treasure, D.C., & Conroy, D.E. (2007). Understanding the dynamics of motivation in sport and physical activity: An achievement goal interpretation. In G. Tenenbaum & R.C. Eklund (Eds.), *Handbook of sport psychology* (p. 3-30). John Wiley & Sons, Inc.

Taylor, I.M., & Bruner, M.W. (2012). The social environment and developmental experiences in elite youth soccer. *Psychology of Sport and Exercise, 13*(4), 390-396.

Tedesqui, R.A., & Young, B.W. (2020). How coaches see conscientiousness-related traits and their impact on athletes' training and expertise development. *International Sport Coaching Journal, 7*(2), 127-138. https://doi.org/10.1123/iscj.2018-0074

Toering, T., Elferink-Gemser, M., Jordet, G., Jorna, C., Pepping, G.J., & Visscher, C. (2011). Self-regulation of practice behavior among elite youth soccer players: An exploratory observation study. *Journal of Applied Sport Psychology*, *23*(1), 110-128.

Toering, T., Elferink-Gemser, M.T., Jordet, G., Pepping, G.J., & Visscher, C. (2012). Self-regulation of learning and performance level of elite youth soccer players. *International Journal of Sport Psychology*, *43*(4), 312.

Toering, T.T., Elferink-Gemser, M.T., Jordet, G., & Visscher, C. (2009). Self-regulation and performance level of elite and non-elite youth soccer players. *Journal of Sports Sciences*, *27*(14), 1509-1517.

Toering, T., & Jordet, G. (2015). Self-control in professional soccer players. *Journal of Applied Sport Psychology*, *27*(3), 335-350.

Toering, T., Jordet, G., & Ripegutu, A. (2013). Effective learning among elite football players: The development of a football-specific self-regulated learning questionnaire. *Journal of Sports Sciences*, *31*(13), 1412-1420.

Vohs, K.D., & Baumeister, R.F. (Eds.). (2016). *Handbook of self-regulation: Research, theory, and applications*. Guilford Press.

Wagstaff, C.R. (2014). Emotion regulation and sport performance. *Journal of Sport and Exercise Psychology*, *36*(4), 401-412.

Young, B.W., & Starkes, J.L. (2006). Measuring outcomes of swimmers' non-regulation during practice: Relationships between self-report, coaches' judgments, and video-observation. *International Journal of Sports Science & Coaching*, *1*(2), 131-148.

Zimmerman, B.J. (2006). Development and adaptation of expertise: The role of self-regulatory processes and beliefs. *The Cambridge handbook of expertise and expert performance*, *186*, 705-722.

Chapter 9

Abdoli, B., Hardy, J., Riyahi, J.F., & Farsi, A. (2018). A closer look at how self-talk influences skilled basketball performance. *The Sport Psychologist*, *32*, 9-15.

Arsal, G., Eccles, D.W., & Ericsson, K.A. (2016). Cognitive mediation of putting: Use of a think-aloud measure and implications for studies of golf-putting in the laboratory. *Psychology of Sport and Exercise*, *27*, 18-27.

Beilock, S.L., & Carr, T.H. (2001). On the fragility of skilled performance: What governs choking under pressure? *Journal of Experimental Psychology: General*, *130*, 701-725.

Bortoli, L., Bertollo, M., Hanin, Y., & Robazza, C. (2012). Striving for excellence: A multi-action plan intervention model for shooters. *Psychology of Sport and Exercise*, *13*, 693-701.

Boutcher, S.H (2008). Attentional processes and sport performance. In T.S. Horn (Ed.), *Advances in Sport Psychology* (3rd ed., pp. 325-338). Human Kinetics.

Bu, D., Liu, J.D., Zhang, C.Q., Si, G., & Chung, P.K. (2019). Mindfulness training improves relaxation and attention in elite shooting athletes: A single-case study. *International Journal of Sport Psychology*, *50*, 4-25.

Derakshan, N., & Eysenck, M.W. (2009). Anxiety, processing efficiency, and cognitive performance: New developments from attentional control theory. *European Psychologist*, *14*, 168-176.

Eccles, D.W., & Arsal, G. (2017). The think aloud method: What is it and how do I use it? *Qualitative Research in Sport, Exercise and Health*, *9*, 514-531.

Englert, C., & Oudejans, R.R. (2014). Is choking under pressure a consequence of skill-focus or increased distractibility? Results from a tennis serve task. *Psychology*, *5*, 1035-1043.

Eysenck, M.W., & Keane, M.T. (2015). *Cognitive psychology: A student's handbook* (7th ed.). Psychology Press.

Eysenck, M.W., & Wilson, M.R. (2016). Sporting performance, pressure and cognition: Introducing attentional control theory: Sport. In D. Groome & M. Eysenck (Eds.), *An introduction to applied cognitive psychology* (pp. 329-350). Routledge.

Galanis, E., Hatzigeorgiadis, A., Comoutos, N., Charachousi, F., & Sanchez, X. (2018). From the lab to the field: Effects of self-talk on task performance under distracting conditions. *The Sport Psychologist*, *32*, 26-32.

Goldstein, E.B. (2011). *Cognitive psychology* (3rd ed.) Wadsworth/Cengage.

Gucciardi, D.F., Longbottom, J.L., Jackson, B., & Dimmock, J.A. (2010). Experienced golfers' perspectives on choking under pressure. *Journal of Sport & Exercise Psychology*, *32*, 61-83.

Hardy, J. (2006). Speaking clearly: A critical review of the self-talk literature. *Psychology of Sport and Exercise*, *7*, 81-97.

Hatzigeorgiadis, A., Zourbanos, N., Galanis, E., & Theodorakis, Y. (2011). Self-talk and sport performance: A meta-analysis. *Perspectives on Psychological Science*, *6*, 348-356.

Hatzigeorgiadis, A., & Biddle, S. J. (2000). Assessing cognitive interference in sport: Development of the Thought Occurrence Questionnaire for Sport. *Anxiety, Stress and Coping*, *13*, 65-86.

Hibbs, D. (2010). A conceptual analysis of clutch performances in competitive sports. *Journal of the Philosophy of Sport*, *37*, 47-59.

Hill, D.M., Hanton, S., Matthews, N., & Fleming, S. (2010). A qualitative exploration of choking in elite golf. *Journal of Clinical Sport Psychology*, *4*, 221-240.

Hill, D.M., Hanton, S., Matthews, N., & Fleming, S. (2011). Alleviation of choking under pressure in elite golf: An action research study. *The Sport Psychologist*, *25*, 465-488.

Kahneman, D. (1973). *Attention and effort*. Prentice-Hall.

Masters, R.S.W. (1992). Knowledge, knerves and know-how: The role of explicit versus implicit knowledge in the breakdown of a complex motor skill under pressure. *British Journal of Psychology*, *83*, 343-358.

Moran, G. (2005, July 12). Oh dear, so near but yet so far away. *The Irish Times*, p. 21.

Moran, A.P. (1996). *The psychology of concentration in sport performers: A cognitive analysis*. Psychology Press.

Moran, A., & Toner, J. (2017). *A critical introduction to sport psychology*. Routledge.

Moran, A., & Toner, J. (2018). Attentional processes in sport and performance. In O. Braddick (Ed.), *Oxford research encyclopedia of psychology*. Oxford University Press.

Newman, P. (2015). Australian Open 2015: Andy Murray left frustrated by repeated Novak Djokovic 'distractions' in final defeat. *Independent*. www.independent.co.uk/sport/tennis/australian-open-2015-andy-murray-left-frustrated-repeated-novak-djokovic-distractions-final-defeat-10016824.html

Nideffer, R.M. (1976). Test of Attentional and Interpersonal Style. *Journal of Personality and Social Psychology*, *34*, 394-404.

Nideffer, R.M., Sagal, M., Lowry, M., & Bond, J. (2001). Identifying and developing world-class performers. In G. Tenenbaum (Ed.), *The practice of sport psychology* (pp. 129-144). Fitness Information Technology.

Oudejans, R.R., & Pijpers, J.R. (2009). Training with anxiety has a positive effect on expert perceptual–motor performance under pressure. *Quarterly Journal of Experimental Psychology*, *62*, 1631-1647.

Oudejans, R.R., & Pijpers, J.R. (2010). Training with mild anxiety may prevent choking under higher levels of anxiety. *Psychology of Sport and Exercise*, *11*, 44-50.

Oudejans, R.R., Kuijpers, W., Kooijman, C.C., & Bakker, F.C. (2011). Thoughts and attention of athletes under pressure: Skill-focus or performance worries? *Anxiety, Stress, & Coping, 24*, 59-73.

Posner, M.I. (1980). Orienting of attention: The VIIth Sir Fredric Bartlett lecture. *Quarterly Journal of Experimental Psychology, 32A*, 3-25.

Reinhart, R.M., McClenahan, L.J., & Woodman, G.F. (2016). Attention's accelerator. *Psychological Science, 27*, 790-798.

Sky Sports. (2015, October 25). Dan Carter insists New Zealand's job is 'not done yet'. *Sky Sports*. www.skysports.com/rugby-union/news/22093/10043212/dan-carter-insists-new-zealands-job-is-not-done-yet

Stoker, M., Lindsay, P., Butt, J., Bawden, M., & Maynard, I. (2016). Elite coaches' experiences of creating pressure training environments for performance enhancement. *International Journal of Sport Psychology, 47*, 262-281.

Stoker, M., Maynard, I., Butt, J., Hays, K., & Hughes, P. (2019). The effect of manipulating individual consequences and training demands on experiences of pressure with elite disability shooters. *The Sport Psychologist, 33*, 221-227.

Swann, C., Crust, L., Jackman, P., Vella, S.A., Allen, M.S., & Keegan, R. (2017). Psychological states underlying excellent performance in sport: Toward an integrated model of flow and clutch states. *Journal of Applied Sport Psychology, 29*, 375-401.

Van Raalte, J.L., Vincent, A., & Brewer, B.W. (2016). Self-talk: Review and sport-specific model. *Psychology of Sport and Exercise, 22*, 139-148.

Wegner, D.M. (1994). Ironic processes of mental control. *Psychological Review, 101*, 34-52.

Whitehead, A.E., Taylor, J.A., & Polman, R.C. (2015). Examination of the suitability of collecting in event cognitive processes using Think Aloud protocol in golf. *Frontiers in Psychology, 6*, 1083.

Woodman, G.F., Carlisle, N.B., & Reinhart, R.M. (2013). Where do we store the memory representations that guide attention? *Journal of Vision, 13*, 1-1.

Chapter 10

Bjørndal, C.T., & Ronglan, L.T. (2019). Engaging with uncertainty in athlete development–orchestrating talent development through incremental leadership. *Sport, Education and Society.* https://doi.org/10.1080/13573322.2019.1695198

Bonner, B.L., & Bolinger, A.R. (2013). Separating the confident from the correct: Leveraging member knowledge in groups to improve decision making and performance. *Organizational Behavior and Human Decision Processes, 122*(2), 214-221. https://doi.org/https://doi.org/10.1016/j.obhdp.2013.07.005

Butler, J. (2016). *Playing fair: Using student-invented games to prevent bullying, teaching democracy, and promote social justice.* Human Kinetics.

Cushion, C.J. (2018). Reflection and reflective practice discourses in coaching: A critical analysis. *Sport, Education and Society, 23*(1), 82-94. https://doi.org/10.1080/13573322.2016.1142961

Delgado-Bordonau, J.L., & Mendez-Villanueva, A. (2012). Tactical periodization: Mourinho's best-kept secret? *Soccer Journal (Tactics) May/June*, 28-34.

Den Hartigh, R.J.R., Van Der Steen, S., Hakvoort, B., Frencken, W.G.P., & Lemmink, K.A.P.M. (2018). Differences in game reading between selected and non-selected youth soccer players. *Journal of Sports Sciences, 36*(4), 422-428. https://doi.org/10.1080/02640414.2017.1313442

Gopnik, A. (2016). *The Gardener and the Carpenter.* Farrar, Straus and Giroux.

Hansen, P., & Andersen, S. (2017). Knowledge integration as co-creation in a high-performance context: Ski-preparation as a knowledge intensive activity under uncertainty. In G. Schiuma, J.C. Spender, T. Gavrilova (Eds). *Proceedings IFKAD 2017* (pp. 1912-1923).

Hodge, K., Henry, G., & Smith, W. (2014). A case study of excellence in elite sport: Motivational climate in a world champion team. *The Sport Psychologist*, *28*(1), 60-74.

Huang, Y., & Hutchinson, J.W. (2013). The roles of planning, learning, and mental models in repeated dynamic decision making. *Organizational Behavior and Human Decision Processes*, *122*(2), 163–176. https://doi.org/10.1016/j.obhdp.2013.07.001

Husebø, S.E., O'Regan, S., & Nestel, D. (2015). Reflective Practice and Its Role in Simulation. *Clinical Simulation in Nursing*, *11*(8), 368-375. https://doi.org/10.1016/j.ecns.2015.04.005

Max-Neef, M.A. (2005). Foundations of transdisciplinarity. *Ecological Economics*, *53*(1), 5-16. https://doi.org/10.1016/j.ecolecon.2005.01.014

Memmert, D. (2015). *Teaching tactical creativity in sport*. Routledge.

Mesagno, C., Hill, D.M., & Larkin, P. (2015). Examining the accuracy and in-game performance effects between pre- and post-performance routines: A mixed methods study. *Psychology of Sport and Exercise*, *19*, 85-94. https://doi.org/10.1016/j.psychsport.2015.03.005

Milch, K.F., Weber, E.U., Appelt, K.C., Handgraaf, M.J.J., & Krantz, D.H. (2009). From individual preference construction to group decisions: Framing effects and group processes. *Organizational Behavior and Human Decision Processes*, *108*(2), 242-255. https://doi.org/10.1016/j.obhdp.2008.11.003

Price, A., Collins, D., Stoszkowski, J., & Pill, S. (2017). Learning to play soccer: Lessons on meta-cognition from video game design. *Quest*, *70*(3), 321-333. doi:10.1080/00336297.2017.1386574

Price, A., Collins, D., Stoszkowski, J., & Pill, S. (2020). Strategic understandings: An investigation of professional academy youth soccer coaches' interpretation, knowledge, and application of game strategies. *International Sport Coaching Journal*, *7*(2), 151-162. https://doi.org/10.1123/iscj.2019-0022

Richards, P., Collins, D., & Mascarenhas, D.R.D. (2012). Developing rapid high-pressure team decision-making skills. The integration of slow deliberate reflective learning within the competitive performance environment: A case study of elite netball. *Reflective Practice*, *13*(3), 407-424. https://doi.org/10.1080/14623943.2012.670111

Richards, P., Mascarenhas, D.R.D., & Collins, D. (2009). Implementing reflective practice approaches with elite team athletes: parameters of success. *Reflective Practice*, *10*(3), 353-363. https://doi.org/10.1080/14623940903034721

Santos, M., & Morgan, K. (2019). Developing creative team games players: From jazz to sport coaching. *International Journal of Sports Science & Coaching*, *14*(2), 117-125.

Seifert, L., Araújo, D., Komar, J., & Davids, K. (2017). Understanding constraints on sport performance from the complexity sciences paradigm: An ecological dynamics framework. *Human Movement Science*, (May), 0-1. https://doi.org/10.1016/j.humov.2017.05.001

Stolz, S., & Pill, S. (2014). Teaching games and sport for understanding: Exploring and reconsidering its relevance in physical education. *European Physical Education Review*, 20, 1, 36-71. https://doi.org/10.1177/1356336X13496001

Vinson, D., & Parker, A. (2019). Vygotsky and sports coaching: non-linear practice in youth and adult settings. *Curriculum Studies in Health and Physical Education*, *10*(1), 91-106. https://doi.org/10.1080/25742981.2018.1555003

Vygotski, L. (1986). *Thought and language*. MIT Press.

Chapter 11

Alvesson, M., & Einola, K. (2019). Warning for excessive positivity: Authentic leadership and other traps in leadership studies. *The Leadership Quarterly*, *30*(4), 383-395.

Bass, B. (1990). From transactional to transformational leadership: Learning to share the vision. *Organizational Dynamics*, *18*(3), 19-31. https://doi.org/10.1016/0090-2616(90)90061-S

Callow, N., Smith, M.J., Hardy, L., Arthur, C.A., & Hardy, J. (2009). Measurement of transformational leadership and its relationship with team cohesion and performance level. *Journal of Applied Sport Psychology*, *21*, 395-412. https://doi.org/10.1080/10413200903204754

Cannon-Bowers, J.A., Salas, E., & Converse, S.A. (1993). Shared mental models in expert team decision making. In N.J. Castellan, Jr. (Ed.), *Current issues in individual and group decision making* (pp. 221-246). Erlbaum.

Chaleff, I. (2003). *The courageous follower: Standing up to & for our leaders*. Berrett-Koehler.

Collins, D., & Collins, L. (2021). Developing coaches' professional judgement and decision making: Using the 'Big 5'. *Journal of Sports Sciences*, *39*(1), 115-119. https://doi.org/10.1080/02640414.2020.1809053

Cruickshank, A. (2019). Culture, leadership, and management with elites. In D. Collins, A. Cruickshank, & G. Jordet (Eds.), *Routledge handbook of Elite Sport Performance.* (pp. 201-211). Routledge.

Cruickshank, A., & Collins, D. (2015). Illuminating and Applying "The dark side": Insights from elite team leaders. *Journal of Applied Sport Psychology*, *27*, 249-267.

Cruickshank, A., & Collins, D. (2016). Advancing leadership in sport: Time to take off the blinkers? *Sports Medicine*, *46*, 1199-1204 https://doi.org/10.1007/s40279-016-0513-1

Cruickshank, A., Martindale, A., & Collins, D. (2018). Raising our game: The necessity and progression of expertise-based training in applied sport psychology. *Journal of Applied Sport Psychology*, *32*, 237-255. https://doi.org/10.1080/10413200.2018.1492471

Eys, M.A., Carron, A.V., Bray, S.R., & Brawley, L.R. (2007). Item wording and internal consistency of a measure of cohesion: The Group Environment Questionnaire. *Journal of Sport and Exercise Psychology*, *29*, 395-402.

Fransen, K., Haslam, S.A., Steffens, N.K., Peters, K., Mallett, C.J., Mertens, N., & Boen, F. (2020). All for us and us for all: Introducing the 5R Shared Leadership Program. *Psychology of Sport and Exercise*, *51*. https://doi.org/10.1016/j.psychsport.2020.101762

Hogan, R., & Hogan, J. (2009). *Hogan Development Survey Manual* (2nd ed.). Hogan Press.

Lyons, A., Fletcher, G., & Bariola, E. (2016). Assessing the well-being benefits of belonging to resilient groups and communities: Development and testing of the Fletcher-Lyons Collective Resilience Scale (FLCRS). *Group Dynamics: Theory, Research, and Practice*, *20*(2), 65–77: https://doi.org/0.1037/gdn0000041

Railo, W. (1986). *Willing to win*. Amas.

Slater, M.J., Coffee, P., Barker, J.B., & Evans, A.L. (2014). Promoting shared meanings in group memberships: A social identity approach to leadership in sport. *Reflective Practice: International and Multidisciplinary Perspectives*, *15*(5), 672-685. https://doi.org/10.1080/14623943.2014.944126

Steinmann, B., Klug, H.J.P., & Maier, G.W. (2018). The path is the goal: How transformational leaders enhance followers' job attitudes and proactive behavior. *Frontiers in Psychology*, *9*:2338. https://doi.org/10.3389/fpsyg.2018.02338

Vallée, C.N., & Bloom, G.A. (2005). Building a successful university program: Key and common elements of expert coaches. *Journal of Applied Sport Psychology*, *17*, 179-196. https://doi.org/10.1080/10413200591010021

Wasserman, S., & Faust, K. (1994). *Social network analysis: Methods and applications*. Cambridge University Press.

Webb, V., Collins, D., & Cruickshank, A. (2016). Aligning the talent pathway: Exploring the role and mechanisms of coherence in development. *Journal of Sports Sciences*. https://doi.org/10.1080/02640414.2016.1139162

Chapter 12

Austin, S. (2017, April 28). How to think like an All Black: No 'dickheads' allowed. *Training Ground Guru.* https://trainingground.guru/articles/how-to-think-like-an-all-black-no-dickheads-allowed

Balague, G. (2012). *Pep Guardiola: Another way of winning.* Orion.

Cole, J.R., & Martin, A. (2018). Developing a winning sport team culture: Organizational culture in theory and practice. *Sport in Society*, *21*(8). https://doi.org/10.1080/17430437.2018.1442197

Colman, M.M., & Carron, A.V. (2001). The nature of norms in individual sport teams. *Small Group Research*, *32*, 206-232.

Costa, A.C., & Anderson, N. (2011) Measuring trust in teams: Development and validation of a multifaceted measure of formative and reflective indicators of team trust. *European Journal of Work and Organizational Psychology, 20*, 119-154.

Coyle, D. (2018). *Culture code: The secrets of highly successful groups.* Bantam Books.

Cruickshank, A. (2019). Culture, leadership, and management with elites. In D. Collins, A.

Cruickshank, & G. Jordet (Eds.), *Routledge Handbook of Elite Sport Performance* (pp. 201-211). Routledge.

Cruickshank, A., & Collins, D. (2012). Culture change in elite sport performance teams: Examining and advancing effectiveness in the new era. *Journal of Applied Sport Psychology*, *24*(3), 338-355

Cruickshank. A., Collins, D., & Minten, S. (2013) Culture change in a professional sports team: Shaping environmental contexts and regulating power. *International Journal of Sports Science & Coaching*, *8*, 190-206

Cruickshank. A., Collins, D., & Minten, S. (2014). Driving and sustaining culture change in Olympic sport performance teams: A first exploration and grounded theory. *Journal of Sport & Exercise Psychology*, *36*, 107-120

Cruickshank. A., Collins, D., & Minten, S. (2015). Driving and sustaining culture change in professional sport performance teams: A grounded theory. *Psychology of Sport and Exercise*, *20*, 40-50

Danielsen, L.D., Giske, R., Peters, D.M., & Høigaard, R. (2019). Athletes as "cultural architects": A qualitative analysis of elite coaches' perceptions of highly influential soccer players. *The Sport Psychologist, 33,* 313-322.

Driskell, J.E. Salas, E., & Hughes, S. (2010). Collective orientation and team performance: Development of an individual differences measure. *Human Factors, 52*, 316-328.

Edmondson, A., & Lei, Z. (2014). Psychological safety: The history, renaissance, and future of an interpersonal construct. *Annual Review of Organizational Psychology and Organizational Behavior*, *1*, 23-43 https://doi.org/10.1146/annurev-orgpsych-031413-091305

Frontiera, J. (2010). Leadership and organizational culture transformation in professional sport. *Journal of Leadership & Organizational Studies*, *17*, 71-86.

Gilmore, S. 2013. Culture change in a professional sports team: Shaping environmental contexts and regulating power – A response to commentaries. *International Journal of Sports Science & Coaching*, *8*(2), 305-307.

Hammerich, K., & Lewis, R.D. (2013). *Fish can't see water: How national culture can make or break your company corporate strateg*y. John Wiley & Sons. https://doi.org/10.1002/9781119207962

Henriksen, K. (2015). Developing a high-performance culture: A sport psychology intervention from an ecological perspective in elite orienteering. *Journal of Sport Psychology in Action, 6*(3), 141-153. https://doi.org/10.1080/21520704.2015.1084961

Henriksen, K., Larsen, C.H., & Christensen, M.K. (2013). Looking at success from its opposite pole: The case of a talent development golf environment in Denmark. *International Journal of Sport and Exercise Psychology, 12,* 134-149.

Henriksen, K., Stambulova, N., & Roessler, K.K. (2010a). Holistic approach to athletic talent development environments: A successful sailing milieu. *Psychology of Sport and Exercise, 11*(3), 212-222.

Henriksen, K., Stambulova, N., & Roessler, K.K. (2010b). Successful talent development in track and field: Considering the role of environment. *Scandinavian Journal of Medicine Science in Sports, 20*(Suppl. 2), 122-132.

Henriksen, K., Stambulova, N., & Roessler, K.K. (2011). Riding the wave of an expert: A successful talent development environment in kayaking. *The Sport Psychologist, 25*(3), 341-362.

Hiddink, G., & Jordet, G. (2019). The coach nomad. In: D. Collins, A. Cruickshank, & G. Jordet (Eds.), *Routledge Handbook of Elite Sport Performance* (pp. 302-309). Routledge.

Holmes, B. (2019). Michelin restaurants and fabulous wines: Inside the secret team dinners that have built the Spurs' dynasty. *ESPN.* www.espn.com/nba/story/_/id/26524600/secret-team-dinners-built-spurs-dynasty

Ingle, S. (2018). 'No jerks allowed': The egalitarianism behind Norway's winter wonderland. *The Guardian.* www.theguardian.com/sport/2018/feb/22/norway-winter-olympics-success

Johnson, T., Martin, A.J., Palmer, F.R., Watson, G., & Ramsey, P.L. (2013). A core value of pride in winning: The All Blacks' team culture and legacy. *The International Journal of Sport and Society, 4,* 1-14.

Jordet, G., & Hartman, E. (2008). Avoidance motivation and choking under pressure in soccer penalty shootouts. *Journal of Sport & Exercise Psychology, 30,* 452-459.

Junggren S.E., Elbæk L., & Stambulova, N.B. Examining coaching practices and philosophy through the lens of organizational culture in a Danish high-performance swimming environment. *International Journal of Sports Science & Coaching, 13*(6),1108-1119. https://doi.org/10.1177/1747954118796914

Kerr, J. (2013). *Legacy: What the All Blacks can teach us about the business of life.* Constable.

Kraus, M.W., Huang, C., & Keltner, D. (2010). Tactile communication, cooperation, and performance: An ethological study of the NBA. *Emotion, 10*(5) http://doi.org/10.1037/a0019382

Larsen, C.H., Alfermann, D., Henriksen, K., & Christensen, M.K. (2013). Successful talent development in soccer: The characteristics of the environment. *Sport, Exercise, and Performance Psychology, 2*(3), 190-206.

Larsen, C.H., Louise, S.K., Pyrdol, N., Sæther, S.A., & Henriksen, K. (2020). A world class academy in professional football: The case of Ajax Amsterdam. *Scandinavian Journal of Sport and Exercise Psychology, 2,* 33-43. https://doi.org/10.7146/sjsep.v2i0.119746

Latané, B. (1981). The psychology of social impact. *American Psychologist, 36*(4), 343-356. https://doi.org/10.1037/0003-066X.36.4.343

Lund Svindal, A., & Ekelund, T. (2019) *Større enn meg: En selvbiografi* [Larger than me: An autobiography]. Pilar Forlag.

Maitland, A., Hills, L., & Rhind, D. (2015). Organisational culture in sport: A systematic review. *Sport Management Review, 18,* 501-516.

Martin, J., & Frost, P. (1996). The organizational culture war games: A struggle for intellectual dominance'. In S.R. Clegg, C. Hardy, & W. Nord (Eds.), *Handbook of Organization Studies (pp. 599-621).* Sage.

Matsumoto, D., Frank, M.G., & Hwang, H.S. (Eds.). (2013). *Nonverbal communication: Science and applications.* Sage.

McDougall, M., Ronkainen, N., Richardson, D., Littlewood, M., & Nesti, M. (2020a). Organizational culture beyond consensus and clarity: Narratives from elite sport. *The Sport Psychologist, 34*, 288-299.

McDougall, M., Ronkainen, N., Richardson, D., Littlewood, M., & Nesti, M. 2020b. Three team and organisational culture myths and their consequences for sport psychology research and practice. *International Review of Sport and Exercise Psychology, 13*, 147-162.

Moll, T., Jordet, G., & Pepping, G.J. (2010). Emotional contagion in soccer penalty shoot-outs: Celebration of individual success is associated with ultimate team success. *Journal of Sports Sciences, 28*(9), 983-992. https://doi.org/10.1080/02640414.2010.484068.

O'Neill, C. (2019). Liverpool players are now allowed to touch 'This is Anfield' sign but only two did ahead of Norwich. *Echo*. www.liverpoolecho.co.uk/sport/football/football-news/liverpool-anfield-klopp-touch-sign-16740748

Pennington, B. (2018, February 15). The ski team that sleeps together wins a lot of gold medals together. *The New York Times*. www.nytimes.com/2018/02/15/sports/olympics/norway-skiing-olympics.html

Potrac, P., & Jones, R. (2009) Power, conflict, and cooperation: Toward a micropolitics of coaching. *Quest, 61*(2), 223-236. https://doi.org/10.1080/00336297.2009.10483612

Prosek, J. 2011. *Army of entrepreneurs: Create an engaged and empowered workforce for exceptional business growth*. Amacom.

Railo, W. (1983). *Best når det gjelder* [Best when it counts]. Norges Idrettsforbund.

Salas, E., Sims, D.E., & Burke, C.S. (2005). Is there a "big five" in teamwork? *Small Group Research, 36*, 555-599.

Schein, E. (1999). *The corporate culture survival guide*. Jossey-Bass.

Schein, E. (2010). *Organizational culture and leadership* (4th ed.). Wiley.

Solomon, C. 2004. *Culture audits: Supporting organizational success*. ASTD Press.

Wagstaff, C.R.D., & Burton-Wylie, S. (2018). Organizational culture in sport: A conceptual, definitional, and methodological review. *Sport and Exercise Psychology Review, 14*, 32-52.

Chapter 13

Arai, S.M. 1997. Empowerment: From the theoretical to the personal. *Journal of Leisurability, 24*(1): 3-11.

Bate, B., & Richards, P. (2011, April 12-13). *Developing decision making in semi-professional footballers*. British Association of Sport and Exercise Conference, University of Chester, Chester, UK.

Burke, V. 2011. Organizing for excellence. In D. Collins, A. Button, and H. Richards, (Eds.), *Performance Psychology: A Practitioners' Guide* (pp. 99-120). Elsevier.

Cannon-Bowers, J.A., Salas, E., & Converse, S.A. (1993). Shared mental models in expert team decision making. In N.J. Castellan, (Ed.), *Individual and group decision making: Current issues* (pp. 221-246). Lawrence Erlbaum.

Caserta, R.J., & Singer, R.N. (2007). The effectiveness of situational awareness learning in response to video tennis match situations. *Journal of Applied Sport Psychology, 19*(2), 125-141.

Eccles, D.W., & Tenenbaum, G. (2004). Why an expert team is more than a team of experts: A social-cognitive conceptualization of team coordination and communication in sport. *Journal of Sport & Exercise Psychology, 26:* 542-560.

Endsley, M.R. (1997). The role of situation awareness in naturalistic decision making. In C.E. Zsambok, & G.A. Klein (Eds.), *Naturalistic decision making* (pp. 269-283). Lawrence Erlbaum.

Gutierrez, L.M. (1999). Working with women of colour: An empowerment perspective. *Social Work, 35*, 149-153.

Hansen, P., & Andersen, S.S. (2014). Coaching elite athletes: How coaches stimulate elite athletes' reflection. *Sports Coaching Review, 3*(1): 17-32.

Kidman, L., & Hadfield, D. (2001). Athlete empowerment. *Sports Coach, 23*(4), 14-15.

Kidman, L. (2001). *Developing decision makers: An empowerment approach to coaching.* Innovative Print Communications Ltd.

Kidman, L., & Hadfield, D. (2001). Athlete empowerment. *Sports Coach, 23*(4), 14-15.

Klein, G.A., Orasanu, J.M., Calderwood R., & Zsambok, C. (1993). Decision making in action: Models and methods. Ablex.

Klein, G., Phillips, J.K., Rall, E.L., & Peluso. D.A. (2007). A data-frame theory of sensemaking. In R. Hoffman (Ed.), *Expertise out of context: Proceedings of the sixth international conference on naturalistic decision making* (pp.113-155). Taylor & Francis.

Klein, G.A. 1993. A recognition-primed decision (RPD) model of rapid decision making. In G. Klein, J. Orasanu, R. Calderwood, and C.E. Zsambok (Eds.), *Decision making in action: Models and methods* (pp. 138-147). Ablex.

Klein, G. 1998. *Source of power: How people make decisions.* MIT Press.

Klein, G. 2008. Naturalistic decision making. *Human Factors: The Journal of the Human Factors and Ergonomics Society, 50*(3), 456-460.

Merola, T., & Richards, P. (2010, September). *Developing decision making skill in youth footballers.* British Association of Sport and Exercise Conference, University of Aberystwyth, Aberystwyth, Wales.

McCauley, C. 1989. The nature of social influence in groupthink: compliance and internalization. *Journal of Personality and Social Psychology. 57*(2), 250-260. https://doi.org/10.1037/0022-3514.57.2.250

Railo, W. (1983). *Best når det gjelder* [Best when it counts]. Norges Idrettsforbund.

Richards, P., Mascarenhas, D., & Collins, C. (2009). Implementing reflective practice approaches with elite team athletes: Parameters of success. *International Journal of Reflective Practice, 10*(3), 353-363.

Richards, P., & Collins, D. (2020, February 7). Commentary: Team cognition in sport: How current insights into how teamwork is achieved in naturalistic settings can lead to simulation studies. *Frontiers in Psychology.* https://doi.org/10.3389/fpsyg.2020.00081

Richards, P. (2020, September). *Understanding Decision-making and operationalising shared mental models in Olympic sports* [Virtual presentation]. EIS Performance Team, English Institute of Sport, Manchester, UK.

Richards, P. (2005, June). *Empowering the decision-making process in the competitive sport environment through using reflective practice.* [Paper presentation] *Can performance intelligence be taught?* 4th Carfax International Conference on Reflective Practice, Gloucester, UK.

Richards, P., Collins, D., & Mascarenhas, D.R.D. (2016). Developing team decision making: A holistic framework integrating both on-field and off-field pedagogical coaching processes. *Sports Coaching Review, 6*(1), 57-75.

Richards, P., Collins, D., & Mascarenhas, D.R.D. (2012). Developing rapid high-pressure team decision-making skills. The integration of slow deliberate reflective learning within the competitive performance environment: A case study of elite netball. *Reflective Practice, 13*(3), 407-424.

Ross, K.G., Battaglia, D.A., Phillips, J.K., Domeshek, E.A., & Lussier, J.W. (2003) *Mental models underlying tactical thinking skills.* Interservice/Industry Training, Simulation, and Education Conference. Orlando, Florida.

Salas, E., Cannon-Bowers, J.A., & Johnston, J.H. (1997). How can you turn a team of experts into an expert team? Emerging training strategies. In C.E. Zsambok & G.A. Klein (Eds.), *Naturalistic decision making* (pp. 359-370). Lawrence Erlbaum.

Westbrook, L. (2006) Mental models: A theoretical overview and preliminary study. *Journal of Information Science, 32,* 563-579.

Sorensen, M., & Roberts, G.C. (2005) Goal orientations and empowerment of individuals with a disability in sports context. *European Bulletin of adapted physical Activity, 2*(2), 1-8.

Williams, A.M. (2009). Perceiving the intentions of others: How do skilled performers make anticipation judgments? In M. Raab, J.G. Johnson, & H.R. Heekeren (Eds.), *Progress in brain research* (pp. 73-83). Elsevier.

Chapter 14

Alfano, H., & Collins, D. (2021). Good practice in sport science and medicine support: Practitioners' perspectives on quality, pressure and support. *Managing Sport and Leisure, 38,* 1-39.

Baumeister, R.F. (1998). The self. In D.T. Gilbert, S.T. Fiske, & G. Lindzey (Eds.), *The handbook of social psychology* (4th ed., pp. 680-740). McGraw-Hill.

Bray, S.R., & Brawley, L.R. (2002). Role efficacy, role clarity, and role performance effectiveness. *Small Group Research, 33*(2), 233-253.

Burke, V. (2011). Organizing for excellence. In D. Collins, A. Button, & H. Richards (Eds.), *Performance Psychology: A Practitioner's Guide* (pp 99-120). Elsevier.

Collins, D., & Collins, L. (2020). Developing coaches' professional judgement and decision making: Using the 'Big 5'. *Journal of Sports Sciences, 39*(1), 115-119. doi.org/10.1080/02640414.2020.1809053

Collins, D., Willmott, T., & Collins, L. (2018). Periodisation and self-regulation in action sports: Coping with the emotional load. *Frontiers in Psychology, 9.* https://doi.org/10.3389/fpsyg.2018.01652

Collins, D., & Taylor, J. (in press, 2019). The Athlete in the Wider Sport Environment. In Davis, Keegan, & Jowett, *Social Psychology of Sport (2nd Edition).* Chapter 26.

Henriksen, K., & Stambulova, N. (2017). Creating optimal environments for talent development: A holistic ecological approach. In J. Baker, S. Cobley, J. Schorer, N. Wattie (Eds.), *Routledge handbook of talent identification and development in sport* (pp. 271-284). Routledge.

Henriksen, K., Stamboulova, N., & Roessier, K.K. (2010). Successful talent development in track and field: Considering the role of environment. *Scandinavian Journal of Medicine and Science in Sports, 20*(2), 122-132. https://doi.org/10.1111/j.1600-0838.2010.01187.x

Jowett, S., & Chaundy, V. (2004). An investigation into the impact of coach leadership and coach–athlete relationship on group cohesion. *Group Dynamics: Theory, Research, and Practice, 8,* 302-311.

Jowett, S., Kanakoglou, K., & Passmore, J. (2012). The application of the 3+1Cs relationship model in executive coaching. *Consulting Psychology Journal Practice and Research, 64*(3), 183-197. https://doi.org/10.1037/a0030316

Kahn, W.A. (1990). Psychological conditions of personal engagement and disengagement at work. *Academy of Management Journal, 33*(4): 692-724. https://doi.org/10.2307/256287

Lickel B., Kushlev, A.K., Savalei, V., Matta, S., & Schmader, T. (2014). Shame and the motivation to change the self. *Emotion, 14*(6), 1049-1061. doi.org/10.1037/a0038235

MacNamara, Á., & Collins, D. (2010). The role of psychological characteristics in managing the transition to university. *Psychology of Sport and Exercise, 11,* 353-362.

Martindale, R. J., Collins, D., & Daubney, J. (2005). Talent development: A guide for practice and research within sport. *Quest, 57*(4), 353-375. https://doi.org/10.1080/00336297.2005.10491862

Mouratides, A., Vansteenkiste, M., Lens,W., & Sideridis, G. (2008). The motivating role of positive feedback in sport and physical education: Evidence for a motivational model. *Journal of Sport & Exercise Psychology*, *30*, 240-268.

Pankhurst, A., Collins, D., & MacNamara, A. (2013). Talent development: Linking the stakeholders to the process. *Journal of Sports Sciences*, *31*(4), 370-380. https://doi.org/10.1080/02640414.2012.733821

Peters, T., & Waterman, R. (1982). *In search of excellence*. Harper & Row.

Sieber, J., & Ziegler, R. (2019). Group polarization revisited: A processing effort account. *Personality and Social Psychology Bulletin*, *45*(10), 1482-1498. https://doi.org/10.1177/0146167219833389

Storm, L.K., Henriksen, K., Larsen, C.H., & Christensen, M.K. (2014). Influential relationships as contexts of learning and becoming elite: Athletes' retrospective interpretations. *International Journal of Sports Science and Coaching*, *9*(6), 1341-1356. https://doi.org/10.1260/1747-9541.9.6.1341

Stoszkowski, J., & Collins, D. (2012). Communities of practice, social learning and networks: Exploiting the social side of coach development. *Sport, Education and Society*, 773-778. https://doi.org/10.1080/13573322.2012.692671

Taylor, J., & Collins, D. (2020). The highs and the lows: Exploring the nature of optimally impactful development experiences on the talent pathway. *The Sport Psychologist*, 34(4), 319-328.

Tuckman, B.W. (1965) Developmental sequence in small groups. *Psychological Bulletin*, *63*(6), 384-399.

Webb, V., Collins, D., & Cruickshank, A. (2016). Aligning the talent pathway: Exploring the role and mechanisms of coherence in development. *Journal of Sports Sciences, 34*(19), 1799-1807.

Chapter 15

Alfano, H., & Collins, D. (2020). Good practice delivery in sport science and medicine support: Perceptions of experienced sport leaders and practitioners. *Managing Sport and Leisure*, *26*(3), 145-160. https://doi.org/10.1080/23750472.2020.1727768

Alfano, H., & Collins, D. (2021). Good practice in sport science and medicine support: Practitioners' perspectives on quality, pressure and support. *Managing Sport and Leisure*. DOI: 10.1080/23750472.2021.1918019

Carson, H.J., Collins, D., & Jones, B. (2014). A case study of technical change and rehabilitation: Intervention design and interdisciplinary team interaction. *International Journal of Sport Psychology, 45*(1), 57-78.

Cole, J., & Martin, A.J. (2018). Developing a winning sport team culture: Organizational culture in theory and practice. *Sport in Society, 21*(8), 1204-1222. https://doi.org/10.1080/17430437.2018.1442197

Collins, D., Willmott, T., & Collins, L. (2018). Periodization and self-regulation in action sports: Coping with the emotional load. *Frontiers in Psychology, 9*, 1652. https://doi.org/10.3389/fpsyg.2018.01652

Cruickshank, A., & Collins, D. (2012). Culture change in elite sport performance teams: Examining and advancing effectiveness in the new era. *Journal of Applied Sport Psychology, 24*(3), 338-355. https://doi.org/10.1080/10413200.2011.650819

Dreyfus S.E., & Dreyfus, H.L. (1980). A five-stage model of the mental activities involved in directed skill acquisition. Operations Research Center, University of California.

Eys, M., Beauchamp, M., & Bray, S. (2006). A review of team roles in sport. In S. Hanton & S. Mellalieu (Eds.), *Literature reviews in sport psychology*, 227-256. Nova Science.

Fletcher, J.D., & Sottilare, R.A. (2018). Shared mental models in support of adaptive instruction for teams using the GIFT tutoring architecture. *International Journal of Artificial Intelligence in Education, 28*, 265-285. https://doi.org/10.1007/s40593-017-0147-y

Floren, L.C., Donesky, D-A., Whitaker, E., Irby, D.M., Ten Cate, O., & O'Brien, B. (2018). Are we on the same page? Shared mental models to support clinical teamwork among health professions learners: A scoping review. *Academic Medicine, 93*(3), 498-509. https://doi.org/10.1097/ACM.0000000000002019

Grace, S.M., Rich, J., Chin, W., & Rodriguez, H.P. (2016). Implementing interdisciplinary teams does not necessarily improve primary care practice climate. *American Journal of Medical Quality, 31*(1), 5-11. https://doi.org/10.1177/1062860614550333

Ingham, S. (2016). *How to support a champion: The art of applying science to the elite athlete.* Simply Said.

Jonker, C.M., van Riemsdijk, M.B., & Vermeulen, B. (2011). Shared mental models. In M. De Vos, N. Fornara, J.V. Pitt, & J. Vouros (Eds.), *Coordination, organizations, institutions, and norms in agent systems VI: COIN 2010. Lecture Notes in Computer Science*, 6541. Springer.

Jonker C.M., van Riemsdijk M.B., Vermeulen B. (2011) Shared Mental Models. In: De Vos M., Fornara N., Pitt J.V., Vouros G. (eds) Coordination, Organizations, Institutions, and Norms in Agent Systems VI. COIN 2010. Lecture Notes in Computer Science, vol 6541. Springer, Berlin, Heidelberg. https://doi.org/10.1007/978-3-642-21268-0_8

Jowett, S. (2017). Coaching effectiveness: The coach–athlete relationship at its heart. *Current Opinion in Psychology*, *16*, 154-158

Jowett, S., & Cockerill, I.M. (2003). Olympic medalists' perspective of the athlete–coach relationship. *Psychology of Sport and Exercise, 4*, 313-331. https://doi.org/10.1016/S1469-0292(02)00011-0

Kramer, R. (2010). Collective trust within organizations: Conceptual foundations and empirical insights. *Corporate Reputation Review, 13*, 82-97. https://doi.org/10.1057/crr.2010.9

O'Connor, M., Fisher, C., & Guilfoyle, A. (2013). Interdisciplinary teams in palliative care: A critical reflection. *International Journal of Palliative Nursing, 12*(3). https://doi.org/10.12968/ijpn.2006.12.3.20698

Reid, C., Stewart, E., & Thorne, G. (2004). Multidisciplinary sport science teams in elite sport: Comprehensive servicing or conflict and confusion? *Sport Psychologist, 18*, 204-217.

Tuckman, B.W. (1965). Developmental sequence in small groups. *Psychological Bulletin, 63*(6), 384-399. https://doi.org/10.1037/h0022100

Youngson, J.W. (2018). *Moving from multidisciplinary to interdisciplinary support teams in high performance sport: A strength and conditioning perspective* [unpublished master's thesis]. University of Canberra.

Chapter 16

Bertollo, M., Bortoli, L., Gramaccioni, G., Hanin, Y., Comani, S., & Robazza, C. (2013). Behavioural and psychophysiological correlates of athletic performance: A test of the multi-action plan model. *Applied Psychophysiology and Biofeedback, 38*(2): 91-99. https://doi.org/10.1007/s10484-013-9211-z

Bertollo, M., Berchicci, M., & di Fronso, S. (2021). Mind-body interaction in sport psychophysiology. In E. Filho & I. Basevitch (Eds.), *The unknown in sport, exercise, and performance psychology: Research questions to move the field forward.* Oxford University Press.

Bertollo, M., di Fronso, S., Conforto, S., Schmid, M., Bortoli, L., Comani, S., & Robazza, C. (2016). Proficient brain for optimal performance: The MAP model perspective. *PeerJ, 4*, e2082. https://doi.org/10.7717/peerj.2082

Bertollo, M., di Fronso, S., Filho, E., Lamberti, V., Ripari, P., Reis, V.M., Comani, S., Bortoli, L., & Robazza, C. (2015). To focus or not to focus: Is attention on the core components of action beneficial for cycling performance? *The Sport Psychologist, 29*(2), 110-119. https://doi.org/10.1123/tsp.2014-0046

Bertollo, M., Doppelmayr, M., & Robazza, C. (2020). Using brain technology in practice. In G. Tenembaum & R. Eklund (Eds.), *Handbook of sport psychology* (4th ed., pp. 666-693). Wiley & Blackwell.

Bortoli, L., Bertollo, M., Hanin, Y., & Robazza, C. (2012). Striving for excellence: A multi-action plan intervention model for shooters. *Psychology of Sport and Exercise, 13*(5), 693-701. https://doi.org/10.1016/j.psychsport.2012.04.006

Carson, H.J., Robazza, C., Collins, D., Toner, J., & Bertollo, M. (2021). Optimizing performance in sport: An action-based perspective. In M. Bertollo, E. Filho, and P.C. Terry (Eds.), *Advancements in mental skills training* (pp. 15-27). Routledge.

Carson, H.J., & Collins, D. (2016a). Implementing the five-A model of technical refinement: Key roles of the sport psychologist. *Journal of Applied Sport Psychology, 28*(4), 392-409. https://doi.org/10.1080/10413200.2016.1162224

Carson, H.J., & Collins, D. (2016b). The fourth dimension: A motoric perspective on the anxiety–performance relationship. *International Review of Sport and Exercise Psychology, 9*(1), 1-21. https://doi.org/10.1080/1750984X.2015.1072231

Carson, H.J., & Collins, D. (2014). Effective skill refinement: Focusing on process to ensure outcome. *Central European Journal of Sport Sciences and Medicine, 7*, 5-21.

Carson, H.J., & Collins, D. (2011). Refining and regaining skills in fixation/diversification stage performers: The five-A model. *International Review of Sport and Exercise Psychology, 4*(2), 146-167. https://doi.org/10.1080/1750984X.2011.613682

Christie, S., Bertollo, M., & Werthner, P. (2020). The effect of an integrated neurofeedback and biofeedback training intervention on ice hockey shooting performance. *Journal of Sport and Exercise Psychology, 42*(1), 34-47. https://doi.org/10.1123/jsep.2018-0278

Collins, D., Burke, V., Martindale, A., & Cruickshank, A. (2015). The illusion of competency versus the desirability of expertise: Seeking a common standard for support professions in sport. *Sports Medicine, 45*, 1-7. https://doi.org/10.1007/s40279-014-0251-1

Davids, K., Araújo, D., Seifert, L., & Orth, D. (2015). Expert performance in sport: An ecological dynamics perspective. In J. Baker & F. Farrow (Eds.), *Routledge handbook of sport expertise* (pp. 130-135). Routledge.

di Fronso, S., Werthner, P., Christie, S., & Bertollo, M. (2020). Using technology for self-regulation in sport. In C. Ruiz & C. Robazza (Eds.), *Feelings in sport: Theory, research, and practical implications for performance and well-being* (pp. 178-186). Routledge.

di Fronso, S., Tamburro, G., Robazza, C., Bortoli, L., Comani, S., & Bertollo, M. (2018). Focusing attention on muscle exertion increases EEG coherence in an endurance cycling task. *Frontiers in Psychology, 9*, 1249. https://doi.org/10.3389/fpsyg.2018.01249

di Fronso, S.D., Robazza, C., Bortoli, L., & Bertollo, M. (2017). Performance optimization in sport: A psychophysiological approach. *Motriz: Revista de Educação Física, 23*(4). https://doi.org/10.1590/S1980-6574201700040001

Filho, E., di Fronso, S., Mazzoni, C., Robazza, C., Bortoli, L., & Bertollo, M. (2015). My heart is racing! Psychophysiological dynamics of skilled racecar drivers. *Journal of Sports Sciences, 33*(9), 945-959. https://doi.org/10.1080/02640414.2014.977940

Frank, C., Linstromberg, G.L., Hennig, L., Heinen, T., & Schack, T. (2018). Team action imagery and team cognition: Imagery of game situations and required team actions promotes a functional structure in players' representations of team-level tactics. *Journal of Sport and Exercise Psychology, 40*(1), 20-30. https://doi.org/10.1123/jsep.2017-0088

Frank, C., Land, W.M., & Schack, T. (2016). Perceptual-cognitive changes during motor learning: The influence of mental and physical practice on mental representation, gaze behavior, and performance of a complex action. *Frontiers in Psychology, 6*, 1981. https://doi.org/10.3389/fpsyg.2015.01981

Gröpel, P., & Mesagno, C. (2019). Choking interventions in sports: A systematic review. *International Review of Sport and Exercise Psychology, 12*(1), 176-201. https://doi.org/10.1080/1750984X.2017.1408134

Hanin, Y., Hanina, M., Šašek, H., & Kobilšek, A. (2016). Emotion-centered and action-centered coping in elite sport: Task execution design approach. *International Journal of Sports Science & Coaching, 11*(4), 566-588. https://doi.org/10.1177/1747954116654782

Hanin, Y., & Hanina, M. (2009a). Optimization of performance in top-level athletes: An action-focused coping approach. *International Journal of Sports Science & Coaching, 4*(1), 47-57. https://doi.org/10.1260/1747-9541.4.1.47

Hanin, Y., & Hanina, M. (2009b). Optimization of performance in top-level athletes: An action-focused coping approach. A response to commentaries. *International Journal of Sports Science & Coaching, 4*(1), 83-91. https://doi.org/10.1260/1747-9541.4.1.47

Harmison, R.J., & Casto, K.V. (2012). *Optimal performance: Elite level performance in "the zone"*. In S. Murphy (Ed.), *The Oxford handbook of sport and performance psychology,* (pp. 707-724). Oxford University Press.

Kamata, A., Tenenbaum, G., & Hanin, Y.L. (2002). Individual zone of optimal functioning (IZOF): A probabilistic estimation. *Journal of Sport and Exercise Psychology, 24*(2), 189-208. https://doi.org/10.1123/jsep.24.2.189

Kimiecik, J.C., & Jackson, S.A. (2002). Optimal experience in sport: A flow perspective. In T.S. Horn (Ed.), *Advances in sport psychology* (pp. 501-527). Human Kinetics.

Land, W., Volchenkov, D., Bläsing, B.E., & Schack, T. (2013). From action representation to action execution: Exploring the links between cognitive and biomechanical levels of motor control. *Frontiers in Computational Neuroscience, 7*, 127. https://doi.org/10.3389/fncom.2013.00127

Latash, M.L., Levin, M.F., Scholz, J.P., & Schöner, G. (2010). Motor control theories and their applications. *Medicina, 46*(6), 382.

Lex, H., Essig, K., Knoblauch, A., & Schack, T. (2015). Cognitive representations and cognitive processing of team-specific tactics in soccer. *PloS One, 10*(2), e0118219. https://doi.org/10.1371/journal.pone.0118219

MacPherson, A.C., Collins, D., & Morriss, C. (2008). Is what you think what you get: Optimizing mental focus for technical performance. *The Sport Psychologist, 22*, 304-315.

Nitsch, J.R., & Hackfort, D. (2016). Theoretical framework of performance psychology: An action theory perspective. In M. Raab, B. Lobinger, S. Hoffmann, A. Pizzera, & S. Laborde (Eds.), *Performance psychology: Perception, action, cognition, and emotion,* (pp. 11-29). Academic Press.

Robazza, C., Bertollo, M., Filho, E., Hanin, Y., & Bortoli, L. (2016). Perceived control and hedonic tone dynamics during performance in elite shooters. *Research Quarterly for Exercise and Sport, 87*(3), 284-294. https://doi.org/10.1080/02701367.2016.1185081

Ruiz, M.C., Bortoli, L., & Robazza, C. (2020). The Multi-States (MuSt) theory for emotion- and action-regulation in sports. In M.C. Ruiz & C. Robazza (Eds.), *Feelings in sport: Theory, research, and practical implications for performance and well-being* (pp. 3-17). Routledge.

Schack, T. (2012). Measuring mental representations. In G. Tenenbaum, R. C. Eklund, & A. Kamata (Eds.), *Measurement in sport and exercise psychology* (pp. 203–214). Human Kinetics. Schack, T., & Frank, C. (2020). Mental representation and the cognitive architecture of skilled action. *Review of Philosophy and Psychology*, 1-20. https://doi.org/10.1007/s13164-020-00485-7

Scholz, J.P., and G. Schöner. 1999. The uncontrolled manifold concept: Identifying control variables for a functional task. *Experimental brain research, 126*(3), 289-306.

Siekanska, M., Bondar, Z., di Fronso, S., Blecharz, J., & Bertollo, M. (2021). Integrating technology in psychological skills training for performance optimization in elite athletes: A systematic review. *Psychology of Sport and Exercise*, 57. doi:10.1016/j.psychsport.2021.102008; https://doi.org/10.1016/j.psychsport.2021.102008

Swann, C., Keegan, R., Crust, L., & Piggott, D. (2016). Psychological states underlying excellent performance in professional golfers: "Letting it happen" vs. "making it happen". *Psychology of Sport and Exercise, 23*, 101-113. https://doi.org/10.1016/j.psychsport.2015.10.008

Wang, K.P., Cheng, M.Y., Chen, T.T., Chang, Y.K., Huang, C.J., Hung, T.M., Feng, J. & Ren, J. (2019). Experts' successful psychomotor performance was characterized by effective switch of motor and attentional control. *Psychology of Sport and Exercise, 43*, 374-379. https://doi.org/10.1016/j.psychsport.2019.04.006

Winter, S., & Collins, D. (2015). Why do we do, what we do? *Journal of Applied Sport Psychology, 27*(1), 35-51. https://doi.org/10.1080/10413200.2014.941511

Chapter 17

Abbott, A., & Collins, D. (2004). Eliminating the dichotomy between theory and practice in talent identification and development: Considering the role of psychology. *Journal of Sports Sciences, 22*(5), 395-408.

Allen, S.V., Vandenbogaerde, T.J., & Hopkins, W.G. (2014). Career performance trajectories of Olympic swimmers: Benchmarks for talent development. *European Journal of Sport Science, 14*, 643-651. https://doi.org/10.1080/17461391.2014.893020

Bailey, R. (2007). Talent development and the luck problem. *Sport Ethics and Philosophy, 1*(3), 367-377.

Bailey, R., & Collins, D. (2013). The standard module of talent development and its discontents. *Kinesiology Review, 2*, 248-259.

Breitbach, S., Tug, S., & Simon, P. (2014). Conventional and genetic talent identification in sports: Will recent developments trace talent? *Sports Medicine, 44*, 1489-1503.

Burnette, J.L., O'Boyle, E., VanEpps, E.M., Pollack, J.M., & Finkel, J.E. (2013). Mindsets matter: A meta-analytic review of implicit theories and self-regulation. *Psychological Bulletin, 139*(3), 655-701.

Cobley, S. (2009). Annual age-grouping and athlete development: A meta-analytical review of relative age effects in sport. *Sports Medicine, 39*, 235-256.

Collins, D, Bailey, R., Ford, P., MacNamara, A., Toms, M & Pearce, P. (2011). Three worlds: New directions in participant development in sport and physical activity. *Sport, Education and Society, 17*(2), 225-243.

Collins, D., MacNamara, Á., & McCarthy, N. (2016). Super champions, champions, and almosts: Important differences and commonalities on the rocky road. *Frontiers in Psychology, 6*, 2009.

Collins, R., Collins, D., MacNamara, A, & Jones, M. (2014). Change of plans: An evaluation of the effectiveness and underlying mechanisms of successful talent transfer. *Journal of Sports Sciences, 32*(17), 1621-1630.

Coutinho, P., Mesquita, I., & Fonseca, A.M. (2016). Talent development in sport: A critical review of pathways to expert performance. *International Journal of Sports Science & Coaching, 11*(2), 279-293.

Côté, J., & Hay, J. (2002). Children's involvement in sport: A developmental perspective. In Silva, J., & Stevens, D. (Eds.), *Psychological foundations of sport (*pp 484-502). Allyn & Bacon.

Credé, M., Tynan, M. C., & Harms, P. D. (2017). Much ado about Grit: A meta-analytic synthesis of the Grit literature. *Journal of Personality and Social Psychology, 113*(3), 492-511.

Dweck, C.S. (2017). *Mindset: How you can fulfil your potential.* Random House.

Duckworth, A.L., & Quinn, P.D. (2009). Development and validation of the Short Grit Scale (GRIT–S). *Journal of Personality Assessment, 91*(2), 166-174.

Duckworth, A.L., Peterson, C., Matthews, M.D., & Kelly, D.R. (2007). Grit: Perseverance and passion for long-term goals. *Journal of Personality and Social Psychology, 92*(6), 1087-101.

Faber, I.R., Nijhuis-Van Der Sanden, M.W.G., Elferink-Gemser, M.T., & Oosterveld, F.G.J. (2015). The Dutch motor skills assessment as tool for talent development in table tennis: A reproducibility and validity study. *Journal of Sports Sciences, 33*, 1149-1158.

Haimovitz, K., & Dweck, C. S. (2016). What predicts children's fixed and growth intelligence mindsets? Not their parents' views of intelligence but their parents' views of failure. *Psychological Science*, 27, 859– 869.

Hill, A., MacNamara, Á., & Collins, D. (2019). Development and initial validation of the Psychological Characteristics of Developing Excellence Questionnaire version 2 (PCDEQ2). *European journal of sport science, 19*(4), 517-528.

Höner, O., Votteler, A., Schmid, M., Schultz, F., & Roth, K. (2015). Psychometric properties of the motor diagnostics in the German football talent identification and development program. *Journal of Sports Sciences, 33*, 145-159.

Kamin, S., Richards, H., & Collins, D. (2007). Influences on the talent development process of non-classical musicians: Psychological, social and environmental influences. Music Education Research, *9*, 449-468.

Kearney, P.E., & Hayes, P.R. (2018). Excelling at youth level in competitive track and field athletics is not a prerequisite for later success. *Journal of sports sciences*, 36(21):2502-2509 1-8.

Louzada, F., Maiorano, A.C., & Ara, A. (2016). ISports: A web-oriented expert system for talent identification in soccer. *Expert Systems with Applications, 44*, 400-412.

MacNamara, Á., Button, A., and Collins, D. (2010a). The role of psychological characteristics in facilitating the pathway to elite performance. Part 1: identifying mental skills and behaviours. *The Sport Psychologist.* 24, 52-73.

MacNamara, Á., Button, A., and Collins, D. (2010b). The role of psychological characteristics in facilitating the pathway to elite performance. Part 2: Examining environmental and stage related differences in skills and behaviours. *The Sport Psychologist*, 24, 74-96.

MacNamara, Á. Collins, D., Bailey, R., Ford, P., Toms, M., & Pearce, G. (2011). Promoting lifelong physical activity and high level performance: Realising an achievable aim for physical education. *Physical Education and Sport Pedagogy, 16*(3), 265-278.

Maddi, S.R., Matthews, M.D., Kelly, D.R., Villarreal, B., & White, M. (2012). The role of hardiness and grit in predicting performance and retention of USMA cadets. *Military Psychology, 24*, 19-28.

Mann, D.L., Dehghansai, N., & Baker, J. (2017). Searching for the elusive gift: Advances in talent identification in sport. *Current Opinion in Psychology, 16*, 128-133.

McCall, A., Fanchini, M., & Coutts, A.J. (2017). Prediction: The modern-day sport-science And sports-medicine "quest for the holy grail". *International Journal of Sports Physiology and Performance, 12*, 704-706.

Miller, P., Cronin, C., & Baker, G. (2015). Nurture, nature and some very dubious social skills: An interpretative phenomenological analysis of talent identification practices in elite English youth soccer. *Qualitative Research in Sport, Exercise and Health, 7*(5), 642-662.

Pinder, R., Davids, K., Renshaw, I., & Arau´jo, D. (2011). Representative learning design and functionality of research and practice in sport. *Journal of Sport & Exercise Psychology, 33*(1), 146-155.

Simonton, D.K. (2001). Talent development as a multidimensional, multiplicative, and dynamic process. *Current Directions in Psychological Science*, *10*, 39-43.

Subotnik, R.F., Olszewski-Kubilius, P., & Worrell, F.C. (Eds.). (2019). High performance: The central psychological mechanism for talent development. In R.F. Subotnik, P. Olszewski-Kubilius, & F.C. Worrell (Eds.), *The psychology of high performance: Developing human potential into domain-specific talent* (pp. 7-20). American Psychological Association.

Taylor, J., & Collins, D. (2019). Shoulda, Coulda, Didnae: Why Don't High-Potential Players Make it? *The Sport Psychologist*, *33*(2), 85-96.

Toering, T., Elferink-Gemser, M., Jordet, G., Jorna, C., Pepping, G-J., & Visscher, C. (2011). Self-regulation of practice behavior among elite youth soccer players: An exploratory observation study. *Journal of Applied Sport Psychology*, 23, 110-128.

Turnnidge, J., Hancock, D.J., & Côté, J. (2014). The influence of birth date and place of development on youth sport participation. *Scandinavian Journal of Medicine and Science in Sports*: *24*, 461-468.

Vaeyens, R., Güllich, A., Warr C.R., & Philippaerts, R. (2009). Talent identification and promotion programs of Olympic athletes. *Journal of Sports Sciences, 27*, 1367-1380.

Van Yperen, N. (2009). Why some make it and others do not: Identifying psychological factors that predict career success in professional adult soccer. *The Sport Psychologist*, *23*, 317-329.

Williams, A.M., Ford, P., & Drust, B. (2020). Talent identification and development in soccer since the millennium. *Journal of Sports Sciences*, *38*(11-12), 1199-1210.

Williams, G., & MacNamara, Á. (2020). I didn't make it but . . . Examining athletes' experiences of deselection. *Frontiers in Sport and Active Living, 2, 24*.

Yeager, D., & Dweck, C.S. (2012). Mindsets that promote resilience: When students believe that personal characteristics can be developed. *Educational Psychologist*, *47*(4), 302-314.

Chapter 18

Acharya, J., & Morris, T. (2014). Psyching up and psyching down. In A.G. Papaioannou & D. Hackfort (Eds.), *Routledge companion to sport and exercise psychology: Global perspectives and fundamental concepts* (pp. 386-401). Routledge.

Balague, G. (2000). Periodization of psychological skills training. *Journal of Science and Medicine in Sport, 3*(3), 230-237.

Bar-Eli, M., (2017). *Boost! How the psychology of sport can enhance your performance in management and work*. Oxford University Press.

Beauchamp, M.K., Harvey, R.H., & Beauchamp, P.H. (2012). An integrated biofeedback and psychological skills training program for Canada's Olympic short-track speed skating team. *Journal of Clinical Sport Psychology, 6*, 67-84.

Birrer, D., & Morgan, G. (2010). Psychological skills training as a way to enhance an athlete's performance in high-intensity sports. *Scandinavian Journal of Medicine & Science in Sports, 20*(2), 78-87.

Blumenstein, B., Lidor, R., & Tenenbaum, G. (2005). Periodization and planning of psychological preparation in elite combat sport programs: The case of judo. *International Journal of Sport and Exercise Psychology, 3*, 7-25.

Blumenstein, B., Lidor, R., Tenenbaum, G. (Eds.). (2007). *Psychology of sport training*. Meyer & Meyer Sport.

Blumenstein, B., & Orbach, I. (2012a). *Mental practice in sport: Twenty case studies*. Nova Science.

Blumenstein, B., & Orbach, I. (2012b). *Psychological skills in sport: Training and application*. Nova Science.

Blumenstein, B., & Orbach, I. (2014a). *Biofeedback for sport and performance enhancement.* Oxford Handbooks Online. https://doi.org/10.1093/oxfordhb/9780199935291.013.001

Blumenstein, B., & Orbach, I. (2014b). Development of psychological preparation for football referees: Pilot study. *Sport Science Review, XXIII*(3-4), 113-126.

Blumenstein, B., & Orbach, I. (2015). Psychological preparation for Paralympic athletes: A preliminary study. *Adapted Physical Activity Quarterly, 32,* 241-255.

Blumenstein, B., & Orbach, I. (2018). Periodization of psychological preparation within the training process. *International Journal of Sport and Exercise Psychology, 18*(1), 1-11. https://doi.org/10.108/1612197X.2018.1478872

Bompa, T., Blumenstein, B., Hoffmann, J., Howell, S., & Orbach, I. (2019). *Integrated periodization in sports training & athletic development: Combining training methodology, sport psychology, and nutrition to optimize performance.* Meyer & Meyer Sport.

Bompa, T., & Buzzichelli, C. (2019). *Periodization: Theory and methodology of training* (6th ed.). Human Kinetics.

Burke, K.L. (2006). Using sport psychology to improve basketball performance. In J. Dosil (Ed.), *The sport psychologist's handbook: A guide for sport-specific performance enhancement* (pp. 121-138). Wiley.

Collins, D., & McPherson, A. (2006). The psychophysiology of biofeedback and sport performance. In E. Acevedo & P. Ekkekakis (Eds.), *Psychobiology of physical activity* (pp. 241-250). Human Kinetics.

Cotterill, S. (2010). Pre-performance routines in sport: Current understanding and future directions. *International Review of Sport and Exercise Psychology, 3*(2), 132-153.

Dosil, J. (Ed.) (2006). Psychological intervention with football (soccer) teams. In J. Dosil (Ed.), *The sport psychologist's handbook: A guide for sport-specific performance enhancement* (pp. 139-158). Wiley.

Elbe, A.M., & Kellmann, M. (2007). Recovery following training and competition. In B. Blumenstein, R. Lidor, & G. Tenenbaum (Eds.), *Psychology of sport training* (pp. 162-185). Meyer & Meyer Sport.

Feltz, D., & Oncu, E. (2014). Self-confidence and self-efficacy. In A.G. Papaioannou & D. Hackfort (Eds.), *Routledge companion to sport and exercise psychology: Global perspectives and fundamental concepts* (pp. 417-429). Routledge.

Freitas, S., Dias, C., & Fonseca, A. (2013). What do coaches think about psychological skills training in soccer? A study with coaches of elite Portuguese teams. *International Journal of Sport Science, 3*(3), 81-91.

Frey, M., Laguna, P.L., & Ravizza, K. (2003). Collegiate athletes' mental skill use and perceptions of success: An exploration of the practice and competition settings. *Journal of Applied Sport Psychology, 15,* 115-128.

Gould, D. (2015). Goal setting for peak performance. In J.M. Williams & V. Krane (Eds.), *Applied sport psychology: Personal growth to peak performance* (7th ed., pp. 188-206). McGraw-Hill.

Henschen, K. (2005). Mental practice: Skill oriented. In D. Hackfort, J. Duda, & R. Lidor (Eds.), *Handbook of research in applied sport and exercise psychology: International perspectives* (pp. 19-36). Fitness Information Technology.

Holliday, B., Burton, D., Sun, G., Hammermeister, J., Naylor, S., & Freigang, D. (2008). Building the better mental training mousetrap: Is periodization a more systematic approach to promoting performance excellence? *Journal of Applied Sport Psychology, 20,* 199-219.

Jacobson, E. (1938). *Progressive relaxation.* University of Chicago Press.

Krane, V., & Williams J. (2015). Psychological characteristics of peak performance. In J.M. Williams & V. Krane (Eds.), *Applied sport psychology: Personal growth to peak performance* (7th ed., pp. 159-175). McGraw Hill.

Lidor, R. (2007). Preparatory routines in self-paced events. Do they benefit the skilled athletes? Can they help the beginners? In G. Tenenbaum & R. Eklund (Eds.), *Handbook of sport psychology* (3rd ed., pp. 445-468). Wiley.

Lidor, R., Blumenstein, B., & Tenenbaum, G. (2007a). Periodization and planning of psychological preparation in individual and team sports. In B. Blumenstein, R. Lidor, & G. Tenenbaum (Eds.). *Psychology of sport training* (pp. 137-158). Meyer & Meyer Sport.

Lidor, R., Blumenstein, & Tenenbaum, G. (2007b). Psychological aspects of training programs in European basketball: Conceptualization, periodization and planning. *The Sport Psychologist, 21*(3),353-367.

Lidor, R., Tenenbaum, G., Ziv, G., & Issurin, V. (2016). Achieving expertise in sport: Deliberate practice, adaptation, and periodization of training. *Kinesiology Review, 5*, 129-141. https://doi.org/10.1123/kr.2015-0004

McCrory, P., Cobley, S., & Marchant, P. (2013). The effect of psychological skills training (PST) on self-regulation behavior, self-efficacy and psychological skills use in military pilot-trainees. *Military Psychology, 25*(2), 136-147.

Moran, A. (2010). Concentration/attention. In S.J. Hanrahan & M.B. Andersen (Eds.), *Routledge handbook of applied sport psychology: A comprehensive guide for students and practitioners* (pp. 500-509). Routledge.

Morris, T. (2010). Imagery. In S.J. Hanrahan, & M.B. Andersen (Eds.), *Routledge handbook of applied sport psychology: A comprehensive guide for students and practitioners* (pp. 481-490). Routledge.

Mujika, I., Halson, S., Burke, M., Balague, G., & Farrow, D. (2018). An integrated, multifactorial approach to periodization for optimal performance in individual and team sports. *International Journal of Sport Physiology and Performance, 13*, 538-561.

Pain, M., & Harwood, C. (2004). Knowledge and perceptions of sport psychology within English soccer. *Journal of Sports Science, 22*(9), 813-826.

Ramsey, R., Cumming, J., & Edwards, M. (2008). Exploring a modified conceptualization of imagery direction and golf putting performance. *International Journal of Sport and Exercise psychology, 6*(2), 207-224.

Vealey, R. (2007). Mental skills training in sport. In G. Tenenbaum & R.C. Eklund (Eds.), *Handbook of sport psychology* (3rd ed., pp. 287-309). Wiley.

Vealey, R., & Forlenza, R. (2015). Understanding and using imagery in sport. In J.M. Williams & V. Krane (Eds.). *Applied sport psychology: Personal growth to peak performance* (7th ed., pp. 240-273). McGraw Hill.

Weinberg, R.S., & Gould, D. (2015). *Foundations of sport & exercise psychology* (6th ed.). Human Kinetics.

Weinberg, R.S., & Williams, J.M. (2015). Integrating and implementing a psychological skills training program. In J.M. Williams & V. Krane (Eds.), *Applied sport psychology: Personal growth to peak performance* (7th ed., pp. 329-358). McGraw Hill.

Zaichkowsky, L.D. (2009). A case for a new sport psychology: Applied psychophysiology and Fmri neuroscience. In R.J. Schinke (Ed.), *Contemporary sport psychology* (pp. 21-32). Nova Science.

Chapter 19

Åkesdotter, C., Kenttä, G., Eloranta, S., & Franck, J. (2020). The prevalence of mental health problems in elite athletes. *Journal of Science and Medicine in Sport, 23*(4), 329-335.

Ardern, C.L., Taylor, N.F., Feller, J.A., & Webster, K. E. (2013). A systematic review of the psychological factors associated with returning to sport following injury. *British Journal of Sports Medicine, 47*(17), 1120-1126.

Bartholomew, K.J., Ntoumanis, N., Ryan, R.M., Bosch, J.A., & Thøgersen-Ntoumani, C. (2011). Self-determination theory and diminished functioning: The role of interpersonal control and psychological need thwarting. *Personality and Social Psychology Bulletin, 37*(11), 1459-1473.

Bartholomew, K.J., Ntoumanis, N., & Thøgersen-Ntoumani, C. (2009). A review of controlling motivational strategies from a self-determination theory perspective: Implications for sports coaches. *International Review of Sport and Exercise Psychology, 2*(2), 215-233.

Bartholomew, K., Ntoumanis, N., & Thøgersen-Ntoumani, C. (2010). The controlling interpersonal style in a coaching context: Development and initial validation of a psychometric scale. *Journal of Sport & Exercise Psychology, 32*(2), 193-216.

Bhavsar, N., Bartholomew, K.J., Quested, E., Gucciardi, D.F., Thøgersen-Ntoumani, C., Reeve, J., Sarrazin, P., & Ntoumanis, N. (2020). Measuring psychological need states in sport: Theoretical considerations and a new measure. *Psychology of Sport and Exercise, 47*, Article 101617.

Bhavsar, N., Ntoumanis, N., Quested, E., Gucciardi, D.F., Thøgersen-Ntoumani, C., Ryan, R. M., Reeve, J., Sarrazin, P., & Bartholomew, K.J. (2019). Conceptualizing and testing a new tripartite measure of coach interpersonal behaviors. *Psychology of Sport and Exercise, 44*, 107-120.

Bissett, J.E., Korshus, E., & Hebard, S. (2020). Determining the role of sport coaches in promoting athlete mental health: A narrative review and Delphi approach. *BMJ Open Sport & Exercise Medicine, 6*(1), Article e000676.

Chan, D., & Hagger, M.S. (2012a). Transcontextual development of motivation in sport injury prevention among elite athletes. *Journal of Sport & Exercise Psychology, 34*(5), 661-682.

Chan, D.K.C., & Hagger, M.S. (2012b). Self-determined forms of motivation predict sport injury prevention and rehabilitation intentions. *Journal of Science and Medicine in Sport, 15*(5), 398-406.

Cheon, S.H., Reeve, J., Lee, J., & Lee, Y. (2015). Giving and receiving autonomy support in a high-stakes sport context: A field-based experiment during the 2012 London Paralympic Games. *Psychology of Sport and Exercise, 19*, 59-69.

Cowden, R.G., & Meyer-Weitz, A. (2016). Self-reflection and self-insight predict resilience and stress in competitive tennis. *Social Behavior and Personality: An International Journal, 44*(7), 1133-1150.

Donald, J.N., Bradshaw, E.L., Ryan, R.M., Basarkod, G., Ciarrochi, J., Duineveld, J.J., Guo, J., & Sahdra, B.K. (2020). Mindfulness and its association with varied types of motivation: A systematic review and meta-analysis using self-determination theory. *Personality and Social Psychology Bulletin, 46*(7), 1121-1138.

Fletcher, D., Hanton, S., Mellalieu, S., & Neil, R. (2006). An organisational stress review: Conceptual and theoretical issues in competitive sport. In S. Hanton & S.D. Mellalieu (Eds.), *Literature reviews in sport psychology* (pp. 321-374). Nova Science.

Gagné, M., Ryan, R., & Bargmann, K. (2003). Autonomy support and need satisfaction in the motivation and well-being of gymnasts. *Journal of Applied Sport Psychology, 15*(4), 372-390

Gerber, M., Best, S., Meerstetter, F., Walter, M., Ludyga, S., Brand, S., Bianchi, R., Madigan, D.J., Isoard-Gautheur, S., & Gustafsson, H. (2018). Effects of stress and mental toughness on burnout and depression symptoms: A prospective study with young elite athletes. *Journal of Science and Medicine in Sport, 21*(12), 1200-1205.

Gaudreau, P., & Antl, S. (2008). Athletes' broad dimensions of dispositional perfectionism: Examining changes in life satisfaction and the mediating role of sport-related motivation and coping. *Journal of Sport & Exercise Psychology, 30*(3), 356-382.

Gillet, N., Vallerand, R.J., Amoura, S., & Baldes, B. (2010). Influence of coaches' autonomy support on athletes' motivation and sport performance: A test of the hierarchical model of intrinsic and extrinsic motivation. *Psychology of Sport and Exercise, 11*(2), 155-161.

Hägglund, M., Waldén, M., Magnusson, H., Kristenson, K., Bengtsson, H., & Ekstrand, J. (2013). Injuries affect team performance negatively in professional football: An 11-year follow-up of the UEFA Champions League injury study. *British Journal of Sport Medicine, 47*, 738-742.Haerens, L., Aelterman, N., Van den Berghe, L., De Meyer, J., Soenens, B., & Vansteenkiste, M. (2013). Observing physical education teachers' need-supportive interactions in classroom settings. *Journal of Sport & Exercise Psychology, 35*(1), 3-17.

Henriksen, K., Hansen, J., & Larsen, C. H. (2020). *Mindfulness and acceptance in sport: How to help athletes perform and thrive under pressure.* Routledge.

Ivarsson, A., Johnson, U., Andersen, M.B., Fallby, J., & Altemyr, M. (2015). It pays to pay attention: A mindfulness-based program for injury prevention with soccer players. *Journal of Applied Sport Psychology, 27*(3), 319-334.

Ivarsson, A., Johnson, U., Andersen, M.B., Tranaeus, U., Stenling, A., & Lindwall, M. (2017a). Psychosocial factors and sport injuries: Meta-analyses for prediction and prevention. *Sports Medicine, 47*, 353-365.

Ivarsson, A., Tranaeus, U., Johnson, U., & Stenling, A. (2017b). Negative psychological responses of injury and rehabilitation adherence effects on return to play in competitive athletes: A systematic review and meta-analysis. *Open Access Journal of Sports Medicine, 8*, 27-32.

Knittle, K., Heino, M., Marques, M.M., Stenius, M., Beattie, M., Ehbrecht, F., Hagger, M.S., Hardeman, W., & Hankonen, N. (2020). The compendium of self-enactable techniques to change and self-manage motivation and behaviour v. 1.0. *Nature Human Behaviour, 4*(2), 215-223.

Kölling, S., Schaffran, P., Bibbey, A., Drew, M., Raysmith, B., Nassi, A., & Kellmann, M. (2020). Validation of the acute recovery and stress scale (ARSS) and the short recovery and stress scale (SRSS) in three English-speaking regions. *Journal of Sports Sciences, 38*(2), 130-139.

Kuettel, A., & Larsen, C. H. (2020). Risk and protective factors for mental health in elite athletes: A scoping review. *International Review of Sport & Exercise Psychology, 13*(1), 231-265.

Langan, E., Blake, C., Toner, J., & Lonsdale, C. (2015). Testing the effects of a self-determination theory-based intervention with youth Gaelic football coaches on athlete motivation and burnout. *The Sport Psychologist, 29*(4), 293-301.

Li, C., Ivarsson, A., Lam, L.T., & Sun, J. (2019). Basic psychological needs satisfaction and frustration, stress, and sports injury among university athletes: A four-wave prospective survey. *Frontiers in Psychology, 10*, Article 665.

Lonsdale, C., Hall, A.M., Murray, A., Williams, G.C., McDonough, S.M., Ntoumanis, N., Owen, K., Schwarzer, R., Parker, P., Kolt, G.S., & Hurley, D.A. (2017). Communication skills training for practitioners to increase patient adherence to home-based rehabilitation for chronic low back pain: Results of a cluster randomized controlled trial. *Archives of Physical Medicine and Rehabilitation, 98*(9), 1732-1743.

Lonsdale, C., & Hodge, K. (2011). Temporal ordering of motivational quality and athlete burnout in elite sport. *Medicine & Science in Sports & Exercise, 43*(5), 913-921.

Maffulli, N., Longo, U. G., Gougoulias, N., Caine, D., & Denaro, V. (2011). Sport injuries: A review of outcomes. *British Medical Bulletin, 97*(1), 47-80.

Mageau, G.A., & Vallerand, R.J. (2003). The coach–athlete relationship: A motivational model. *Journal of Sports Sciences, 21*(11), 883-904.

Moreland, J.J., Coxe, K.A., & Yang, J. (2018). Collegiate athletes' mental health services utilization: A systematic review of conceptualizations, operationalizations, facilitators, and barriers. *Journal of Sport and Health Science, 7*(1), 58-69.

Nilsson, T., Östenberg, A.H., Alricsson, M. (2016). Injury profile among elite male youth soccer players in a Swedish first league. *Journal of Exercise Rehabilitation, 12*(2), 83-89.

National Safety Council. (2021, October 12). *Injury Facts.* https://injuryfacts.nsc.org/home-and-community/safety-topics/sports-and-recreational-injuries/

Ntoumanis, N. (2012). A self-determination theory perspective on motivation in sport and physical education: Current trends and possible future directions. In G.C. Roberts & D.C. Treasure (Eds.), *Advances in motivation in sport and exercise* (pp. 91-128). Human Kinetics.

Ntoumanis, N., & Mallett, C.J. (2014). Motivation in sport: A self-determination theory perspective. In A.G. Papaioannou & D. Hackfort (Eds.), *Routledge companion to sport and exercise psychology: Global perspectives and fundamental concepts* (pp. 67-82). Routledge.

Nylandsted Jensen, S., Ivarsson, A., Fallby, J., Dankers, S., & Elbe, A.-M. (2018). Depression in Danish and Swedish elite football players and its relation to perfectionism and anxiety. *Psychology of Sport and Exercise, 36*, 147-155.

Park, S., Lavallee, D., & Tod, D. (2013). Athletes' career transitions out of sport: A systematic review. *International Review of Sport and Exercise Psychology, 6*(1), 22-53.

Pelletier, L.G., Fortier, M.S., Vallerand, R.J., & Brière, N.M. (2001). Associations among perceived autonomy support, forms of self-regulation, and persistence: A prospective study. *Motivation and Emotion, 25*, 279-306.

Podlog, L., Dimmock, J., & Miller, J. (2011). A review of return to sport concerns following injury rehabilitation: Practitioner strategies for enhancing recovery outcomes. *Physical Therapy in Sport, 12*(1), 36-42.

Purcell, R., Gwyther, K., & Rice, S.M. (2019). Mental health in elite athletes: Increased awareness requires an early intervention framework to respond to athlete needs. *Sports Medicine – Open, 5*, Article 46.

Reynders, B., Vansteenkiste, M., Van Puyenbroeck, S., Aelterman, N., De Backer, M., Delrue, J., De Muynck, G.-J., Fransen, K., Haerens, L., & Broek, G.V. (2019). Coaching the coach: Intervention effects on need-supportive coaching behavior and athlete motivation and engagement. *Psychology of Sport and Exercise, 43*, 288-300.

Rocchi, M., Pelletier, L., & Desmarais, P. (2017). The validity of the Interpersonal Behaviors Questionnaire (IBQ) in sport. *Measurement in Physical Education and Exercise Science, 21*(1), 15-25.

Ryan, R.M. (1995). Psychological needs and the facilitation of integrative processes. *Journal of Personality, 63*(3), 397-427.

Ryan, R.M., & Deci, E.L. (2017). *Self-determination theory: Basic psychological needs in motivation, development, and wellness.* Guilford Press.

Sarkar, M., & Fletcher, D. (2014). Psychological resilience in sport performers: A review of stressors and protective factors. *Journal of Sports Science, 32*(15), 1319-1434.

Schinke, R.J., Stambulova, N.B., Si, G., & Moore, Z. (2018). International society of sport psychology position stand: Athlete's mental health, performance, and development. *International Journal of Sport and Exercise Psychology, 16*(6), 622-639.

Smith, N., Quested, E., Appleton, P.R., & Duda, J.L. (2016). A review of observational instruments to assess the motivational environment in sport and physical education settings. *International Review of Sport and Exercise Psychology, 9*(1), 134-159.

Standage, M., & Ryan, R.M. (2020). Self-determination theory in sport and exercise. In G. Tenenbaum & R.C. Eklund (Eds.), *Handbook of sport psychology* (4th ed., pp. 37-56). Wiley.

Stenling, A., Lindwall, M., & Hassmén, P. (2015). Changes in perceived autonomy support, need satisfaction, motivation, and well-being in young elite athletes. *Sport, Exercise, and Performance Psychology, 4*(1), 50-61.

Teixeira, P.J., Silva, M.N., Carraça, E.V., & Marques, M. (2013). *Physical activity, eating behavior, and weight control* [Pre-conference presentation]. 5th International Conference on Self-Determination Theory. Rochester, NY.

Topp, C.W., Østergaard, S.D., Søndergaard, S., & Bech, P. (2015). The WHO-5 Well-Being Index: A systematic review of the literature. *Psychotherapy and Psychosomatics, 84*(3), 167-176.

Truong, L.K., Mosewich, A.D., Holt, C.J., Le, C.Y., Miciak, M., & Whittaker, J.L. (2020). Psychological, social and contextual factors across recovery stages following a sport-related knee injury: A scoping review. *British Journal of Sports Medicine, 54*, 1149-1156.

Wiese-Bjornstal, D. (2010). Psychology and socioculture affect injury risk, response, and recovery in high-intensity athletes: A consensus statement. *Scandinavian Journal of Medicine and Science in Sports, 20* (Suppl. 2), 103-111.

Wiese-Bjornstal, D.M., Wood, K.N., & Kronzer, J.R. (2020). Sport injuries and psychological sequelae. In G. Tenenbaum & R.C. Eklund (Eds.), *Handbook of sport psychology* (4th ed., pp. 711-737). Wiley.

Epilogue

Arch J.J., & Craske, M.G. (2008). Acceptance and commitment therapy and cognitive behavioral therapy for anxiety disorders: Different treatments, similar mechanisms? *Clinical Psychology: Science and Practice, 15*(4), 263-279.

Azjen, I. (1991). The theory of planned behavior. *Organizational Behaviour and Human Decision Processes, 50*, 179-211.

Carson, H.J., & Collins, D. (2015). The fourth dimension: A motoric perspective on the anxiety–performance relationship. *International Review of Sport and Exercise Psychology. 9*(1), 1-21. https://doi.org/10.1080/1750984X.2015.1072231

Cruickshank, A., Martindale, A., & Collins, D. (2020). Raising our game: The necessity and progression of expertise-based training in applied sport psychology. *Journal of Applied Sport Psychology, 32*, 237-255. https://doi.org/10.1080/10413200.2018.1492471

Martindale, A., & Collins, D. (2005). Professional judgment and decision making: The role of intention for impact. *The Sport Psychologist, 19*(3), 303-317.

Maw, G. (2019). Effective performance support: An integrated view. In Collins, D., Cruickshank, A., & Jordet, G. (Eds.), *Routledge Handbook of Elite Sport Performance.* Oxford: Routledge.

Neenan, M., & Dryden, W. (2011). *Rational emotive behaviour therapy in a nutshell.* Sage.

Peters, S. (2012). *The chimp paradox: The mind management programme for confidence, success and happiness.* Vermilion.

Prochaska, J.O., DiClemente, C.C., & Norcross, J.C. (1992). In search of how people change: Applications to addictive behaviors. *American Psychologist, 47*, 1102-1114.

Tetlock, P.E. (2006). *Expert political judgment: How good is it? How can we know?* Princeton University Press.

Tinsley, H.E.A., Bowman, S.L., & Barich, A.W. (1993). Counseling psychologists' perceptions of the occurrence and effects of unrealistic expectations about counseling and psychotherapy among their clients. *Journal of Counseling Psychology, 40*, 46-52.

Winter, S., & Collins, D. (2015). Why do we do, what we do? *Journal of Applied Sport Psychology, 27*(1), *35-51.* https://doi.org/10.1080/10413200.2014.941511

Winter, S., & Collins, D. (2016). Applied sport psychology, *are* we a profession? *The Sport Psychologist, 30*, 89-96. https://doi.org/10.1123/tsp.2014-0132

INDEX

Note: The italicized *f* and *t* following page numbers refer to figures and tables, respectively.

goodness of fit 36
great person theory 12
grit 275-276
group. *See also* team
    conflict in 220
    differences of opinion in 199
    higher-ability 220
    influence across 172-173, 175-177, 180-181
    lower-ability 220
Group Environment Questionnaire 175
groupthink 200
growth mindset 67-68, 275-276
Guardiola, Pep 193

H
haka 92, 92*f*, 183, 184*f*
hierarchy of needs 78
high-level performance 55, 59
high-performance coaches 46
high-performing cultures. *See also* culture
    behavioral norms of 189
    coach's influence on 195
    connection cues in 189
    example of 183
    leadership aspects for optimizing of 194-195
    optimization of 191-197
    in orienteering 187
    performance standards in 191, 193
    punctuality of 193
    relevance of 184
    studies of 185-186
    team orientation in 193-194
high-performing environments (HPE) 200, 205, 219, 224, 229
high-pressure training 148
holistic approach 57-58, 58*t*
holistic athletic career (HAC) model 41-42, 45, 49
holistic-ecological approach 40
Honnold, Alex 74
horizontal coherence
    macrostructures 216-219
    mesosystems and 220-222
    in talent development environments 221
horizontal integration 11

I
identification-control-correction (ICC) program 258*t*, 259, 261
imagery. *See also* mental imagery
    description of 29
    intrusive visual 111-112
    self-efficacy affected by 100
    team confidence affected by 103
implicit psychology work 9
in-action training 210-211
indirect selling 12

individual athlete plans (IAPs) 87-88
influence
    across group 172-173, 175-177, 180-181
    leadership and 168-169, 171
informal leaders 173
informal leadership 195-196
injury recovery 117-118, 248
injury rehabilitation
    confidence in 96
    mental imagery for 108, 117-118
    need support for 318
    self-determination theory and 313-314
instructional self-talk 146
intelligent action 154-155
intelligent learning 151
interdisciplinary approach 241-242
interdisciplinary support team (IST) 69
interdisciplinary teams 248
internal alignment 56, 56*f*
internal distractions 139
Interpersonal Behaviors Questionnaire (IBQ) 317
interpersonal conflicts 47
interpersonal functioning 29
interpersonal relationships 30, 222-223
intervention goals 62
interviews 31-33, 82
intrinsic motivation 78-79, 79*f*
intrusive visual imagery 111-112
involuntary mental imagery 111-112
I-shaped practitioners 328, 329*f*
issue conceptualization
    assessment of 34
    case study of 25-26, 37
    knowledge bases in 27-28
    optimization of 34-35
    purpose of 27

J
James, LeBron 149-150
Jansrud, Kjetil 183
Jordan, Michael 74, 74*f*
Jowett, Sophia 12, 222

K
Kahneman's capacity theory 137-138
Klopp, Jürgen 192
knowledge 154-155, 201
knowledge bases 27-28

L
Lang's bioinformational theory 110
layered stimulus response training (LSRT) 110-111, 118
leader
    effective 171
    informal 173
    thinking skills of 174
    trust building by 251

ABOUT THE EDITORS

Dave Collins, PhD, earned a doctorate in psychology from the University of Surrey in 1990. He is currently the director of Grey Matters UK, a performance-focused company that offers applied consultancy services in sport, business, performing arts, and more. He is also a professor at Edinburgh University, an institution ranked in the world's top 20 by QS World University Rankings. Dr. Collins has written over 350 peer-reviewed publications and has authored or contributed to 80 books. His research interests include performer and coach development, expertise, and peak performance. As a practitioner, Dr. Collins has worked with more than 70 world-class athletes or Olympic medalists as well as professional athletic teams and performers. He is the director of the Rugby Coaches Association and is a fellow of the Society of Martial Arts, a fellow of the British Association of Sport and Exercise Sciences (BASES), and an associate fellow of the British Psychological Society. Dr. Collins is a former Royal Marine and a fifth-degree dan in karate.

Andrew Cruickshank, PhD, earned a doctorate in sport psychology from the University of Central Lancashire in 2013. He has led or contributed to more than 40 peer-reviewed publications and book projects, all with direct relevance to elite performance. He is a former professional soccer player who now works with Grey Matters UK as a senior performance psychologist. Within his applied activities, Dr. Cruickshank is currently working with performance directors, coaches, support staff, and athletes in international golf; Olympic, Paralympic, and national judo; and professional rugby. Previous consultancies have included work in a range of other elite-level sports, including soccer, cycling, motor sports, and hockey, as well as other performance domains, including business and policing. Dr. Cruickshank is also a qualified coach and an associate fellow of the British Psychological Society, and he supervises psychologists working toward professional accreditation.

ABOUT THE CONTRIBUTORS

Maurizio Bertollo, PhD, is a professor of methods and didactics of physical activity at G. d'Annunzio University of Chieti–Pescara in Italy, where he is the rector's delegate for international cooperation and partnership. He is also a visiting professor of human performance at the University of Suffolk in the United Kingdom. He is currently serving as vice president of the European Federation of Sport Psychology (FEPSAC). His research area is motor behavior and psychology of sport and exercise, with emphasis on performance optimization, stress-recovery balance in sport, psychophysiology and neuroscience in sport, biofeedback and neurofeedback in sport, bio-psycho-physiological states underpinning performance, and the individual zone of optimal functioning (IZOF) model. He worked as scientific consultant, psychologist, and coach for many Italian sport clubs, sport federations (e.g., modern pentathlon, triathlon, swimming, rink hockey, soccer, cycling, track and field, and shooting), and the Italian and Romanian Olympic committees. He has written over 200 papers and publications in peer-reviewed journals, books, and book chapters.

Boris Blumenstein, PhD, is a full professor in sport psychology in the School of Behavioral Sciences at the College of Management Academic Studies in Rishon LeZion, Israel. He is former director of the department of behavioral sciences at the Ribstein Center for Research and Sport Medicine at the Wingate Institute in Israel. He is the author of over 100 publications, including seven books, 35 book chapters, and about 70 peer-reviewed journal articles. He has given more than 80 scientific presentations at international and national conferences and workshops. As an applied practitioner over the past 40 years, he has provided psychological support to more than 200 international and professional elite athletes, including world-class athletes and Olympic medalists. He has worked as the Israeli sport psychology practitioner at four Olympic Games and in more than 50 international events. His research focuses on psychological preparation with biofeedback training and the periodization of psychological skill training.

Humberto Moreira Carvalho, PhD, is an assistant professor at the School of Sports at the Federal University of Santa Catarina in Brazil. His research focuses on understanding and improving the development of youth athletes. This includes promoting multidisciplinary research in youth sports and the use of advanced statistical analysis. Carvalho has extensive experience as a basketball coach.

Antonio De Fano is an exercise specialist and PhD student in neuroscience and imaging at the Behavioral Imaging and Neural Dynamic Center at G. d'Annunzio University of Chieti–Pescara in Italy. His current research focuses on the kinematic and neurophysiological underpinnings of nonverbal joint action. De Fano is also a professional break-dancer, teacher, and personal trainer. He is currently the strength and conditioning trainer of the Italian National Team of Breaking for Paris 2024.

Rune Giske, PhD, is a professor in sport psychology and coaching at the University of Stavanger in Norway. He teaches and conducts research on topics related to team performance, decision-making, leadership, learning, and applied sport psychology. In addition, he is a sport psychology practitioner who works with athletes and has comprehensive experience in delivering mental training in a military setting. His coaching experience is primary from team ball games at a range of performance levels (youth to national elite).

Carlos Eduardo Gonçalves, PhD, is an associate professor in the faculty of sport sciences at the University of Coimbra in Portugal, where he teaches sport pedagogy. He has decades of experience as a basketball coach, at the professional and international levels, and as a coach educator. His main research interests are the sport specialization process and its implications for athletes, coaches, families and society.

Denis Hauw, PhD, is a psychologist with a doctorate in sport psychology from the University of Paris X. He joined the Institute for Sport Studies at the University of Lausanne in 2012. He teaches sport psychology to bachelor's and master's degree students and is responsible for a postgraduate program for certification of sport psychologists in Switzerland. His research interests include talent development, elite performance, doping, discrimination, harassment, and abuse in sport. As a psychologist, he has been delivering psychological and coaching services to athletes, teams, and coaches at the national and international levels for more than 20 years.

Andreas Ivarsson, PhD, is an associate professor at Halmstad University and an associate professor in the department of sport science and physical education at the University of Agder. His research interests include psychological aspects related to sport injuries, health and well-being in athletes, factors influencing participation in sport and physical activities, and statistical and methodological issues in psychological research. He is currently the sport psychology practitioner for the Norwegian female national soccer team as well as the coordinator of the Psychology Science Network at the Swedish Ice Hockey Federation.

Geir Jordet, PhD, is a professor of sport psychology and soccer at the Norwegian School of Sport Sciences in Oslo, Norway. Here he teaches and conducts research on topics such as visual perception and cognition, performance under pressure, effective learning, and applied sport psychology. In addition, he is a sport psychology practitioner specializing in soccer. Over the last 20 years, he has worked with many leading professional soccer clubs, national soccer associations, and individual professional players. He also cofounded a software company, Be Your Best, that provides digital simulation training for soccer players.

Andreas Küttel, PhD, is an assistant professor at the Institute of Sports Science and Clinical Biomechanics at the University of Southern Denmark. As a former elite athlete representing Switzerland in several Olympics and world championships as a ski jumper, he has gathered firsthand experience about the dynamic state of mental health in high-performance sports. His research interests are athletes' transitions and dual careers, with a focus on mental health. Since 2017, he has served the Swiss ski jumping national team as a sport psychology practitioner, applying a holistic approach to athletes' development in sport and life.

Geoff P. Lovell, PhD, is an accomplished researcher, having published almost 100 peer-reviewed research articles. Lovell is an applied psychologist who has supported medal-winning performances in the Commonwealth Games, Paralympic Games, and Olympic Games. He has also coached kayaking at Olympic levels. Lovell studied and trained as a sport and exercise psychologist in the United Kingdom, completing his undergraduate degree at St. Mary's University–Twickenham. He earned his doctorate at Manchester Metropolitan University. After working at a number of U.K. universities and having supported a range of elite sporting teams and individuals, Lovell and his family moved to Australia, where he works at the University of the Sunshine Coast as an associate professor and registered psychologist. Lovell continues to work in private practice with sport and nonsport populations, focusing on injury rehabilitation and well-being and supporting athletes of all levels to realize their full potential.

Áine MacNamara, PhD, is an associate professor of elite performance at Dublin City University and is the chair of the professional doctorate program in elite performance (sport). MacNamara's background is in physical education, youth coaching, and talent development. She has worked in a range of sport environments as an educator, coach educator, and consultant. Her main research interests are talent development, coaching, and the design and implementation of systems and policies in sport. She has published widely, including over 50 peer-reviewed journals, 15 book chapters and technical reports, and three books. She has been a consultant to a range of sporting organizations in the United Kingdom and Ireland—including the Gaelic Athletic Association, England Golf, Munster Rugby, Welsh Rugby Union, Leinster Golf, Irish Hockey, and Leinster GAA— to help them develop talent development pathways and policies as well as provide coach and parent education to support the implementation of these ideas. MacNamara frequently engages with national governing bodies of sport by contributing to coach education and player development workshops.

Amanda Martindale, PhD, is a chartered psychologist (CPsychol), a registered practitioner psychologist, and a senior lecturer in sport and performance psychology at the University of Edinburgh. As a practitioner, she has provided sport psychology support for over 20 years to high-level athletes, coaches, and teams preparing for major tournaments and events. Her research involves the application of psychology to high-performance domains, including sport, forensics, medicine, and academia, and she has over 40 research outputs. Martindale is particularly interested in accessing expert cognition and enhancing professional judgment and decision-making expertise in hyperdynamic environments.

Iris Orbach, PhD, is the head of the master's program in sport and exercise psychology at the College of Management Academic Studies in Rishon LeZion, Israel. She is a researcher and a sport psychology practitioner in the department of behavioral sciences at the Ribstein Center for Sport Medicine Sciences and Research at Wingate Institute, and she is the head of the health promotion program at the Nat Holman School for Coaches and Instructors at Wingate Institute. In the past she worked as an assistant professor in the department of sport, fitness, and leisure studies at Salem State University in the United States. Orbach has published numerous peer-reviewed journal articles, three books, and book chapters and has given presentations at national and international conferences on topics related to sport psychology. Orbach's current research interests include psychological preparation with biofeedback training, young female athletes, and motivation in sport. In her free time, she enjoys running, bicycling, swimming, weightlifting, and all kinds of fitness activities.

John K. Parker, PhD, PGCHE, has been an active researcher and applied sport psychologist for over 15 years. Early in his career, Parker became a PGA-qualified golf professional before entering into academia, and he continues to be active in golf at professional and recreational levels. Parker completed an undergraduate degree in psychology at University College Worcester before getting a master's degree in cognitive neuropsychology at Oxford Brookes. His doctorate was completed at the University of Gloucestershire and focused on the characteristics of imagery use among youth sport performers. Parker is a reader in sport psychology at Hartpury University, contributing to undergraduate and postgraduate sport and exercise psychology provision. Parker is a chartered psychologist (CPsychol) and an associate fellow of the British Psychological Society (AFBPsS). His applied practice spans a number of sports at various competitive levels with a view to maximizing performance and enhancing athlete well-being.

Artur Poczwardowski, PhD, is a professor at the University of Denver and is a fellow of the Association for Applied Sport Psychology (AASP) and the International Society of Sport Psychology (ISSP). He is certified by AASP as a mental performance consultant (CMPC) and is listed in the United States Olympic and Paralympic Committee Sport Psychology Registry and the ISSP Registry. Since 1991, Poczwardowski has provided consulting services to athletes, coaches, and teams from numerous sports (e.g., tennis, golf, hockey, judo, soccer, track and field, cycling, speed skating, and esports). Most recently, he has delivered mental training services to three U.S. Paralympic teams. Poczwardowski has written over 60 publications and delivered over 200 professional presentations that focus on sport and performance psychology practice for performance enhancement and psychological well-being, coach–athlete relationships, and coping strategies in elite performers.

Pam Richards, PhD, is a former national field hockey coach and a world-qualified coach (certified as a high performance coach by FIH) with 19 years of international coaching experience. Richards has been actively involved in research and applied work relating to high-pressure team decision-making for over 25 years, and she leads the University of Central Lancashire research theme "Developing Expertise in Individuals and Teams." She supervises doctoral students in elite sport, military, police, fire, and medical contexts. Richards focuses on the development and operationalization of shared mental models in high-pressure settings, exploring both the psychomotor and psychosocial aspects.

David Shearer, PhD, is a professor of elite performance psychology at the University of South Wales and is a sport and exercise psychologist certified by the Health and Care Professions Council (HCPC). He has consulted extensively with world-class athletes and Olympic and Paralympic athletes in wheelchair basketball, golf, swimming, athletics, and shooting. He also works with several extreme and adventure athletes. Shearer has published extensively on a range of topics in psychology and sport science and specializes in elite performance research on team dynamics (e.g., collective efficacy), psychological and physical factors related to recovery (e.g., mood, sleep, hormones), and psychological factors underpinning extreme sport participation. He is the performance psychology lead for the Welsh Institute of Performance Science, which conducts performance solution–driven research to help Welsh athletes perform at Commonwealth and Olympic Games.

Andreas Stenling, PhD, is an associate professor in the department of psychology at Umeå University and an associate professor in the department of sport science and physical education at the University of Agder. His research interests span the areas of health psychology and epidemiology (e.g., physical activity and fitness), sport psychology (e.g., athletes' physical and mental health, motivational processes), and work and organizational psychology (e.g., leadership). Stenling is currently on the scientific advisory board at the Swedish Ice Hockey Federation, where he is involved in the development and evaluation of coach education programs.

Tynke Toering, PhD, is a sport scientist and performance psychology consultant. In her research, she focuses on performance psychology, learning, and expertise development in sport and other performance domains. Toering has experience with various types of performance psychology consulting work—working with management, coaches, and players in multiple European countries.

John Toner, PhD, is a chartered psychologist (CPsychol) and lecturer in sport coaching and performance in the department of sport, health, and exercise science at the University of Hull in the United Kingdom. He is the coauthor of the textbook *A Critical Introduction to Sport Psychology* and the forthcoming book *Continuous Improvement: Intertwining Mind and Body in Athletic Expertise*. His research and teaching interests include skill acquisition, expertise in sport performance and pedagogy in sport coaching.

Tom Willmott, DProf, is head coach of the park and pipe program for Snow Sports New Zealand. He has coached free skiing and snowboarding at all levels over the past two decades and has helped his athletes achieve medal success at major events, including the Winter Olympics. Willmott has a professional doctorate in elite performance from the University of Central Lancashire in the United Kingdom. He has published a number of journal articles and book chapters. A keen snowboard mountaineer, he also works as a heliski guide and split-board guide in New Zealand and internationally.

Find other outstanding resources at

US.HumanKinetics.com
Canada.HumanKinetics.com

In the **U.S.** call 1-800-747-4457
Canada 1-800-465-7301
International 1-217-351-5076

 HUMAN KINETICS